The Sugar Smart Diet

Stop cravings and lose weight
while still enjoying the sweets you love!

ANNE ALEXANDER

Editorial Director of **Prevention** *with Julia VanTine*

Foreword by Delos M. Cosgrove, MD
Chief Executive Officer and President of Cleveland Clinic

RODALE.

The trade edition was published by Rodale Inc. in December 2013.

© 2013 by Rodale Inc.
Photographs © 2013 by Rodale Inc.

Mentor photographs by Glenn Glasser (page 61), Matt Rakola (page 83), Andrew Duany Photography (page 114), Landria Voight (page 140), courtesy of Morristown Medical Center, Morristown, NJ (page 167), David Carlson (page 198); success story Before photographs by Trisha Calvo; success story After photographs and exercise photographs by Mitch Mandel/Rodale Images (pages 263–284).

Book design by Joanna Williams

Library of Congress Cataloging-in-Publication Data is on file with the publisher.

ISBN 978-1-62336-280-5   direct hardcover

4   6   8   10   9   7   5   3   direct hardcover

We inspire and enable people to improve their lives and the world around them.
For more of our products, visit **prevention.com** or call 800-848-4735.

To the sweetest treats

in my life:

Casimir, Katie, and Charlotte

CONTENTS

ONE NATION, UNDER SUGAR
1

THE THREE FACES OF SUGAR
13

ANATOMY OF A SUGAR BELLY
29

UNDERSTANDING THE ATTRACTION
45

THE SUGAR SMART DIET RULES
57

THE SUGAR STEP-DOWN:
DAYS 1–5
71

FOREWORD

Americans eat a lot of sugar. They eat a lot of everything. Doctors know this better than anyone. We see the consequences of overeating every day in our practices. Almost 70 percent of American adults are overweight. Half of all overweight Americans are obese. Something is clearly out of hand. We need new strategies to address America's—and the world's—epidemic of obesity.

The health problems associated with obesity almost defy enumeration. Obese individuals die at an earlier age; they are at higher risk of hypertension, stroke, coronary artery disease, venous thromboembolism, some cancers, sleep apnea, liver disease, pancreatic disease, even some psychiatric disorders. They are at higher risk of diabetes, which directly raises the risk of deadly heart disease.

Now there is even more alarming news. Studies have shown an association between obesity and Alzheimer's disease. With our nation's aging demographic, this is cause for particular concern. It could spell a perfect storm of cardiovascular disease, diabetes, and dementia—with no one to blame but us and our poor lifestyle choices.

As one of America's leading health-care institutions, Cleveland Clinic has a particular responsibility to set a good example in health and wellness. In 2006, we launched a series of programs to promote healthy lifestyles among the 40,000 caregivers across all our facilities. We offered free smoking cessation classes, fitness club memberships, yoga and relaxation programs to all members of our employee health plan. We also took a good look at the foods we served in our hospital, cafeterias, and vending machines. We banned all trans fats from our kitchens. Sugary soft drinks and snacks were removed from vending machines and dining areas and replaced with sugar-free or lower-sugar alternatives.

Like Cleveland Clinic, Anne Alexander and the team at *Prevention* are committed to promoting healthier lifestyles. *The Sugar Smart Diet* is an approach that merits serious consideration. It targets sugar as a major driver of unwanted weight gain. It points out the strong association of excess belly fat with heart disease and diabetes. It offers personal testimony from individuals who have changed their diets and improved their prospects for better health. Best of all, it offers its recommendations as part of a lifestyle that includes better all-around nutrition and exercise.

My thanks to Anne Alexander for raising awareness of sugar in the American diet and for her positive approach to better health. I hope that everyone who reads this book will take its message to heart.

—Delos M. Cosgrove, MD, chief executive officer and
president of Cleveland Clinic, Cleveland, OH

ACKNOWLEDGMENTS

Personally and professionally, I am indebted to CEO Maria Rodale for her inspiring leadership, encouragement to pursue this project, and regular edict to trust my gut. I am so grateful to work at a very special company where the corporate mission is to inspire and enable people to improve their lives and the world around them.

I am also profoundly grateful for the kismet that brought Julia VanTine into this project in the nick of time. Her relentless research and laugh-out-loud funny, extremely talented writing turned this idea into a real book. A thousand thank-yous, Julia!

I'm lucky enough to be surrounded by a team of highly talented people every day, and many of them played an important role in the creation and execution of this book. Editorial Director Anne Egan jumpstarted this project, and Editorial Director Jennifer Levesque, Executive Editor Trisha Calvo, and Editorial Assistant Jessica Fromm pulled things together. The book looks as great as it does thanks to Jeffrey Batzli, Chris Gangi, Amy King, and Joanna Williams. Hope Clarke, Sara Cox, and Chris Krogermeier kept everyone organized and on track. Thanks to the entire *Prevention* and prevention.com staff, especially Polly Chevalier, Siobhan O'Connor, Lauren Paul, Amy Rushlow, Amy Beal, and Melissa Roberson.

Many thank-yous to Stephanie Clarke, RD, and Willow Jarosh, RD, owners of C&J Nutrition in New York City, for their nutrition guidance. The meals and recipes they created truly made getting sugar smart a satisfying, flavorful pleasure.

Thanks to *Prevention*'s former fitness director, Michele Stanten, who developed the Sugar Smart Workout and coordinated our test panel. Kelly Hartshorne, RN, offered invaluable assistance. And much gratitude goes to our test panelists Lisa Dickinson, Robyn Endress, Nora Haefele, Chrissie Hartner, Patricia Huxta, Gayle Hendricks, Colleen Krcelich, Jessica Lievendag, Scott

Lievendag, Renee Marchisotto, Jeanne McDonald, Lisa Miller, Robin Molnar, Kathy Rocchetti, Carol Stiegler, Myra Stoudt, David Sun, and Stephanie Zwetolitz. Thank you for putting this plan to the test and for sharing your journey. Your feedback made this plan better, and your stories and experiences are an inspiration to everyone aiming to eat healthfully.

You can't get sugar smart without addressing your emotional connection to sugar. These three emotional eating experts provided a number of the highly effective craving-controlling strategies you'll find in this book. Thank you to:

- Susan Albers, PsyD, a psychologist at the Cleveland Clinic Family Health Center and author of *Eat Q: Unlock the Weight-Loss Power of Emotional Intelligence*
- Karen R. Koenig, LCSW, MEd, author of *The Food and Feelings Workbook: A Full Course Meal on Emotional Health*
- Jennifer L. Taitz, PsyD, author of *End Emotional Eating: Using Dialectical Behavior Therapy Skills to Cope with Difficult Emotions and Develop a Healthy Relationship to Food*

I'd also like to thank our Sugar Smart mentors Arthur Agatston, MD; Tasneem Bhatia, MD; David Katz, MD, MPH; Ashley Koff, RD; Pam Peeke, MD, MPH, FACP; and Andrew Weil, MD, for their contributions to this book, as well as for the expertise they've shared with *Prevention* and the support they have given us over the years as members of our advisory board, columnists, story sources, and guides to all things health.

And finally to my children: Thank you for your forbearance all those times Mommy was on the computer and for helping me scope out sugar bombs in the grocery store!

INTRODUCTION

Welcome to the Sweet Life!

When I was a kid, sugar was a treat. It was dessert on weekends—a piece of pie or a bowl of ice cream. The miracle of Easter morning was a Russell Stover chocolate bunny and a few Peeps waiting just for me. Once a year, for the Super Bowl, my parents would open a bottle of Coke, and my brothers and I savored one glass each of that rare flavor rush. Sugar was simple: white and sweet and pure. It had its place—in a little bowl on the breakfast table.

Little did I know it, but over the next 40 years, sugar would leave its innocent perch and creep into almost every refined food on the grocery store shelf. Like most everyone else, I didn't notice this sugary invasion until I suddenly stumbled upon it with the fresh eyes of an outsider.

That's because about 15 years ago, when I was an editor-in-chief at Rodale, my family and I had the chance to move first to London and, later, Eastern Europe. As the mother of three small children, healthy eating was a priority for me—and a no-brainer in Warsaw. Fresh food markets were everywhere, and processed foods were hard to find! We ate according to the seasons and lived on real, whole food—grilled meats, fruits and locally grown veggies, thick yogurt, and dense loaves of bread flecked with chunks of whole wheat and rye kernels, so chewy and filling that one slice satisfied both belly and soul. We savored *młoda kapusta* (young cabbage) with fresh dill, heads of broccoli as big as watermelon, with such flavor my kids never resisted, and *chłodnik*, a chilled yogurt soup colored a delightful pink by fresh beets and filled with chopped fresh veggies. In the spring, fruit sellers would appear on street corners all over Warsaw. Every few weeks, a new fruit was featured as it came into season—mountains of strawberries, raspberries, blackberries, or cherries. Some nights,

I would pick up a kilo (more than 2 pounds) of fresh cherries on my way home from work, and my kids and I would polish off the whole bowl and call it dinner!

That didn't mean we didn't love our sweets, though. There's nothing like a Sunday stroll through one of Warsaw's beautiful parks with *lody* (ice cream) served in golf ball–size scoops and balanced on top of a waffle cone. We treasured our Sunday *lody* the same way I treasured having a little bowl of ice cream on the weekends as a child.

Prompted by my desire to raise my children in America, we decided to move back to the States. On my first trip to the supermarket, I filled my cart with healthy choices, including whole grain cereal, whole wheat bread, and low-fat yogurt. Nothing new there—these were staples of our Eastern European diet.

What *was* new: my appetite. I was ravenous. All the time.

In the first weeks after our arrival, we lived in a temporary apartment about 45 minutes from my kids' new school. Each morning, we shared a healthy breakfast of whole wheat toast, fruit, and bran cereal or yogurt, then piled into the car. But by the time we arrived at their school, I was *starving*. I could barely focus on kissing my kids good-bye for the day. I had a must-eat-something-*now* kind of hunger that was off the charts. I was eating my Warsaw-style breakfast every morning—what was going on?

One day, after experiencing this relentless out-of-control hunger, I drove straight back to our apartment and read the nutrition labels on my "healthy" cereal, bread, and yogurt. *Every single item* listed sugar or high-fructose corn syrup as the second or third ingredient. I went through all of my cabinets, stocked with what I thought were healthy foods, and, damn it, sugar was everywhere: in our soups, our pasta sauce, our packaged noodle dinners, our cans of chili, our cooking sauces, our rice dinners, even in our whole wheat crackers that we liked to munch on during the car ride home after school.

I was shocked. Having been out of the States for a decade, returning once a year for family visits, I was, in some sense, a newbie to the American diet, looking at these supposedly healthy foods with fresh, wide-open eyes. And I was ticked off. *What the hell was all of this sugar doing in my food? What was it doing to my family's health? And how could I possibly stop this secret invasion of sugar into my family's food supply and rumbling stomachs?*

That lightbulb moment—followed by many others—led to this book. *The Sugar Smart Diet* is the revolutionary result of asking one simple question: How can we free ourselves from sugar overload and reclaim its simple, sweet pleasure?

The answer lies in achieving what I call sugar freedom—breaking the powerful hold that invasive sugar has on both your body and your mind. Get ready to lose weight and belly fat, reenergize your body, and reinvigorate your mind. The sweet life awaits you!

WHAT'S THE SWEET LIFE?

When you live the sweet life, you assert your sugar freedom—enjoying the pleasure of sugar, but not letting it run your show. You call the shots. Not your cravings. Not the doughnuts in the break room. Not the food industry. *You.*

To take control, it's vital to make friends with sugar—to respect its power yet regard it as just one pleasure in the banquet of life. And that's coming from a woman who savors dark chocolate almost every day and devotes a cabinet above her refrigerator to sugary goodies! I enjoy sugar, yet I'm free. You can be, too.

Having choices doesn't make you free. *Making* choices—smart, informed ones—does. This plan gives you the knowledge you need about sugar: the forms it takes, which kinds are healthiest, and how to satisfy your natural desire for it in ways that empower you. It also offers you a framework for building a full and satisfying life so that you can right-size sugar's place in your diet and savor it in the ways that give you the most pleasure.

Once you've learned about sugar's effects on your health and well-being, you can make those smart choices while continuing to enjoy your favorite treats. Every choice that elevates your health, your happiness, and your dreams and aspirations represents one step on the path to the sweet life. But to make such savvy choices, you have to be informed about sugar. Sad to say, it seems that the less you know about it, the better the food industry likes it.

THE SUGARJACKING OF THE AMERICAN DIET

Now that I'm back at Rodale and am editorial director of *Prevention*, the top health magazine in the country, I read a *lot* of medical journals and health books and talk to a variety of experts to stay on top of hot-button public health issues. After my lightbulb moment, I set my sights on added sugars and found study after disturbing study about their impact on health. A *New York Times Magazine* cover story on sugar was particularly illuminating. Evidence of the deleterious health effects of sugar overload has been amassing for decades. It's just been kept quiet. Until recently.

As part of my investigation, I met with Robert Lustig, MD, of the University of California at San Francisco, whose explosive YouTube video, *Sugar: The Bitter Truth*, first sounded the alarm about the added sugars in our diet—on the eve of publishing his game-changing book *Fat Chance*. I'd read an early copy of his book and found his conclusions jaw-dropping. Talking with him about how the food industry had sugarjacked America's food choices was like meeting Deep Throat (minus the clandestine garage setting), and it compelled me to dig even further into the research. From the American Heart Association and the Centers for Disease Control to the Harvard School of Public Health, scientists are reaching consensus: The huge amount of sugar we consume, often unknowingly, is a public health crisis that can lead to obesity, type 2 diabetes, and heart disease.

Specifically, research implicates fructose, a simple sugar found naturally in fruit that's also present in refined sugars. At one time, most of the fructose in our diets came from natural foods like honey and fruit. The healthy fiber in fruit slows our bodies' absorption of fructose and acts as a natural brake on our intake of this sugar. (Can *you* eat 10 apples in one sitting?) But now fructose in the form of high-fructose corn syrup is ubiquitous in our diets. Why? As high-fructose corn syrup became cheaper to make, food manufacturers began to add it to everything—not just soda, but jarred sauces, canned soups, crackers, and prepared foods. And although manufacturers of infant formula are not required to list the sugar content of their formulas, some brands add sucrose. That's white table sugar in baby food!

When even infant formula contains added sugar, you know our food supply has been "sugarjacked." In the past 40 years, sugars have become cheap, ubiquitous food additives—key ingredients that an enormous industrial food complex uses to sell more and more food products to a tired, busy, overworked, time-stretched, hungry populace.

You're likely paying the price even if you rarely eat sweets or drink soda. Added sugars have seeped into virtually every food in a bottle, jar, box, or bag— even "whole grain" breakfast cereals and "100 percent whole wheat" breads aren't the solution. Sure, these foods contain whole wheat or whole grains. But they're highly *processed* whole wheat or whole grains. And during processing, their fiber—the stuff that slows the digestion—is pulverized. As far as your body is concerned, highly refined whole grain crackers or fluffy whole wheat bread aren't much better than a cupcake. (Of course, portion sizes matter, too.)

To add insult to injury, added sugars seem to supercharge our appetites. In a study published in the *Journal of the American Medical Association,* researchers looked at brain imaging scans after people consumed fructose or another simple sugar called glucose. Fructose altered bloodflow in areas of the brain that stimulate appetite, the study found; glucose did not. What this means is that eating refined sugars may trigger cravings for more of the stuff that thickens our waists and threatens our health! No wonder I had such intense cravings when I moved back to the United States—my brain was being flooded by the sudden surge in refined sugary foods.

THE PATH TO SUGAR FREEDOM

I admit it: As I pored over the research, sugar became an obsession. I'd go to the supermarket, pick up items at random, read their Nutrition Facts labels, and gasp out loud. Seriously? Thirty-three grams of sugar in a cup of yogurt? Twenty-five grams in a frozen entrée? And those kid-friendly tubes of yogurt that I thought were such a brilliant invention for moms and used to feel good about putting in my kids' lunch boxes? Ten grams of sugar per 2-ounce tube— that's 2½ teaspoons of sugar I was encouraging my kids to eat every day. And I was looking at the "healthy" brands! I could feel my blood boiling. Why, I wondered, are we being forced to swill these obscene amounts of sugar, when the research linking overconsumption to obesity and disease is so clear? And why is it in *everything*?

Deep in my sugar-outrage stage, I unthinkingly bought potato salad from the deli section of my supermarket for a party. I opened the lid, sampled a forkful, and—*what*? Even my kids, who love their cookies and ice cream, thought it was sickeningly sweet. What is sugar doing in potato salad?

There's this feeling I get when I know I *have* to write a book. That no-turning-back moment was sealed after meeting with my longtime colleague and *Prevention* advisor Andrew Weil, MD. I asked him what one change he would recommend to *Prevention* readers that could dramatically reduce their risk of chronic disease.

"Cut out sugar-sweetened drinks," he replied.

I nodded my agreement. I'd read the studies linking sweetened drinks with obesity, diabetes, and heart disease, and the debate over New York City's "Big Gulp ban" had reached critical mass. But then I thought, *What about people who don't drink soda, who think they're eating healthy? They're getting sugar in "healthy" cereals and whole wheat breads. Jarred pasta sauce. Frozen diet entrées. Frozen pizza. What can they do to break free?*

My mission: to devise a plan that would break the powerful grip sugar exerts on people's bodies and minds so they could lose weight and improve their health while still enjoying nature's greatest treat. I didn't want to demonize sugar (You'll have to pry Oreos cookies-n-cream ice cream from my cold, dead hands!); I wanted to reclaim it by steering our desire for it back to healthy, natural sources of sweetness and by indulging in decadent sugar splurges when we consciously choose to and not because crazed cravings tell us we need to (or because we couldn't have imagined that our "healthy" frozen dinner was a sugar bomb).

Fired up, I welcomed the challenge. I felt like Mel Gibson in *Braveheart*: They can spike our potato salad with high-fructose corn syrup, but they can't take our sugar freedom!

ROAD TESTED AND APPROVED!

My expectations for the Sugar Smart Diet were high. It had to reduce belly fat and result in a loss of up to 2 pounds a week, improve insulin sensitivity, reduce blood pressure, lower triglycerides, and slash the risk for type 2 diabetes and other chronic diseases. The meals and snacks had to be delicious and based on whole foods packed with flavor to seduce sugar-logged taste buds and hearty enough to prevent hunger and sugar cravings. Finally, because so many people felt "addicted" to sugar, I wanted to build in strategies used by experts to help "comfort eaters" forge a healthier relationship with sugar and silence those cravings.

That's a pretty big wish list. But my crack team of registered dietitians, emotional-eating experts, and an experienced personal trainer were up to the task. They developed the plan, found 18 people who struggled with sugar cravings or their weight, and had them follow it for 32 days. We even formed a private Facebook group for them called the Sugar Crushers. Having had the pleasure of meeting them personally, I cheered them on from my desk every day—I refreshed their page constantly when I should have been answering e-mails or returning phone calls.

The results: nothing less than spectacular. The Sugar Smart Diet's effectiveness lies in its three-pronged approach to sugar:

It addresses your body's physiological "pull" toward sugar as well as the powerful emotional connection that many people experience. Our healthy and lip-smackingly delicious whole foods eating plan short-circuits cravings and satisfies hunger and our inborn desire for sweetness by bringing levels of hormones that drive hunger, fullness, and cravings into harmony. (Before the sugarjacking of our food supply, they harmonized a lot better.) The exercise part of the plan is short and sweet, the way most of us like it, but keeps blood sugar and insulin levels steady so you burn fat instead of store it.

If you tend to soothe stress or negative emotions with food, the expert-recommended coping strategies give you positive alternatives to "cookie therapy." Unlike a fistful of Chips Ahoy!—a temporary fix, at best—these techniques offer the lasting comfort, calm, and sense of control you seek. I know, I've been there. In college, I discovered the dark side of sugar. Stressed by exams and looking to fuel all-night study sessions, I turned to things like Snickers bars for quick energy only to realize that the sugar rush put me on an express lane to a sugar binge. Fortunately, I learned how to recognize when such a tsunami of sugar cravings is building and how not to channel those feelings into a sugar raid, and you will, too.

It reduces intake of added sugars automatically and deliciously. Our plan slashes the "straight-up sugars" in sweets and sodas as well as the "secret sugars" that lurk in foods you'd never think of. But you're not likely to miss them for long—the menu is fabulous. (Mustard-glazed salmon, anyone?) It's filling, too. Many of our panelists were so full after meals, they had to force down their snacks!

It sets its sights on Sugar Mimics. I've already mentioned the pitfalls of refined carbs and highly processed whole grain products. On this plan, you'll dramatically reduce your intake of both, swapping them for healthier alternatives that taste just as good.

In short, you'll reap benefits sweeter than a handful of gummy bears. By cutting added sugars and adding pleasure to every day, the Sugar Smart Diet will help you:

- Crush cravings for sugar and carbs
- Lose weight
- Flatten a sugar belly
- Flip the switch from tired out to fired up

- Turn back the clock on aging skin, making it glow again
- Cut your risk of diabetes, heart disease, and other chronic diseases
- Enjoy sugary treats when you choose to, not because you need to

The cherry on top? Personal advice, tips, and recipes from *Prevention* advisors, including Dr. Andrew Weil, Dr. Arthur Agatston, Dr. Tasneem Bhatia, and Dr. David Katz, along with pros like Dr. Pamela Peeke and Ashley Koff, RD. They're Sugar Smart mentors at your service.

THE PROMISES OF THE SWEET LIFE

As I was writing this introduction, one of my favorite sayings from Mohandas Gandhi kept running through my head: "Happiness is when what you think, what you say, and what you do are in harmony." Gandhi's nonviolent approach to tyranny inspired a nation and changed the world. And similarly, we can take a quiet, but effective approach to changing our relationship with sugar. We don't need to fight with sugar or even go to battle with the evil geniuses who are spiking our food supply with it. We simply need to find that kind of balance that Gandhi talks about: aligning our new knowledge about sugar with making conscious choices to eat in a way that makes us happy.

When you gain new information, as you will in this book, your thinking changes. You have your own lightbulb moment. The negative chatter in your head that stops you from giving your diet, your health, and your life the care it deserves is silenced, and a new, empowering inner voice emerges. And when *that* happens, you begin to treat your body and your soul with the same nurturing care that you lavish on those you love. It's pretty simple: When you know better, you do better and feel better—about everything in your life, not just your diet.

We've all swan-dived into sugar to cool stress or hide from feelings or situations we'd rather not deal with. But on the Sugar Smart Diet, the *only* good reason to eat sugar is a positive one—to gift our tongues and (as you'll learn) our brains with its pleasures. Stick to that one reason, and sugar returns to its proper place in your diet: as a treat to be savored with eyes-closed bliss.

It's amazing how stripping the excess sugar from your diet sweetens your life. On this plan, you'll ask yourself questions like, How can I nurture myself right now? Do I "need" this chocolate, or is a hug, a long walk, or a shoulder to cry on what I'm craving? What did I do today just for fun? What choices can I make today that will empower and revitalize me?

One of the best things about the Sugar Smart Diet (besides the weight loss, of course) is that it makes sugar special again. After periods of eating it mindlessly, not really tasting my share of doughnuts and candy bars, I came full circle to my experience of sugar as a kid: It's a treat again. But so is listening to the cicadas on your porch on a summer evening, or racing downhill on a sled with your kids for the first time in years, or choosing a pedicure over folding the laundry because pretty toes make you feel good.

My point: In this food-centric society, we rarely deprive ourselves of food. It's plentiful, quick, and often cheap. It's the other, more deeply satisfying pleasures that we cut out because we are too busy. I think we have it backward. This plan will change your weight, no question. The proof is in those before-and-after photos. But if you let it, it might also change your life.

We'll talk more about the perks of putting yourself first later in the book. Before I do that, I need to tell you what's been going on with our food supply for the past 40 years. You may be shocked. You may get angry. But at long last, you'll learn the truth about the rising tide of added sugars implicated in obesity and chronic disease and get a glimpse of the solution that will take you to your sugar-smart, sweet life.

ONE NATION, UNDER SUGAR

Think back to that recent birthday party, baby shower, or wedding. There was a cake, of course. Whether vanilla or chocolate, sheet or layer, decorated with icing roses or Scooby-Doo, each sweet, moist, melt-in-your-mouth bite was a celebration of family, tradition, life's meaningful transitions–life itself.

But the truth must be told: Sugary foods are no longer just an obvious treat, taking center stage. It's likely that you are eating far more sugar than you realize and getting it from places you would never suspect. Ever-increasing amounts of sugar have invaded the American diet in the past 40 years, and it's not because we're eating more oranges and apples. The average American consumes 130 pounds of *added* sugar per year–that is, sugar that's an ingredient in food rather than sugar that's naturally occurring in food. Since sweetened beverages get most of the bad press, you might think that the majority of our added sugar intake comes from soda, juice, and specialty coffee drinks. Nope. Sweetened drinks account for only one-third of that amount.

You might also think that most of that added sugar gets consumed away from home. The cheesecake chaser after a nice dinner, fast-food pit stops, convenience store snatch-and-grabs–nope again. We consume two-thirds of that 130 pounds at home.

Which means, *the sugar is coming from inside your house.* Indeed, one study that analyzed almost 86,000 packaged foods over a 4-year period found that 75 percent contained added sweeteners. The vast majority of it is in the form of white table sugar and the syrupy goo called high-fructose corn syrup (HFCS).

On top of all that sugar, we are also drowning in highly refined carbohydrates. The average daily calorie intake in the United States has risen nearly 25 percent since the 1970s. More than half of that increase has come from grains and sugar. We eat *11 servings* of grains and grain products on average per day–about twice as many as we should be eating–and we aren't talking quinoa and wheat berries. Most of those servings come in the form of refined grains. This category doesn't just include white flour, bagels, muffins, and white bread. Pretzels, crackers, pita chips, white rice, pasta, and pizza crust are also part of that group. So are highly processed whole grain products–such as brown rice cakes, whole wheat bread, breakfast cereals (like whole grain flakes, cream of wheat, and instant oatmeal), and whole wheat crackers. These foods may have fiber and labels touting the grams of whole grains they contain, but because of the way they're processed, they behave like sugar in your body. On top of that, grain products are often sweetened with sugar!

Not you, you say. You don't eat that much sugar. Maybe you don't. But maybe, just maybe, you do and you don't even know it. After all, research has found that we think we consume fewer calories than we do. It isn't a stretch to say that you may be seriously underestimating your intake of sugar, especially when it goes by so many different names and masquerades as healthy foods.

How did we arrive at this sugar-drenched state of affairs? Blame it on fat phobia.

REVENGE OF THE SNACKWELL'S

In 1978, disco was in full swing, and American obesity rates were steady: 13 percent of men and 17 percent of women were obese (meaning a BMI of over 30). By the late 1980s, those rates had risen to 18 and 25 percent, respectively. By 2003, 2 years after Americans first heard the phrase "obesity epidemic," a stunning 32 percent of men and 35 percent of women were obese. In 25 years, obesity rates in America had more than doubled. Rates of type 2 diabetes and metabolic syndrome–both associated with obesity–had skyrocketed, too (see page 37).

What happened? It's complicated; there's no one cause of obesity. However, two significant diet-related changes occurred during that 25-year period.

The first change: the rise of the low-fat diet–SnackWell's Madness, if you will. In 1977, 3 years before the introduction of the Dietary Guidelines for Americans, a Senate report recommended that we reduce our intake of dietary fat. We listened, drastically cutting back on even those fats that current research shows are healthy.

In response to our fat phobia, the food industry swung into action, rolling out fat-free everything–chips, ice cream, granola bars, muffins. SnackWell's cookies were born, with just as many empty calories, but zero fat, and they sold like gangbusters. (Of *course* I bought them. I could eat cookies? And not get fat? Ah, the wonders of science!) Even manufacturers of cereals, bagels, and pasta–which have just traces of fat to begin with–got into the act, slapping "naturally fat-free" on their labels. America became a fat-free wonderland, and refined carbs were king. By the mid-1990s, SnackWell's Madness was in full swing. The number of new reduced- or low-fat products rose steeply, reaching 2,076 in 1996 before sinking to 481 in 1999.

These products may have contained little or no fat, but many *did* contain sugar. Lots of it. (And those that didn't contain sugar were comprised primarily of white flour.)

And that was the second major dietary change: HFCS became the nation's primary caloric sweetener. Between 1970 and 1990, its use skyrocketed 1,000 percent. (Seriously. One thousand . . . one with three zeros.)

High-Fructose Corn Syrup: Sweet Madness

It's in soda. It's in cereal. It's in beef jerky, for goodness' sake. It's high-fructose corn syrup, prized by food manufacturers, reviled by food activists, and maddening to anyone who tries mightily to stick to a healthy diet. This syrupy goo has infiltrated our food supply. What is it, and why is it added to virtually everything?

Until the 1970s, most American foods were sweetened with cane sugar. Then, capitalizing on earlier American attempts to transform glucose to fructose, Japanese researchers figured out how to convert cornstarch, the powder made from the inside of corn kernels, into a substance sweet enough to replace the costlier cane sugar. That substance: HFCS, which bears only a passing resemblance to actual corn syrup, the thick, clear bottled liquid in the baking aisle of your supermarket.

Corn syrup proper is cornstarch, broken down into individual glucose molecules, which is essentially 100 percent glucose. To make HFCS, enzymes are added to corn syrup to convert some of the glucose to fructose. The result: corn syrup on steroids, so aggressively sweet that even a grandma baking a pecan pie might make a face. Compared to the pure glucose in corn syrup, HFCS is high in fructose.

A paper published in an obscure journal devoted to California agriculture way back in 1979 made a prediction that would have escaped the notice of pretty much everyone but a handful of researchers and the food industry. Today, the paper's title gives it away: "High Fructose Corn Syrup: An Important New Sugar Substitute." And the prediction was: "Adoption of HFCS is projected to be rapid between 1978 and 1984 and would be essentially completed by 1990." As it turned out, a 1990 Yale study conducted on 14 healthy kids found that those who ate the sugar equivalent of two frosted cupcakes a day had a tenfold increase in adrenaline and exhibited abnormal behavior. People began cutting their intake of cane sugar (white table sugar). In response, food companies pulled a switcheroo, using less sugar and more HFCS.

Food manufacturers make different formulations of HFCS. The most common forms contain either 42 percent or 55 percent fructose. HFCS 42 is mainly used in processed foods, cereals, baked goods, and some beverages, while HFCS 55 is used primarily in soft drinks. Food manufacturers use HFCS for several reasons: It improves the consistency of processed foods and extends shelf life. It also makes sweet foods cheaper—good for food manufacturers, but not so good for you! As you'll see, the large amounts of fructose we're consuming—much of it in the form of HFCS—is being implicated as a primary factor in overweight and chronic disease.

High-fructose corn syrup had replaced cane sugar in sodas by the end of the 1980s; food manufacturers began using the goo in their products soon after. That's why the earliest research on the potential link between obesity and HFCS focused on soft drink consumption.

Full-bore SnackWell Madness is long gone. We cook with olive oil, snack on nuts and seeds, and stud our salads with avocado chunks. We've made peace with these and other heart-healthy fats. But the added sugars that gave low-fat and fat-free foods their appeal remain in virtually all processed foods, and our consumption of added sugars, particularly fructose, has doubled in the past 30 years. Doubled!

OUR GROWING SUGAR BELLIES

This sugar- and carb-drenched diet may be taking its toll on your weight, energy, mood, and health. In fact, without knowing it, you may be experiencing some of its symptoms right now. Do you start your day with a container of fruited yogurt or a "healthy" fast-food smoothie, only to feel famished an hour later? Turn to cookies as a reward after a brutal day or as comfort when you feel low? Steer clear of soda and sweets, and choose wheat bread and whole grain cereal, but still struggle with fatigue and intense cravings? Do you find your weight edging upward, or have a bigger belly than you'd like? Do you spend your day fighting your cravings—and doing your best to ignore that little voice inside that whispers, while you're at work, "Sneak out to the corner store—chocolate is 5 minutes away!"

These are all signs of a physical and emotional tie to the added sugars in processed foods and drinks that, over time, can lead to a big gain in body fat, especially around your middle. This is what I call a *sugar belly,* and it can cause more than just a bad day in the department store dressing room. There's mounting evidence that consuming too much of one type of sugar—in particular, fructose—is a major player in the epidemic-level rates of obesity and diabetes. Fructose causes you to pack on fat and may bypass many of the body's "I'm full" signals, which may promote overeating, weight gain, and insulin resistance, a body chemistry glitch considered a risk factor for diabetes and heart disease.

"Well, okay," you say, "but my belly is just fine, thank you. What I'm doing must be working." *Au contraire, mon ami.* Even if you're rocking size-8 jeans, a sugary diet may be packing on fat where you'd never see it: in your liver. As you'll see in Chapter 3, a fatty liver may tip the body into metabolic disarray and disease.

The bitter truth is that the food industry has hijacked our natural attraction to sugar and easy-to-digest carbs–a desire that's both physical and emotional–and radically altered our expectations of "sweet." But we've got sweet news: *You can shrink your sugar belly without swearing off sugar forever.* Talk about having your cake and eating it, too! When *you* take control of your sugar intake and outsmart hidden sugars, you can lose weight, protect your health, and enjoy one of nature's greatest treats on *your* terms.

That's what the Sugar Smart Diet is all about. Yes, I am going to help you dial down the amount of sugar you eat–not to deprive you, but so you can

The Tongue's "Sweet Spot" Doesn't Exist

Maybe you've heard that certain parts of the tongue register specific tastes. According to this "tongue map," the taste buds that register sweet tastes nestle on the tip; those that detect salt are found near the front of either side; those discerning sour lay behind them; and those that identify bitter are found on the back. This idea, which dates back to 1901, was pretty much disproved in 1974 by scientist Virginia Collins, to the notice of no one.

Actually, Collins *did* find variations in how receptors in different areas of the tongue detect tastes. But the differences were so small as to be insignificant. However, wineglass manufacturers have been known to cite the map, playing up the variations part but ignoring the "insignificant" part.

What science shows now: Every part of the tongue can register every taste, as well as an odd "fifth taste" dubbed umami, the result of tasting glutamate (found in monosodium glutamate, or MSG). While the taste buds on the sides of the tongue *are* more acute than those in the middle, those at the back are even more discerning: They are exquisitely sensitive to bitter tastes, probably, experts believe, to sound the alarm ("yuck") if we ingest poisonous or spoiled foods before we swallow them.

retrain your taste buds and your habits. I'm also going to show you how you can bring it back into your diet in a healthful way. You'll learn how much added sugar you should be eating on a typical day and when it's appropriate to treat yourself to a little extra (and the right way to do that). This plan puts you on the path to the sweet life of sugar freedom.

But first you have to understand just what I mean when I say *sugar.*

SUGAR BASICS

For 10 seconds, forget about your weight, the ice cream in the freezer, and every talk show segment or Internet headline you've caught about sugar and health. Drag everything you think you know about the sweet stuff to your mental recycle bin and hit delete.

Now, consider your flower or vegetable garden, or the prettiest tree in your backyard, or the plant on your sunniest windowsill. Sugar helps it grow. Sugar keeps it alive.

All green plants are sugar factories. Using the sun's energy and the green pigment in plants called chlorophyll (in a process called photosynthesis), plants convert carbon dioxide and water into oxygen and glucose, a type of sugar and one of the building blocks of carbohydrates. Glucose is the fuel your body runs on, too. (Sorry, Dunkin' Donuts.)

NASA has even discovered sugar in space. Sugar is *life.*

We need to see sugar for what it is and what it's not. Ditto for carbohydrates, sugar's "packaging." The "good carbs, bad carbs" trope obscures a simple truth: Not all simple carbs (sugars) are bad, and not all complex carbs (starches) are good. Yet somehow, the idea that carbohydrates are the Snidely Whiplash of nutrition, tying us to the train tracks of obesity and disease, persists.

That characterization is too easy. And there's nothing simple about sugar or its role in our psychology, our diets, and our health.

When you use the word *sugar,* context is key. There's the sugar your body, and most life-forms, use for energy. There's the naturally occurring sugar in the plants we eat. And there are the refined sugars that food companies add to their products, often in entirely insane amounts. You need to know about all of these sugars because that's the only way you'll know how to deal with any of them.

THE CHEMISTRY OF SUGAR, IN COLOR

Any discussion about dietary sugar (whether it's from plants or Big Gulps) begins with carbohydrates, which are known in chemistry labs as saccharides. Sugars are the building blocks of all carbs, whether you're talking ice cream or quinoa. To get a handle on the chemical structure of sugar, let's employ a visual: those colorful Snap-Lock Beads babies play with.

In your mind, hold one green bead. That's glucose, found naturally in honey, maple syrup, and other naturally occurring foods. Glucose is the primary form of energy for the muscles and the brain.

Pick up a pink bead. That's fructose, the sugar found naturally in fruit.

There's one more sugar, galactose, found only in milk. Make that one a blue bead.

Glucose, fructose, and galactose are monosaccharides, consisting of one molecule of sugar. Eventually, any type of sugar or starch that passes your lips, whether you're savoring chocolate truffles or wild ones, ends up as a monosaccharide in your body. As you'll learn, glucose and fructose are the ones that have the greatest impact on your weight and health.

Now, pop two of those beads together. Bingo—you've made a disaccharide, a sugar comprised of two molecules of sugar.

Snap the green and pink beads together. One molecule of glucose plus one molecule of fructose adds up to sucrose—plain old white table sugar, derived from sugar beets or sugarcane.

Join the green and blue beads (glucose plus galactose), and you've got lactose, the sugar in milk.

Connect two green beads together, and you get maltose, the sugar that results from the fermentation of the starch in grains (such as in making bread or brewing beer).

That's where the bead game ends. You don't have the time, or beads, to model the sugars in complex carbs, which are long chains of hundreds or even thousands of glucose molecules. These polysaccharides put the *complex* in complex carbohydrates. There are two basic types of polysaccharides in plant foods: starch and fiber. Starch is found in corn, legumes such as peas and beans, grains, and tubers like potatoes. Fiber, found in varying amounts in plant foods, passes through our stomach and intestines largely undigested. But don't think it's useless–fiber helps you feel full, slows the breakdown of sugars and starches, and helps feed the trillions of friendly bacteria that promote a healthy gut, which itself plays a key role in your mood, energy level, and perhaps even your weight.

And there you have it. In general, simple carbohydrates = simple sugars, whether derived from fruit salad, carrots, Skittles, or frozen entrées. Complex carbohydrates from starchy veggies and whole grains = complex chains of glucose molecules "packaged" in fiber, nutrients, and health-promoting plant chemicals.

This little trip back to chemistry class will come in handy as you read through the next chapters. Mostly, it helps you understand what your choices are–and you do have them. The Sugar Smart Diet gives you choices. Choices are power.

You are about to make a change that will have a real impact on how you feel and look and that will add years to your life (and ensure those years are infused with strength and vitality). You can outsmart the food industry's tricks that are fattening America while you reclaim the role of sugar in your life–as a source of delightful, rewarding pleasure–in ways that make you healthier, more energized, and fueled to be your best self. Let me show you what I mean.

LISA MILLER

BEFORE

LISA ALWAYS KNEW SHE HAD A SWEET TOOTH. In fact, she made it a point to add something sweet to every meal. "I'd have juice or pastries with breakfast, chocolate after lunch, and when I was making dinner, I was already thinking about dessert," she says. But until she started the Sugar Smart Diet, she didn't realize just how much sugar she was getting in a day—more than three times the recommended level—or where exactly it was coming from. "I started reading food labels. I couldn't believe the foods I thought were healthy—like whole grain cereals, instant oatmeal, and fruit-flavored yogurt—contained so much sugar!" she says. "I also didn't know that pretzels and other white-flour foods acted like sugar in your body. My whole diet was packed with terrible carbs!"

Once she got all the "crap" out of her body and reset her taste buds, she began to appreciate the natural flavors of food in a whole new way. "Veggies are so delicious. I just use a little drizzle of olive oil and vinegar. It's like eating them for the first time." The one sugary treat that Lisa allows herself is hazelnut creamer in her coffee. "I could give up desserts, chocolate, soda. The creamer was what I chose to bring back, but now I'm satisfied with just one tablespoon compared to three. It's my little bit of heaven for the day."

Vegetables and creamer aren't the only things Lisa is reconsidering. "I tended to wear loose-fitting clothes because of my belly and muffin top." But after losing almost 4 inches from her waistline and firming up her arms and legs, she's ready for a new, show-off-her-figure wardrobe. "We spent the day at the beach recently. Before, I'd stay covered up. Now, I didn't even hesitate to slip into my bathing suit. I'm looking forward to going shopping for the first time in years. I want more form-fitting, sexy outfits. This plan gave me the body and the confidence to pull them off!"

6.6
POUNDS LOST

AGE:
51

**ALL-OVER
INCHES LOST:**
9

SUGAR SMART WISDOM
*"Skip the commercial salad
dressings that are loaded
with sugar and make your
own. My favorite is a
little bit of olive oil and
Dr. Bragg's apple cider
vinegar."*

THE THREE FACES OF SUGAR

Remember that brilliant surprise ending to the 1999 film *The Sixth Sense*, starring Bruce Willis? Of *course* Willis was a ghost. How could we have missed it? The clues were right there in front of our noses.

We're at a similar forehead-slapping moment in science: Sugar is everywhere we look, haunting the health of this country, trying to turn us into sugar-crazed zombies. Sugar is bliss, but we are drowning in sugar overload—and food manufacturers aren't helping. What are the roots of our potentially fatal attraction? There are three main factors that affect our intake:

1. Our bodies' normal, natural attraction to sugar, which is a part of our human circuitry, as well as the emotional connection to sugar that some people experience
2. The sugars added to processed foods, both obvious and hidden

3. The foods that don't taste sweet but act like sugar in the body, fueling cravings for sugar and other refined carbs

Let's examine these factors one by one.

YOUR STONE-AGE SWEET TOOTH

As our ancestors roamed the open grasslands of east Africa, where humans most likely originated, they could never have imagined deep-fried Oreos. Yet even five million years ago, they preferred plants that tasted sweet.

Some things never change. Our preference for sweet is part of our human hardware, an evolutionary thing. For most of us, sweet is the most alluring of the four common tastes, which also include sour, salty, and bitter. It's the one that gooses our 10,000 taste buds, minuscule collections of cells that connect to nerves running straight to the brain.

The sweet tooth played a key role in human evolution. It's thought that our ancestors associated a sweet taste with energy-dense plant foods like the fruit plucked from trees. With their entire existence centered on getting enough to eat—an arduous task, with unpredictable results—every calorie counted, and sweetness meant "food" and "safe." (They associated a strong bitter taste with potentially poisonous plants, but our taste buds have evolved to accept foods with a mild bitterness, from coffee and beer to kale and Brussels sprouts.)

For a while, calorie-dense fruit and honey were virtually all we knew of sweet. In the Paleolithic era, a period of half a million years that ended around 10,000 years ago, fruits and veggies made up an estimated 65 percent of humans' diet. Fred Flintstone's brontosaurus burgers would have been a treat, and a fig or a dollop of honey the caveman's version of Hershey's Kisses.

Things started to change with the birth of agriculture. Humans began to rely on cereal grains, and fruit and veggie consumption dropped to 20 percent or less. And sugar—derived from sugarcane and cultivated in tiny amounts at first—began its delicious, relentless seduction. Our bodies were designed to

Added Sugars Stoke Appetite

As we've established, gorging on high-calorie foods was a wise strategy for Stone Age humans who didn't know when they'd eat again. But today, foods packed with Straight-Up and Secret Sugars are available 24/7—and these sugars may be stoking our desire for sugary, high-fat, high-calorie fare.

In a study of how the brain responds to food cues and how that increases hunger and desire for certain foods, researchers at the University of Southern California found that young women who looked at pictures of cupcakes and other tempting edibles experienced cravings, especially if they drank a sugary beverage at the same time.

In this study, using functional magnetic resonance imaging, researchers measured the brain responses of 13 young women as they looked at pictures of both high-calorie and low-calorie foods. The women's brains were scanned twice as they viewed images of cookies, cakes, burgers, and fruits and vegetables. After seeing all the images, they were asked to rate their hunger as well as their desire for sweet or savory foods.

Halfway through the scans, the women drank 50 grams of glucose, which is similar to drinking a can of sugary soda. In a separate instance, they drank 50 grams of fructose.

The researchers had hypothesized that the reward areas in the women's brains would be activated as they looked at the pictures of the high-calorie foods—and they were right. "What we didn't expect was that consuming the glucose and fructose would increase their hunger and desire for savory foods," said the study's principal investigator, Kathleen Page, MD. And fructose resulted in more intense cravings and hunger among the women than glucose. "This stimulation of the brain's reward areas may contribute to overeating and obesity, and has important public health implications," she said.

As you'll learn, research is pointing to fructose, in particular, as a real dietary menace and appetite-gooser. In a study of 20 healthy people published in the *Journal of the American Medical Association*, Yale researchers looked for appetite-related changes in bloodflow in the hypothalamic region of their brains after they ingested either glucose or fructose. The study's findings suggested that glucose may reduce blood flow in parts of the brain that govern appetite, which may help inhibit the desire to eat. That wasn't so for fructose, according to the findings.

crave sugar, store it easily, and use it fast. But we live in high-tech times, and while we're still hardwired to seek sugar, we store more than we use. And we're not climbing trees to pluck fruit, either. We're hitting drive-thrus and calling for free delivery. Never fear. The Sugar Smart Diet is full of strategies to work with your body's natural attraction to sugar and its healthy nutritional needs. As you'll discover, something as simple as eating breakfast—and packing it with protein—helps rein in your appetite during the day and reduces snacking on high-sugar foods at night.

THE EMOTIONAL CONNECTION

We love sweets. Our taste buds, our eyes, our emotions crave the delightful reward of sugar. We love the taste, the way it makes us feel, and the emotional connection that sweets provide: comforting warm fuzzies at the end of a long day. From time to time, we all succumb to sugar's sweet but empty promise: relief. Horrendous day at the office? Ice cream. Crushing worries about your aging mom or slacker teen? Ice cream. Feeling fat and friendless? You get the idea.

Eating in response to emotions as varied as boredom, loneliness, or anxiety—what's called *emotional eating*—is real. I told you about my stress-induced binges on sugar as a college student. Those episodes didn't lead to much weight gain. The drama around food played out in my head rather than on my body. Back then, I honestly thought those candy bars would help me power through final exams. Now I know that sugar had its hooks in me, emotionally speaking. I was lucky. Those hooks only "pulled" when I was under stress. But for some people (maybe you), the dig of those hooks is constant; they struggle with cravings every day.

More than one person on our test panel described the connection to sugar as feeling like addiction. One told me she'd find herself leaving work in the middle of the day to drive to the corner pharmacy for chocolate, thinking, "What am I doing?" Another described himself as obsessed with sugary foods— "I feel like I spend my whole day thinking about sugar."

In fact, in a study of 40 women of varying body sizes (some lean, some overweight) published in the *Archives of General Psychiatry*, those who scored higher on a scientifically designed food-addiction scale showed more activity in the parts of the brain associated with drug and alcohol addiction when they were shown pictures of chocolate milkshakes.

One sign of using sugar to manage emotions is that responding to a sugar craving—eating, say, chocolate or ice cream to satisfy it—doesn't alleviate it. Rather, trying to satisfy the craving prompts a desire for more.

Memory plays a key role in the link between sugar and feelings. Many of the sugary foods we love and crave transport us back to times when we felt loved and cared for. Maybe fresh-from-the-oven cookies remind you of your beloved Nana. Perhaps you unwind with a bowl of ice cream in front of the TV every night because as a little kid, you did the very same thing with your dad, and that was your time together. Habit ties into the emotional attraction, too. If you're used to having a muffin for breakfast, cookies in the afternoon, or dessert after dinner, something feels off if you skip it.

NOW YOU SEE THEM, NOW YOU DON'T

We all know that regular soda is liquid sugar. For a while, you couldn't turn on the news without hearing about the controversial "Big Gulp ban" in New York City. But you rarely hear that kind of passion over a turkey sandwich on whole wheat bread, which can have 2 teaspoons of added sugar per slice, or a bowl of raisin bran, which contains $4^{1}/_{2}$ teaspoons—some of it from the raisins, but most of it added. (As I'll explain later, you should be consuming only 6 to 9 teaspoons of added sugar per day.) It's one thing to know you're eating a sugar bomb. It's quite another to learn that many foods you consider healthy or don't even think of as sweet can be sugar bombs, too.

There are two main types of added sugars in foods: the kind you know about and the kind you don't.

Straight-Up Sugar. Found in candy, sweetened soft drinks (sodas, juice drinks, flavored milks, coffee drinks), sweetened breakfast cereals, energy and

Yeah, That's Sugar

Unfortunately, food manufacturers are not required to distinguish between natural and added sugars on a food label. All you'll see is a gram amount for sugars. That can make determining your intake of added sugar tricky. For instance, you could pick up a 6-ounce cup of plain low-fat yogurt, look at the Nutrition Facts label, and see that it has 12 grams of sugar. You might think that sounds like a lot, but that's not *added* sugar—it's the sugar naturally present in dairy products. Look at the ingredients list and you won't see any form of added sugar listed, so you know it's free of added sugar.

But what about fruit yogurt? Fruit has natural sugar, and the yogurt has natural sugar. Does that mean that the 26 grams of sugar listed on the label for a 6-ounce container of low-fat blueberry yogurt is natural sugar? Check the list.

Added sugar goes by many names. Anything that ends in –*ose* is sugar, and so is anything with *sugar* or *syrup* after the name. If you see any of the words in the list on a food's ingredients label, the product contains added sugar.

Next, check out how many sources of sugar there are on the label. Ingredients are listed in order of predominance by weight. That means the product contains more of the first ingredient than any other single ingredient. Since sugar comes in a variety of forms, it is possible that sugar could be the predominant ingredient when you combine them together.

For example, the blueberry yogurt ingredients list reads:

> Cultured grade A low-fat milk, blueberries, **sugar, fructose syrup, high-fructose corn syrup,** contains less than 1% of modified cornstarch, pectin, kosher gelatin, sodium phosphate, malic acid, natural flavor, calcium phosphate. Contains active yogurt cultures including *L. acidophilus*.

The ingredients highlighted in bold are all forms of sugar. Add them together and chances are there's more added sugar in this yogurt than blueberries! It's impossible to tease out exactly how much added sugar this yogurt contains, but if you're armed with some back knowledge, you can make a reasonable guess.

We said above that 6 ounces of plain low-fat yogurt has 12 grams of sugar. So right there you know that about 14 grams of the sugar in the yogurt don't come from the milk. Maybe

cereal bars, and desserts, this type of sugar is right out there, loud and proud. While it's often listed as "sugar" on a food's ingredient label, it might also be called by any number of different names (see "Yeah, That's Sugar").

a few of those grams come from the blueberries themselves. Let's be generous and say there's ¼ cup of blueberries in that yogurt. That amount has 4 grams of sugar. You're left with 10 grams or 2½ teaspoons of added sugar in the yogurt. (Every teaspoon of sugar has 4 grams and 6 calories.) Given the fact that you should be getting only 6 to 9 teaspoons of added sugar on a typical day, is this the way you want to use a third of them?

By getting a general idea of how much natural sugar there is in various grains, fruits, dairy products, and vegetables, you will find it easier and easier to guesstimate the amount of added sugar in packaged products.

These are all different names for sugar:
- Agave nectar
- Barley malt
- Beet sugar
- Brown rice syrup
- Brown sugar
- Buttered sugar
- Cane crystals
- Cane juice
- Cane sugar
- Caramel
- Carob syrup
- Castor sugar
- Coconut sugar
- Corn sweetener
- Corn syrup
- Corn syrup solids
- Crystalline fructose
- Date sugar
- Dextrose
- Evaporated cane juice
- Fructose
- Fruit juice concentrates
- Glucose
- High-fructose corn syrup
- Honey
- Invert sugar
- Lactose
- Maltose
- Malt syrup
- Molasses
- Muscovado sugar
- Raw sugar
- Rice bran syrup
- Rice syrup
- Sorghum
- Sorghum syrup
- Sucrose
- Sugar
- Syrup
- Turbinado sugar

Even if you're aware that these foods pack sugar, you may not realize just how much. For instance, doesn't raspberry iced tea sound a lot better than Coke? A 16-ounce Coke has 52 grams, or 13 teaspoons, of sugar. A 16-ounce bottle of Snapple Raspberry Tea has 36 grams of sugar, or 9 teaspoons—better, but not by much.

Secret Sugar. Wander down any center aisle of your supermarket. Pick up bottles, jars, and boxes at random. More often than not, you're likely to find sugar listed as an ingredient, even if you don't recognize its alias.

True to their name, however, Secret Sugars lurk in foods you don't even think of as sweet. These include pasta sauce, frozen entrées (low calorie or otherwise), packages of ramen noodle soup (the sugar is in the packet of broth, which tastes salty!), salad dressings, ketchup, barbecue sauce, and some deli meats and breakfast sausages. There are also sweeteners that you may not realize are sugar. For example, despite its Garden of Eden name, agave nectar contains more fructose than table sugar. And a popular brand of yogurt came under legal fire in 2012 for its simultaneous use of evaporated cane juice and claim of "no sugar added." It's frustrating, but once you're familiar with the many words for sugar that appear in a product's ingredients list, you'll be better prepared to control your sugar choices.

SUGAR IN ITS SNEAKIEST FORM

Sugar Mimics are foods that don't typically taste like sugar but mimic its action in the body. Foods like crackers, pretzels, potato chips, bagels, white rice, and pasta may not contain sugar per se, but they might as well—they're digested as rapidly as sugar. And they have the same effect on the body: Glucose floods the bloodstream, triggering a rise in the fat storage hormone insulin and disruptions in other hormones that control appetite. Thus, Sugar Mimics have the same harmful effects as Straight-Up and Secret Sugars.

Maybe you already know that a steady diet of such refined carbohydrates, stripped of their fiber and nutrients, is associated with overweight and chronic disease. Not your problem, you say. You start the day with whole wheat toast or bran cereal. You snack on whole grain crackers and hummus. Occasionally, you splurge on a whole grain bagel. Whole grain equals healthy. Right?

Not quite. If your whole grain intake consists mostly of foods made with

From Stevia to Splenda: Taste Bud Teases

On a recent trip to the supermarket, I came across a beverage sweetened with erythritol that, according to its nutrition label, contained 5 calories and 1 gram of sugar per serving. I'd never heard of erythritol, so I decided to investigate.

What I found: erythritol (pronounced ih-RITH-ri-tawl) is a sugar alcohol, one of several (such as xylitol and sorbitol) that are used to sweeten beverages, candies, gum, jams, and yogurt with few or no calories.

Sugar alcohols as well as the natural sweetener stevia and artificial sweeteners such as sucralose (marketed as Splenda) are all safe, according to the FDA. But after some research and discussions with *Prevention* advisory board members, the nutritionists who developed this plan and I decided not to include *any* sugar substitutes in the Sugar Smart Diet. Not even zero-calorie stevia, derived from an herb, which is as natural as it gets.

Why? Because they deliver hundreds of times the sweetness of white table sugar, with few or no calories. And evidence suggests that exposing your taste buds to these high-intensity sweeteners makes them less receptive to natural sources of sweetness such as fruit. For example, sucralose is 600 times sweeter than sucrose; stevia, 200 to 300 times as sweet. Neotame, a relatively new zero-calorie sweetener, is more than *7,000 times* sweeter than white table sugar! Remember the name. While not yet widely used, neotame is expected to find its way into beverages, dairy products, frozen desserts, baked goods, and gums. High-intensity sweeteners undermine sugar freedom because they reduce your appreciation for the true taste of sweet—the kind that comes from actual food rather than from vats in industrial parks.

More worrisome: the link between the use of artificial sweeteners and an increased risk of obesity and type 2 diabetes. The theory is that exposing our bodies to sweetness without calories can lead to an outpouring of insulin, thereby leading to insulin resistance. For example, a study published in *Diabetes Care* found that diet soda drinkers had an increased risk for type 2 diabetes, and several large studies have associated the use of artificial sweeteners with weight gain.

On the Sugar Smart Diet, you'll stick to natural sweeteners like honey, maple syrup, and dried fruit most of the time, indulging in decadent sugar splurges when you choose to. Once you eliminate diet drinks, artificially sweetened yogurt, or those pink, blue, or yellow packets that you stir into your morning coffee, you likely won't miss them. After Phase 2, the flavor of whole foods and natural sweeteners will seem incredibly intense. Skeptical? One of our test panelists, Nora, described the taste of broccoli as "sweet as candy" and Pellegrino with a slice of lemon as "an explosion of flavor." She rightsized her "sweet buds," and so can you.

whole grain flours, such as whole wheat English muffins or whole grain cereals and crackers, you can also grow a sugar belly.

The FDA has a strict definition of whole grains: cereal grains that consist of the intact, ground, cracked, or flaked kernel, which includes the bran (where most of the fiber is), the germ (chock-full of protein and healthy fats), and the starchy innermost portion (the endosperm). (In contrast, refined grains contain only the endosperm.)

Whole grains themselves—brown rice, steel-cut and rolled oats, wheat berries—meet that criteria, and brim with fiber and nutrients. It takes longer for digestive enzymes in the stomach to reach the starch inside whole grains or grains cracked into large pieces, which slows down the conversion of starch to sugar.

For products such as bread or pasta to be labeled whole grain, the FDA says, the grain can be ground, cracked, or flaked, but must retain the same proportions of bran, germ, and endosperm as the intact grain. So far so good.

However, in the process of making whole wheat or whole grain flour, the kernels are pulverized practically to dust, so they're digested about as quickly as white flour, table sugar, or HFCS. This means that they can spike blood sugar and insulin levels, leading to hunger and prompting you to reach for more of these foods. You're caught in an unending cycle of cravings and consumption.

But that cycle can be broken, and the Sugar Smart Diet can help you do it. What makes the Sugar Smart Diet unique is that it helps you get at sugar in *all its guises and from all angles*. You learn to identify and cut back on Straight-Up Sugars, Secret Sugars, and Sugar Mimics. You learn to face and manage the physical and emotional pull of sugar. Our 32-day plan combines the power of healthy, whole foods, physical activity, emotional coping strategies, and sugar know-how to help you outsmart sugar cravings without feeling hungry or deprived—and lose weight and improve your health in the process. It will get you off that sugar merry-go-round and quench those nearly unstoppable cravings once and for all, by showing you how to hit your sugar reset button.

RESETTING YOUR SUGAR THERMOSTAT

Next to the lid-up, lid-down discussion, many couples engage in small-scale thermostat wars. He likes the house toasty. She prefers Arctic-like temperatures. Or vice versa. To make peace, you agree to set the thermostat to a temperature that keeps your environment neither too hot nor too cold.

You can think of your desire for sugar just like this. When you settle on that perfect number—and this plan will help you do that—your attraction to sugar isn't so "hot" that it contributes to belly fat, weight gain, and a higher risk of disease; and isn't so "cold" that you're deprived of the pleasure of a square or two of exquisite chocolate after dinner or a couple of cookies during the day.

This plan's gift to you is sugar freedom. To receive it, you must reset your sugar thermostat. This helps you achieve sugar freedom in two ways:

It dials down your body's physical attraction to sugar and cools your emotional connection with it. On this plan, you reduce your sugar intake in stages, then cut it out completely for less than a week as you learn practical tools that temper sugar withdrawal and replace the reward of a sugar rush with healthier pleasures. This strategy resets your taste buds. Once you reintroduce sugar to your diet, it will taste intensely sweet, and you'll be satisfied with less (way less).

It sets the stage for metabolic harmony. Dramatically curtailing your sugar consumption also resets your metabolism. Your insulin levels will fall, and your body's ability to burn fat will improve. Levels of the hunger hormone ghrelin will drop, and your response to the appetite-quelling hormone, leptin, will improve. As insulin, ghrelin, and leptin once again work in concert to manage hunger and cravings, metabolic harmony is achieved, the sugar belly flattens, and the risk of disease falls. (We'll explain exactly how these hormones can go awry and affect your appetite and cravings in the next chapter.)

Once you begin to introduce sugars back into your diet, you'll add them slowly and in a particular way, so you can determine how you feel without all that sugar in your system. You'll learn how to enjoy it without triggering fatigue, weight gain, or negative health effects—and how to keep the physiological/emotional pulls of sugar at comfortable levels.

THE SUGAR SMART DIET PLAN

How will we get you to this point? The Sugar Smart Diet is a 32-day plan that ensures your success through a diet based on whole, natural foods, physical activity, emotional coping strategies, and other tips to outsmart sugar cravings without feeling hungry or deprived. It gradually weans you off both obvious and hidden sugars and refined carbs so you can reintroduce sugar in a healthy, balanced way.

How do we define success? Of course, you'll see desired changes in your weight and measurements. But you will also achieve so much more—more energy; better sleep; improved cholesterol, blood pressure, and blood sugar levels; and fewer cravings. When it comes to sugar, we're lovers, not fighters, so our plan is designed to help you make peace with sugar, not banish it from your life forever. Take a look at what's ahead, and you'll see that it offers everything you need to make that peace: knowledge, practical ways to apply that knowledge to everyday life, and—above all—choices.

Days 1–5: The Sugar Step-Down. During this time, you'll assess your current intake of sugar and refined grains, and you will gradually eliminate them. In just 72 hours, you begin to transform your physiological and emotional connection and reduce sugar overload's harmful effects.

Days 6–11: The Tough Love Turnaround. *Tough*, because this phase removes all sugar—even from fruit—from your diet. *Love*, in that you will love the results: Our test panelists lost an average of 4 pounds by Day 11. You also won't be eating any processed grain products, refined or whole grain. It's an adjustment, I know, but I've given you strategies that temper sugar withdrawal and replace the reward of a sugar rush with healthier routes to pleasure. The delicious, sugar-balancing meals we've provided will help, too.

Days 12–18: Fruit Feast! Fruit is back in healthy amounts. You'll be amazed at how satisfying it will taste now that you've begun to reset your sugar thermostat. Low-sugar whole grain bread products return, too—one serving per day.

Days 19–25: A Spoonful of (Natural) Sugar. To help make whole, nutritious foods even more enjoyable, this phase reintroduces honey and maple syrup. We chose these sweeteners because they have some nutritional value, they are straight from nature, and they are sweeter than cane sugar, so you don't need to use as much of them. You're allowed 1 teaspoon a day. Whole grain pasta and bread are also included; you can continue to have them once a day.

Days 26–32: Hello, Sugar! You'll be consuming approximately 6 teaspoons of added sugar in this phase, which is the amount you should eat on most days for good health. We have some delicious treats in store for you that contain no more than 3 teaspoons of added sugar. You can still have fruit and a meal that includes honey or syrup. And you can have processed whole grain products—regular or whole wheat—once a day.

All Month Long: The Sugar Smart Workout. The more muscle you have, the better equipped your body is to process sugar and carbs. Exercise also helps boost mood and control stress (a contributor to a sugar belly). And, oh yeah, it burns calories and fat. If you're already exercising, good for you! You can stick with what you're doing. But I encourage you to give the Sugar Smart Workout a try. It has a number of features that will help you get that sugar belly off fast.

That's 32 days to sugar freedom, with bennies right away. So prepare to enjoy one of nature's greatest treats on your own terms, in ways that enhance your health and well-being without skimping on pleasure. Sugar freedom, here you come!

GAYLE HENDRICKS

BEFORE

WHEN SHE STARTED THE SUGAR SMART DIET, Gayle was averaging 36 teaspoons of sugar a day. "I'm an emotional eater. The last time I cut out sugar, I went bonkers!" she says. "On the day after my sugar fast ended, I couldn't get enough of the stuff. If it had sugar in it, I ate it!" This time, Gayle's experience was very different.

At first, Gayle was worried. "I looked at the meals and thought: This is going to be very, very tough. I wasn't expecting a structured meal plan, and I wasn't crazy about a lot of the recipes." During Phase 1 of the plan, she felt tired and cranky.

The build-your-own meal alternative was what turned Gayle around. "Once I realized I could combine my own lean proteins, good carbs, vegetables, and healthy fats, it got easier. I could choose what was fresh at the farmers' market and take responsibility for my choices and the outcome." Still, the recipes taught her an important lesson. "Because they were single servings, I got a handle on portions. I used to go back for seconds just because they were there." She even found a few new favorites, such as the Tangy Mediterranean Tuna Salad (page 128) and Hearty Lentil Sauté with Bulgur (page 128). "I think I'm becoming addicted to the Banana-Coconut Roll." (Find it on page 150.)

Of course, the results she got were encouraging, too. In addition to her 2-pound-a-week weight loss, her cholesterol level dropped from 152 to 134. Most surprising, though, was the change in the intensity of her cravings. "During Phase 4, I was out with friends and they wanted to stop for frozen yogurt. Because dessert was on the menu during this phase, I didn't have to say no and watch the others eat. I just had my dessert at 2 in the afternoon—3½ ounces of strawberry frozen yogurt. A month ago I would have filled a jumbo cup, piled on all sorts of toppings, and then ate dessert after dinner, too! Now, I feel more in control. I don't deprive myself, but I no longer go off the deep end with sugar and carbs. If I'm offered a cookie, I eat one—not the whole box. If I have soda, I drink only a little. I'm satisfied with just a taste of something sweet."

8.6
POUNDS LOST

AGE:
57
**ALL-OVER
INCHES LOST:**
9.75

SUGAR SMART WISDOM
"You'll be less likely to snack or overeat if you always put your food on a plate or in a bowl. Since I hate washing dishes, the thought of dirtying another one stops me in my tracks."

ANATOMY OF
A SUGAR BELLY

Virtually every TV news report about America's collective weight problem uses the same stock footage: obese men and women walking on a city street, filmed from the waist down. We've seen that footage so often, it barely registers anymore. But those anonymous bodies tell the story behind the story: In the past 30 years, as the amounts of refined sugars in our food supply skyrocketed, so did the rates of obesity and obesity-related diseases such as metabolic syndrome, type 2 diabetes, and cardiovascular disease.

The American Heart Association (AHA) knows that backstory. In 2009, alarmed by America's sugar-dipped diet, the AHA issued a scientific statement on the added sugars in our diet. The news was decidedly sour. The added sugars in processed foods—primarily sucrose and HFCS—are likely responsible for our increased calorie consumption and contribute to the twin epidemics of obesity and type 2 diabetes, the AHA said. The statement also issued guidelines for added sugar: no more than 6 teaspoons (100 calories, 25 grams) a day for women, and no more than 9 daily teaspoons (150 calories, 37.5 grams) for men.

We need an intervention. Now. That's because the average American consumes 22 teaspoons of added sugars a day, according to the AHA. That's 366 calories. And that's a conservative estimate. Some run even higher (see "From Sugar Bust to Sugar Crush"). And much of it is ending up on bellies.

THE SUGAR-BELLY CONNECTION

What links a sugary diet with overweight and disease? Belly fat, which wraps around your heart, liver, and other vital organs. Researchers call it visceral fat. *Vicious* is more like it.

The pinchable fat that pads our thighs and butt and causes those maddening bra rolls is called subcutaneous fat. It provides padding and insulation and is a storage depot for energy. But belly fat is active fat—so active that it's now described as an organ in its own right. Belly fat churns out nasty substances that impair the healthy functioning of the liver, pancreas, heart, blood vessels, brain, and even the tissue in a woman's breasts.

For example, deep abdominal fat secretes inflammatory proteins called cytokines. The ongoing slow burn of chronic inflammation has emerged as a link between obesity and insulin resistance, diabetes, and cardiovascular disease.

Science hasn't found such risks in those with curvy hips and thighs. In fact, large studies involving both men and women show that people who store most of their fat in these areas tend *not* to get obesity-related diseases such as diabetes and heart disease. And a study published in the *International Journal of Obesity* found that gluteofemoral fat—an elegant term that simply means butt and thigh fat—actually traps the fatty acids produced by belly fat and prevents them from doing their damage.

How does belly fat develop? It begins with your body's ability to balance glucose and insulin. During digestion, your body breaks down food into its individual components: namely amino acids (from protein), fatty acids (from fat), and glucose (from carbs). Your muscles and brain rely on glucose for energy. Insulin is a hormone that is released by the pancreas to help move glucose from the bloodstream into the cells that use it. The more glucose in your blood, the more insulin you require.

And there's where problems can start. Carbohydrates that are digested quickly flood the blood with glucose and result in a large output of insulin. Which carbs are digested quickly? I'm sure you guessed that sugar is one of them. But so are refined carbohydrates, like white flour and products made with it as well as many processed whole grain products. For instance, the kind of whole wheat bread typically used for sandwiches and white bread are digested at about the same rate and cause about the same rise in blood glucose levels, and therefore require the same amount of insulin to clear the bloodstream of glucose.

Over time, continual spikes in insulin have several detrimental effects. First your cells become less responsive to it. This condition, called insulin resistance, results in your pancreas producing even more insulin to compensate. Glucose levels remain high, and in large amounts glucose can damage blood vessels and nerves.

On top of that—and here's the link to your sugar belly—all that extra insulin floating around causes your body to store more fat than it normally would.

From Sugar Bust to Sugar Crush

I'm not a math geek, but this nugget on sugar consumption in the 1800s, from the USDA, made me reach for a calculator: In 1822, it took the average American 5 days to consume the amount of sugar in a single 12-ounce can of soda. That amount of soda can contain anywhere from 10 to 12 teaspoons of sugar (40 to 48 grams). This means that in 1822,

a citizen of Anywhere, USA, consumed slightly more than 2 teaspoons of sugar a day.

According to one USDA estimate, the average American consumes 10 to 12 teaspoons *every 7 hours*. That's significantly more than the AHA estimate of 22 teaspoons—it comes out to roughly 33 teaspoons a day, or 550 calories. Yikes.

It also prevents your body from using fat for energy between meals. It's as though the insulin has put your fat in Alcatraz—once it enters, it's not coming out. And because your body isn't able to use your stored fat for fuel, you get more hungry, more often. You produce more insulin, you store more fat. The more fat you have, the more your cells become resistant to insulin. It's a vicious cycle.

Insulin resistance promotes fat storage everywhere. Fructose, on the other hand, contributes to belly fat specifically, according to some studies. It's found naturally in fruits and some veggies that are packaged with vitamins, minerals, phytochemicals, and fiber. As any nutrition expert would tell you, though, fruit salad isn't the problem.

The real issue: The amounts of fructose we're consuming in added sugars, such as table sugar (cane or white sugar) and HFCS, are swelling our bellies and menacing our health. Our bodies were designed to handle fructose in small amounts (i.e., in a few servings of fruit or a little honey a day), not the 60 pounds of HFCS a year the average American consumes, often unknowingly. And in this form, you aren't getting any of the good stuff along with it.

Too much fructose takes a toll on even the youngest hearts, according to a study published in the *Journal of Nutrition*. The study found that teens who consumed the most fructose had higher blood pressure and blood sugar levels than those who ate the least, and it linked high-fructose diets to increases in visceral fat.

FROM SUGAR BELLY TO FATTY LIVER

My son and I were in the supermarket recently. As we rolled our cart down the cookie aisle, he asked me why his friend gets to have *seven* chocolate chip cookies in his lunch, while he and my other kids get two a day, max (*after* they've done the dishes and their homework). I said, "Well, let me tell you about nonalcoholic fatty liver disease." I'll tell you what I told him: When you overdo the cookies or other sugary foods, your liver takes the fructose hit.

Located on the right side of your abdomen, tucked behind your lower ribs, your liver is the body's alchemist. One of its most critical jobs is to turn toxins—both formed naturally in the body and man-made, such as from prescription or over-the-counter medications, street drugs, and alcohol—into harmless substances. This hardworking organ uses about 20 percent of the calories you take in to fuel itself and its critical work, which also includes converting proteins and sugars from food into energy for your body, aided by insulin.

Recent research suggests that calories from different types of food are metabolized differently in the body. Every single one of your body's 10 trillion cells can metabolize glucose. But only the liver can metabolize fructose. Sucrose, or table sugar, is half fructose, so it puts some burden on the liver; the glucose it contains is processed by the rest of the body. HFCS contains about 10 percent more fructose than sucrose, making the liver's job that much harder. Worse, these sugars are found in foods that sound healthy. Let's say your standard breakfast is a 16-ounce, 250-calorie strawberry-banana smoothie, which you pick up every morning at the local drive-thru. Strawberries. Banana. Only 250 calories. Sounds healthy. Sweet.

You have no idea. That wholesome-sounding smoothie packs 54 grams of sugar, almost all of it added, and the yogurt base contains straight-up fructose. The added sugars are coming from the "strawberry banana fruit base," which implies whole fruit but is not. The ingredients list reveals "puree" of both strawberry and banana, along with grape juice concentrate, something called clarified demineralized pineapple juice concentrate, and plain old sugar (sucrose).

Your liver must work much harder to break down all that fructose than if you ate a 250-calorie bowl of, say, steel-cut oatmeal topped with half a sliced banana—because these foods contain much less total sugar, and the fiber in the oatmeal slows the absorption of sugar into the bloodstream. Since the smoothie's sugars come in liquid form, they reach your liver fast. Imagine wading in the ocean, and out of nowhere a huge wave smashes into you, knocking you off your feet. Figuratively speaking, that's how a large influx of fructose hits your liver.

Consume a high-fructose diet for long enough, and globules of fat begin to form in the cells of the liver. Before 1980, doctors rarely saw this fatty buildup, known as nonalcoholic fatty liver disease (NAFLD). Now, it affects 30 percent of US adults. It's worth noting that the rise in the incidence of NAFLD parallels the increase in obesity and diabetes, and that the condition affects between

70 and 90 percent of those who are obese or have type 2 diabetes. In fact, experts consider NAFLD a hallmark of a condition characterized by the cluster of obesity-related conditions known as metabolic syndrome. (More on that condition in a bit.)

This buildup of fat in the liver isn't necessarily obvious on your thighs, either. A 2012 study in the *American Journal of Clinical Nutrition* found that people who ate 1,000 extra calories of sugary foods for 3 weeks saw just a 2 percent increase in body weight, but a 27 percent increase in liver fat.

When you lose weight, liver fat returns to normal levels. But if NAFLD isn't caught in time, the liver can become inflamed, which can lead to a more severe liver condition known as nonalcoholic steatohepatitis (*steato* means fat, and hepatitis is liver inflammation). If the inflammation becomes severe enough, scar tissue replaces healthy tissue, impairing the liver's ability to perform its many crucial functions. When that happens, it's called cirrhosis. (Cirrhosis only happens with really severe alcoholism, right? At least that's what I always thought. Now, it appears, an excessively sugary diet could play a role, too. Amazing.) A fat-riddled liver may become resistant to the action of insulin. As the pancreas churns out more and more of this fat-storage hormone to prod the liver into doing its job, insulin levels increase—and so does body fat.

FRUCTOSE: THE QUICKER FATTER-UPPER

As you'll recall, one of the liver's jobs is to convert the sugars in food into fuel for the body. It's also tasked with turning excess energy into body fat. This process is called lipogenesis, and at least theoretically, research suggests, the body may turn fructose into body fat more efficiently compared to sucrose and glucose.

An early study that looked for a link between fructose consumption and body fat was conducted on mice. German researchers allowed them to freely drink either plain water or fructose-sweetened water—the rodent version of soft drinks—for 10 weeks. Though the fructose-sipping mice regularly ate fewer calories from solid food, they gained weight and ended up with 27 percent more body fat than the mice that drank plain water. Because fructose doesn't need insulin to enter the cells, it floods the body and is quickly stored as fat, the study found.

Another study, this one on people, addressed the question of whether fructose really does cause the body to pack on fat. Researchers at the University of Texas Southwestern Medical Center fed "breakfast" to six volunteers—four men and two women. That morning meal was actually 8 ounces of lemonade that contained three different combinations of sugar—100 percent glucose, an equal mix of glucose and fructose, and 25 percent glucose and 75 percent fructose.

Immediately after the volunteers had breakfast, the team measured the conversion of the sugars to fat in the liver. Four hours later, the volunteers ate lunch—turkey sandwiches, salty snacks, and cookies. Each volunteer's lunch contained different amounts of sugars based on body weight. Then the researchers measured how the food was metabolized.

The results: Lipogenesis rose 17 percent when the volunteers had the fructose-containing drinks, compared to 8 percent for the glucose drink. Simply put, their bodies made fat more efficiently. Further, after metabolizing fructose in the morning, the liver increased the storage of fats eaten at lunch. As the study's lead researcher, Elizabeth Parks, PhD, put it: "The carbohydrates came into the body as sugars, the liver took the molecules apart like Tinkertoys, and put them back together to build fats. All this happened within 4 hours after the fructose drink. As a result, when the next meal was eaten, the lunch fat was more likely to be stored than burned." Although this research is preliminary, it certainly raises important questions about starting your day with a fructose-filled sugary drink.

Most likely, these results underestimated the effect of fructose because the test subjects consumed the sugar drinks while fasting and because they were healthy and lean, and could presumably process the fructose quickly, according to Dr. Parks. So the fat-packing potential of fructose may be worse if you're overweight, because this process may be already revved up.

MAKING THE METABOLIC CONNECTION

As you may know, carrying extra pounds sets the stage for a host of metabolic diseases. You're familiar with the BOGO sales at stores? With metabolic syndrome, you "buy" the extra pounds, and you're likely to get all the nasty freebies—belly fat, high blood pressure, high fasting blood sugar, low HDL ("good") cholesterol, and high triglycerides (fatty substances in the blood).

You don't have to be overweight to have metabolic syndrome, which is the name for the bundle of risk factors listed above that raise your odds for heart disease, diabetes, and stroke. Up to 40 percent of normal-weight adults have it. But weight—healthy or no—isn't the defining characteristic of metabolic syndrome. Insulin resistance is.

A team of researchers, including Robert Lustig, MD, author of *Fat Chance*, advanced a theory of exactly how metabolic syndrome—and its disastrous, system-wide consequences—might occur. The process, described in an article published in *Pediatrics*, is extraordinarily complex. But it begins with the body being forced to store excess fat in the liver, as well as in the tissue around the internal organs. This excess fat makes the liver resist the action of insulin. In response, the pancreas produces more insulin to prod the liver into doing its job. Insulin levels rise even higher and cause even more energy to be stored in subcutaneous fat tissue (like your thighs or butt). This is the fat you see in the mirror, the kind you moan over.

The liver tries to export the excess fat that is damaging it in the form of a specific type of blood fat called triglycerides. But too many triglycerides floating around in your bloodstream can be just as problematic. High triglycerides may raise your risk of coronary artery disease, especially if you're a woman.

There's more to this insidious progression of system-wide havoc. But the bottom line is, high insulin levels affect every part of the body—including your belly. In a study published in the *Journal of Clinical Investigation*, 32 overweight men and women drank either glucose- or fructose-sweetened drinks three times a day, along with following a standard diet for 10 weeks. The drinks totaled 25 percent of their daily calories.

At the end of the study, all the participants had gained weight. But CT scans showed that the fructose group mostly gained belly fat. They were actually growing sugar bellies! On the other hand, most of the glucose group's fat gain was subcutaneous. Compared to the glucose group, the fructose group also had higher total cholesterol and LDL ("bad") cholesterol, plus greater insulin resistance—consistent with metabolic syndrome.

BELLY FAT AND DIABETES

So if a sugary diet appears to promote the storage of this deep and dangerous belly fat, it's reasonable to conclude that type 2 diabetes can't be far behind. Indeed, research already links sugar intake to the development of type 2 diabetes, independent of its role in obesity. In other words, it's possible that people develop diabetes because they're overweight or obese. But it may *also* be possible that they develop it because they're consuming added sugars to excess.

One recent study found a smoking gun: an independent, direct link between sugar in the food supply and risk of developing type 2 diabetes. The findings give weight to the still-controversial hypothesis that it's not obesity that's driving this now global pandemic, but the rising consumption of sugar worldwide.

In this study, published in *PLoS ONE,* researchers from the Stanford University School of Medicine, the University of California, Berkeley, and the University of California, San Francisco, analyzed a decade's worth of health data from the United Nations, including diabetes rates and sugar availability, across 175 countries. After controlling for factors like obesity, aging, income, and total calories, the link between sugar and diabetes remained significant. For every extra 150 calories from sugar available per person each day, diabetes prevalence rises by 1.1 percent, the study found. (By the way, 150 calories is just a little more than the number of sugar calories in a 12-ounce can of soda.) Conversely, reduced exposure to sugar was linked to a drop in diabetes prevalence.

This relationship was unique among food types. Categories like protein, fat, and fiber didn't show a significant link to diabetes. Neither did total caloric intake.

While the findings don't prove that sugar causes type 2 diabetes, they do support the ever-expanding body of research—in test tubes, animals, and humans—that suggests sugar affects the liver and pancreas in ways that other

We're Sweeter—and Sicker

In the past 30 years, as our sugar consumption skyrocketed, so did rates of obesity, diabetes, lipid problems, high blood pressure, and heart disease—collectively termed metabolic syndrome. Research is starting to show that that's not a coincidence. Here are the numbers, then and now.

Overweight/obesity. In 1980, obesity rates—which had held steady in the 20 years prior—rose significantly. Until 1980, just 15 percent of American adults had a BMI above the 85th percentile, suggesting either overweight or obesity. Now, it's 55 percent.

Type 2 diabetes. From 1990 through 2010, the annual number of new cases of diagnosed type 2 diabetes almost tripled.

Metabolic syndrome. In 1990, an estimated 50 million US adults had metabolic syndrome. In 2000, that figure rose to 64 million, a 28 percent jump. A 2010 study revised that figure upward yet again—to 68 million, a further increase of 6 percent.

Heart disease. While death from cardiovascular disease fell nearly 33 percent from 1999 to 2009, it still accounted for nearly one in three deaths. And projected increases in obesity and type 2 diabetes, among other factors, may slow that positive change in heart health to only 6 percent.

---

types of foods don't. Another study, published in *Global Public Health*, found that as a nation's fructose intake rises, so do levels of type 2 diabetes. Again, the study didn't prove a direct cause-and-effect link, but did conclude that the prevalence of type 2 is about 20 percent higher in countries where use of HFCS is high, compared to nations where consumption is lower.

SUGAR BELLIES AND SWEET HEARTS

Heart disease is still the number one killer of Americans. Being overweight or having type 2 diabetes raises the risk. Given that previous research links a diet high in sugary soft drinks with obesity and type 2 diabetes, might consuming a steady stream of liquid sugar increase heart disease risk as well?

Yes. In a 2009 study published in the *American Journal of Clinical Nutrition*, Harvard researchers followed the health and habits of 88,520 women enrolled in the famed Nurses' Health Study for 24 years. Compared to women who rarely drank sugary beverages, those who drank more than two a day had a 40 percent higher risk of heart attacks or death from heart disease, the study found.

Maybe you think a daily Big Gulp doesn't matter if you're at a healthy weight or eat a basically healthy diet. Nope. While eating well and maintaining a healthy weight are both important, neither did much to reduce the heart disease risk associated with sugary beverage consumption, the study found.

Other studies suggest that a high-sugar diet does nasty things to your blood vessels, too. For example, high insulin levels cause the smooth muscle cells around each blood vessel to grow faster than normal. This growth tightens artery walls, promoting high blood pressure and thereby raising the risk of heart attack and stroke.

Added sugars in processed foods may also increase cholesterol. A study in the *Journal of the American Medical Association* analyzed 7 years of data from the National Health and Nutrition Examination Survey, administered annually by the Centers for Disease Control and Prevention. The data tracks such things as diet, body mass index, cholesterol level, and blood pressure, as well as behaviors like smoking, exercise, and alcohol consumption.

After excluding people with diabetes and high cholesterol, and those who were excessively overweight, the researchers found that adults consumed an average of 21.4 teaspoons of added sugar a day. Alarmingly, as the number of added-sugar calories increased, the levels of HDL cholesterol went down, and LDL cholesterol and triglyceride levels went up. These associations held true even after the researchers controlled for other risk factors for high cholesterol and heart disease. How and why added sugars increase cholesterol aren't yet clear, but one theory is they cause your liver to secrete more "bad" LDL cholesterol and interfere with the body's ability to get rid of it.

THIS IS YOUR BRAIN, ON DOUGHNUTS

A rat brain ravaged by insulin resistance—significantly punier than a healthy rat brain—is not a pretty sight. And worse, there's evidence that a steady diet

A Moment on the Lips, Forever on the Face?

Pricey firming creams, filler injections, and antiaging facials will always be here. But to have supple, radiant skin in your midthirties and beyond, dermatologists have a tip for you: Lay off the sugar. A lifetime of overdoing it on sugar may accelerate age-related damage.

The culprit: the natural process glycation, in which the sugar in your bloodstream attaches to proteins to form harmful new molecules called advanced glycation end products. (Researchers called them AGEs for short. Too perfect!) The more sugar you eat, the theory goes, the more AGEs you develop. As AGEs build up, they damage the proteins nearby.

Most vulnerable to damage are the protein fibers collagen and elastin, which keep skin firm and elastic. Once they're damaged, these fibers go from springy and resilient to dry and brittle, leading to wrinkles and sagging. These age-related changes to the skin start at about age 35 and increase rapidly after that, according to a study published in the *British Journal of Dermatology*.

But a high-sugar diet doesn't just damage collagen. It also affects the *type* of collagen you have, another factor in skin's resistance to wrinkling. Skin's most abundant collagens are types I, II, and III, with type III lasting the longest. Glycation can transform desirable type III collagen into the more fragile type I, making it look and feel less supple. To add insult to injury, AGEs also deactivate your body's natural antioxidant enzymes. That leaves your skin more vulnerable to sun damage, which is still the main cause of skin aging.

You take care of the sunscreen—we'll help with the eating. The Sugar Smart Diet ferrets out not just obvious Straight-Up Sugars like sweets and soda, but the Secret Sugars and the Sugar Mimics that act like sugar in your body and may show up on your face.

of sugary, processed foods can mess with insulin in *our* brains, triggering what some experts are calling type 3 diabetes, better known as Alzheimer's disease.

Suzanne de la Monte, MD, a neuropathologist at Brown University whose team coined the term type 3 diabetes, was among the first to uncover the link between insulin resistance and a high-fat diet in brain cells. In a paper published in *Current Alzheimer Research*, de la Monte reviewed the growing body of evidence suggesting that Alzheimer's is fundamentally a metabolic disease in which the brain's ability to use glucose and produce energy is impaired. The evidence, she writes, suggests that Alzheimer's has "virtually all of the features of diabetes [mellitus], but is largely confined to the brain."

In one study, de la Monte and her team disrupted the way rats' brains respond to insulin. The rats developed all the brain damage seen in Alzheimer's disease. For example, areas of the brain associated with memory got clotted with toxic protein fragments called beta-amyloid plaques. The rats were unable to learn their way through a maze. In other experiments where insulin resistance was induced, they developed many of the features of Alzheimer's disease.

People with type 2 diabetes are significantly more likely to suffer from Alzheimer's. While the disease doesn't necessarily *cause* Alzheimer's, researchers believe that both diseases may share the same root: insulin resistance, which can be caused by eating too much sugary, fatty junk food. When researchers fed healthy men and women a high-saturated-fat diet loaded with refined grains and sugary foods for a month, their insulin levels rose—and the levels of beta-amyloid in their spinal fluid rose significantly, an *Archives of Neurology* study reported. A control group on a low-saturated-fat/healthier-carb diet showed reductions in both. Dr. de la Monte's research is ongoing, but the implications are clearly pointing toward an adverse connection between sugar consumption and Alzheimer's. Remember that the next time you're tempted to swap a snack of almonds and a piece of fruit for a blueberry muffin as big as your fist slathered with jam. Your brain's counting on you to make the healthier choice.

It's easy to be hooked on sweet flavors thanks to so much fructose hiding in processed foods. But once you reset your taste buds, you'll find that whole, natural foods deliver just the right amount of sweetness. There's nothing like enjoying a slice of sun-warmed cantaloupe or forking up some tender beets, knowing that you're savoring the true taste of sweet. You'll discover all this when you begin the Sugar Smart Diet. First, though, there's just one more aspect of sugar I want you to understand: why we're so drawn to it.

NORA HAEFELE

BEFORE

"THIS HAS BEEN A MIRACLE DIET FOR ME," says Nora, who has been battling her weight for 45 years and was diagnosed with type 2 diabetes 7 years ago. "I've never lost weight this quickly with so little pain or effort."

Previously, Nora had focused mainly on increasing exercise. "I walk every day and do a race on most weekends," she says. "I realized that I was doing 5-Ks but eating for marathons—and I wasn't paying attention to the quality of the calories I was eating," she says. "On this plan, it became clear to me that when I avoided sugar and refined carbohydrates and ate good carbs, lean protein, and healthy fats instead, I was able to have smaller portions without feeling hungry."

Nora discovered many new favorite dishes while on the Sugar Smart Diet meal plans. "I love, love, love the Fiesta Egg Salad and when I had my first Banana-Coconut Roll, I thought I'd died and gone to heaven!" she says. However, she wasn't completely comfortable in the kitchen at first. "All the planning, shopping, cooking, and cleaning up were cutting into my exercise time," she says. As she became more familiar with the dishes and created a system for meal prep, it got easier. Now on Sundays, Nora plans her meals for the week, shops, and cooks ahead, broiling chicken breasts, cooking bulgur, and hard-cooking eggs.

On top of losing more than 16 pounds and almost 11 inches (2½ of them from her waist) during the 32-day plan, Nora lowered her borderline high blood pressure a total of 26 points and cut her triglycerides 66 points. She also improved her fasting glucose level by 13 points, getting her down to a healthy level.

Nora's decided that Phase 2 of the Sugar Smart Diet is what she wants to follow for life. "I feel like I've literally been freed from an addiction," says Nora, an alcoholic who's been sober for 25 years. "Just like I can't have one beer, I learned on this plan that I can't have one piece of cake. I don't have to think about if I want it or should I have it. It's just no, that's not good for me. For the first time, I'm hopeful that I will get down to a healthy weight."

16.2
POUNDS LOST

AGE:
56

ALL-OVER
INCHES LOST:
10.75

SUGAR SMART WISDOM
"You can break that soda habit! Try drinking orange-vanilla seltzer instead. It tastes like a creamsicle."

UNDERSTANDING THE ATTRACTION

Cravings are like itches—often they don't stop until you scratch. Yet you probably know someone who, when they crave a brownie or Frappuccino, can easily sidestep it or can enjoy the treat and go on with their lives. Why do so many others—maybe even you—seem locked in sugar's subtle but powerful grip? It happens when the hardwiring of the brain intersects with your life's experiences with sugar.

SUGAR ON THE BRAIN

In the late '60s, quite by accident, a graduate student in upstate New York discovered that the lab rats in his care went nuts for Froot Loops. So powerful was their lust for the sugary cereal, it drove them into the center of their roomy, brightly lit cages.

Any researcher who works with rats knows that rats prefer cramped, dark surroundings.

The Froot Loop epiphany was one budding psychologist's bread crumb on a trail that will someday lead to a full understanding of what happens in the brain to trigger the compulsion to use substances that snare the body and the brain. Those substances include alcohol, nicotine, street drugs—and food.

In certain areas of the brain, the pursuit of pleasure merges with the drive to survive. This is the hedonic pathway, the brain's reward system. Give it natural rewards, like food and sex, and it activates, reacting like a slot machine releasing its jackpot. It's also activated by artificial rewards such as addictive drugs. To paraphrase the writer Elizabeth Wurtzel, the hedonic pathway knows just three words: more, now, again.

The hedonic pathway is composed of two brain areas: the VTA and the NA (the ventral tegmental area and the nucleus accumbens, respectively). This pathway to pleasure is attuned to two brain chemicals, opiates and dopamine. It's important to understand that foods or activities we associate with bliss—say, ice cream or sex—aren't inherently blissful. The real cause of the delight is those pleasure chemicals flooding our brains. The more important of these chemicals is dopamine.

Working in tandem, the VTA and the NA—which is dubbed the brain's reward center—release dopamine, resulting in what researchers call a "feeling of reward" and we call pleasure. That fluttery anticipation you feel just before you bite into a brownie? Thank your dopamine supply for hot-wiring your hedonic pathway.

But eat brownies or other sugar-laden treats too often, and over time the brain adapts to the surges in dopamine by producing less of it or reducing the number of dopamine receptors in the reward circuit. With the impact of dopamine reduced, you need more of the substance to achieve the same dopamine high.

This effect, called tolerance, occurs with street drugs. And it may occur with sugar, too. Research shows that sugar triggers the release of opioids and dopamine, as addictive drugs do, and more lab studies on rodents suggest evidence of sugar addiction. The parallels are stunning.

- Rats given daily access to sugar in the form of a sugar solution, only to have it taken away, will binge when it's given back to them.
- When sugar is taken away, their teeth chatter, they develop tremors and the shakes, and, when put into mazes, demonstrate anxiety—all signs of withdrawal.
- After 2 weeks of abstinence from sugar—imposed by the researchers—they begin to seek and crave it, as demonstrated by repeatedly pressing a lever to self-administer it. (Luckily, you're a lot smarter than a rat, and can actually learn to protect your health and short-circuit your sugar cravings.)

As it turns out, these findings have implications for humans.

SUGAR, CARBS, AND ADDICTION

Say that you're "addicted" to chocolate (or jelly beans or chips—insert your must-have carb of choice here) and somewhere, a registered dietitian sighs. Nutrition experts have spent considerable time and energy saying that there are no bad foods. And they're right, providing you don't eat so much of them that they threaten your health, make you feel terrible about yourself, or otherwise hurt your quality of life.

But what if you *do* consume sugar to excess and can't stop, no matter how much you want to? Is it possible for humans to be literally addicted to sugar?

There's no simple answer. As the rodent studies discussed above suggest, a pattern of avoiding sugar and then bingeing on it can lead to behavior and neurochemical changes that resemble the effects of substance abuse. And researchers have long known that sugar affects the same feel-good brain hormones, dopamine and opioids, as street drugs.

Jokes about your daily sugar fix aside, there's evidence to suggest that some people may abuse sugar. Take, for example, a 2008 study conducted on 61 overweight women, all self-reported carb cravers. The carbs these women craved weren't in apples or quinoa, but in chocolate, gummy bears, chips, pasta, bread, pretzels—foods that are high in easy-digested carbs and/or sugar.

The researchers didn't take the women's claims of carb-craving at face value. To participate in the study, the women had to meet a list of stringent criteria. To name just a few, they had to report eating carb-rich snacks with a specific ratio of carbs to protein between meals at least four times a week, in the afternoon or evening, and that they either felt blue before eating them or felt their low mood lift when eating them.

The researchers wanted to know about carb-rich foods' "abuse potential"— a phrase that refers to a drug used in nonmedical situations, repeatedly or sporadically, for its positive effects, including sedation, euphoria, and mood changes. Drugs with abuse potential can produce psychological or physical dependence and may lead to addiction.

The findings, published in the journal *Psychopharmacology*, are interesting. Given a choice between a carb-rich drink and a protein-rich one, and with no information about what the two beverages contained, the majority of these carb cravers preferred the carb-rich beverage. But here's where it gets *really* interesting. The responses of the women who *consistently* preferred the carb-y beverage indicated a key criterion of substance dependence: tolerance.

The study was broken into two 3-day sessions that occurred over 2 weeks. For the first 2 days of each "exposure" session, researchers asked the women to recall and focus on a sad memory as they listened to a piece of classical music shown in previous studies to invoke a melancholy mood. (For the record, it was *Russia Under the Mongolian Yoke*, by Sergei Prokofiev.)

Once they'd lowered their moods, the women were given either the carb drink (100 percent carbohydrate, from a variety of refined sugars) or the protein drink (37 percent whey protein, 0 percent fat, and 63 percent carbohydrates from refined sugars and food starch). Each volunteer was given one of the beverages in a red-topped cup on one day and the other beverage in a blue-topped cup on the other day; the same drink appeared in the same cup color across both weeks. The third day of each session was the test session: After again self-inducing a bad, sad, or low mood, the women were asked to choose and drink the beverage that had most lifted their moods. By a significant margin, the women reported better moods when they drank the carbohydrate drink.

Even more noteworthy: In the women who consistently preferred the carb drink, their liking for it grew over time, whereas the drink's ability to lift their negative mood decreased over time. This suggests tolerance—the need for more of a substance to get the same effect, or when the same amount produces less of a "rush" with continued use.

The study's conclusion? Sugary, starchy foods *do* show abuse potential, but only in those who crave them. In other words, it's possible to develop a dependence on these foods' ability to alter your mood.

SUGAR, HUNGER, AND HORMONES

Maybe you don't feel that you're addicted to sugar, have an intense emotional relationship with chocolate, or turn to food when life gets hard. In fact, you might think you're eating just great. You're microwaving oatmeal for breakfast and packing Greek yogurt for lunch and eating diet entrées for dinner, plus forking up salads with that amazing low-fat Asian ginger salad dressing. But the jeans ain't getting any looser. You're eating healthy food. What's going on?

The incredible truth is that even if you avoid Straight-Up Sugar, there's a good chance you're consuming Secret Sugar—every day, and more than is healthy. The foods it's added to would shock you.

But you don't know that. You just wonder why you're hungry, starving, famished all the damn time.

Recent studies suggest that chronic sugar intake messes with our brain's ability to tell us to stop eating. Basically, eating too much added sugar allows the fructose in white sugar and HFCS to send your hunger hormones—the ones that tell your brain you're full—into a tailspin.

Here's what's supposed to happen. Your stomach produces a hormone called ghrelin. That's your brain's cue to send out the "chow down" signal. As you eat, your stomach begins the process of digestion, breaking down your meal or snack and converting it to glucose, which enters your bloodstream.

In response to that influx of blood sugar, your pancreas releases the hormone insulin. Insulin in turn triggers your fat cells to send out a third hormone, leptin, which decreases your appetite. Basically, rising leptin lets your brain know that you've had enough, thank you very much, and you can put the fork down and step away from the table.

Here's where things can go right or wrong.

If your cells are sensitive to the effects of insulin, your body uses glucose properly, ghrelin and leptin stay in balance, and you are unlikely to overeat. But if your cells resist insulin's effects—which is likely if you're carrying extra pounds or have type 2 diabetes—your appetite doesn't diminish and glucose is more likely to be stored as fat.

In addition, research suggests that consuming large amounts of fructose can wreak havoc on these hormones of metabolism. That's because leptin, insulin, and ghrelin do not respond to fructose as they do to glucose, so your body doesn't know when it's had enough to eat. Without those internal controls—and *with* a steady diet of fructose foods—you're liable to gain weight. The worst part: The fructose in these foods is often hidden, so you may not even know you're consuming it.

FROM RUSH TO CRASH: SUGAR AND MOOD

In an ad campaign for a popular energy bar, elite athletes waxed philosophic about the beauty of competition. These dudes and chicks are *warriors*. What's in that 2.3-ounce bar—sold in every drugstore, supermarket, and big-box store—that delivers such energy, such endurance?

Twenty grams of sugar, according to the Nutrition Facts label. The first ingredients listed: organic evaporated cane juice syrup, maltodextrin, fructose, and dextrose. That's three sugars and a starch (maltodextrin)!

Athletes engaged in high-intensity competition can use the bar's quick burst of energy. For those of us who tear it open and call it breakfast or lunch, not so much.

Food manufacturers often describe their sugary wares as offering quick energy. It's quick, all right. Sugar can raise levels of the mood-boosting neurotransmitter serotonin in much the same way as a nutritious, fiber-filled bowl of steel-cut oatmeal. But that sugar rush soon evaporates, and your energy and mood deflate like one of those holiday lawn ornaments on a timer. Your timer: 30 minutes or less, the time it takes from sugar rush to sugar crash. Sugary pick-me-ups can set you up for fatigue, low moods, and more unhealthy eating.

Let's say you grab a sugary energy bar or coffee drink or a food that acts like sugar in the body—a package of cheese crackers or a big bag of pretzels. Their refined carbs are digested quickly and speed into the bloodstream as glucose. This rapid breakdown triggers a flood of insulin to transport that glucose into the cells. Shortly thereafter, blood sugar levels nose-dive, you get hungry, you reach for another pick-me-up, and the cycle continues. Sugar also triggers the release of serotonin—which regulates sleep as well as mood—causing postsugar drowsiness. You may crave more sweets to regain that sugar high or brighten your mood.

Sugar's link to full-on clinical depression is complex. One theory about depression holds that it's caused by a deficiency of brain serotonin. Antidepressants such as Wellbutrin and Prozac increase this serotonin. So does eating carbohydrates. People with serotonin-deficient brains may well medicate with carbs, especially sugary carbs. But over time, it takes more and more sugar to achieve the same boost in brain serotonin. Sounds like a great way to pack on the pounds, no?

So in the long run, sugar does not stabilize mood. It's an unreliable friend—it drains you and leaves you feeling worse after your encounter rather than better. This was shown in a study published in *Public Health Journal.* A group of Spanish researchers examined the relationship between the incidence of depression and eating sugary sweets and fast food in 8,964 people. The researchers collected data on other variables that could influence the relationship between eating habits and depression, including age and sex, BMI and physical activity level, and total calorie intake and healthy food consumption.

After following the group for 6 years and adjusting for the variables noted above, the researchers determined that those who ate the most junk food had a 37 percent greater risk of developing depression compared to those who consumed the least.

And here's another way sugar betrays you. What if a major part of the brain's reward region reacted to the consumption of sugar in an abnormal way:

by not offering much of a reaction at all? This brain glitch may have its roots in yet another glitch, one of metabolism: insulin resistance, which is associated with an increased risk of type 2 diabetes. Scientists compared the brains of people with insulin resistance to those of insulin-sensitive people (whose cells absorb glucose efficiently). They found that, in people with insulin resistance, the nucleus accumbens (NA) released significantly lower levels of dopamine, compared to people whose cells responded normally to insulin's effects.

The bottom line? The overeating and weight gain that often precedes type 2 diabetes might be related to these abnormally lower levels of dopamine release.

In the study, presented at a 2013 annual meeting of the Society of Nuclear Medicine and Molecular Imaging, researchers had two groups of people consume sugar (a glucose drink). One group was insulin resistant. The other group was sensitive to insulin's effects. On a separate day, both groups drank an artificially sweetened beverage.

After both groups consumed each drink, the scientists scanned their brains to compare the release of dopamine in the NA. The results were then matched with the answers to a questionnaire that asked the volunteers to document their eating behaviors, so the scientists could catch anything abnormal.

After drinking the artificially sweetened beverage, dopamine receptors in the brain worked normally in both groups, the scientists found. Not so with the sugary drink. Compared to the insulin-resistant group, the NA of the insulin-sensitive group released significantly more dopamine. The brains of the insulin-resistant volunteers did not receive the same reward.

The bottom line: If you're insulin-resistant, your brain may not reward you when you eat sugar by releasing normal amounts of dopamine. In other words, you may not be getting that sugar rush you want so badly. Trying to get that pleasure, you eat more, gain weight, increase your risk of diabetes, and feed that sugar belly.

If you suspect your love of sugar is messing with your mood, job one is to steady your insulin and blood sugar levels. Big spikes and dips can zoom you to the bright mood and energetic buzz of a sugar high, followed soon after by a crash that leaves you moody and tired. The Sugar Smart Diet can help get those blood sugar levels rock-steady. It can also help put you in touch with what sugar means to you, what it does for you, and how to make healthy changes in the amount and type of sugars you choose to eat.

You can do this. We'll do it together. The next chapter gives you an overview of the Sugar Smart Diet Rules. Read them now, and tomorrow you can take that first step toward sugar freedom. It might be a little rocky at first, but we'll stick with you every step of the way, offering words of support and practical ways to make it through. Sooner than you think, your jeans will be looser; your energy higher; and your mood brighter. And in just 32 days, you'll have kicked sugar overload to the curb, given food manufacturers a run for their money, and made your peace with sugar, reclaiming it as the pleasure it was always meant to be.

CAROL STIEGLER

BEFORE

WHEN CAROL WAS GETTING READY for her Sugar Smart photo shoot, she asked her family for their opinion on what to wear. As she modeled several outfits, everyone reached a consensus—she had to go shopping. "Nothing fit; everything was too big!" she said proudly. "When I went shopping, I bought size 6s. I couldn't believe it! I haven't been that size in 20 years. It's a great feeling."

With her new svelte figure, "Shopping was fun; the way it used to be before I gained all the weight," said Carol. "After I had a hysterectomy in my forties, I noticed it was harder to lose weight. When I quit smoking in my fifties, I got into the habit of snacking, and the weight really piled on. I'd always been a runner, and I even increased my mileage over the past 4 years. When I started running more, though, I started eating more at night, snacking on all the wrong things like cheese crackers, Chex Mix, and licorice. I had a licorice addiction. I'd eat a whole bag in a day."

Carol started the Sugar Smart Diet because she wanted to get her snacking—and her licorice habit—under control. The first week was hard, and Carol was feeling sluggish during her runs. However, she adjusted the timing of her meals and snacks so she was eating enough before she hit the pavement. Now she has so much energy, she has increased her workouts from 4 days a week to every day, often doing multiple activities such as running and walking or walking and inline skating. Healthwise, Carol had big drops in her total cholesterol (64 points, the best result in our test panel) and triglyceride levels.

And Carol succeeded in breaking her excessive snacking habit. "After you clean out the sugar and junk in your body, you start to lose the cravings for those things. You feel better and want to continue," says Carol. "I've lost the desire for snacking and for sweetness." She does allow herself a treat once a week—a handful of licorice. "It's easy to stop now. I've worked so hard to lose this weight, and I don't ever want to gain it back."

10.8
POUNDS LOST

AGE:
60

ALL-OVER INCHES LOST:
10.25

SUGAR SMART WISDOM
"Set a goal and just start. If you want to become more physically active, walk or do another activity you enjoy every day, and before you know it, it will become a habit."

THE SUGAR SMART DIET RULES

Ready to kick some sugary butt? Good! Over the next 32 days you are going to break the hold sugar has on your body and your brain and shrink your sugar belly for good. And it is going to be simpler—and sweeter—than you might think. The Sugar Smart Diet infuses each day with health and pleasure, always including some way to tantalize your taste buds. Brownies are delightful, ice cream divine, but the sweet life outshines even their considerable charms.

Before you begin, get familiar with these eight rules. Each addresses a small but crucial component of sugar freedom. Some of them guide you toward eating the right foods in the right ways, but they focus on more than what to eat and what not to eat. (That sounds too much like a diet!) Others are designed to help you find pleasure and comfort without turning to sugar. In every phase of the plan, we offer practical ways to put each one into daily practice. Commit to them, and they'll lead you to a life of joy and good health, punctuated with the pleasure of a sweet treat Every Single Day. Once you're free of the sugary shackles that bind you, what *can't* you accomplish if you want to?

Does that sound like an exaggeration? Let me assure you, it's not. I can honestly say that once I got sugar smart and changed my relationship with sugar, it changed my life. Read any of our test panelists' success stories and you'll see that it changed theirs, too. Now it's your turn. Here's a snapshot from your future: You've shrunk your sugar belly, but you've also accomplished so much more. You're healthy and energized, calm and craving free. You've crushed your dependence on sugar but reclaimed the pleasure. You're in control. These eight guidelines can set you free.

SUGARSMART RULE# 1 | Begin your day with breakfast— and pack it with protein.

You've probably heard this a million times, but breakfast really is the most important meal of the day, especially if you're looking to slim down. In fact, eating a morning meal is a common habit among people who have lost weight and kept it off. Breakfast skippers are 4.5 times more likely to be obese than breakfast eaters, a study in the *American Journal of Epidemiology* showed. Another study from the Harvard Medical School found that eating breakfast led to better blood sugar control, cutting in half the odds of having high glucose levels.

What you eat is important, though. Start your day with a bowl of cold cereal (even whole grain), a bagel, a muffin, or some fruit, and chances are you will be ravenous in just a few hours. Why? Those meals are primarily carbohydrates—and quickly digested ones at that. Glucose levels spike and insulin is released, glucose levels drop precipitously and you're left scrounging for something else to eat.

The antidote: Pump up the protein. It slows digestion, and research shows that calorie for calorie, protein is more filling than carbohydrates or fat.

Researchers at Saint Louis University found that overweight women naturally took in about 160 fewer calories at lunch when they ate protein-packed eggs in the morning versus a bagel.

Other research shows that protein in the morning makes it difficult for sugar cravings to take hold later on. University of Missouri researchers had 20 overweight young women who routinely skipped breakfast either eat one of two morning meals, cereal or eggs and beef, or no breakfast at all for 7 days. On that last day, the women took part in a 10-hour test that included an all-you-can-eat dinner of microwaveable pizza pockets, as well as an unlimited evening snack of foods such as cookies, cakes, apple slices, and yogurt. The results? The high-protein egg-beef group produced less of the hunger-stimulating hormone ghrelin and more PPY (a hormone that, like leptin, signals fullness) than those who ate cereal. MRI scans showed reduced activity in areas of the brain associated with cravings. In the end, the protein group reported a 30 percent increase in feelings of fullness and consumed 170 fewer calories from their evening snack smorgasbord.

Breakfasts on the Sugar Smart Diet are hearty—around 300 calories, with at least 20 percent of those calories coming from protein. Your breakfasts will include plenty of lean-protein items, from Greek yogurt and peanut butter to eggs and low-fat cheese. (If you haven't tried the fluffy, high-protein grain called quinoa, you're in for a treat!)

Can't stomach food too early in the morning? No problem. Eat it by 10 a.m. and breakfast will still help quell late-day cravings.

SUGAR SMART RULE #2 | Never go hungry—eat five times a day.

We told you why you shouldn't skip breakfast. Now we'll tell you why you shouldn't skip lunch, dinner, or snacks, either. We know—sometimes that's unavoidable. You're staring down a can't-miss deadline. Your pet is ill, and the vet appointment trumps lunch. Or you're just honest-to-goodness not hungry, so you figure that if you skip a meal you don't want anyway, you'll save a few calories.

But there's danger in meal skipping—weight and sugar belly peril. If you cut down on the amount of food you eat for an extended period of time, your body is going to slow things down to conserve its energy supply. If you're looking to flatten your sugar belly, that "starvation response" is the last thing you need. Meal skipping is also a guaranteed way to fire up sugar cravings. Skipping meals lowers blood sugar levels and causes you to overeat the rest of the day to make up for missed calories.

However, we're predicting that you won't want to miss any meals or snacks while you're following the Sugar Smart Diet. Made with nourishing and delicious whole foods—such as whole grains, beans, lean meats/poultry/fish, nuts, unsweetened low-fat dairy, eggs, and veggies—they'll fill you up and give you the ideal balance of lean protein, energizing carbohydrates, and healthy fats to steady your blood sugar and insulin levels and extinguish cravings for sugar.

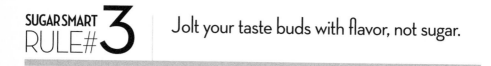

SUGAR SMART RULE #3 | Jolt your taste buds with flavor, not sugar.

What's the difference between the two? As delightful as sugar is, it always tastes the same, with variations on sweet and sickeningly sweet. On the other hand, flavor is wonderfully diverse and surprising. If you've ever laid a branch of fresh rosemary on chicken as it bakes, seeded a deliciously fragrant vanilla bean for a special dish, or topped a sliced tomato with basil leaves still warm from the garden, you know how much flavor fresh herbs and spices can add to everyday fare. And as you'll learn, sweet spices, such as cinnamon, can ease cravings for sugar, which can help you stick to a healthy eating plan.

The dried herbs and spices in your spice rack are the workhorses of everyday cuisine, but when a dish calls for fresh herbs, do your best to use them. Leafy basil, cilantro, parsley, mint, dill, and thyme are far more flavorful than their dried counterparts. And when you chop them, the fragrance they release is an olfactory delight.

And don't forget other flavor boosters—balsamic vinegar, lemon and orange zest, roasted peppers, hot sauce, toasted nuts, and sugar-free salsa, to name a few. One of my favorites is extra-virgin olive oil. I love its grassy, fruity

SUGAR SMART MENTOR

Andrew Weil, MD

GIVE IT A WEEK. The taste buds soon habituate to a lower overall level of sweetness in the diet—this starts to happen in as little as a week. Foods that once seemed palatable soon seem cloyingly, even sickeningly sweet. A side benefit is that reducing sugar consumption and heightening your sensitivity can reveal a wonderful, subtle sweetness in foods that once seemed to have no sweet notes at all. Certain oolong teas, for example, have a pronounced natural sweetness that I came to appreciate only after I had ratcheted down my consumption of sweet foods.

MAKE SUGAR PART OF A MEAL. Generally, the only added sugar I consume is the modest amount that is added to high-quality dark chocolate (70 percent cacao). My reasoning is that the fat in the chocolate slows the spikes and dips in insulin and blood sugar. If you do eat a food with added sugar, the healthiest way to do so is to make sure that the amount of sugar it contains is modest and to have it with foods that are full of fiber, protein, and fat to slow metabolism and control the rise and fall of insulin.

DON'T SIP SUGAR. The least healthy way to consume added sugar is to drink it in the form of a sweetened beverage. The sugar dissolved in soda is maximally bioavailable. The rise in blood sugar is nearly vertical, and the upcoming dip is correspondingly precipitous.

GET BACK TO BASICS. Added sugar is a relatively recent invention in human evolutionary history, and we have absolutely no need for it. Added, refined sugar in the diet appeared only in the last 1,500 years or so and in abundance only in the last century. There has not been nearly enough time for human beings to metabolically adapt to consuming copious amounts of sugar. When it comes to imagining life without it (or less of it), imagine yourself as the end product of hundreds of thousands of years of evolution and as a creature exquisitely adapted to thrive on a diet of unprocessed whole foods.

ANDREW WEIL, MD, *a leader and pioneer in the field of integrative medicine, is founder and director of the Arizona Center for Integrative Medicine at the University of Arizona in Tucson, where he is also the clinical professor of medicine and professor of public health and holds the Jones-Lovell Endowed Chair in integrative rheumatology. He is the author of numerous books including* True Food: Seasonal, Sustainable, Simple, Pure *and* Spontaneous Happiness.

flavor on salads and vegetables and in soups; even a little drizzle gives me that "I'm full" feeling. I used to think that was because of the fat, but get this—the oil's aromatic compounds seem to be a factor that makes it so satisfying. Just getting a whiff reduced the number of calories people consumed at a meal and even improved their blood sugar response, according to a study from the German Research Center for Food Chemistry. Amazing!

As you move through the phases of the plan, identify which flavors thrill your taste buds and commit to exploring the diverse array of flavors that nature offers. Have you drizzled really good balsamic vinegar over poached pears? Have you grated fresh ginger or chopped citrus-scented cilantro to create a homemade salsa? Enjoy the spiciness of freshly cracked pepper on your salads, or treat yourself to fresh vanilla beans. Stir your coffee or tea with a stick of cinnamon. Toss a serving of plain, air-popped popcorn with a teaspoon of smoked paprika—its deep color and intense flavor go way beyond what you get from the regular type. The more adventuresome you are, the more you'll grow to appreciate flavor and put sugar in its rightful place in your daily diet.

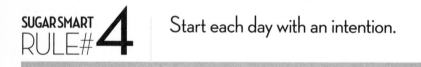

SUGAR SMART RULE #4 | Start each day with an intention.

Yesterday is gone. Tomorrow isn't here yet. Today is what you have to work with. Setting an intention—a personal goal or hope for the day—each morning can help you make the most of this unique 24-hour slice of your life. It opens you to the opportunities for joy, growth, and wisdom that are unique to you and that help you place sugar in the right context: a pleasure, to be savored mindfully in healthy amounts.

It took me a while to learn the importance of setting a daily intention. I figured it out one morning at 5 a.m. As was my habit, I was checking my e-mail while waiting for my coffee to brew. (I can get a *lot* of e-mail overnight!) This particular morning, I had a lightbulb moment: Why was I starting my day with a slew of other people's to-dos at the top of my own to-do list? Then and there, without realizing it, I set my first daily intention: to spend that 5 a.m. quiet time on *me*.

Now, as my coffee brews, I read, meditate, do yoga, or just think about my personal priorities, from big-picture goals to what I need to accomplish that morning. My daily intention can be as practical as, "Today I will order that book on Amazon I've been meaning to read," or as lofty as, "Today I will not let fear motivate me—I will move toward bringing more joy and happiness in my life." This hour of "me" time has made a real difference in my life—every day.

Beginning in Phase 1, you'll set an intention before you begin your day. I'll explain how in Chapter 7, but for now, know this: You'll come to rely on those few minutes, which are completely and entirely all about you and your success.

SUGAR SMART RULE #5 | Add some joy to your life each day.

We can almost hear you now: With what time? Well, maybe the time you spend shaking your fist at the heavens over traffic jams, schedule snafus, and other common stresses you can't control. To lose weight and shrink your sugar belly, it's vital to commit to everyday R&R. Otherwise, chronic stress may eventually gain the upper hand and grind your physical and emotional well-being to dust.

Chronic stress—a daily assault of stress hormones from a demanding job or a life in turmoil—grinds away every cell in your body. That wear and tear comes at a price. Numerous emotional and physical disorders have been linked to stress, including depression, anxiety, heart attacks, stroke, hypertension, digestive problems, even autoimmune diseases like rheumatoid arthritis.

You may also hit the cookies and ice cream pretty hard. When you're stressed, your body releases the hormone cortisol, which signals your brain to seek rewards. Foods loaded with sugar and fat apply the brakes to the stress system by blunting this hormone. When you reach for food in response to stress, you inadvertently create a powerful connection in your brain. The food gets coded in your memory center as a solution to an unpleasant experience or emotion. Face that same problem again, and your brain will likely tell you, "Break out the cupcakes!"

While you can't banish stress from your life completely, you can create an oasis of calm in your daily routine. Managing your stress requires that you find and maintain a balance between the stressful activities that drain you and the relaxing activities that refresh and renew your body and spirit. In each phase of the Sugar Smart Diet, you'll discover stress-management techniques you can build into your day. These simple but powerful strategies don't have to disrupt your busy schedule.

For example, if you like oranges, pick up a bottle of orange-scented aromatherapy oil or spray and treat yourself to a hit of "sweet" without the sugar. In a study published in the *Journal of Alternative and Complementary Medicine*, participants who endured a stressful test felt much less anxious when they sniffed orange essential oil 5 minutes before the exam. Best of all, the effects followed them throughout the day. I've used scent as a stress buster for years—it works! I keep a few aromatherapy sprays at home and in my office drawer and choose depending on my mood: lavender for calming, tangerine to brighten my day, peppermint for energizing. Keeping a scented oil or spray at your desk can truly save the day. When you're in crunch time, pause and take a deep whiff. Bam—the modern-day equivalent of stopping to smell the roses. We've got a ton more relaxation strategies in store. Small things can deliver such sweet rewards!

SUGAR SMART RULE# 6 | Sleep more to eat (and crave) less.

One important goal of the Sugar Smart Diet is to restore metabolic harmony between the hormones ghrelin (an appetite trigger) and leptin (which signals satiety), along with insulin. When these hormones are working in concert, the result is fewer cravings and less propensity to store fat. But if you get less than the recommended 7 to 9 hours of sack time, you may be undercutting this goal. In a University of Chicago study, a few sleepless nights were enough to drop levels of leptin by 18 percent and boost levels of ghrelin by about 30 percent. Those two changes alone caused appetites to kick into overdrive, and cravings for sugary foods like cookies and bread jumped 45 percent.

Another reason to get to bed at a decent hour: Sleep deprivation may not only make sugary, fatty foods more appealing, it may also lower your ability to resist them, according to two small yet intriguing studies presented at a 2012 annual meeting of sleep researchers.

In one study of 25 men and women, researchers at Columbia University and St. Luke's/Roosevelt Hospital used brain scans to compare activity in the brain's reward regions after 5 nights of either normal sleep (9 hours) or restricted sleep (4 hours). The scans were performed as the researchers showed their volunteers pictures of both healthy foods (fruit, veggies, oatmeal) and unhealthy foods (candy, pizza). The reward regions were more active when the volunteers were sleep deprived than when they were well rested—especially when the sleepy subjects viewed the pictures of the candy and pizza.

Worse, the parts of your brain that usually put the brakes on cravings aren't as active when you're tired, research conducted at the University of California, Berkeley, found. Scientists had 16 people rate their desire for various foods—once after a night of normal sleep and once after 24 hours without sleep—as they administered brain scans. The volunteers expressed a stronger preference for junk food when they were deprived of sleep. But the scans didn't just show more activity in reward regions. They also showed less activity in regions involved in decision making. The upshot? When you're tired, you may be drawn to sugary, fatty foods partly because your ability to process information and make sound decisions is impaired.

If there's anything humans should know how to do perfectly, it's sleep. However, our tech-heavy, stress-laden lifestyles can make it hard to do what should come naturally. Each phase of the plan offers simple ways to slide into the restful slumber you deserve—every night.

SUGAR SMART RULE# 7 | Move away from cravings.

Exercise has a positive effect on appetite and blood sugar metabolism. But I know how tough it is to fit a workout into a busy day. That's why I worked with the *Prevention* fitness team to create a workout that was convenient, pleasurable (nothing too sweaty or grueling), and effective at helping to shrink a sugar belly. The Sugar Smart Workout in Chapter 12 combines cardio exercise, strength training, and yoga for a triple whammy attack on blood sugar and cravings.

If you're plagued by strong sugar cravings, getting more active may help deactivate them. According to a study published in *Applied Physiology, Nutrition, and Metabolism,* the more you sit, the greater your appetite—even if your body doesn't need the calories. In fact, sedentary subjects felt 17 percent hungrier than those who moved around during the day, possibly because inactivity spurs secretion of ghrelin.

Moderate exercise also helps keep muscle cells sensitive to insulin. Even better, strength training builds muscle density—stronger muscles that use more glucose. And, like cardio, strength training aids weight loss.

Even if you don't want to follow the Sugar Smart Workout, any physical activity that you actually enjoy will help get sugar off your brain—and belly. Brisk walking and tai chi both rev metabolism as they quiet and divert the mind. If you'd rather swim, cycle, do yoga, or dig in your garden, that's fine, too. The point is: The more you move, the faster your sugar belly will melt away.

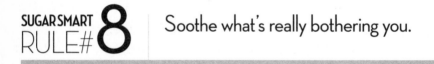

SUGAR SMART RULE #8 | Soothe what's really bothering you.

You don't remember this, but from the moment you were born, you associated sugar with comfort. Held to the breast, newborns derive comfort from skin-to-skin contact, sucking, and mother's milk, rich in lactose and naturally sweet. (Even if you were a bottle baby, you got the sweetness of lactose in your formula.)

The link between comfort and sweets is primal—and persistent. Rewarded with candy while growing up? You may still treat yourself to dessert for a job well done. Handed cookies so you'd stop crying? You may unknowingly have linked sweets to being soothed. Do you associate sweets with periods in your life when you felt safe and loved? You may try to re-create those positive feelings every time you pick up a fork. Did you push back the confusion and loneliness of adolescence with candy bars? Are you doing it today, to push back those same feelings? You may not know the answers to these questions, yet intuitively know they're worth exploring.

We've all read enough magazine articles to make at least a hazy connection between how we feel and what we eat. But the first step to breaking that emotional connection to sugar is to become aware of the feelings that drive you to it. Not after the fact—*the very moment* you reach for sugar. To get a split second of clarity as your fingers close in on your coworker's candy dish: *Why am I reaching for this?*

Years ago, in college, I took part in a cognitive behavioral stress-eating study. All the participants were asked to keep a food journal and to write down the feeling that accompanied every decision to eat. I followed those instructions to the letter.

Keeping that diary showed me that I ate a lot of doughnuts—something I already knew. But why? On paper, the reason fairly leaped off the page: Each and every time I'd eaten my favorite doughnut, I'd been stressing about exams.

Later in the study, the leaders taught us a slogan: "Stop. Slow down. Think." I did that, too, and learned to recognize the rush of stress that made my brain switch gears from fretting about exams to plotting a doughnut run to the local Italian bakery, which specialized in extra-thick frosting—the kind so sweet it makes your teeth hurt and your eyes bug out. More important, I learned to respond to my desire for sugar with a question: "Do I *really* want this, or am I just feeding my stress?"

That phrase, from decades ago, is still embedded in my brain. So today, when I reach for something sweet, it's because I've stopped, thought, and consciously *chosen* to indulge in the pleasure that a sweet treat offers. And then I savor every bite.

In each phase of the Sugar Smart Diet, you'll learn emotional coping strategies to help you do just that. Whether or not to eat a doughnut isn't about need. It's about a decision. On the road to sugar freedom, making a conscious choice about sugar, regardless of how you feel, is an important milestone.

DAVID SUN

BEFORE

DAVID DIDN'T HAVE A LOT OF WEIGHT TO LOSE, but he knew he had a serious sugar problem. "I couldn't resist the temptation of soft ice cream and would often have two cones a day," admitted David. In all, he ate about 62½ teaspoons of sugar per day—that's the equivalent of 25 glazed donuts!

After some prodding from his children, David made a New Year's resolution to get healthier. But instead of cutting out sweets, he eliminated meat and wheat. "I lost about 20 pounds but felt dizzy and weak. I looked pale, and people often asked me what was wrong." His fasting blood glucose level was also high, meaning he was at risk of developing diabetes, and his triglycerides were borderline high.

When he started the Sugar Smart Diet, David was dreading his family's nightly trips for ice cream because he wouldn't be able to partake. "I was able to control my desire because it was my choice to not eat ice cream." And his family made it easier for him by not hanging out at the ice cream store, which is what used to lead to David getting a second helping. "They get their ice cream and then move onto a walk. Family time feels more like time together now rather than time with sweets," he says.

And the results showed. When David walked in for his final weigh-in, he looked energized and had a healthy glow. "I feel stronger," he reported, adding that he ran for the first time in more than 30 years.

The change in his health was even more impressive. "I hadn't eaten meat for several months and was worried that my cholesterol would go up," he said. Quite the opposite: His total cholesterol dropped 36 points, his LDL (bad) cholesterol decreased 28 points, and his borderline high triglyceride level plummeted an incredible 115 points! What's more, his HDL (good cholesterol) rose 15 points, and he lowered his fasting glucose level by 13 points, significantly reducing his risk for diabetes.

"I had been thinking about losing weight for more than 10 years," says David. "I am so happy that I finally did something about it."

5.2
POUNDS LOST

AGE:
54
ALL-OVER
INCHES LOST:
5.5
SUGAR SMART WISDOM:
*"Do it now! Don't
procrastinate!"*

6

THE SUGAR STEP-DOWN

You may have heard it said that our personalities are as unique as snowflakes. Your relationship with sugar, shaped by your personal history, is similar. At some point in your life, you learned to prefer sugary foods over others or sugar snuck into your diet without your realizing it. The Sugar Smart Diet is designed to help you unlearn those preferences and rightsize sugar's role in your diet—as a small but enjoyable part of an overall wholesome and nutritious food plan. And it all begins with this Sugar Step-Down.

The purpose of the Step-Down is twofold. First, just like diving into chilly water, going from a sugar-packed diet to a sugar-smart one in a single leap can be a shock to your system. Over the next 5 days, you'll follow your regular diet as you gradually taper your intake of sugars from all three sources—Straight-Up Sugars, Secret Sugars, and Sugar Mimics. This approach gives you time to adjust and time to really understand the role that sugar plays in your diet. That brings us to our second purpose: to increase your sugar awareness.

During the first 2 days, you'll eat the way you normally do and keep a food log, which you'll use to help you examine your sugar preferences and patterns. On Days 1 through 3, you'll complete an exercise designed to reveal three crucial facets of your unique sugar profile: the sugar sources that appeal to you most, the emotions that trigger your desire for sugary foods, and the habits of sugar consumption you follow. When you become conscious of these aspects of your current relationship with sugar, you can make better choices in the future.

During Days 3 through 5, you'll take one practical action to prepare for Phase 1 of the Sugar Smart Diet, where you'll be eliminating all forms of sugar, including fruit, for 6 days.

Days 1-2

Goals for Days 1 and 2

- Eat the way you normally do.
- Explore your relationship with sugar.
- Keep a food log.

Assess: The reasons you eat sugar

I can't make this point strongly enough: You're *supposed* to enjoy a chocolate chip cookie or a dish of premium ice cream. Humans are hardwired to desire sweet foods, so if you swoon for them, you're only following nature's operating instructions. Because food is a key part of socializing and celebrating, we're especially prone to indulging when we dine out or on special occasions.

But if an out-of-control sweet tooth threatens your health or leads to weight gain that causes emotional pain, it's likely that you overeat sweet foods for reasons other than pleasure. Two of the most common are stress relief and emotional comfort.

When you're drowning in stress, sugar can seem like the friend who understands. But the relief it offers is temporary, and there's a price to pay: You can begin to associate sweet foods with comfort. Gradually, you may turn automatically to that immediate, sweet shot of relief and away from healthier stress management techniques, like a daily brisk walk or some quality alone time.

Just as sugary foods can momentarily relieve stress, they can also soothe emotions you may want to suppress or ignore. But when you eat to fill yourself up emotionally, even the most delectable dessert or starchy comfort food can't satisfy emotional hunger.

Often, bottled-up emotions are expressed through overeating. People who eat in response to emotions may snack when they're not physically hungry,

(continued on page 76)

How Intense Is Your Emotional Connection to Sugar?

Discover how strong sugar's pull is for you by taking this simple quiz. When you're finished, add up your score and compare it to the rankings below.

1. **You find it difficult to say no to your favorite sweets.**

   Always. Place a 4 in column A.

   Usually. Place a 3 in column A.

   Sometimes. Place a 2 in column A.

   Rarely or never. Place a 2 in column B.

2. **When you've tried to cut back on sugar in the past, how intense were your cravings?**

   Very strong. You typically ate what you were craving. Place a 4 in column A.

   Strong, but more often than not, you were able to satisfy your craving with something healthier than what you wanted (for instance, fruit instead of cookies). Place a 3 in column A.

   Noticeable. Sometimes you ate what you were craving and sometimes you didn't. Place a 2 in column A.

   Minor. It took some effort, but more often than not, you distracted yourself and the craving passed. Place a 1 in column B.

   Ignorable. You were able to get past it pretty easily or you didn't have any cravings. Put a 2 in column B.

3. **You find yourself thinking about sugary foods _____ times a day.**

   More than 4 times. Place a 3 in column A.

   3–4 times. Place a 2 in column A.

   2–3 times. Place a 1 in column A.

   Rarely or never. Place a 2 in column B.

4. **Once you start to eat sugary foods, it's hard to stop.**

   Always. Place a 5 in column A.

   Usually. Place a 4 in column A.

   Sometimes. Place a 3 in column A.

   Rarely or never. Place a 2 in column B.

	A	B
1		
2		
3		
4		
5		
6		
7		
8		
9		
10		
11		
	total A	total B
	—	

Add up your score in each column. Subtract your B score from your A score.

5. **Your mood and/or energy level rise right after you eat, but you tend to crash or feel hungry an hour or two later.**

   Always or often. Place a 3 in column A.
   Sometimes. Place a 2 in column A.
   Rarely or never. Place a 2 in column B.

6. **You often feel guilt or shame after you eat sugar.**

   Yes. Place a 2 in column A.
   No. Place a 2 in column B.

7. **You seek refuge in sweets to avoid feelings like anger, loneliness, sadness, or powerlessness.**

   Always or often. Place a 3 in column A.
   Sometimes. Place a 2 in column A.
   Rarely or never. Place a 2 in column B.

8. **You reward yourself with sugar after a challenging task—you feel you "deserve" it.**

   Always or often. Place a 3 in column A.
   Sometimes. Place a 2 in column A.
   Rarely or never. Place a 2 in column B.

9. **You overeat sugary foods when you're under stress.**

   Always or often. Place a 3 in column A.
   Sometimes. Place a 2 in column A.
   Rarely or never. Place a 2 in column B.

10. **At least one of your favorite sweet treats is fused to a memory of feeling loved and cared for.**

    Yes. Place a 1 in column A.
    No. Place a 2 in column B.

11. **The more you indulge in sugar, the less it satisfies—but the more you seem to "need" it.**

    Yes. Place a 2 in column A.
    No. Place a 2 in column B.

Results

A negative number. Your emotional connection to sugar is balanced or nonexistent. But you can still benefit from the Sugar Smart Diet. You may be consuming more sugar than is healthy, either from the Straight-Up Sugars you are eating or from Secret Sugars you may be consuming in amounts far greater than you think. The good news is that you'll have an easy time on the plan.

0–10. You have your occasional struggles with sugar, but overall have your cravings pretty much under control. You could still be consuming more than you realize, though, and you're likely to notice a difference in the way you feel after following the plan.

11–20. Sugar is one of your go-to coping mechanisms. You use it to soothe or distract you, and you're likely consuming much more of it than is healthy. You may have some withdrawal symptoms as you go through the plan, but the strategies I provide throughout will help you take the edge off. You will likely experience noticeable results in your weight, cravings, and mood by the end of Phase 1.

20+. You're very sensitive to sugar's emotional effects and very susceptible to its charms. Phase 1 may be a challenge. But—deep breath—you can reset your sugar thermostat and get back to a place where sugar is a pleasure, not a compulsion. Stick with the plan and you will see dramatic results: The Sugar Smart Diet is your answer to emotional equilibrium and a healthy, happy weight.

experience intense cravings for a particular food, and feel unsatisfied even after they finish a hearty meal. They may also eat during or after a stressful experience or to numb their feelings. In a culture that pushes instant gratification, reaching for food is one of the fastest ways to cope with emotions that can be hard to express or even acknowledge.

The jury's still out on whether it's possible to be physically addicted to sugar. However, there's no doubt that it can certainly feel that way. While not scientific, the quiz on page 74 can help you gauge the intensity of your emotional tie to sugary or starchy foods. If your results suggest a powerful bond, take heart. It is possible to break that food feelings connection, and this plan can help you begin.

Prep: Track your sugar intake

Quick—what did you eat yesterday? Did you hit the drive-thru for a mega-sugary coffee drink and a bagel in the morning? Did you grab a smoothie after you went to the gym? Perhaps you relied on sweetened soda, a handful of candy from your coworker's desk, or a second coffee drink to get you through the afternoon? Did you nibble on pretzels while you watched TV? Maybe you made healthy choices all day, but blew it by eating nearly an entire pint of ice cream or a "Nutella nightcap" (the jar and a spoon) before bed?

I'm guessing, of course. But to lose your sugar belly for good, you'll need to identify the type of sugar you gravitate toward and how much of it you consume. That's why I want you to keep a food log for 2 days. Record what you eat for breakfast, lunch, and dinner and for snacks each day.

Look, I know you may not be a fan of tracking what you eat. Or maybe you're eager to begin the plan and want to just get to it. But the information you'll discover over this 48-hour period will be revolutionary. It certainly was for our test panelists. Most of them were getting around 20 teaspoons of added sugar a day, which is comparable to the national average. But Gayle and David were shocked: Gayle was eating 36 teaspoons and David 63! Jot down every bite, sip, and nibble for just 2 days. You can simply note what you eat, but if you want more information, add the serving size of each food.

What's key is to track your mood and your hunger level before and after you eat. Both pieces of information are going to tell you a lot about your emotional and physiological connection to sugar. You'll be able to spot patterns that will increase your awareness of what you eat, when you eat, and why you choose the foods you do. That's the first step to healthy change. You don't have to write pages and pages. Just a few words will do. See the sample entry on page 78 to get an idea. And we've made the hunger assessment easy. Just jot down the appropriate number. Before you eat, rank your hunger level on a scale of 1 to 5.

1. Starving
2. Hunger pains
3. Hunger
4. Slight hunger
5. Neutral

Then do the same after you eat:

1. Still hungry. You could use a second helping.
2. Full, but not quite satisfied.
3. Content.
4. Stuffed. Your stomach may hurt because it's so full of food.
5. Nauseous. You're so full that you may feel sick.

Hang on to those logs. You'll be looking at them closely over the next 3 days. As you do, a picture of your sugar habits will emerge in stark relief. No matter what you discover, the news is good. Once you're aware of your high-sugar preferences—which is not always the case if you tend to eat without thinking—you can swap them for healthier alternatives that are lower in sugar but please your "sweet buds" just as much.

For example, you might be shocked to find that although you're not a sweets eater, you pack away a ton of foods that act like sugar in your body. Or that your standard diner breakfast—scrambled eggs and homefries with ketchup—is full of Secret Sugar. Every tablespoon of ketchup contains a teaspoon of added sugar. If you're a woman and use 5 tablespoons on your scrambled eggs and homefries—not hard to do if you don't stay aware of portion sizes—you're consuming practically all of your recommended daily intake of added sugar in ketchup alone.

FOOD LOG

Weak point	When it occurs
Doughnuts in the coffee room at work— it's an office "perk." The HR department provides two dozen every day.	9 a.m., right when I get to work.

Why it makes me "need" sugar	Positive alternative I can use to meet that need
Work is so stressful—too much to do and not enough people to help. I'm in a panic most of the day. Plus, I'm always starving when I get to work, and the doughnuts are right there.	I could make a healthy breakfast at home and eat it at work. I could take a brisk walk around the parking lot before I enter the building.

Day 3

Goals for Day 3

- Identify the Straight-Up Sugar sources that matter most to you.
- Eliminate all of the Straight-Up Sugar you eat, except for your favorites.

Assess: Your intake of Straight-Up Sugars

Grab your food log. Today you're going to look for foods that contain Straight-Up Sugar—SUS for short. Write SUS next to each item that you know contains sugar. These foods include:

- Any food or beverage you added sugar to—for instance, a few teaspoons in your coffee or tea or on your morning cereal
- Agave syrup, honey, maple syrup
- Sugar-sweetened beverages—soda, juice, lemonade, iced tea, fruit-flavored drinks, chocolate or strawberry milks, sports drinks
- Jams and jellies
- Chocolate and pancake syrups
- Chocolate in its many forms—puddings, snack cakes, candy, cocoa
- Candy—jelly beans, gummy candy, licorice sticks, mints, hard candies
- Sweetened cereals
- Granola or energy bars
- Cookies, doughnuts, packaged snack cakes, frosted toaster pastries, muffins, pies, and other bakery items
- Cake, muffin, or sweet bread mixes
- Ice cream or frozen yogurt
- Fruit or flavored yogurt

Count the number of items and note that in your log. If you chose to write down your serving sizes, you can estimate the grams of sugar you are getting from these foods. For assistance, look at the item's Nutrition Facts label. Total your grams and divide by 4 to get the number of teaspoons of Straight-Up Sugars you typically eat—there are 4 grams of sugar in 1 teaspoon. Recall that the Sugar Smart Diet is designed to get you to 6 to 9 teaspoons of added sugar per day. Are you close? Congratulations! If not, don't worry. Use that number as motivation as you go through the plan.

Produce: The Real Good-Mood Food

What would you rather eat when you feel exhausted, stressed, or blue: a classic comfort food like ice cream or mac and cheese, or a cup of fresh blueberries or baby carrots? If you're like most people, sugar and starch win hands down. However, in a study published in the *British Journal of Health Psychology*, it was actually fruits and vegetables that promoted feelings of well-being, rather than sugary, fatty junk.

In a 21-day study, 281 students completed an online daily food diary, logging in each night to describe their feelings from a long list of positive and negative words. The negative words the students could choose included *angry, anxious, short-tempered,* and *sad*; the positive words included *relaxed, happy, content,* and *calm*. The students were also asked to describe their menu each day, including the number of servings of five specific foods—fruits, veggies, cookies, chips, and cake.

When the researchers analyzed both the students' food choices and their feeling words, they found a strong relationship between positive moods and higher intake of fruits and vegetables, but not the sweets and starches. That means on days when the students ate more produce, they reported feeling happier, calmer, and more energetic. The therapeutic "dose" of fruits and veggies that resulted in positive moods—7 to 8 servings a day—sounds like a lot, but you can get that amount in a cup of berries in the morning, a salad at lunch, a plate of crudités as a midafternoon snack, and a veggie at dinner.

Was it the positive moods that came first or the healthy amount of produce? When the researchers conducted additional analyses to find out, they discovered that eating fruits and vegetables on one day tended to improve mood the next.

The team wasn't sure whether the students' good moods were because of the high amount of nutrients in produce, or because people tend to feel good when they make healthy food choices. You'll have a prime opportunity to find out—you'll be eating lots of fresh produce on the Sugar Smart Diet. Might you experience a lift in energy and mood? If you're anything like our test panelists, the answer is yes!

Assess: Your sugar preferences

Next, take a close look at all of the Straight-Up Sugars you eat. What time of day did you eat them? How were you feeling when you ate them? (This is where the mood and hunger information on your food log comes in handy.) Are there some you ate out of habit rather than pleasure?

Note any cravings that pop up at the same time each day. For example, let's say you "need" ice cream after dinner. Why is that? After some thought, you may conclude that without that nightly indulgence, you feel deprived. Probe a bit deeper, and you may also realize that it doesn't matter how much sugar you consume during the day, you still want that bowl of ice cream in front of the TV at night. Noticing—and honoring—such cravings can help you say no to sugary items during the day, for the most part. You realize that these foods don't come close to satisfying like your nightly dish of ice cream does—at least for now. At the end of your 32 days on the Sugar Smart Diet, your preferences may change, or they may stay the same.

Here's the question I want you to think hardest about: Which of the Straight-Up Sugars you ate did you *really* enjoy? Or, to put it another way, if you could only have one sweet hit, which one would it be? Maybe a morning without a doughnut feels like a day without sunshine, or you're wedded to your 8 p.m. ice-cream fix, or you must have cookies and tea at your desk midafternoon. Your favorite one or two treats are your key sugar sources. Have them, but otherwise don't eat any other Straight-Up Sugars today.

Prep: Kitchen makeover, part 1

Today you'll remove all of the Straight-Up Sugars that lurk within your refrigerator, freezer, and pantry—except for those one or two treats you truly love—to make room for the new, healthy foods you'll soon enjoy.

Start with your refrigerator first, then move to your freezer and pantry. Most of the sources will be obvious to you, but refresh your memory if you need to with the list beginning on page 87. Place all the Straight-Up Sugar sources on your kitchen island or countertops.

When you're done, take one last look at these items—the granola bars that

SUGAR SMART MENTOR

Pam Peeke, MD, MPH,
FACP

RECOGNIZE THE SUGAR/BRAIN CONNECTION. Refined or processed sugar is ubiquitous in our food. As a result, the brain's reward center is constantly being ignited, stirring up an endless appetite for these empty calories. In vulnerable individuals, consuming refined and processed sugar to excess results in an addictive process. It's impossible to eliminate sugar entirely as it is present in so many foods. But you can minimize it significantly. If someone has a high level of sugar addiction, the intake should be very minimal. The key is to know how much of which food will trigger a feeling of loss of control and overeating or a binge. For instance, a regular chocolate bar with a high level of refined sugar is too much for most people and may result in overeating. However, an organic bar, with at least 70 percent cacao may not, as it has so much less sugar. The source of sugar is important.

PICK THE BEST APPROACH FOR YOU. There are a number of ways to cut back on sugar. You can wean yourself—for example, from six sugar sodas down, then on to diet sodas, then to seltzer water, and finally to plain water perhaps flavored with lemon or orange slices. But if you are addicted to the stuff, an immediate detox may be necessary for you to break free and stop caving to the craving. Whichever path you take, get going on a healthy lifestyle overhaul. Increasing physical activity is wonderful to help regulate appetite and hunger. So is getting 7 to 8 hours of high-quality sleep.

REACH FOR PROTEIN. The only time I crave refined sugar is when I'm stressed out. When that toxic stress hits, there's an instant urge to grab something sweet. It's like a knee jerk reaction. At that very moment, I'll grab something with protein and fiber that will kill the craving. Peanut or almond butter on a piece of fruit like apple slices or a banana works well, as does yogurt with walnuts and berries.

SET YOURSELF UP FOR SUCCESS. As a preemptive strike against sugar cravings, I meditate twice a day for 20 minutes each time. Meditation increases your ability to draw upon your prefrontal cortex (the CEO of the brain) to stay vigilant and make the right decisions.

PAM PEEKE, MD, MPH, FACP *is an assistant clinical professor of medicine at the University of Maryland. An internationally renowned expert on nutrition, metabolism, stress, and fitness, she is the author of* Body for Life for Women, Fight Fat after Forty, *and* Fit to Live. *Her most recent book is* The Hunger Fix: The Three-Stage Detox and Recovery Plan for Overeating and Food.

pack 25 grams of sugar per serving, the pancake syrup that's pure HFCS, the candy you retrieved from your secret stash so the kids wouldn't find it. Sure they taste good, but these sugary seducers have had their shot—it's time to move on. Dispose of them or box them up for friends or the food bank, except for the one or two sweet foods and beverages you love most. Those items are your key sugar sources, and you're free to enjoy them for the rest of the Step-Down.

This long good-bye to your sugary foods can make it a bit easier to let them go temporarily. Just as important, it introduces the idea of "spending" sugar on the foods where you notice and enjoy it most. Remember, the more sugar you eat, the more it takes to satisfy you and the less of a treat it is. Conversely, the less sugar you consume, the more special it becomes and the less you'll "need" it.

Even though you can still have your key sugar sources today, you can choose to cut back on them so it won't be as hard to give them up on day 6. For many people, key sources are sweetened beverages, desserts, and ice cream. These tips can help.

If you're a soda sipper or juice guzzler: Today: Sip the full-sugar variety, but step down to a smaller bottle or can. Tomorrow or the day after, swap every other serving with ice water or seltzer with a twist of lime.

If you're a dessert lover: Today: Have your regular dessert. Tomorrow: Opt for a fruit-based dessert, like a baked apple or poached pear. The day after: Step down to raw fruit. Splurge on the varieties you love most—mangoes, berries, purple or red seedless grapes.

If you're an ice-cream junkie: Today and tomorrow: Eat one serving, then give away or dispose of the carton. (If you've got a family of ice-cream lovers, place it below your line of sight in the freezer.) The day after: If you want ice cream, go for it, but drive to the local ice-cream shop. Going forward, you might set an ice-cream ground rule: You can have it if you go out for it—but only on a Friday or a Saturday.

"Need" Chocolate? Walk Off Those Cravings

It's 2 hours before quitting time. You're so lethargic you're about to slide off your chair, and chocolate is whispering your name. Before you open your mouth, get to your feet: A short walk can short-circuit chocolate cravings, according to a study published in the journal *Appetite*.

To observe the effect of physical activity on chocolate cravings, researchers recruited 25 "regular chocolate consumers" for their study. This designation was precise. To get chosen for the study, they had to report scarfing at least 3.5 ounces of the sweet stuff every day. To ignite their volunteers' cravings, researchers had them abstain from their favorite sweet for 3 days and told them not to exercise or have caffeine 2 hours before their test periods.

The research team set up two test sessions and held them on separate days. At the first session, one group of chocolate lovers sat quietly while the other group walked briskly on a treadmill for 15 minutes. At the second ses-sion, the walkers sat and the sitters hit the treadmill. During each test session, volunteers filled out a scientific questionnaire designed to assess food cravings but adapted to measure chocolate cravings specifically.

After each session, both groups sat quietly for 10 minutes. Then every volunteer performed two 3-minute tasks, with 10 minutes between each task. In the first, the volunteers took a computerized test known to cause psychological stress. The second task? Testers presented the volunteers with a selection of chocolate bars and asked them to open and handle—but not eat—the bar they'd chosen. (If that's not stressful, we don't know what is!)

The sweet results? Compared to how they were at the start of the study, the walkers' cravings dropped by 12 percent, while the sitters' cravings actually intensified. Like chocolate, exercise may increase the levels of feel-good chemicals in the brain's reward regions, thus reducing a desire for sweets, the study said.

Day 4

Goals for Day 4

- Uncover your hidden sugar triggers.
- Identify and eliminate the Secret Sugars in your diet.
- Identify and eliminate the Sugar Mimics in your diet.

Assess: The situations that lead you to reach for sugar

Cravings and food preferences aren't the only things that draw us toward sugar. Habit, external cues, or the situations we're in are also a factor. Today, you'll review your typical routine to identify the times and situations that trigger a desire for sugar or starches. For instance, maybe you're in the habit of multitasking as you eat. If so, practicing mindful eating may help you feel more satisfied, with less sugar.

A study published in the journal *Psychological Science* found that people who eat or drink while they're distracted require greater intensities of taste—sweetness included—to feel satisfied. In one part of the study, people who made and tasted lemonade as they memorized a seven-digit number ended up with a 50 percent higher sugar concentration in their drink than when they had to memorize just one number. In other words, a healthy meal may be flavorful if you eat it mindfully, but bland if you're distracted with work or TV, prompting you to eat more sugar after dinner to feel satisfied.

Look back at your food log again, think about the triggers that led you to reach for sugar, and jot them down in a chart like the one on pages 78–79. I've given you an example of the kind of detail that will be helpful. Really try to pinpoint the reason each weak point increases your vulnerability to sugary foods, and come up with solutions. Going forward, you'll find them invaluable when you're in similar circumstances.

Assess: Your intake of Secret Sugars and Sugar Mimics

I've combined identifying Secret Sugars and Sugar Mimics into one step because often—but not always—the two categories come as a package in foods. I'll explain more ahead, but for now, similar to what you did yesterday for Straight-Up Sugars, place an SS—Secret Sugar—next to all the foods that you may not think of as containing added sugar, but that do. (On the list below, I've noted which foods tend to contain Secret Sugars, which are Sugar Mimics, and which are sources of both.) Do the same for Sugar Mimics—use SM as your notation. Here's what to look for.

Refrigerator

Ketchup SS

Barbecue sauce SS

Teriyaki sauce, plum sauce, or other Asian sauces SS

Low-fat or fat-free salad dressings and marinades SS

Dips and spreads, such as onion dip SS

Side dishes from the supermarket deli, such as macaroni salad, potato salad, or coleslaw SS, SM

Canned biscuits and pizza dough SS, SM

Leftovers from take-out meals, such as pizza or that sweet-and-sour chicken from your favorite Chinese place SS, SM

Freezer

Look past the ice cream—if it's still there, it's one of your key sugar sources. Focus on:

Frozen entrées (low-calorie or otherwise) SS, SM

Processed meats (sausage, hot dogs) SS

Frozen veggies prepared with sauces SS

Breakfast sandwiches SS, SM

Mini pizza bagels or pizza rolls, or pocket sandwiches SS, SM

Frozen bread and rolls SS, SM

Potpies SS, SM

Pantry

The pantry is a gold mine for Secret Sugars and Sugar Mimics. You'll find them in:

Saltines or oyster crackers SM

Pretzels, chips, or other salty snack foods SM

Pasta sauce SS

Pasta, regular and whole wheat SM

Couscous SM

White rice SM

Rice mixes SS, SM

Instant flavored oatmeal SS, SM

Granola or fruit and grain bars (whole grain varieties included) SS, SM

Sweetened cornbread mix SS

Whole grain cold cereals (Even the ones that are sugar free and
   contain fiber are processed and can spike your blood sugar. You can
   reintroduce whole grain cereals with 0 grams sugar and at least
   3 grams fiber on Phase 2 of the plan.) SS, SM

Flour, all-purpose or whole wheat SM

Bread, whole grain and white SS, SM

Baked beans SS

Trail mix SS

Whole grain crackers SS, SM

English muffins SS, SM

Pita bread SS, SM

Tortilla wraps SS, SM

Taco shells SS, SM

Rice cakes SM

Yogurt, fruit or flavored SS

Prep: Kitchen makeover, part 2

Second verse, same as the first! After you review your food log, head to your
refrigerator, freezer, and pantry, and load up your countertops with the sources
of Secret Sugar and Sugar Mimics you find. But this time, there's an extra step.
Read the ingredients list on the back of the food's package before you make a

decision about what to do with it. Look for sugar by one (or more) of its many names. I listed the various names for sugar in Chapter 2, but I think committing them to memory is so important that I've listed them again in the box below. Not every salad dressing or frozen dinner or what have you will contain them. As for Sugar Mimics—those processed grain products, both wheat and whole grain—as I said, most of them (like whole wheat bread, instant oatmeal, and breakfast cereal) contain added sugar as well.

The following foods are reintroduced in Phase 2, so you can stash them in your freezer or pantry if you like until then: tortillas, wraps, pita bread, and whole wheat pasta. But as for the others? Dispose of these items in the way you've decided. Toss 'em out, box 'em up, get 'em out—you don't need them anymore. You're taking control of your weight and your health, and becoming sugar smart.

Sugar by Any Other Name Is Still Sugar!

Agave nectar	Corn syrup	Maltose
Barley malt	Corn syrup solids	Malt syrup
Beet sugar	Crystalline fructose	Molasses
Brown rice syrup	Date sugar	Muscovado sugar
Brown sugar	Dextrose	Raw sugar
Buttered sugar	Evaporated cane juice	Rice bran syrup
Cane crystals	Fructose	Rice syrup
Cane juice	Fruit juice concentrates	Sorghum
Cane sugar	Glucose	Sorghum syrup
Caramel	High-fructose corn	Sucrose
Carob syrup	syrup	Sugar
Castor sugar	Honey	Syrup
Coconut sugar	Invert sugar	Turbinado sugar
Corn sweetener	Lactose	

Day 5

- Identify healthy "treats."
- Eliminate fruit juice.
- Get ready for Phase 1.

Assess: Sugar-free ways to soothe cravings

To break the cycle of reaching for sugar when you are either biologically or emotionally cued to, you have to have something that will short-circuit your reflex response. When you begin Phase 1 of the Sugar Smart Diet on Day 6, you'll find many strategies designed to disconnect your body and your brain from sugar. Each day offers an action you can take to ease stress in the moment and help manage it consistently—and encourage you to become aware of and accept uncomfortable feelings, so you can learn to manage them without sweets.

As you've learned, there's evidence that highly palatable food—brownies and ice cream definitely qualify—can activate the brain reward system. In fact, a personality trait called reward sensitivity may predispose some people to be highly responsive to cues linked with pleasurable food, like TV ads, according to research presented at an annual meeting of the Society for the Study of Ingestive Behavior. To turn the tables on your pleasure-seeking brain, create a "rewards card"—a list of nonfood treats that give it (and you) the bliss it seeks, sans sugar. And that discovery process can be a pleasure in itself!

Most of the activities that curl your toes, float your boat, or make your heart sing are simple and fit into even the most harried schedule. For a few years, I kept a list of 20-minute pleasures on my fridge. Whenever I found myself heading to the kitchen for a treat, I'd see the list and realize how many more calorie- and sugar-free options I could enjoy, right then and there. So many of the things that delight me were available to me, pretty much anytime.

Doing yoga. Listening to music—from Johnny Cash to Krishna Das. Hanging out with my kids.

My greatest pleasure? Daydreaming. Letting your mind wander where it will is part of the beauty of life. Give yourself permission to indulge! Sure, you're busy—me, too. But making time to daydream can lead you to your vision of how you want to live, what you want to do, who you want to be.

These days, I don't need to keep my list on my fridge. It's in my head. Taking a long, deep drink from the well of pleasure each day—doing something just for you, and just because—can help ensure that you don't feel pleasure-deprived and turn to food to make yourself feel happy, nurtured, or loved.

MAKING A "REWARDS CARD"

Now it's time to create your own personal Rewards Card to be whipped out anytime you find yourself heading to the fridge absentmindedly. Your rewards should be things you can do instantly and that last for the 15 to 20 minutes you otherwise might spend indulging in a sugar episode. They should also elicit the same pleasure you feel when you indulge in your favorite dessert. From now on, instead of treating yourself to food, you can treat yourself to pleasure. This strategy—*pleasure-focused redirection*, you might call it—will work like a charm to keep you focused on nonfood sources of pleasure. Not used to rewarding yourself with anything but sugary treats? Consider devoting your daily intention to enjoying one of the pleasures on your card until treating yourself to nonfood pleasures becomes second nature.

Copy the blank form below, fill it out, and keep it with you wherever you go. (You might even laminate it, so it won't bend or tear.) Here are some of my personal 20-minute pleasures. Feel free to steal a few for your Rewards Card— but don't pass up the chance to think up your own. Discovering your personal pleasures is almost as fun as actually indulging in them!

- Listen to music
- Dance like crazy
- Call a really good friend

- Paint my toenails
- Daydream
- Spritz perfume on my wrists or neck
- Take a nap
- Go for a walk, a bike ride, or a run, or stretch
- Pet the cat
- Take the dog to the park
- Watch junky TV
- Watch something silly on YouTube
- Browse a pretty catalog
- Goof off with my kids
- Draw or paint
- Do needlepoint (so relaxing and addictive!)
- Weed the garden (yes, it's actually relaxing)
- Rake leaves
- Fill the bird feeder and wait for birds
- Give myself a facial
- Finally use those lovely bath salts/scrubs
- Take some cool photographs
- Post something on Facebook; scan others
- Plant a flower box for the windowsill
- Plan a dream vacation
- Lie down and look up at the sky

While you can still have favorite sweets today, at least once pull out your card and indulge in a treat that won't spill over your waistband later. Often, you can stop a craving in its tracks with a small, simple action—a brisk walk around the parking lot, a trip to the library on a rainy day, or a call to your best friend who can stage a sugar intervention. But sometimes, only a treat from your Rewards Card, or the promise of one, will do. What's more indulgent, really—a professional pedi with a happy color, or half a pan of brownies made from a cheap mix?

Rewards Card

The pleasure of sugar is fleeting.
   Instead, I choose to treat myself to . . .

1. _____

2. _____

3. _____

4. _____

5. _____

6. _____

7. _____

8. _____

9. _____

10. _____

Prep: Shop for reset

Today, you'll go to the supermarket to shop for Phase 1 of the Sugar Smart Diet. Review the quick and easy meal options that begin on page 126 and pick a few that appeal to you. (If you are cooking for more than one, all you have to do is multiply the ingredients by the number of servings you need. Your results will be just as delicious!) Or you can turn to Chapter 11 and peruse the Sugar Smart Diet recipes. They're a little more involved, but I promise the extra effort is worth it.

Make a list of the items you need. Once you get your groceries home, follow the strategies below to give healthy items prime real estate in your refrigerator, freezer, and pantry, and continue your strategic shelving as you progress through the phases.

Place favorite items at eye level. Location, location, location. That's where it's at in real estate—and in your kitchen. A study published in the *American Journal of Public Health*, which staged a nutritional "intervention" in a large hospital cafeteria, found that color-coding foods and beverages based on their healthiness, and making healthy items more visible, led people to make healthier choices.

Whether you're opening your refrigerator, freezer, or pantry, your eyes should fall right on the foods you love most. Place veggies, yogurt, and lean protein (salmon, grilled chicken breast) front and center in the refrigerator; your air-popped popcorn and rolled or steel-cut oats on an eye-level pantry shelf; your package of frozen edamame where you'll see it, so you'll remember to thaw it.

Prep foods for faster meals. As soon as you get home from the supermarket, wash, slice, and peel your crudités, avocado, and salad vegetables and place them in see-through containers. Hard-cook eggs and prepare grains the night before you plan to eat them. When you walk in the door hungry, you'll be able to whip up a healthy meal without a lot of tedious prep work.

Hide the junk. If your family will continue to eat foods not on your plan, keep their options—especially the sweets and treats—on the bottom shelf of the refrigerator, on the lower shelf in your freezer, and in high or low shelves in your pantry, where you're less likely to see them.

Shop European style. Especially if you shop for your family, hit the supermarket more often and buy only for their next few meals, rather than lay in supplies for the week. An overload of choices at home may deplete your willpower, a *Journal of Consumer Psychology* study found.

YOU'RE READY FOR PHASE 1!

Now that you've identified your sugar profile and swapped the sugar bombs in your kitchen with whole, natural foods, you're ready to start your journey to sugar freedom. The first step? Removing all sugar from your diet—temporarily, we promise. We'll stick with you every step of the way, offering practical ways to prevent and relieve cravings and curb any crankiness. The benefits you stand to gain in Phase 1 far outweigh any short-term discomfort you may experience. Less than a week from now, your jeans will be looser, your energy higher, and your mood brighter.

Day 5

Just as important, you'll have turned your diet around in ways that maybe you didn't think were possible. You, passing up your morning bagel and coffee drink or kicking your 2-liter-a-day cola habit or eliminating those nightly ice-cream fests? Yes—and that's just for starters. The sweet life is within your grasp. Turn the page and reach for it.

ROBIN MOLNAR

BEFORE

"SUGAR IS THE LAST THING YOU NEED!" That was Robin's response when a coworker was complaining that she was tired and needed sugar. She should know! The Sugar Smart Diet gave Robin a huge energy reboot. On a single weekend during her time on the plan, she took a 14-mile hike and walked 10 miles on a rail trail. To top it off, she logged another 6 miles on Monday. Now she's training to walk a half-marathon. "I feel better today than I did in my twenties," she gushes. "When I say this plan changed my life, I mean it with every ounce of my being."

But Robin could relate to her coworker's desire for sugar. "I used to have chocolate every afternoon as a pick-me-up, and I missed it at first," she says. However, Robin was surprised to discover that she didn't think twice about the ice cream, pastries, and other sugary foods she typically ate. To deal with her chocolate cravings, she'd take a short walk. "It really helped! And pretty soon I was able to simply talk myself out of wanting the candy. For me, realizing that I didn't need sugar was very freeing." Even staring down aisles of cookies and bakery cases full of treats didn't put a dent in Robin's resolve. "I needed to order some cupcakes for friends, and when I walked into the bakery, I was amazed—nothing even appealed to me. I walked out with a huge smile. Life without sugar is grand."

Robin knew she was losing weight and inches—2¼ inches off her waist and 4 off her thighs—and that she was getting healthier. Robin's high cholesterol level went from 268 to 221 and her LDL dropped from 198 to 153. Her borderline high blood pressure dropped a total of 36 points, getting her into the healthy zone. She didn't realize just how much she had changed, though, until her husband returned from a business trip. "He was gone the entire 4 weeks I was on this plan. When he came home, he couldn't believe his eyes. He kept staring at me and telling me how great I looked, even a week later!"

9.4
POUNDS LOST

AGE:
43

**ALL-OVER
INCHES LOST:**
10.5

SUGAR SMART WISDOM
*"I feel like I'm shopping in
my own closet. I tried on an
outfit that I haven't worn in
6 years, and it fit!"*

7

Phase 1: Days 6-11

THE TOUGH LOVE TURNAROUND

Catch your breath: In the past 5 days, you've done a lot of challenging but eye-opening work. You've assessed your unique emotional connection to sugar. Discovered where it's lurking in your diet. Determined how much you're currently consuming. Identified the sweets that matter most to you. Learned about the major sugar bombs in the American diet. In short, you've amassed crucial knowledge about yourself and the role that sugar plays in your diet and your life—knowledge you're about to put into action to slim your body and safeguard your health.

Welcome to Phase 1. This is where the rubber meets the road, where the determined take action.

When a toddler melts down in aisle 4 of the market, or a

Q: What About the Sugar in Milk Products?

A: Milk and yogurt contain lactose, a type of sugar (a combination of glucose and galactose). We haven't eliminated them from the Sugar Smart Diet, though. Lactose is digested more slowly than other types of sugar, and therefore does not have as big an impact on your blood sugar and insulin response. Milk and yogurt are also packed with protein, which further slows digestion, and calcium, which you need for a healthy heart and bones. Finally, these products don't taste sweet in the way most of us think of as sweet, so they are less likely to trigger cravings.

teenager howls "it's not fair!" as she stomps to her room, loving parents do what they need to do—put them on time-out or ground them—because they care. Faced with an unruly sweet tooth that wants what it wants when it wants it—*Doughnut! Now!*—you need to exert the same tough love. During this phase, you will remove sugar from your diet. Even fruit. That's the only way to break sugar's grip on you.

Why no fruit? Fruit is good for you. But you need to readjust your palate and get your metabolism running smoothly. That's why we don't want you to have *any* sugar. To that end, this phase also cuts out two vegetables that rival fruit in sugar content: sweet potatoes and beets. Like fruits, these are incredibly nutritious, packed with fiber and antioxidants, and, along with fruit, can come back into your diet in Phase 2.

To further help you quell cravings, improve the quality of your diet, and rebalance the way your body uses glucose and insulin, there are no processed grain products—white or whole wheat—in this phase. Because it can be hard to go without bread or pasta for very long, we begin to bring them back in Phase 2 in limited amounts. However, you don't have to eat them.

We can't sugarcoat it: We call this phase the Tough Love Turnaround because we know that it may not be easy. But we promise you'll love the results! For the first several days, you may not feel at your best, physically or emotionally. Did you ever quit smoking or know someone who did? Do you recall the fatigue and irritability? You may experience similar symptoms, such as headaches, fatigue, and edginess, and the cravings may get intense. Your score on the quiz you completed on Day 1 or 2 (page 74) will give you an indication of how strong your sugar cravings are likely to be. But don't let that scare you—let it be a motivation. Take a cue from one of our test panelists, Lisa. On the first day of the Tough Love Turnaround, she posted a picture of a 5-pound bag of sugar on Facebook, with the caption: "I'm breaking up with you! I CAN do this!" Let your score spur you on.

The good news: It's all over in 6 days, and the meals you'll be eating are designed to keep you satisfied, keep your blood sugar levels steady, and keep cravings at bay. All of the meals and recipes (see Chapter 11) were developed by Stephanie Clarke, RD and Willow Jarosh, RD, who ensured that they contained the right balance of protein, carbohydrates, and fat to prevent the wild swings in blood sugar and insulin that trigger cravings and promote fat storage.

But in no way did Stephanie and Willow sacrifice flavor. These meals are delicious! How does Fiesta Egg Salad (page 128) sound? Or Potato, Pepper, and Chicken Sausage Sauté (page 129)? Or Steak and Roasted Baby Potatoes and Carrots (page 129)? Every one of the meals and snacks will dim your palate's demand for sugar by providing you with vibrant, straight-from-nature flavors. One of our test panelists, Robyn, said that the Broiled Mustard Salmon with Roasted Broccoli and Quinoa (page 129) "was as good as anything you might order at a five-star restaurant!" I've included a daily food log with all of your options on Phase 1—I encourage you to make copies of the log and check off what you eat each day.

Plus, I'm giving you two ways to make the process as painless as possible. Each day, you'll follow a *Cravings Crusher* tip and a *Sweet Freedom* strategy. Cravings Crushers come straight from the latest scientific research. They're designed to help you overcome the physical symptoms that may occur when you remove sugar from your diet or better manage your blood sugar levels. Sweet Freedom strategies are so named because they soothe stress or offer emotional comfort *better* than sugar. (You can also turn to rewards you identified and jotted down on your Rewards Card, page 93.) When you use all of these tools faithfully, you create a positive spiral that sparks your motivation to stay on track. And because you'll carry the strategies you learn each day into the next, your discomfort eases day by day. Any symptoms you may experience typically fade, replaced by a positive upswing in energy and mood.

By Day 9, you should begin to notice just how good you feel. More energy, a brighter mood, and sound sleep are just the start. As your body regains its sensitivity to insulin and maintains steadier blood-sugar levels, sugar's iron grip on your body and mind will loosen.

So will your waistband. By Day 11, if you've followed the Turnaround faithfully, you can expect to lose an average of 7 pounds and nearly 8 inches all over, nearly 2 inches from your waist and hips, and an inch off your thighs. Those numbers aren't theoretical—they're the average losses experienced by our test panelists. Women and men just like you, who broke their health-threatening dependence on sugar, shrank their sugar bellies, and retrained their taste buds to savor the sweetness of whole, natural foods. These rewards aren't temporary, like a sugar buzz. They're lasting, and the benefits only get better as you progress through the plan.

Days 6-11

What to Do

- **Have breakfast every morning.** As I explained in the Sugar Smart Diet Rules, breakfast goes a long way toward keeping cravings at bay. Choose from the six high-protein options you'll find on pages 126–127 or try one of the breakfast recipes in Chapter 11. Breakfasts have about 300 calories and at least 15 grams of protein.

- **Mix-and-match the lunch and dinner options.** They're interchangeable from a calorie and a nutritional perspective. Lunches and dinners contain 400 to 450 calories and, of course, they contain no added sugar. Have something different every day, or stick to three or four meals you love—it's up to you. Every meal is easy and quick to prepare. When you feel like doing more cooking, you can choose from the recipes labeled "Phase 1" in Chapter 11. If you're pressed for time, we offer a few restaurant options in this phase. If you just want something familiar, you can always have 4 ounces of lean protein (chicken or turkey breast; pork tenderloin, loin, or chops; lean beef like sirloin or eye of round; fish; or tofu), 1 to 2 cups of vegetables, 1 cup of a whole grain or a medium potato, and 1 to 2 teaspoons of butter or oil or 2 tablespoons of nuts or seeds.

- **Don't forget to snack!** Eating every few hours prevents the blood sugar dips that trigger appetite and sugar cravings. When you have the snacks is up to you. You can snack midmorning to tide you over until lunch or in the afternoon to hold you over until dinner. Or you can save your snack for after dinner. Just aim for eating something about every 4 hours. One of your snacks contains 100 calories and the other 150 calories.

Q: Why do these meals have any sugar?

A: As you may recall from Chapter 2, grains, beans, dairy products, nuts, vegetables, and milk contain sugar naturally (as do fruits). Not much, mind you, but when you combine foods in a meal, it adds up. This is not added sugar, the kind you need to worry about; food manufacturers don't distinguish between natural sugar and added sugars on their products. But because we created these meals and recipes, we know exactly what went into them. I've given you the total amount of sugar in the dish, and I hope that you'll be able to get a sense of which foods contain sugar naturally and how much, so you can make healthy food choices when the food label is confusing.

● **Avoid the following foods:** Fruit, fruit juice, dried fruit, sweet potatoes, beets, processed grain products (both white and whole wheat), and sugar in any of its many forms (including the table sugar you might add to foods, honey, and maple syrup).

● **Set your daily intention.** I firmly believe that spending a few minutes at the beginning of each day acknowledging what you hope to achieve that day, practically or spiritually, and giving thanks for what is good in your life is beneficial to your health, your weight, and your overall well-being. As I mentioned, setting an intention every morning helped me put my own health and my well-being first. Today (and every day throughout this plan), set your daily intention. The box below shows you how.

Setting an Intention

● **Begin each morning with thanks.** Whether or not you're a person of faith, beginning your day with what you're grateful for sets a positive tone for the entire day. I start my day usually with something as simple as, "Thank you for one more day to be on this planet, seeing my children grow and blossom into the special people that they are."

● **Pick a focus.** Once you've given thanks, pick one area of your life that you want to improve or decide on something you want to accomplish. Then create an intention around it and write it down. Intentions sound something like this:

Today, my intention is to be strong and to nourish myself with love. I want to become aware of how I feel, physically and emotionally.

Today, my intention is to do one thing that gives me pleasure.

Today, my intention is to take steps to ease my stress.

Today, my intention is to start my day with a protein-rich breakfast.

Today, my intention is to stick to three meals and two snacks.

● **Move into a few minutes of meditation.** It will help calm your mind and help you stay focused on the intention you've just set. A study in the journal *Emotion* showed that a type of meditation called mindfulness—which requires you to tune in to your thoughts, feelings, and physical sensations—significantly improved people's working memory, the short-term memory needed to manage emotions and solve problems. The result: You'll feel more centered, less stressed, and have more energy to create a healthy, balanced life you'll love.

Day 6

If you feel a bit nervous today, I totally get it—your key sugar sources are gone, and today is D-Day (Ditch Sugar Day). To spark your resolve, remember this: Today, you begin to break sugar's grip on your mind and body, free yourself from insatiable food cravings, and kick-start a full-body health revolution.

It's difficult to predict how you'll feel today. However, we suspect that, at least for today, your desire for sugar will stem more from habit than physiology. Or it might just be a bit of resistance. One of our test panelists, Colleen, told us at the start of the plan that she's not normally a chocolate lover, but she found herself craving it just because she knew she couldn't have it! Remind yourself that this plan is about *gaining* things—health, vitality, and freedom from sugar cravings so you can enjoy it again guilt-free—rather than giving things up.

That said, I won't discount the possibility that you may feel a strong urge for something sweet. While it would be too early for physical symptoms to occur (*if* they occur—they may not!), you may feel strange without having your regular go-to sugars within arm's reach. If you get a craving, turn to one of the nonfood rewards you jotted down on your Rewards Card on Day 5 of the Sugar

Q: Can I swap ingredients in a meal?

A: Yes, as long as the ingredients are in the same food group and you are eating phase-appropriate foods. So, for example, you can have brown rice instead of quinoa, mozzarella cheese in place of feta, replace dairy milk with soy milk, chickpeas for kidney beans, green beans for broccoli, and chicken for fish, if you like. Be sure to keep your portion sizes about the same, too.

Step-Down. Or you can use today's Sweet Freedom strategy to get the stress relief or emotional comfort you're used to getting from sugar.

In fact, you might think about the power of habits today. So many of the food decisions we make aren't decisions at all. How often did you consume sugary foods mindlessly, without thinking about or even enjoying them? No worries. Before long, consuming sugar will be a mindful choice—for pleasure, not out of habit.

Cravings Crusher: Supplement with calcium and vitamin D

Supplements can't take the place of a healthy diet, but they may make eating one easier. How? By possibly helping to quell cravings and accelerate weight loss—if you're taking the right ones: calcium and vitamin D.

Extra body fat holds on to vitamin D so that the body can't use it. This perceived deficiency interferes with the action of leptin, the hormone that tells your brain you're full. In a study of 1,800 overweight people being treated at a weight loss clinic, the heavier the participants, the lower their vitamin D levels tended to be. According to the study, which was published in the *Journal of Nutrition,* it may be that people who are overweight are less able to convert vitamin D into its hormonally active form.

Moreover, if you're deficient in calcium, your body can experience up to a fivefold increase in the fatty acid synthase, an enzyme that converts calories into fat. In a study published in the *British Journal of Nutrition,* 63 overweight women were put on a 15-week diet and took 1,200 milligrams of calcium and 400 IU of vitamin D a day. The women who had adequate intake of calcium at the start of the study did not see any benefit, but those with low intakes (600 milligrams or less)—a situation many women find themselves in—lost six times more weight than women who followed the diet but did not take a supplement.

While you'll be getting plenty of calcium on the Sugar Smart Diet, a bit of extra nutrition "insurance" can't hurt. Try taking a multi that supplies 25 percent of the DV for calcium (250 milligrams) and at least 400 IU of vitamin D, preferably in the form of D_3 (cholecalciferol). which is better used by the body than other forms. You might just find your cravings lessen while your weight loss speeds up.

Sweet Freedom: Eat with awareness

"Be here now!" That '60s-era figure of speech is truly full of ancient wisdom. It perfectly illustrates the idea of mindfulness, a way of thinking and focusing rooted in Buddhist meditation. In the West, mindfulness has come to mean cultivating a moment-by-moment awareness of your thoughts, feelings, bodily sensations, and environment. When you practice mindfulness, you don't judge what you're thinking or how you're feeling. You just accept where you're at in this moment, rather than fret about the past or worry about the future.

You can do anything in a mindful way—walk, wash dishes, even eat. Especially eat. A large body of research has sprung up around mindful eating. The findings are overwhelmingly positive: Study after study suggests that eating "in the moment" promotes weight loss and healthier choices. When you eat in a mindful manner, you're fully aware of and appreciate the flavors, textures, and aromas of each and every bite. You're equally tuned in to your thoughts, feelings, and sensations of hunger and fullness as you eat. The dual payoff: You enjoy your food more and don't need as much of it to feel satisfied.

Starting with your next meal, try mindful eating for yourself. There are dozens of versions of this exercise, but they all teach the same thing: When you eat, focus on nothing else. No reading, watching TV, paying bills, or texting or talking on your cell phone. Always, you sit to eat, and do nothing but focus on your food, bodily sensations, and thoughts and feelings.

Try this exercise alone the first few times, so that you experience it fully without feeling self-conscious. After a time or two, you should feel comfortable eating mindfully when you're eating with others.

1. Sit at the table, with your plate in front of you. Before you pick up your fork, take a couple of deep breaths to allow your body and mind to settle.
2. Look at your food. Really look at it and ponder its origins. The Vietnamese Buddhist monk, teacher, writer, and peace activist Thich

Nhat Hanh developed an exercise where you imagine the life cycle of your food. He does a meditation on an orange that I love and cherish. You imagine the blossom, the fruit growing and ripening, and appreciate how long it has taken to grow, along with the sun that

Snap a Photo, Snap Out of Temptation

It's good advice you've heard before: When you're trying to lose weight, keep a food diary. People who do so lose more weight, research shows. But not everyone likes to record everything they eat on paper—and that does mean *everything*, from the mouthful to the spoonful. If that sounds like you, consider a higher-tech type of food diary: Snap a photo of every meal or snack before you eat it.

In a study published in the *International Journal of Consumer Studies*, researchers had 43 people keep a traditional, on-paper food diary *and* take photos of their meals and snacks with disposable cameras for a week. Both before and after the experiment, the researchers interviewed the volunteers about their eating habits and their thoughts about the experience.

The results? The on-paper diary carried the day; 19 of the volunteers preferred it, compared to nine preferring the photo method, and seven not having a preference. But all reported that the act of taking the photos, and the photos themselves, raised their awareness of what they were eating in a way that the paper diaries didn't. When participants took pictures of their food, they often changed or adjusted their choices because they could see what they were going to eat before they ate it—and reconsidered their selections.

People often record what they eat *after* they eat it, the study noted. With photo food diaries, you have to snap the picture *before* you eat—and that action can snap you out of an unhealthy choice. As one study participant said in a post-study interview, "Who wants to take a photo of a jumbo bag of M&Ms and write it down?"

Although disposable cameras were used in this study, you can use the camera on your cell phone. The rule is, put all meals and snacks on a plate before you take a picture. That minute of delay may be all you need to decide that you've put too much on your plate or that you could choose a better option.

While you're at it, why not download the daily photos of your meals and snacks on Pinterest or Facebook? You can share them with supportive pals and encourage them to do the same. Together, day by day, you can raise your awareness of what you choose to eat (or not), and ooh and aah over each other's healthy plates. As your eating habits change for the better, you may discover that you're a darn good photographer or food stylist. Who knew?

nourished it, the farmer who picked it, the driver who carried it, the store person who displayed it—all of the phases it has passed through to come to you. You thank them, the tree, the sun, the people. It's really powerful. This kind of gratitude is at the heart of mindfulness.

3. Take a bite, taking time to observe your fork rising to your mouth, the way your mouth opens to receive it. Notice the shape and size of the morsel, as well as its color, texture, and scent. Place it on your tongue and chew, tuning in to its flavor, temperature, and texture. Do you detect a hint of ginger, cinnamon, or other natural flavor?

4. Chew each bite for at least 20 seconds. By turning your focus inward and concentrating on sensations such as taste and smell, eating—an activity you may have performed on autopilot for a long time—can feel brand new.

5. Notice your thoughts and feelings. Do you like what you're eating? Do you wish it were sweeter, saltier, spicier? Are you comparing it to previous meals? Are you still hungry or getting full? Do you wish you had more, or are you feeling satisfied?

6. As you finish, take a few deep breaths, then leave the table. Remind yourself of how the plate looked when it was full and how it looks now. When you focus on your food, you're less likely to overeat and consume things that don't truly nourish you.

Seven Ways to Stay Energized During Phase 1

How's your energy? If you're dragging a bit, don't panic. You may be experiencing sugar "withdrawal," which can cause some people to experience temporary fatigue or mental fogginess. While some of our test panelists breezed through Phase 1, others felt a bit pooped, especially in those first few sugar-free days.

If this sounds like you, the tips below can help perk up both your body and your brain. And hang in there; the fatigue will pass. In fact, all our panelists felt *more* energized as time went on!

Revive with rosemary. This herb's pleasant, spicy scent is an eye-opener, suggests a study published in the *International Journal of Neuroscience*. Researchers gave 40 volunteers electroencephalograms (EEGs), which measure the brain's electrical activity, and had them smell rosemary for 3 minutes both before and after they did a simple math test.

The volunteers' EEGs showed reduced certain brain waves in the frontal cortex, which indicates increased alertness. And while the scent didn't increase the accuracy of their test results, the volunteers did report feeling less anxious, and more relaxed and alert. Essential oil of rosemary is sold in most natural foods stores. You might keep a small bottle in your purse and inhale when that mental fog rolls in.

Stoke your cellular power plants. Regular exercise is a time-tested energy booster, and the benefits start at the cellular level. Your cells contain tiny structures called mitochondria. These cellular "power plants" convert food molecules into adenosine triphosphate (ATP), a form of energy your cells can use.

Interestingly, exercise stimulates the development of mitochondria. This means, over time, your body will be able to produce more ATP, which can energize both your body *and* your brain. In fact, experiments conducted at California State University showed that a brisk 10-minute walk increased energy *better than eating a candy bar*, and the energizing effects lasted up to 2 hours!

Take flight. If you're low on energy, you might want to head for the elevator. But for instant pep, take the stairs! It will get your heart pumping, allowing oxygen-rich blood to surge through your entire body, including your brain.

So if your eyelids start to droop, get up, head for the stairs, and climb a flight as quickly as you can. Walk at a normal pace on the way down. Repeat, and see if you don't feel more alert!

Take a break for tea. Like coffee, tea contains energy-boosting caffeine. Yet it is known and loved for its calming effects. Its ability to deliver a relaxed state of alertness may be due to the amino acid L-theanine. Research indicates that tea's combo of caffeine and L-theanine delivers the same amount of energy as caffeine alone but without the jitters.

Studies suggest that L-theanine stimulates alpha waves in the brain, which are associated with alertness. One study examined the effects of 50 milligrams of L-theanine, the amount found in 2 cups of tea. Researchers gave 16 volunteers

EEGs as they relaxed with their eyes closed. Compared with 19 other people who did not receive L-theanine, those who consumed this amino acid showed increased alpha-wave activity, indicating a relaxed but alert mental state.

Another reason tea may be the perfect energizing beverage? If you're dehydrated—a definite mood- and energy-sapper—even the water in tea may perk you up. If you're sensitive to caffeine, opt for green tea, which contains less caffeine per cup than black tea (36 versus 60 milligrams).

Rejuvenate with ginseng. Panax ginseng is another herb known for its energizing qualities. In a 12-week study of 501 men and women, a group of participants given a multivitamin supplement that included ginseng reported having more energy and greater well-being than a group that received a ginseng-free supplement. Try 200 milligrams of a standardized extract taken as 100 milligrams twice daily. And stick with brands that are standardized to 4 percent ginsenosides.

Step outside the box. The "box" is the four walls of your office or house. A series of studies found that spending just 20 minutes outside in nature can invigorate you.

In these studies, the researchers conducted separate experiments of 537 college students. In one experiment, students were led on a walk either indoors or outside along a tree-lined river path. In another, they looked at photos of buildings or landscapes. Other experiments had the students keep diaries in which they tracked their moods and energy levels throughout the day.

The results? The students consistently felt more energetic in natural settings or by imagining themselves in them.

Breathe in some energy. A simple yoga breathing exercise can clear your mind and raise your energy in minutes. It's called *bhastrika*, which translates as "bellows breath." Here's how to do it.

- Sit comfortably. Relax your shoulders and take deep breaths.
- Begin to inhale and exhale rapidly through your nose, keeping your mouth closed but relaxed. Your breaths in and out should be equal in duration but as short as possible. This is a noisy breathing exercise.
- Try for three in-and-out breath cycles per second. This produces a quick movement of the diaphragm, suggesting a bellows. Breathe normally after each cycle.
- Do this for 15 seconds or less on your first try. Each time you practice, increase your time by 5 seconds or so, until you reach a full minute.
- If you feel light-headed, stop for a minute, then start again in a less forceful manner.

One more thing: Don't try bellows breathing before bed. It may pep you up too much to fall asleep!

Day 7

Check-in time: Have any sugar cravings cropped up? They may not, but it can't hurt to focus today's intention on what you'll do if your taste buds start demanding your usual morning whipped-cream coffee drink or an afternoon nibble of chocolate. Regardless of how you're feeling (or whether you're hungry), whip up that protein-packed breakfast to keep the cravings at bay, and remember that if one does hit, it's likely to pass in 15 minutes or less. Treating yourself to one of the items on your list of nonfood rewards can help you power through!

Cravings Crusher: Add PB to breakfast

Besides being warm, creamy, and packed with flavor, there's yet another reason to enjoy your bowl of Microwave Peanut Butter Oats (page 126) in the morning: Eating PB or peanuts at breakfast curbs hunger and controls blood sugar levels throughout the day, according to a small study published in the *British Journal of Nutrition.*

Researchers tested the effects of peanuts and peanut butter in three phases. In one phase, the participants breakfasted on orange juice, hot cereal, and 1.5 ounces of peanuts. In another phase, they had 3 tablespoons of peanut butter instead of the peanuts. In a third "control" phase, they had just the juice and cereal. The volunteers were also fed a lunch guaranteed to raise blood sugar levels: white bread and jam.

For 3 hours after breakfast and lunch, researchers collected blood samples to track the volunteers' blood sugar, and the volunteers completed a questionnaire that had them rate their feelings of hunger and fullness. They were also asked to keep a food diary for the rest of the day after they left the testing site.

The volunteers' blood sugar levels did not rise as much after breakfasts that included peanuts and peanut butter, the study found. Nor did they rise as much as they might have after their sugary lunch, even though they didn't eat peanuts or PB for lunch. But that wasn't the end of the benefit. The study found that adding either peanuts or peanut butter to breakfast also reduced the volunteers' appetites for up to 12 hours by ramping up production of the appetite-suppressing hormone peptide YY (PYY for short).

Peanut butter had a slightly stronger effect, the study found. But in both cases, peanuts' package of high protein, high fiber, and healthy fats were credited with helping to steady blood sugar levels and quell hunger. Why not try those peanut butter oats this morning?

Sweet Freedom: Circle breathing

Like credit card late fees, stress is a reality of life. While you'll never banish it from your life permanently, you can employ a host of techniques that help relieve it without tearing through a jumbo bag of Swedish Fish.

Circle breathing is a simple way to relieve stress fast and fits well into any stress-management plan. When you're anxious, off center, or feel like you'll explode if you don't have your Frappuccino, do a round of circle breathing—5 to 10 breaths. During Phase 1, aim to use this centering exercise 5 or more times a day, to help your body and mind form a strong, positive habit. What's more, according to a recent study in the *Journal of Alternative and Complementary Medicine*, relaxation breathing after meals helps prevent glucose spikes.

1. Inhale and stretch your arms over your head. Exhale, giving a sigh of relief as you lower your arms. Relax and keep your arms lowered for the rest of the exercise.
2. Now imagine that you're inhaling a stream of peaceful energy into a spot a few inches below your navel.
3. Continue inhaling, imagining the energy traveling to the base of your spine, then imagine it traveling up your back to the top of your head.
4. Exhale, and mentally follow that breath back down the front of your body to the point below your navel where you'll begin the next inhale. Your breath has now made a full circle—up the back of your body, down the front, and back to the starting place below your navel.
5. Do 5 to 10 circle breaths. You can also use circle breaths for a longer period as a relaxing form of meditation.

SUGAR SMART MENTOR

Arthur Agatston, MD

BE A SUGAR SLEUTH. It's important to remember that sugar isn't just found in the sugar bowl. It's added to a vast array of products from salad dressings and soups to tomato sauce and peanut butter, and found naturally in carbohydrate-rich foods like bread and potatoes.

FIBER MATTERS! The more highly processed and lacking in fiber the foods you eat are, the more they can cause the swings in blood sugar that can lead to cravings for more refined sugars and starches. It's a vicious cycle. A substantial part of your diet should consist of nutrient-dense, high-fiber real foods—fruits, vegetables, and whole grains—that will keep you feeling satisfied longer and make you less likely to overeat.

CUT BACK GRADUALLY. Getting used to less sugar can be tough for some people, so I recommend that you start by eliminating the foods that are the biggest problems—soda and fruit drinks, candy, sweet bakery goods like cookies and muffins, and ice cream. It may take a few days for your body to adjust to going cold turkey on refined sugar, but I guarantee that if you do so, your cravings for it will disappear.

TAP INTO THE POWER OF THREE. On special occasions, most people (including myself) want to enjoy a decadent dessert. For such times I recommend the South Beach Diet Three-Bite Rule: Have three bites and then put the dessert aside for a few minutes or pass your plate to a fellow diner or the busboy. You'll find that three bites of any dessert will satisfy you without triggering your desire to keep eating. Having a small piece of dark chocolate (at least 70 percent cacao) after a meal instead of dessert can also do the trick. Several studies have shown that eating dark chocolate in moderation can lower blood pressure (probably due to the beneficial effects of its polyphenols on blood vessel elasticity and blood flow) and reduce levels of C-reactive protein (CRP) in the body, a powerful predictor of heart disease and type 2 diabetes. The flavonoids in dark chocolate and cocoa powder may also help protect against certain forms of cancer and diabetes.

ARTHUR AGATSTON, MD, is the medical director of Wellness and Prevention for Baptist Health South Florida and a clinical professor of medicine at the Florida International University Herbert Wertheim College of Medicine. He is the creator of the bestselling South Beach Diet book series. Most recently, he is the author of The South Beach Diet Gluten Solution and The South Beach Diet Gluten Solution Cookbook.

Day 8

If you're going to experience cravings, they're likely to hit today. You may get a headache, feel more tired than usual, or snap at the people around you. No, it's not fun (for you or for them), but look at it this way: Such symptoms mean that the sugar is leaving your body and will soon make its absence felt in your mood and on the scale. And any symptoms you're experiencing aren't likely to last much longer. Be gentle on yourself today, and when a craving hits, do a round of circle breathing or sip a cup of tea and read a good book (see below). It gets easier from here!

Cravings Crusher: Relax with a cup of tea and a novel

There's nothing new about advice to carve out "me" time. What's new is a study from England's University of Sussex that found reading can slash stress by 68 percent! Other methods the study tested that also work are listening to music (61 percent) or sipping a cup of tea (54 percent). It's a great way to divert yourself when you get that urge to munch. Pick a quiet spot where you won't be interrupted and brew a cup of a calming tea, such as chamomile, to sip while you turn the pages.

Sweet Freedom: Listen to your belly, not your head

Although eating is meant to be a pleasure, it's helpful to know the difference between physical hunger and appetite. I asked you to rate your hunger when you were keeping your food log on Days 1 and 2. It's a good idea to get in the habit of asking yourself "How hungry am I?" before a meal and after—before you reflexively reach for a second helping (or later on, dessert). It may mean the difference between staying on plan or overeating when you're not truly in need of fuel for energy.

Brew Up "Green" Blood Sugar Control

No matter what phase of the Sugar Smart Diet plan you're on, drinking green tea is a tasty, natural way to manage your blood sugar, according to an analysis of 17 studies of green tea published in the *American Journal of Clinical Nutrition*. The analysis linked this fragrant, mild-tasting tea to lower fasting levels of blood sugar and also to lower levels of HbA1c, which indicates the presence of long-term glucose in the blood.

Those benefits to blood sugar control are on top of previous research that links frequent consumption of green tea to a reduced risk of heart disease and some cancers and to lower cholesterol and blood pressure. (One study even found that green tea increases the body's ability to burn fat!)

Green tea's health-promoting effects are attributed to plant compounds called catechins, which belong to the flavonol family of compounds. A flavonol called epigallocatechin gallate, or EGCG, is among the most-tested—and potent—catechins in green tea. Nine of the 17 studies in the analysis used green tea extracts in capsule form, in dosages of 200 to 800 milligrams of EGCG. The other studies used the tea itself. The catechin dosages in all 17 studies ranged from 208 to 1,207 milligrams.

Because of the wide variations in catechin dosages and the different forms of green tea extract used, the analysis didn't recommend a cup-a-day amount to improve blood sugar or benefit that all-important HbA1c level. However, consider drinking 4 cups a day. In a previous meta-analysis involving more than 300,000 people, those who sipped that daily amount reduced their risk of type 2 diabetes by 20 percent, compared with those who drank less or none.

You may be wondering if you can get these benefits from bottled teas. Not likely. In an independent test of four bottled green teas, only two contained catechins: Teavana had the most, followed by Lipton Green Tea. What bottled teas are more likely to contain is sugar. When it comes to green tea, brew it yourself. And when you reach Phase 3, a teaspoon of pure honey can sweeten up your cup.

Hunger is a physical feeling that develops when you have not eaten for several hours or you skip a meal. Appetite is a psychological feeling, often prompted by the sight or smell of food. For example, you may want a cupcake when you pass a bakery and see them displayed in the window, or you may want dessert even after a large meal.

When you're not sure if you're hungry—which can happen if you're used to eating what you want, when you want it—use the hunger scale I introduced in Chapter 6 (I've reproduced it below). Taking a few minutes to rate your hunger can help you decide if what you're feeling is true physical hunger or simply a desire to eat for other reasons. It also is helpful to use during a meal to monitor how full you're getting. It's a simple but effective technique.

Before you eat, rank your hunger level on a scale of 1 to 5:

1. Starving
2. Hunger pains
3. Hunger
4. Slight hunger
5. Neutral

Then do the same after you eat:

1. Still hungry. You could use a second helping.
2. Full, but not quite satisfied.
3. Content.
4. Stuffed. Your stomach may hurt because it's so full of food.
5. Nauseous. You're so full that you may feel sick.

As a general rule, eat when you rate your hunger at 3 or 4. You should start to feel hungry and want to eat every 3 to 4 hours. Don't let your hunger get down to 1 or 2, or you may overeat when you finally do have the time to eat.

As you progress through the phases, try to use the scale before and during each meal and snack. Before long, you should be in tune with when you're truly hungry—or when you want to eat because stress, the sight or smell of food, or uncomfortable feelings are pushing your appetite buttons. If you want to lose weight and keep it off, knowing the difference can keep you slim for good.

Day 9

If you've been feeling tired and headachy the past few days, or so irritable you'd consider selling your mother for a Tootsie Pop, just breathe: The worst of these physical symptoms should begin to pass today. However, it's just as likely that you woke up this morning feeling calm and craving free. Set your daily intention and use the Cravings Crushers and Sweet Freedom strategies you've learned so far to manage any stress you may feel today. Each time you replace sugar with a healthy alternative, that healthy habit becomes more firmly rooted in your mind and your behavior. Keep it up—you're almost there!

Cravings Crusher: Wake up your taste buds, lower your blood sugar

Now that you've tossed out those sugar-laden bottled salad dressings, give your taste buds and blood sugar a treat: Dress those baby greens with fresh herbs, extra-virgin olive oil, and the vinegar of your choice. In a study published in the journal *Diabetes Care,* people with insulin resistance or type 2 diabetes had lower blood sugar levels when they consumed just over a tablespoon of vinegar immediately before a high-carb meal.

In this study, researchers fed 10 people with type 2 diabetes, 11 people with insulin resistance, and eight people with no blood sugar issues a sugary, starchy breakfast: orange juice and a bagel, which packed a hefty dose of carbs (87 grams). However, 2 minutes before the meal, half the participants drank a "vinegar cocktail"—4 teaspoons of apple cider vinegar and a teaspoon of saccharin (which we don't recommend) in an 8-ounce glass of water. The remaining volunteers were given a placebo drink. Everyone's blood sugar was measured both before and after the breakfast.

A week later, the researchers repeated the experiment, with those who'd received the vinegar getting the control drink and vice versa.

All three groups had better blood sugar readings after meals begun with those vinegar cocktails. But those with insulin resistance saw a 34 percent reduction in their postmeal blood sugar levels, while those with type 2 diabetes experienced a 19 percent reduction.

The acetic acid in vinegar may inactivate certain starch-digesting enzymes, slowing carbohydrate digestion, the study said. In fact, the researchers noted that vinegar's effects may be similar to those of the blood sugar–lowering medication acarbose (Precose).

The bright, tart taste of natural vinegar puts the flavor of many of those bottled dressings to shame. You can use any kind of vinegar—red wine, apple cider, or balsamic. Consume the vinegar at the start of your meal, as the people in the study did. We suppose you could make your own "vinegar cocktail"— minus the saccharin—but it's much tastier drizzled over a salad. And a tablespoon of balsamic brings out the flavor of meat or veggies.

Sweet Freedom: Practice radical acceptance

Allowing yourself to investigate the emotions that may be driving you to reach for sugar and learning to respond to them in ways that don't involve food will help neutralize their power. Accepting things as they are, without reservation, is called radical acceptance. When we submit to what is, we've taken the first step to moving forward into positive action. This exercise can help you be open to the moment and to yourself.

The first step: Think of a situation in your life right now that you find challenging and difficult (perhaps your struggle with weight or sugary foods), yet possible to accept.

Now do the following:

1. Consider the facts. If you notice judgment or your personal opinions creeping in, let them go. Return to the facts as you know them.
2. Tense your body as you think or write about this situation. You might raise your hands and clench your fists while making a classic angry

face—eyes narrowed, lips open, teeth clenched. How do you feel? What thoughts do you notice? What sensations do you notice in your body as you think about this situation?

Remain in this position for a minute or so, noticing your thoughts and feelings as they float through your mind, without labeling them as good or bad.

3. Now, relax your body and assume a pose that expresses acceptance. You might raise your arms to the sky and open your hands, close your eyes, or put a half-smile on your face as you sit with the facts as you've presented them. This is you, accepting the reality of the situation you've chosen to focus on.

Remain in this position for a minute, allowing your thoughts and feelings to go where they will. What do you notice about them? Does the reality of your situation seem like something you can accept and change? Do you feel more hopeful and peaceful, less so, or about the same?

Here's an example of what radical acceptance might look and feel like in this exercise.

1. I weigh 40 pounds more than I'd like or that is healthy for me. I've been gaining about 2 pounds a month for the last 2 years. It's hard for me to lose weight without changing my eating. [facts]
2. As I tense my body, I feel even heavier and more uncomfortable. The extra pounds seem to weigh more in my mind and body. [physical sensations]
3. As I release, I feel like I can look at the facts more openly and move forward. I feel less heavy and more ready to commit to a plan. [openness to change]

Although this technique may feel like a stretch for you, try to keep an open mind and go with it.

Day 10

At the beginning of your fourth day without sugar, you should be noticing some positive changes. Feel less tense? Are you a couple of pounds lighter? Are you sleeping better or feeling more positive overall? If so, take a moment to acknowledge how good you feel—and to pat yourself on the back for taking action. Each positive change that you may notice today is a gift that you've given yourself and one that you've earned. Savor it!

Cravings Crusher: Drink up to quell cravings

If your sweet tooth is on overdrive, turn on the tap and drink up. Dehydration can spike cravings for sugar and junk food dramatically, some experts say—and take a toll on your mood as well. Recent studies have linked mild dehydration to fatigue, anxiety, poor concentration, and even your cranky midday slump.

Two Fabulous Flavored Waters

Missing soda? Try jazzing up plain water! It's simple to do: Put the ingredients in a 2-quart jar, muddle with a wooden spoon or spatula, cover with 6 cups of ice, fill the jar with water, and stir. Pop it in the refrigerator for 2 hours to chill and let those luscious flavors mingle. Strain before drinking. Each recipe makes 2 quarts and will keep in the refrigerator for 2 or 3 days. In Chapter 9, we'll introduce more flavored waters, made with sweet and luscious fruit.

Cucumber-Jalapeño Quencher

2 cucumbers, peeled and thinly sliced
2 jalapeño peppers, seeded and sliced (wear plastic gloves when handling)

Vanilla Latte

2 vanilla beans, crushed with a wooden spoon
2 cups whole coffee beans

Despite the frequent bathroom trips, drinking water throughout the day is worth it. It may promote weight loss by speeding up metabolism, according to a study published in the journal *Obesity*. The latest guidelines from the Institute of Medicine recommend that women get 91 ounces of water a day—more than 11 cups! You might be relieved (no pun intended) to know that not all of it has to come from the tap. In fact, at least 20 percent of the water you get will come from food. If you eat lots of fruits and veggies, as you will on this plan, you'll make a hefty dent in your water needs. Try our fabulous flavored waters (page 121). Coffee and tea count, too. Diet soda, however, does not—and as you've already read, the artificial sweeteners it contains may be a secret plumper-upper.

Sweet Freedom: Climb the feelings ladder

In the midst of a stressful situation, have you ever talked to yourself in a soothing voice, offering yourself words of comfort? Often, this instinctive reaction to stress does make you feel better.

That's because altering an intense feeling in this way can make it easier to bear. Perhaps you didn't know you had that ability. But now that you do, you can consciously lower the intensity of any feeling that triggers your impulse to eat chocolate, ice cream, or any other food, so you won't need to use those foods to soothe yourself. The exercise below can help you change the way you think and talk to yourself.

1. Choose a feeling that you find difficult to cope with. (Let's use anger as an example.)
2. Imagine yourself standing at the bottom of a ladder. The top represents the peak of the emotion. At the bottom, where you're standing, the emotion is mild—perhaps you feel somewhat irritated, but not really angry.
3. Now, "connect" to that feeling. It can be helpful to call up a powerful memory of a particular situation in which you experienced intense anger.
4. Maintaining that connection, picture yourself slowly climbing the ladder as your anger intensifies with each step upward. You'll know you've reached the top when your anger reaches its full intensity.

5. Pause at the top of the ladder for a moment, then begin to climb down. With every step down, lower the intensity of your anger until you're on the ground again.

6. If you wish, repeat the exercise with another emotion you find difficult to manage.

Take a moment to reflect on your reaction to this exercise. Did you feel scared or not? Did you take your time going up the ladder or ascend quickly? How did you feel de-escalating the intensity of your emotion as you descended the ladder?

Day 11

Wow. You made it. That's got to feel pretty sweet. Six days of healthy eating. Six days of countering sugar cravings with healthy actions. Six days of setting positive intentions and making them happen. By this time, most people experience a surge in energy and mood, and the headaches, fatigue, and crankiness have faded away. If you can get through this, what can't you do? Continue to use the tips and techniques you've learned in this phase as you launch into Phase 2 tomorrow and bring fruit back into your diet. You'll find even more tools to help you sail through occasional cravings and really start loving your new, low-sugar life.

Cravings Crusher: Spice it up

You'll notice that we use cinnamon and ginger quite often in our meals and recipes. That's because these warm spices (nutmeg and allspice are others) along with vanilla extract give you tons of flavor with none of the sugar. Plus, they seem to quell a sweet tooth. And cinnamon, in particular, may do even more: In 60 people with type 2 diabetes, just a teaspoon a day for 20 days improved insulin response and lowered blood sugar by up to 20 percent, according to the study, published in the journal *Diabetes Care*.

For the best flavor, buy whole cinnamon sticks and grind them in a spice or dedicated coffee grinder. Store the sticks or powder in an airtight container in a cool, dark place. Then try these tasty ideas (if you like things spicy, add nutmeg, too):

- Stir your herbal tea with a cinnamon stick and let it steep as you sip.
- Cinnamon and low-fat dairy were made for each other. In this phase, you're already sprinkling it over your oatmeal and yogurt. But in later

phases, it sweetens up popcorn and part-skim ricotta cheese, which is divine when spread onto whole grain toast. Along with a dash of vanilla extract, cinnamon also sweetens up a pre-bedtime cup of steamed fat-free milk.

- Cook your grains with a cinnamon stick and maybe a bay leaf. It gives them a wonderful depth of flavor.

Sweet Freedom: Assume a sugar-free stance

Yoga, for sugar cravings? Absolutely! It can help relax and quiet the mind, so cravings won't gain traction in your brain.

The most common type of yoga practiced in the United States, hatha yoga combines physical poses (called asanas), breathing techniques, and a period of relaxation or meditation. Even simple asanas require you to focus intently on what your body is doing. This intense awareness has a way of calming the mind. The breathing techniques help tame the stress response, so that you can respond rationally to cravings, rather than react emotionally to them. And relaxation or meditation can help you begin to tune in to desires that ice cream can't satisfy. These desires might include more joy in your life, emotional closeness with others, meaningful work to do, or the courage to follow a true passion or lifelong dream. Once you're in touch with these desires, you can take steps to make them happen, rather than use sugar to suppress them.

Q: Can I have a beer or a glass of wine?

A: Do not drink any alcohol during Phase 1. We recommend that you skip alcohol during the entire plan. It just adds extra calories and can make it more challenging to stick with healthy eating choices.

If during Phase 2 and beyond you decide to have a drink, stick to light beer (12 ounces), wine (5 ounces), or 1 shot of spirits (vodka, gin, rum, Scotch, bourbon), and count it as your 100-calorie snack for that day. Most mixers—even tonic water—have added sugar or are fruit juice–based. Do not have those. Limit your drinks to two per week maximum.

The Sugar Smart Workout includes two yoga routines—one to energize you and one to help you relax (see page 272). If you have time, do one of them when you feel frantic. But if you only have a minute or two, a simple standing forward bend can help you relax and decompress your mind, letting you reflect on the emotion that's driving you to eat. Here's how to do it:

1. Stand with your back about a foot from a wall and your feet hip-width apart.
2. Lean back onto the wall. Then gently bend your knees and fold forward, bringing your belly and chest to your thighs. Take 6 to 12 breaths, focusing on the exhalation.
3. Slowly roll up one vertebra at a time, until your back is leaning up against the wall again. Close your eyes and take a few breaths. Repeat 3 to 5 times.

PHASE 1 QUICK & EASY MEALS

Have three meals and two snacks every day from the options below. You can also choose from the Phase 1 recipes in Chapter 11.

Breakfast

Mediterranean Scramble

Whisk 1 egg and 1 egg white together with 1 tablespoon water. Heat 1 teaspoon olive oil in a nonstick skillet over medium-high heat and scramble eggs together with ⅓ cup chopped tomato, ⅓ cup rinsed and drained canned white beans, 2 tablespoons feta cheese, and ½ cup roughly chopped baby spinach.

Nutrition per serving: 291 calories, 20 g protein, 23 g carbs, 5 g fiber, 3 g total sugar, 14 g fat, 5 g saturated fat, 454 mg sodium

Microwave Peanut Butter Oats

In a medium microwaveable bowl, combine 1 cup fat-free milk (or unsweetened soy milk), ½ cup rolled oats, and a pinch of salt. Microwave on high for 2 minutes, then stir in 2 teaspoons natural almond or peanut butter and ground cinnamon to taste. Microwave on high for another 30 seconds, or until oats are soft. Stir before eating.

Nutrition per serving: 300 calories, 16 g protein, 42 g carbs, 5 g fiber, 13 g total sugar, 8 g fat, 2 g saturated fat, 107 mg sodium

Loaded Breakfast Potato

Use a fork to poke holes in 1 small russet (baking) potato. Place it in a microwaveable bowl and microwave on high for 3 to 4 minutes, or until soft. Split the potato in half and top with 1 scrambled egg and egg white, 1 slice cooked and chopped turkey bacon, 2 tablespoons salsa, and 2 tablespoons 0% plain Greek yogurt.

Nutrition per serving: 292 calories, 20 g protein, 34 g carbs, 4 g fiber, 4 g total sugar, 8 g fat, 3 g saturated fat, 660 mg sodium

Tip: If you're short on time, instead of scrambling the egg and egg white, place them in a small microwaveable bowl or mug and microwave on high for 1½ minutes.

Tip: Bake or microwave a few potatoes ahead of time—they'll keep for up to 4 days in the refrigerator.

On-the-Go Breakfast

Pair 1 hard-cooked egg with 1 part-skim string cheese and 8 celery sticks dipped in ⅓ cup hummus.

Nutrition per serving: 312 calories, 18 g protein, 19 g carbs, 4 g fiber, 2 g total sugar, 18 g fat, 6 g saturated fat, 511 mg sodium

Crunchy Almond Yogurt

Stir 1 tablespoon natural almond or peanut butter into 1 cup fat-free plain yogurt until smooth. Gently stir in 2 tablespoons sliced almonds and ground cinnamon to taste.

Nutrition per serving: 311 calories, 20 g protein, 25 g carbs, 4 g fiber, 20 g total sugar, 16 g fat, 2 g saturated fat, 225 mg sodium

Cashew-Coconut Muesli Yogurt

Combine ⅓ cup rolled oats, 1½ tablespoons chopped cashews, and 1½ tablespoons unsweetened shredded coconut. Stir ¼ teaspoon ground ginger and ¼ teaspoon ground cinnamon into ½ cup 0% plain Greek yogurt and gently fold in oat mixture.

Nutrition per serving: 283 calories, 18 g protein, 28 g carbs, 4 g fiber, 5 g total sugar, 12 g fat, 5 g saturated fat, 47 mg sodium

Fiesta Egg Salad

Mash ¼ avocado with 2 teaspoons lemon juice and a pinch of ground cumin and black pepper. Combine with 1 hard-cooked egg and 1 hard-cooked egg white, both chopped. Toss with 1 cup rinsed and drained canned black beans and 3 tablespoons salsa. Serve over 2 cups baby spinach.

Nutrition per serving: 416 calories, 29 g protein, 51 g carbs, 20 g fiber, 3 g total sugar, 13 g fat, 3 g saturated fat, 558 mg sodium

Tangy Mediterranean Tuna Salad

Whisk together 1½ teaspoons olive oil, 1½ tablespoons red wine vinegar, ¼ teaspoon minced garlic, and ½ teaspoon Dijon mustard. Gently combine half of a 5-ounce can drained water-packed tuna with 1¼ cups rinsed and drained canned chickpeas and toss with the dressing. Stir in 2 tablespoons sliced kalamata or green olives and serve over 2 cups roughly chopped romaine lettuce.

Nutrition per serving: 453 calories, 28 g protein, 56 g carbs, 3 g fiber, <1 g total sugar, 14 g fat, 2 g saturated fat, 617 mg sodium

Cool Cucumber, Tomato, Black Bean, and Barley Salad

Whisk together 1 tablespoon red wine vinegar, 2 teaspoons olive oil, ¼ teaspoon dried oregano, and ½ teaspoon minced garlic. Toss together ½ cup halved grape tomatoes, ½ cup chopped cucumber, 2 tablespoons finely chopped red onion, ½ cup cooked barley, ¾ cup rinsed and drained canned black beans, and the dressing.

Nutrition per serving: 449 calories, 18 g protein, 63 g carbs, 19 g fiber, 4 g total sugar, 15 g fat, 2 g saturated fat, 410 mg sodium

Crunchy Sesame Chicken and Bulgur Bowl

Whisk together 2 teaspoons toasted sesame oil, 1 tablespoon rice wine vinegar, ½ teaspoon minced garlic, and ¼ teaspoon reduced-sodium soy sauce. Using a fork, shred a 3-ounce piece of grilled skinless chicken breast. Toss 1⅔ cups cooked bulgur with 1 cup roughly chopped spinach. Top with 2 tablespoons chopped scallion, ⅓ cup shredded carrot, the shredded chicken, and 1 tablespoon chopped roasted salted peanuts. Drizzle with the dressing.

Nutrition per serving: 447 calories, 29 g protein, 49 g carbs, 13 g fiber, 3 g total sugar, 17 g fat, 3 g saturated fat, 414 mg sodium

Hearty Lentil Sauté with Bulgur

Over medium-high heat, cook ¼ cup finely chopped onion and ½ cup shredded carrot in 2 teaspoons olive oil for 5 minutes, or until soft and golden. Add 1 teaspoon minced garlic, ⅛ teaspoon ground cumin, ⅓ cup dried lentils, ⅔ cup low-sodium chicken or vegetable broth, and ⅔ cup water and simmer for 10 to 15 minutes, or until all of the liquid is absorbed into the lentils. Serve lentil mixture over 1 cup cooked bulgur.

Nutrition per serving: 403 calories, 18 g protein, 52 g carbs, 20 g fiber, 6 g total sugar, 15 g fat, 2 g saturated fat, 227 mg sodium

Broiled Mustard Salmon with Roasted Broccoli and Quinoa

Combine ¼ teaspoon minced garlic, ¼ teaspoon dried oregano, ¼ teaspoon balsamic vinegar, and 1 teaspoon Dijon mustard. Spread onto a 3-ounce salmon fillet. Toss 2 cups broccoli florets with a pinch of salt and pepper and 2 teaspoons olive oil. Spread broccoli on a baking sheet and bake at 375ºF for 20 minutes. Turn oven to broil, place salmon onto the baking sheet with the broccoli, and broil, stirring broccoli so it doesn't burn, for 7 to 8 minutes, or until salmon is just cooked through. Serve salmon over ¾ cup cooked quinoa with broccoli on the side.

Nutrition per serving: 436 calories, 29 g protein, 50 g carbs, 9 g fiber, 4 g total sugar, 14 g fat, 2 g saturated fat, 155 mg sodium

Potato, Pepper, and Chicken Sausage Sauté

Heat 2 teaspoons olive oil in a nonstick skillet over medium-high heat. Add ¾ cup chopped potato and cook for 8 minutes, or until potatoes begin to soften and brown. Add 1 cup sliced bell pepper (any color) and ⅓ cup sliced onion and cook for 5 minutes, or until onion is tender. Add 1 finely chopped cooked chicken sausage and cook for 4 minutes, or until lightly browned.

Nutrition per serving: 412 calories, 22 g protein, 51 g carbs, 5 g fiber, 7 g total sugar, 16 g fat, 3 g saturated fat, 516 mg sodium

Blue Cheese, Walnut, Chicken, and Quinoa Salad

Cook 2 cups arugula and ⅛ teaspoon salt in ½ teaspoon olive oil over medium-high heat for 3 minutes, or until wilted. Whisk together 1 teaspoon olive oil, ½ teaspoon minced garlic, and 1 tablespoon balsamic vinegar. Toss the arugula with ¾ cup cooked quinoa and top with 3 ounces chopped roasted skinless chicken breast, 2 teaspoons chopped walnuts, 2 teaspoons crumbled blue cheese, and the dressing.

Nutrition per serving: 455 calories, 29 g protein, 45 g carbs, 6 g fiber, 5 g total sugar, 17 g fat, 3 g saturated fat, 553 mg sodium

Steak and Roasted Baby Potatoes and Carrots

Toss ¾ cup halved baby potatoes and 1 cup baby carrots with 1 teaspoon olive oil and a pinch of salt and pepper. Roast at 375ºF for 20 minutes. Heat 1 teaspoon olive oil over medium-high heat in an ovenproof skillet and sear a 4-ounce sirloin steak for 3 to 4 minutes, or until it develops a crust on the bottom. Remove potatoes and carrots from the oven, turn the oven to broil, and place the skillet with the steak under the broiler for 4 minutes (for medium). Remove from the oven and let rest for 3 to 4 minutes. Serve with carrots and potatoes.

Nutrition per serving: 450 calories, 33 g protein, 56 g carbs, 8 g fiber, 9 g total sugar, 12 g fat, 3 g saturated fat, 207 mg sodium

Grilled Shrimp Salad with Potato, Sunflower Seeds, and Goat Cheese

Cut a red potato into wedges, toss with 1 teaspoon olive oil, ⅛ teaspoon salt, and a pinch of black pepper and bake at 350°F for 25 minutes, or until soft on the inside and golden on the outside. Toss 4 ounces large shrimp with ½ teaspoon olive oil and ¼ teaspoon garlic powder. Grill for 2 minutes on each side, or until pink. Whisk together 1 teaspoon olive oil, 1 tablespoon balsamic vinegar, and ¼ teaspoon minced garlic. Toss 2 cups mixed greens with ½ cup chopped cucumber and the dressing. Top with shrimp, potato, 2 teaspoons roasted and salted sunflower seeds, and 2 teaspoons crumbled goat cheese.

Nutrition per serving: 477 calories, 32 g protein, 44 g carbs, 7 g fiber, 7 g total sugar, 20 g fat, 4 g saturated fat, 428 mg sodium

Build-Your-Own Meal

- 4 ounces lean protein (lean beef, pork tenderloin or a pork loin chop, chicken or turkey breast without skin, fish, or shellfish)
- 1–2 cups vegetables* (with 1–2 teaspoons olive oil or butter for flavor; or 1 tablespoon nuts or seeds; use herbs or spices, too)
- 1 cup whole grain (bulgur, quinoa, brown rice, amaranth, farro, wheat berries, oats) or 1 medium potato

Sweet potatoes and beets are not Phase 1 choices. They can be reintroduced in Phase 2.

Starbucks Hearty Veggie & Brown Rice Salad Bowl

Nutrition per serving: 430 calories, 10 g protein, 50 g carbs, 8 g fiber, 8 g total sugar, 22 g fat, 3 g saturated fat, 640 mg sodium

Outback Steakhouse Victoria's 6-oz Filet

Order with grilled asparagus and half a baked potato with a dollop of sour cream.

Nutrition per serving: 420 calories, 42 g protein, 35 g carbs, 7 g fiber, 8 g total sugar, 16 g fat, 5 g saturated fat, 723 mg sodium

Snack (100 calories)

Pick one per day.

Turkey and Cheese Wrap

Wrap a 1-ounce piece of turkey breast (1 deli slice) around 1 part-skim string cheese.

Nutrition per serving: 106 calories, 11 g protein, 2 g carbs, <1 g fiber, <1 g total sugar, 6 g fat, 4 g saturated fat, 343 mg sodium

Crudités and Hummus

Dip ½ cup sliced cucumber and 5 grape tomatoes in 3 tablespoons hummus.

Nutrition per serving: 98 calories, 5 g protein, 12 g carbs, 4 g fiber, 3 g total sugar, 5 g fat, <1 g saturated fat, 176 mg sodium

Pick one per day.

Cashew-Ginger Coconut Muesli

Mix together 2 tablespoons rolled oats, 1 tablespoon chopped cashews, 1 tablespoon unsweetened shredded coconut, ⅛ teaspoon ground ginger, and ⅛ teaspoon ground cinnamon. Add ¼ cup fat-free milk and stir to combine.

Nutrition per serving: 155 calories, 5 g protein, 14 g carbs, 2 g fiber, 4 g total sugar, 9 g fat, 5 g saturated fat, 30 mg sodium

Pumpkin Pie Trail Mix Popcorn

Toss 1 cup air-popped popcorn with 2 tablespoons pumpkin seeds, 1 tablespoon unsweetened coconut, and a pinch of pumpkin pie spice and/or ground cinnamon.

Nutrition per serving: 153 calories, 6 g protein, 10 g carbs, 3 g fiber, <1 g total sugar, 11 g fat, 5 g saturated fat, 6 mg sodium

16-Ounce Fat-Free Latte

Order with soy milk or fat-free cow's milk and pair with 7 almonds.

Nutrition per serving: 161 calories, 12 g protein, 17 g carbs, 1 g fiber, 15 g total sugar, 4 g fat, <1 g saturated fat, 140 mg sodium

Cheesy Popcorn with Almonds

Toss 1 cup air-popped popcorn sprinkled with 1 tablespoon Parmesan cheese. Have with 16 almonds.

Nutrition per serving: 162 calories, 7 g protein, 11 g carbs, 4 g fiber, 1 g total sugar, 11 g fat, 2 g saturated fat, 77 mg sodium

Turkey, Cheese, and Veggies

2 ounces low-sodium deli turkey, 1 cup red bell pepper slices*, 1 part-skim string cheese, regular or jalapeño flavored

Nutrition per serving: 159 calories, 20 g protein, 7 g carbs, 2 g fiber, 4 g total sugar, 6 g fat, 4 g saturated fat, 511 mg sodium

Can substitute 7 baby carrots or 1 cup whole cherry tomatoes for the red bell pepper; the calories and sugar content are approximately the same.

PB Celery and Milk

1 tablespoon natural peanut or almond butter spread on 4 small stalks celery and ½ cup fat-free milk

Nutrition per serving: 146 calories, 9 g protein, 11 g carbs, 2 g fiber, 9 g total sugar, 7 g fat, 2 g saturated fat, 109 mg sodium

Caprese

1 large beefsteak tomato, sliced and topped with the following: fresh basil (or the fresh or dried herb of your choice), pinch of salt, freshly ground pepper to taste, and 1 teaspoon olive oil. Serve with 1 ounce fresh mozzarella (or 1 part-skim string cheese).

Nutrition per serving: 195 calories, 9 g protein, 8 g carbs, 2 g fiber, 5 g total sugar, 7 g fat, 3 g saturated fat, 185 mg sodium

DAILY FOOD LOG

Date:

Today's intention:

Place an X next to the meals and snacks you ate today. An asterisk denotes a recipe that can be found in Chapter 11.

BREAKFAST

Hunger level ____

__ Cashew-Coconut Muesli Yogurt
__ Crunchy Almond Yogurt
__ Crustless Mini Broccoli and
Cheese Quiche*
__ Loaded Breakfast Potato

__ Mediterranean Scramble
__ Microwave Peanut Butter Oats
__ Mushroom-Quinoa Frittata*
__ On-the-Go Breakfast
__ Sausage-Potato Hash and Eggs*

LUNCH AND DINNER

Hunger level ____

__ Barley Risotto with Chicken and
Asparagus*
__ Blue Cheese, Walnut, Chicken,
and Quinoa Salad
__ Broiled Mustard Salmon with
Roasted Broccoli and Quinoa
__ Build-Your-Own Meal
__ Cool Cucumber, Tomato, Black Bean,
and Barley Salad
__ Crunchy Sesame Chicken and
Bulgur Bowl
__ Fast, Hearty Turkey Chili*
__ Fiesta Egg Salad
__ Grilled Shrimp Salad with Potato,
Sunflower Seeds, and Goat Cheese

__ Hearty Lentil Sauté with Bulgur
__ Outback Steakhouse Victoria's
6-oz Filet
__ Potato, Pepper, and Chicken
Sausage Sauté
__ Roasted Veggie, Bulgur, and
Chickpea Salad with Feta Dressing*
__ Starbucks Hearty Veggie & Brown
Rice Salad Bowl
__ Steak and Roasted Baby Potatoes
and Carrots
__ Sugar Smart Marinara Sauce*
__ Tangy Mediterranean Tuna Salad
__ Vegetarian Stuffed Portobello*

DAILY FOOD LOG *(cont.)*

SNACKS AND SIDES (100 CALORIES)

Hunger Level____

__ Turkey and Cheese Wrap

__ Crudités and Hummus

SNACKS AND SIDES (150 CALORIES)

Hunger Level____

__ 16-Ounce Fat-Free Latte
__ Caprese
__ Cashew-Ginger Coconut Muesli
__ Cheesy Popcorn with Almonds
__ Crunchy Roasted Rosemary Chick-
peas*

__ PB Celery and Milk
__ Pumpkin Pie Trail Mix Popcorn
__ Tuna-Potato Wrap*
__ Turkey, Cheese, and Veggies

Additional Foods:

Notes:

MYRA STOUDT

MYRA NEVER SAW HERSELF as a person with a lot of will-power until she tried the Sugar Smart Diet. Phase 1 of the plan coincided with a family beach vacation—it was a scary proposition, but Myra was prepared. She studied the meal plans and stocked up on the healthy, sugar-free foods she could eat.

"Every day I took a can of nuts in my beach bag to snack on while my husband ate licorice," she says. She was able to resist the temptations of the boardwalk—like pizza and soda—and was satisfied sipping unsweetened iced tea and feasting on a freshly grilled chicken sandwich loaded with crispy lettuce and a thick slice of tomato, minus the bun. "I was so proud of myself." She was rewarded for all her hard work when she stepped on the scale 10 days into the plan. "I lost 6 pounds—on vacation, no less!"

So what gave her this infusion of determination? "I'm in my fifties and was feeling like it was the last chance to change my life," she says. "My father has diabetes, and I saw that as the path mapped out for me. Doing this plan gave me an opportunity to change." Not only did Myra lose weight, she improved her cholesterol, blood pressure, and triglyceride levels, thereby reducing her risk of heart disease.

And the changes she experienced went beyond the physical. "The most amazing part is that you really can conquer the cravings that you think have control over you," she says. "I used to know where to find chocolate anywhere and couldn't imagine how I'd exist without it. Now I don't need chocolate. I feel more in control and care about the kind of fuel that I put into my body."

That success gave Myra the confidence to become more physically active. "I never thought the exercise world was for me," says Myra. But the Sugar Smart Workout didn't feel intimidating, and soon she found that she was waking up looking forward to exercise. "There's no better feeling than getting out for a walk in the morning. It's spiritual. It's me out there saying, 'I can do this! It's not impossible! I'm sticking with this!' I'd still like to lose more weight, and for once I feel like I might just do it for good!"

7.8
POUNDS LOST

AGE:
52

ALL-OVER
INCHES LOST:
7.5

SUGAR SMART WISDOM
"I invited three friends to join me for a trail walk. It was fun and refreshing to be outside in beautiful scenery rather than sitting inside complaining over coffee."

8

Phase 2: Days 12-18

FRUIT FEAST!

Phase 2 reintroduces nature's original dessert: fruit. Trust me, after 6 days without any sugar at all, your brain's reward region will experience that first bite of juicy pear, luscious grape, or crunchy apple as an explosion of sweetness—a marching band of flavor led by high-stepping, baton-twirling beauty queens. Your "sweet buds" will be just as satisfied with this phase's delectable, fruit-filled menu.

I want to remind you that the sugar in fruit is not added sugar and therefore does not count toward the 6 teaspoons of added sugar (or 9 teaspoons for men) that eventually is your goal on most days. Fruit is also packed with fiber and nutrients. Why then did we eliminate it on Days 6–11 of the Sugar Smart Diet? Our palates have been so over-sugared that we've lost the ability to really taste and appreciate the sweetness in fruit. Eliminating it for those 6 days helped to reset your sugar thermostat—you've got a clean slate when it comes to sugar. And by reintroducing it now when you are still avoiding any added sugars, you reclaim the sweet pleasure fruit can provide.

Yes, fruit has sugar. And yes, the sugar is more or less chemically the same as the sugar in candy (table sugar and the sugar in fruit have approximately the same proportion of fructose and glucose). But fruit has less of it, and the body has a harder time extracting the sugar from a piece of fruit than it does from a piece of candy. That's because fruit is packed with fiber, which slows the breakdown of the food in your digestive system, leading to a far more gradual release of sugar into your body. This means that a flood of glucose does not hit your bloodstream, and your liver is not overwhelmed by fructose. Add to that the fact that studies have directly linked fiber to long-term weight loss. So when you enjoy the sweetness of fruit, you're less likely to reach for processed, nutritionally bereft items instead.

Days 12-18

What to Do

● **Have breakfast every morning.** Just as you did in Phase 1, you'll be eating a protein-packed breakfast to keep appetite and blood sugar on an even keel. In this phase, you'll find some terrific fruit options. When fruit is paired with protein and fat, it's even more satisfying.

● **Mix and match the lunch and dinner options.** You can keep eating any of the Phase 1 meals, but we have eight new quick and easy meals and four new recipes to put into rotation. Just like the Phase 1 meals, these are centered on fresh, whole foods—grains, vegetables, low-fat dairy, and lean protein.

● **Have one serving of a processed whole grain product, if you like.** Ideally, all of your grain intake would be from whole unprocessed grains. I can't stress enough that even whole grains—once they're pulverized into flour and restructured into cereal, bread, or noodles—are digested nearly as quickly as sugar. But we all live in the real world, when a bowl of cold cereal makes for a quick breakfast, a bowl of pasta is calling your name, or you want the convenience of a sandwich. That's why we've brought back processed whole grain products in this phase, but just once a day. A note about bread: It can be tough to find a commercial one that doesn't contain added sugar, so the bread we use on this phase comes in the form of tortillas and pitas, which tend to have about 1 gram or less. If you choose to eat one of our wrap or burrito options, you'd be taking in a minuscule amount of added sugar. If you opt for cereal, pick one with 0 gram of sugar and 3 or more grams of fiber per serving.

● **Have fruit up to three times a day.** For all its nutritious goodness, fruit's sugar content means it's higher in calories than vegetables. So to keep your weight in check, you don't want to go overboard on the fruit. Whether you snack on it, serve it for dessert, or eat it as part of a meal, you can have fruit as long as you don't eat more than three servings a day. (A serving is a cup of sliced fruit or one medium piece of whole fruit.) If strong sugar cravings have been an issue in the past, you may want to choose low-sugar fruits more often. The chart on page 148 gives you the sugar content of different fruits.

● **Don't forget to snack!** Eating every few hours is just as important in this phase as it was in the last one. You'll still be eating one 100-calorie and one 150-calorie snack per day at the times of your choosing. And while you can have a juicy piece of fruit, I suggest that you pair it with protein or a fat in order to control your blood sugar response and satisfy your appetite even more. See the chart on page 149 for some ideas.

● **Avoid the following foods:** White flour and products made with it, white rice, fruit juice, and sugar in any of its many forms (including the table sugar you might add to foods, honey, and maple syrup).

● **Set your daily intention.** You may be feeling more in control of your cravings and your diet during this phase, but reminding yourself every morning of your wish to live Sugar Smart and announcing to yourself how you'll do that in a small way each day helps ensure you'll reach your goal.

SUGAR SMART MENTOR

Tasneem Bhatia, MD

DON'T LET HEALTH HALOS FOOL YOU. Health claims on packaged products can be misleading. Packaged organic products can still be packed with sugar. Whole wheat cookies are still cookies. Since I'm gluten-free, I'm especially careful about reading food labels. Sugar is the first item on the ingredients list in many packaged gluten-free products.

FIND FRUIT FABULOUS. I try to limit my added sugar intake to a few teaspoons per day. I'd take a crisp apple or a perfectly ripe peach over cookies or candy any day! Plus, fruit is buffered with fiber, which helps avoid the spikes in glucose and insulin that trigger cravings and contribute to health problems. In fact, one study found that people who ate at least 3 servings of fruit a day had a 12 percent decline in diabetes risk. Apples, blueberries, and grapes were particularly protective. If I need a little more sweetness, I use honey, a superfood with immune-boosting properties.

MAKE A DATE WITH DESSERT. I've made it a rule to not keep sugary foods in the house. If my family and I want ice cream or dessert, we go out for it. You make more conscious choices that way, and I think you enjoy the treat more because it's an event.

CALM DOWN, CRAVE LESS. Managing stress lessens the lure of sugar. Most of us seek sugar when we're tired or depressed. When I'm particularly busy or tired, I make it a point to drink green tea throughout the day and to fit in exercise. Self-care, nurturing, breathing, and exercise are my secrets to combating sugar cravings.

TASNEEM BHATIA, MD, *is an integrative medicine expert and medical director of the Atlanta Center for Holistic and Integrative Medicine. She is the author, with the editors of* Prevention, *of* What Doctors Eat.

LIVING SUGAR SMART IN PHASE 2

Now that you've reset your sugar thermostat, your cravings should be gone, or nearly so. It's truly amazing how small, simple changes—like clearing your schedule for a dose of "me" time or a nightly walk around the neighborhood—can elicit such positive changes in mood and energy. As a result, you probably don't need day-by-day tips and tricks. You can always use the Cravings Crushers and the Sweet Freedom strategies you learned in Phase 1. But still, I've given you some Phase-2-specific tips to help keep you calm but energized, well-rested, and positive during this phase, along with an especially delightful way to soothe yourself if a craving should pop up. (Use it to crush stress, too!)

EXPAND YOUR FRUIT HORIZONS

Think of fruits as crayons. You wouldn't use just red and yellow, right? You want the whole colorful box to pick from. It's the same with fruit. All fruit contains fiber, vitamins, minerals, and various disease-fighting nutrients like antioxidants and phytochemicals. The different colors are indicators of different nutritional profiles. Red watermelon and grapefruit are great sources of lycopene. The dark reds, purples, and purple-blues in fruits like cherries, plums, and blueberries are rich in anthocyanins. Mangoes, peaches, nectarines, apricots, and

Guava, Demystified

Native to the American tropics, this fragrant, exotic fruit—which resembles a pear on the outside and watermelon on the inside—is likely in your supermarket's produce aisle. Don't shy away. It can be a delicious addition to Phase 2 eating. Its tangy sweetness is a nice alternative to cherries and berries.

Depending on the variety, guavas may have light-green or yellow skin, and pink, red, yellow, or even white flesh.

Ripe guavas have a fragrant aroma that ranges from strong and penetrating to mild and pleasant. Give them a gentle squeeze before you buy. Guavas sold in markets are usually quite firm, so you should let them sit for a few days at room temperature before you use them, to allow them to ripen. They're ripe when they yield to a gentle squeeze. Refrigerate ripe guavas immediately, and use them within a day or two.

cantaloupe pack carotenoids, like beta-carotene. The more colors you choose, the more health benefits you'll reap.

As it turns out, consuming smaller amounts of many phytochemicals may benefit health more than larger amounts of fewer phytochemicals, according to a study published in the *Journal of Nutrition*. Researchers had 106 women eat 8 to 10 servings of fruit a day (veggies, too) for 8 weeks. Half the women chose from 18 different varieties (including kiwi, peaches, berries, grapes, and pineapple), while the others ate the same five fruits over and over again.

Two weeks later, blood tests showed that compared to the low-variety group, the high-variety group had less DNA damage, possibly making their bodies more resilient against disease.

THROW SOME FRUIT ON THE BARBIE

To truly appreciate the sweetness of fruit, you've *got* to grill it, at least once. Grilling fruit causes its sugars to caramelize, creating a unique, smoky flavor that's perfect for a side dish or dessert that tastes decadent.

You can grill any fruit large and firm enough to take the heat—apples, pears, pineapple, peaches, oranges, even strawberries—if you put them on skewers. If you want to try grilling smaller fruits, like grapes or blueberries, use a grill pan to hold them above the flames or coals.

To prep a fruit for grilling, wash and slice it in half, or cut it into large

How to Cut a Mango

We know people who won't buy mangoes, claiming that they're too hard to cut. Not true! This simple four-step method ensures a perfect, nonmutilated mango.

1. With a sharp knife, cut both sides of the mango lengthwise along the pit, as close to the pit as possible.
2. Lay each half, skin side down, on a cutting board.
3. Score the flesh into 1-inch squares, without cutting through the skin.
4. Invert the skin side so the fruit pops out.

chunks. Leave the skin on to help hold the fruit together as it cooks. Next, soak the fruit in 1 to 2 cups cold water for about 30 minutes. This step maximizes the fruit's water content so it stays juicy as it grills. For extra flavor, spice up the soaking water with ground cloves, cinnamon, or nutmeg.

Now you're ready to grill. To prevent sticking, brush the fruit on both sides with about a teaspoon of olive oil. Most fruits need only 3 to 4 minutes of grilling per side. Grill over medium-low heat and don't walk away while it's cooking. When it's done, slide it onto a plate, top with a dollop of Greek yogurt, and dust with cinnamon.

TRY "SLEEPY BREATHING"

Is your busy brain keeping you awake at night? Long, slow abdominal breathing can reduce anxiety and arousal, making that hamster in your head get off its wheel and relax. In a small Harvard study using yoga breathing techniques to treat insomnia, all volunteers reported that the quality and quantity of their sleep improved. To sleep better tonight, try one breathing technique called the 4-7-8 breath exercise. With your tongue resting on the roof of your mouth, just behind your upper teeth, exhale completely. Close your mouth and inhale through your nose for four counts. Hold your breath for seven counts. Then exhale (with your tongue in the same position) while mentally counting to eight. Repeat the cycle three more times.

SOOTHE WITH SCENT

Self-soothing techniques help you tolerate strong or overwhelming emotions, so you can manage them in a positive way, rather than reflexively reaching for a sugary treat. Activating the senses, such as inhaling a pleasant scent, is a helpful reminder to enter the present. To try this exercise, you'll need a bottle of eucalyptus oil, available at natural foods stores, and a small washcloth (make it a pretty one).

Add 2 drops of eucalyptus oil to 1 cup of water in a bowl and stir. Soak a washcloth thoroughly in the scented water. Squeeze out the excess water,

Q: Can I swap dried fruit or fruit juice for fresh fruit?

A: Dried fruit has all the fiber, nutrients, and sugar of fresh, but concentrated into a smaller portion. For instance, ½ cup of fresh apricot halves has 37 calories and 7 grams of sugar. Half a cup of dried apricot halves supply 157 calories and 35 grams of sugar. Rather than snacking on it out of hand, I like to think of it as an added sugar, like honey or maple syrup, and use it as an ingredient in recipes to enhance the flavor of whole foods. (Some dried fruit, like cranberries and tart cherries, is sweetened with sugar.) As such, the meals in this phase don't contain any dried fruit. We bring it back as an ingredient in meals in Phase 3.

As for fruit juice, no. If your goal is to shrink your sugar belly, it's best to satisfy your sweet tooth with fruit. Fruit juice has more sugar than fruit, and even though that sugar is natural, it contributes calories. For instance, an 8-ounce glass of orange juice has 112 calories, 21 grams of sugar, and 0.5 gram of fiber. A medium navel orange has 69 calories, 12 grams of sugar, and 3 grams of fiber. The juice will be converted into blood sugar more quickly than the orange will. Moreover, calories that you drink simply don't fill you up. That's because liquids don't trigger your satiety mechanism the same way whole foods do, and juice doesn't have the critical fiber component that whole fruit offers.

You might also be wondering about canned fruit. That's a little tricky. Certainly avoid those packed in heavy or light syrup—that's code for sugar. As for varieties canned in fruit juice, they have more calories and sugar than fresh or frozen (unsweetened) fruit. You can cut back some by draining the juice before you eat the fruit. Water-packed fruits are often sweetened with artificial sweeteners, but if you can find a water-packed brand that isn't, that's a fine choice.

then roll it up neatly and place it in a plastic bag in your refrigerator, where you can see it.

When a craving hits, retrieve your scented washcloth and drape it gently over your face. Bring your full attention to the sensations you notice—the roughness of the cloth, its coolness, its scent—as you inhale deeply and exhale fully. Be still for a minute or two, continuing to inhale and exhale, focusing on the scent and your sensations.

After your soothing session, check in with your feelings. Did your urge to eat go up, go down, or remain the same? Did soothing yourself without food help you move away from the impulse to eat?

PHASE 2 QUICK & EASY MEALS

Have three meals and two snacks every day from the options below. You can also choose from the quick and easy meals in Phase 1 and the Phase 1 and Phase 2 recipes in Chapter 11.

Breakfast

Apricot-Almond Breakfast Wrap

Stir ⅛ teaspoon ground cinnamon, ¼ teaspoon vanilla extract, and 1 tablespoon sliced almonds into ¼ cup part-skim ricotta cheese. Spread on an 8" whole wheat tortilla and top with 2 sliced apricots. Fold the sides of the tortilla in and roll.

Nutrition per serving: 288 calories, 14 g protein, 41 g carbs, 6 g fiber, 7 g total sugar, 9 g fat, 3 g saturated fat, 331 mg sodium

Spicy Avocado Breakfast Bowl

Toss ⅔ cup cooked quinoa with 1 egg and 2 egg whites, scrambled or hard-cooked, ⅛ avocado, and ¼ cup pico de gallo (fresh salsa). Add salt, pepper, and chili powder to taste.

Nutrition per serving: 303 calories, 20 g protein, 31 g carbs, 6 g fiber, 3 g total sugar, 11 g fat, 2 g saturated fat, 457 mg sodium

Strawberry-Kiwi Crunch Yogurt

Mix ½ cup sliced strawberries with 2 chopped kiwis. Toss with 3 tablespoons sliced almonds and ½ cup nonfat plain yogurt.

Nutrition per serving: 318 calories, 23 g protein, 39 g carbs, 8 g fiber, 24 g total sugar, 10 g fat, <1 g saturated fat, 67 mg sodium

Turkey Sausage, Spinach, and Cheddar Wrap

Cut a cooked 1-ounce turkey breakfast sausage link into pieces. Sprinkle ¼ cup shredded reduced-fat Cheddar cheese over an 8" whole wheat tortilla and top with 1 cup spinach leaves and the sausage. Microwave the tortilla until the cheese melts, then wrap and eat.

Nutrition per serving: 289 calories, 18 g protein, 31 g carbs, 4 g fiber, <1 g total sugar, 11 g fat, 4 g saturated fat, 661 mg sodium

Apple-Cinnamon Oats with Walnuts

Bring ¾ cup fat-free milk to a boil and stir in ⅓ cup rolled oats. Reduce heat to a simmer and cook for 10 minutes, or until thick. Two minutes before the oats are finished cooking, stir in ½ apple, chopped, and a dash of ground cinnamon. Remove from the heat and stir in ¼ cup 0% plain Greek yogurt and top with 1 tablespoon walnuts.

Nutrition per serving: 295 calories, 17 g protein, 43 g carbs, 5 g fiber, 21 g total sugar, 7 g fat, <1 g saturated fat, 0 mg sodium

Picnic Breakfast

Have 1 ounce reduced-fat Cheddar cheese with 1 slice deli ham, 2 walnut halves, 1 pear, and a 12-ounce cafe au lait (6 ounces warm fat-free milk mixed with 6 ounces hot coffee).

Nutrition per serving: 297 calories, 21 g protein, 36 g carbs, 5 g fiber, 26 g total sugar, 9 g fat, 4 g saturated fat, 581 mg sodium

Starbucks Spinach & Feta Breakfast Wrap

Nutrition per serving: 290 calories, 19 g protein, 33 g carbs, 6 g fiber, 4 g total sugar, 10 g fat, 4 g saturated fat, 830 mg sodium

Lunch and Dinner

Spinach and Grapefruit Salad with Wheat Berries and Grilled Chicken

Whisk together 1 tablespoon apple cider vinegar, 2 teaspoons olive oil, ¼ teaspoon dried thyme, and ¼ teaspoon minced garlic and set aside. Toss 2 cups baby spinach with 1 cup cooked wheat berries and the dressing. Top with ½ cup grapefruit segments and 3 ounces chopped grilled chicken.

Nutrition per serving: 388 calories, 28 g protein, 45 g carbs, 9 g fiber, 9 g total sugar, 12 g fat, 2 g saturated fat, 148 mg sodium

Bento Box

Have 1 hard-cooked egg with 1 ounce Cheddar cheese, 1 cup grape tomatoes, ¼ cup hummus, and half of a 6" whole wheat pita.

Nutrition per serving: 412 calories, 21 g protein, 38 g carbs, 7 g fiber, 5 g total sugar, 21 g fat, 8 g saturated fat, 613 mg sodium

Fennel Slaw with Salmon and White Beans

Whisk together 1 tablespoon apple cider vinegar, 2 teaspoons olive oil, ½ teaspoon dried oregano, and ½ teaspoon Dijon mustard. Toss together 1 cup thinly sliced fennel bulb, ⅓ cup shredded carrot, ⅓ cup thinly sliced cucumber, 1 cup rinsed and drained canned white beans, and the dressing. Gently stir in half of a drained 5-ounce can wild salmon.

Nutrition per serving: 463 calories, 31 g protein, 55 g carbs, 16 g fiber, 6 g total sugar, 14 g fat, 2 g saturated fat, 497 mg sodium

Whole Wheat Tuna Pasta Salad over Mixed Greens

Whisk together 1 tablespoon lemon juice, 2 teaspoons olive oil, ¼ teaspoon dried basil, and ¼ teaspoon minced garlic. Toss 1⅓ cups cooked and cooled whole wheat spiral pasta, 3 tablespoons sliced black olives, half of a 5-ounce can drained water-packed tuna, and the dressing. Serve over 1 cup mixed greens.

Nutrition per serving: 396 calories, 22 g protein, 54 g carbs, 7 g fiber, 2 g total sugar, 13 g fat, 2 g saturated fat, 406 mg sodium

Garlic-y Shrimp 'n' Grits

Boil 1½ cups water and stir in ⅓ cup grits or coarse cornmeal. Reduce heat to low and cook, stirring constantly, for 10 minutes, or until thickened. Stir in ¼ teaspoon minced garlic, 1 teaspoon olive oil, and pepper to taste. Set aside. Cook ⅓ cup sliced onion in 1½ teaspoons olive oil over medium-high heat for 4 minutes, or until tender. Add 1 cup spinach and 3 ounces large shrimp and cook until shrimp turn pink. Add ½ cup no-salt-added canned tomatoes, ¼ teaspoon minced garlic, and ¼ teaspoon dried oregano and simmer until heated through. Serve shrimp over grits.

Nutrition per serving: 406 calories, 23 g protein, 51 g carbs, 5 g fiber, 5 g total sugar, 13 g fat, 2 g saturated fat, 139 mg sodium

Chicken Sausage and Veggie Pita Pizza

Heat 1 teaspoon olive oil over medium heat and add ¼ cup finely chopped onion and ¼ cup chopped mushrooms and cook for 5 minutes, or until soft. Add 2 cups baby spinach and cook for 2 minutes, or until wilted. Spread ⅓ cup no-sugar-added marinara sauce on a 6" whole wheat pita, top with spinach mixture, a small chopped cooked chicken sausage patty or link, and 2 tablespoons shredded part-skim mozzarella cheese. Broil on high for 4 minutes, or until cheese is melted.

Nutrition per serving: 408 calories, 28 g protein, 41 g carbs, 8 g fiber, 9 g total sugar, 15 g fat, 5 g saturated fat, 1,181 mg sodium

Chipotle Burrito Bowl

Order a burrito bowl with steak or chicken, black beans, fajita vegetables, roasted chili-corn salsa, fresh tomato salsa, and lettuce. Skip the rice.

Nutrition per serving (steak): 435 calories, 42 g protein, 49 g carbs, 17 g fiber, 11 g total sugar, 9.5 g fat, 2 g saturated fat, 1,620 mg sodium

Nutrition per serving (chicken): 435 calories, 44 g protein, 48 g carbs, 17 g fiber, 11 g total sugar, 9.5 g fat, 2 g saturated fat, 1,670 mg sodium

Panera Bread Chopped Chicken Cobb with Avocado

Ask for the Greek/Herb Vinaigrette dressing on the side and use half of it. Skip the side of bread.

Nutrition per serving: 470 calories, 38 g protein, 14 g carbs, 6 g fiber, 2 g total sugar, 30 g fat, 8 g saturated fat, 900 mg sodium

Snacks (100 calories)

Pick one per day.

PB&J Yogurt

Stir ½ tablespoon natural almond or peanut butter into ⅓ cup fat-free plain yogurt until smooth. Gently stir in 8 sliced grapes.

Nutrition per serving: 106 calories, 7 g protein, 11 g carbs, <1 g fiber, 9 g total sugar, 4 g fat, <1 g saturated fat, 65 mg sodium

Fruit and Protein Combo

For a 100-calorie snack, pick one item from each of the two charts that follow on pages 148–149. None of these foods contain any added sugar.

FRUIT

Serving of fruit*	Calories	Carb (g)	Fiber (g)	Sugar (g)
Apple, 1 cup sliced	57	15	3	11
Banana, ½ large	61	16	2	8
Blackberries, 1 cup	62	14	8	7
Blueberries, ¾ cup	63	16	3	11
Cherries, 12	62	15	2	13
Clementines, 2	70	18	3	14
Figs (fresh), 2	74	19	3	16
Grapefruit, 1 large	53	13	2	12
Grapes, 20	68	18	<1	15
Guava, 2	74	16	6	10
Kiwi, ½ cup sliced	55	13	3	8
Mango, ½ cup chunks	50	12	1	11
Melon, 1 cup chunks	61	15	1	14
Orange, 1 medium	65	16	3	13
Papaya, 1 cup chunks	62	16	3	11
Peach, 1 medium	58	14	2	13
Pear, ¾ cup slices	60	16	3	10
Pineapple, 1 cup chunks	62	16	2	12
Plums, 2 medium	61	15	2	13
Raspberries, 1 cup	64	15	8	5
Starfruit, 1 cup sliced	33	7	3	4
Strawberries, 1 cup sliced	53	12	4	8
Tangerine, 1 medium	47	12	2	9
Watermelon, 1 cup balls	37	9	<1	8

*Fruit contains 1 gram or less of protein and fat and minimal sodium.

PROTEIN SNACKS

Serving of protein	Calories	Protein (g)	Carb (g)	Fiber (g)	Sugar (g)	Fat (g)	Sat Fat (g)	Sodium (mg)
Almond butter, ½ Tbsp	49	2	2	<1	<1	4	<1	18
Almonds, 6	41	2	2	<1	<1	4	<1	0
Cashews, 4	49	1	3	<1	<1	4	1	1
Peanut butter, ½ Tbsp	47	2	2	<1	<1	4	<1	37
Pistachios, 10	40	1	2	<1	<1	3	<1	0
Walnuts, 3 halves	46	1	1	<1	<1	5	<1	0
Cheddar cheese, low-fat, 1 oz	48	7	1	0	<1	2	1	171
Cottage cheese, low-fat, ¼ cup	41	7	2	0	2	<1	<1	229
Ricotta, part-skim, ⅛ cup	39	3	2	0	<1	2	1	35
Swiss cheese, low-fat, 1 oz	48	8	1	0	<1	1	<1	73
Yogurt, Greek, 0% plain, ¼ cup	50	9	3	0	3	<1	<1	31
Yogurt, regular, fat-free plain, ⅓ cup	46	5	6	0	6	<1	<1	63
Roast beef, deli, 3 slices	48	7	1	0	0	1	<1	366
Turkey, deli, 2 slices	55	13	0	<1	2	<1	<1	432

Snacks/Desserts (150 calories)

Pick one per day.

Banana-Coconut Roll

Roll 1 small banana in 1½ tablespoons unsweetened coconut flakes.

Nutrition per serving: 152 calories, 2 g protein, 25 g carbs, 4 g fiber, 13 g total sugar, 6 g fat, 6 g saturated fat, 5 mg sodium

Pear Wedges with Blue Cheese and Walnuts

Cut ½ pear into 4 wedges and top each with a walnut half and 1 teaspoon crumbled blue cheese.

Nutrition per serving: 151 calories, 4 g protein, 15 g carbs, 3 g fiber, 9 g total sugar, 9 g fat, 3 g saturated fat, 189 mg sodium

DAILY FOOD LOG

Date:

Today's intention:

Place an X next to the meals and snacks you ate today.
You can mix and match your meals and snacks from Phases 1 and 2. **Boldface** indicates an option added in this phase; an asterisk denotes a recipe that can be found in Chapter 11.

BREAKFAST

Hunger level _____

__ **Apple-Cinnamon Oats with Walnuts**
__ **Apricot-Almond Breakfast Wrap**
__ **Banana Cream Pie Overnight Oats***
__ **Breakfast Quesadilla***
__ Cashew-Coconut Muesli Yogurt
__ Crunchy Almond Yogurt
__ Crustless Mini Broccoli and Cheese Quiche*
__ Loaded Breakfast Potato
__ Mediterranean Scramble
__ Microwave Peanut Butter Oats

__ **Mushroom-Quinoa Frittata***
__ On-the-Go Breakfast
__ **Picnic Breakfast**
__ Sausage-Potato Hash and Eggs*
__ **Spicy Avocado Breakfast Bowl**
__ **Starbucks Spinach & Feta Breakfast Wrap**
__ **Strawberry-Kiwi Crunch Yogurt**
__ **Turkey Sausage, Spinach, and Cheddar Wrap**

DAILY FOOD LOG (cont.)

LUNCH AND DINNER

Hunger level ____

__ Barley Risotto with Chicken and Asparagus*

__ **Bento Box**

__ Blue Cheese, Walnut, Chicken, and Quinoa Salad

__ Broiled Mustard Salmon with Roasted Broccoli and Quinoa

__ Build-Your-Own Meal

__ **Chicken Sausage and Veggie Pita Pizza**

__ **Chipotle Burrito Bowl**

__ Cool Cucumber, Tomato, Black Bean, and Barley Salad

__ Crunchy Sesame Chicken and Bulgur Bowl

__ Fast, Hearty Turkey Chili*

__ **Fennel Slaw with Salmon and White Beans**

__ Fiesta Egg Salad

__ **Fish Tacos with Mango-Lime Salsa in Crispy Corn Tortillas***

__ **Garlic-y Shrimp 'n' Grits**

__ Grilled Shrimp Salad with Potato, Sunflower Seeds, and Goat Cheese

__ Hearty Lentil Sauté with Bulgur

__ Outback Steakhouse Victoria's 6-oz Filet

__ **Panera Bread Chopped Chicken Cobb with Avocado**

__ **Penne with Meatballs***

__ **Pork Tenderloin with Roasted Pear-Cabbage Medley and Barley***

__ Potato, Pepper, and Chicken Sausage Sauté

__ Roasted Veggie, Bulgur, and Chickpea Salad with Feta Dressing*

__ **Spinach and Grapefruit Salad with Wheat Berries and Grilled Chicken**

__ Starbucks Hearty Veggie & Brown Rice Salad Bowl

__ Steak and Roasted Baby Potatoes and Carrots

__ Sugar Smart Marinara Sauce*

__ Tangy Mediterranean Tuna Salad

__ **Turkey-Veggie Lasagna***

__ Vegetarian Stuffed Portobello*

__ **Whole Wheat Tuna Pasta Salad over Mixed Greens**

SNACKS AND SIDES (100 CALORIES)

Hunger level ____

__ Crudités and Hummus

__ **Fruit and Protein Combo What combo?** _____

__ **PB&J Yogurt**

__ Turkey and Cheese Wrap

DAILY FOOD LOG *(cont.)*

SNACKS, SIDES, AND DESSERTS (150 CALORIES)

Hunger level _____

__ 1 cup air-popped popcorn with 1 tablespoon Parmesan cheese and 16 almonds
__ 16-Ounce Fat-Free Latte
__ **Banana-Coconut Roll**
__ **Berry-Veggie Smoothie***
__ Caprese
__ Cashew-Ginger Coconut Muesli
__ **Chocolate-Cherry Smoothie***
__ **Creamy Dark Chocolate–Banana-Coconut Pudding***
__ Crunchy Roasted Rosemary Chickpeas*

__ **Easy Cinnamon Apple Cobbler***
__ PB Celery and Milk
__ **Peachy Ginger All-Fruit Soft Serve***
__ **Pear Wedges with Blue Cheese and Walnuts**
__ Pumpkin Pie Trail Mix Popcorn
__ **Roasted Fennel with Pine Nuts***
__ **Roasted Lemon-Ginger Pears with Pecan Yogurt***
__ Tuna-Potato Wrap*
__ Turkey, Cheese, and Veggies
__ **Yogurt-Covered Blueberries***

Additional Foods:

Notes:

ROBYN ENDRESS

BEFORE

ROBYN HAD ALREADY LOST about 35 pounds by the time she started the Sugar Smart Diet. Her secret: cutting sugar (except fruit) and carbs, limiting dairy, and walking regularly. "The neuropathy in my feet was so bad, I stopped eating refined sugars," she says. "Within 2 days, there was no longer pain in my feet."

So why did she need this plan? "I was worried that I wasn't eating balanced meals. Also, while I had stopped bingeing on sugary foods, I was still eating large quantities of roasted almonds, especially at night. And I wanted to get good carbs back into my diet without triggering cravings or stalling my weight loss."

When Robyn eliminated fruit and foods, like salad dressing, that contained hidden sugars in Phase 1, she was surprised that she didn't miss them. Instead, she enjoyed trying new foods like quinoa and bulgur, and for the first time, she was feeling full. But she was still worried about adding carbs back into her diet in Phase 2. "I thought it might make me want more," she says. But it didn't. The only time Robyn found herself craving sugar was when she went too long between meals. Now she's careful about eating at regular intervals and carries snacks like almonds with her in case food isn't readily available. "As I was eating more balanced meals, I had more energy and no more cravings."

In addition, Robyn added the Sugar Smart strength workouts to her walking routine. "My muscles feel stronger and I have a brisker stride," she says. "My teenage daughter and I walk together. At first, she was setting the pace. Now she has to keep up with me!"

Robyn's doctor also has to keep up with all of the improvements in Robyn's health. Her cholesterol levels are all healthy now. Her triglycerides went down 53 points, total cholesterol 48 points, and LDL cholesterol 39 points. He was able to take her off of two blood pressure medications. Her sleep apnea, a condition that results from obesity, has also improved enough that she no longer has to sleep with a device that helps her to breathe.

"This has been a magic formula for me. I am in control again. I can choose not to eat a treat without feeling deprived or struggling with the decision. It is truly liberating."

15

POUNDS LOST

AGE:
52

ALL-OVER
INCHES LOST:
16.5

SUGAR SMART WISDOM
"I find the smell of sweet treats can be almost as appetizing as eating them. It's as if I can taste the fragrance and need nothing more."

Phase 3: Days 19–25

A SPOONFUL OF (NATURAL) SUGAR

If you've ever tasted pure maple syrup, you know that its flavor is galaxies away from the goo sold in the supermarket next to the pancake mix (which, by the way, is primarily high-fructose corn syrup and caramel color). Likewise, there's a vast difference between the flavor of a good local honey you might pick up at the farmers' market and the stuff that fills those bear-shaped bottles. Like fine coffee or tea, these natural sweeteners possess subtle flavors that make each batch unique. They're special, precious (and expensive) sweet delights. But they still count as added sugar in your diet.

I wanted to make that point clear up front, because while this phase reintroduces good-quality honey and real maple syrup—along with fruit spread, fruit juice (not to drink, but to use in a dressing, marinade, or sauce), and dried fruit (which, despite its fiber and nutrients, I consider an added sugar because of its concentrated sugar content)—that doesn't mean you should go crazy. In this phase, you are limited to one meal that contains these intense natural sweeteners per day. The maximum amounts are 1 teaspoon of honey or maple syrup, 2 teaspoons of 100 percent fruit spread, 2 to 3 tablespoons of dried fruit, and fruit juice only as an ingredient in a recipe (no more than $\frac{1}{4}$ cup per serving). This is to keep your calories in check and to ensure you don't stir up your sugar cravings. But to your now exquisitely sensitive taste buds, those amounts are plenty.

In this phase, the natural sweeteners are used as ingredients in dishes, not just to give you a sweet hit but to make healthy foods more enjoyable. That's a really important point. If serving Brussels sprouts with a mustard–maple syrup sauce makes you eat more Brussels sprouts, or drizzling a little honey over fat-free plain yogurt increases your consumption of this protein- and calcium-rich food, you are promoting your health.

You might wonder, though, how this is different from the sugar that gets added to jarred tomato sauce, vegetable soup, or chocolate milk. The answer is: less sweetener of a higher quality. Pure honey and maple syrup and dried fruit come packed with disease-fighting antioxidants. Imagine that you were still consuming more than 30 teaspoons of added sugars a day from processed foods. (Perish the thought!) If you eliminated them and replaced them with an equal amount of a natural sweetener, you'd add the antioxidant equivalent of a serving of nuts or berries to your diet, according to a study published in the *Journal of the Academy of Nutrition and Dietetics*. (But don't! Although healthier than refined sugars, natural sweeteners are calorie dense and can contribute to weight gain if not used sparingly.)

We've expanded your bread options in this phase, too, to include whole grain English muffins, rolls, bagels (small ones), or sliced bread. These products tend to contain added sugar, so we set a sugar content limit of 2 grams per slice of bread, English muffin, or burger bun/roll and 6 grams or less per bagel (bagels tend to contain more because the sugar helps the chewy crust form during cooking). However, your best bread choice would be a dense, seed-caught-in-your-back-tooth bread, rather than a fluffy loaf. (I usually buy breads by Ezekiel. Widely available in regular grocery stores, they come in a variety of flavors and contain no added sugar. The slices are sturdy enough to enjoy as an open-face sandwich, and toast up deliciously.) And we still recommend having processed grain products no more than once a day. Between the natural sweeteners and the added sugar in bread products, you could be taking in 2 teaspoons of added sugar a day in this phase, depending on what you choose to eat.

Now, let's take a closer look at the natural sweeteners you'll be dipping into.

HONEY: ALL-NATURAL SUGAR BUZZ

The thick, delectable liquid we spoon into tea or spread on toast starts as nectar from flowers, including clover, buckwheat, orange blossoms, and many more. Hardworking honeybees break down that nectar into simple sugars. Packed into honeycombs and fanned constantly by bee wings, the nectar evaporates. Presto! Honey.

Like wine, olives, and maple syrup, honey's flavor is influenced by region and environmental conditions. Depending on the type of nectar that bees collect, honey can be nearly colorless or dark amber; its taste delicate or robust. As a general rule, however, the lighter the honey, the milder the flavor.

But all honey is complex. It contains an estimated 180 different substances—proteins, enzymes, amino acids, minerals, vitamins, phytochemicals—that may account for its health-promoting effects. For example, gram for gram, honey is as rich in antioxidants as some fruits and veggies. Of course, we eat honey in small quantities (at least we should, to keep sugar bellies in check), so it can't replace produce. But even small amounts may offer some protection against cancer and promote heart health. In test-tube studies, honey—the darker the better—slows the oxidation of LDL ("bad") cholesterol in human blood. Oxidized LDLs are the foundation of dangerous plaque deposits in blood vessel walls that can lead to heart attack and stroke.

Compared to clover honey, the variety easiest to find in most supermarkets, buckwheat honey contains eight times the antioxidant punch. Sunflower honey boasts three times as many antioxidants, and tupelo honey packs twice the antioxidant punch as clover honey. Or check out your local farmers' market for honey that's been produced near you. I love taking my kids to the Saturday morning farmers' market and taste-testing different honeys. My kids usually opt for mellow flavors, while I lean toward those that are rich and dark.

Wherever you buy your honey, when you find the real deal that sends your taste buds on a happy dance, store it at room temperature (your kitchen counter or pantry shelf is ideal). It will keep indefinitely. (If it crystallizes, just place the jar in warm water and it will clear.)

MAPLE SYRUP: LIQUID BLISS

Pure maple syrup—the kind you buy on weekends spent in Vermont or New Hampshire—is pricey, which is why many people make do with HFCS-laden imitators. By law, pure maple syrup can be made only by the evaporation of pure maple sap, and by weight may contain no less than 66 percent sugar. But in the amounts that you'll use it in this plan, it will last a long time. And you don't need more than a teaspoon to reach maximum, eyes-shut-in-delight pleasure.

As with honey or wine, no two bottles of pure maple syrup taste exactly the same. There are more than 300 different natural compounds found in pure maple syrup, but only one (sugar furanone) is linked to the maple flavor present in all maple syrup. The flavor is affected by a variety of factors, including the genetics of the tree the sap was tapped from, the composition of the soil, weather conditions, and the time during the season when the sap was collected. Besides that can't-be-replicated maple flavor, you might taste subtle hints of caramel and vanilla, nuts or butter, chocolate or coffee.

Regardless of flavor, all pure maple syrup is rich in antioxidants. Researchers at the University of Rhode Island College of Pharmacy have repeatedly investigated the compounds in maple syrup. To date, they've discovered more than 50. Among them: polyphenols, which appear to slow enzymes that help convert carbohydrates to sugar. This particular ability raises the possibility of a new way to manage type 2 diabetes.

Maple syrup is classified by its color. The darker the syrup, the more intense its flavors. You'll find two types on the market:

Grade A. Syrup classified as grade A comes in three amber shades: light, medium, and dark. The flavor profile ranges from mild and delicate to strong and caramel-like. Medium amber is probably the most popular.

Grade B. This is darker and more maple-y than syrup rated grade A, and until recently it was mostly used commercially. Now you can find it on store shelves, and it is typically less expensive than grade A.

Buy your maple syrup in a bottle, rather than a plastic container. Plastic can affect the syrup's color and flavor after 3 to 6 months of storage. Glass, while more expensive, protects the quality of the syrup for a longer period. Unopened, maple syrup will stay fresh for more than a year. After you open it, it will keep in your refrigerator for about 6 months.

DRIED FRUIT: NATURE'S CANDY

Each time I stir raisins into my oatmeal or nibble dried figs or dates, I'm bowled over anew by the intense sweetness of dried fruit. But *why* is it so sweet? Because as the dehydration process removes the fruit's water, it intensifies its natural sugars. That shrinkage doesn't just amp up the sweetness. Nutritionists consider dried fruit "energy dense," which means that it packs a ton of calories into a small portion.

That's why the Sugar Smart Diet limits the serving size to 2 to 3 table-spoons at a time. That amount yields about 80 calories, around the same number of calories in a piece of whole fruit. But that small amount is plenty sweet for a snack in place of fresh fruit, to sweeten salads, and to savor in the Fruity Trail Mix featured in this phase. Your newly sugar-sensitive taste buds will rejoice. However, before you buy dried fruit, check the ingredients list for added sugars. Most commercially available dried fruit is filled with them. Pass them by and choose dried fruit with no sugar added. Dried cranberries are the one exception. Because of their natural tartness, the added sugar brings their sugar up to that of other dried fruit.

Your local supermarket or natural foods store should carry at least a few brands of dried fruits, either packaged or in bulk-bin containers. Even if you shop at natural foods stores, check those ingredients lists: Some natural dried fruit is sweetened with added sugar, and you'll want to avoid those. Dried fruit doesn't require refrigeration; store it in airtight containers so it doesn't absorb moisture and attract the interest of insects. On occasion, the natural sugars in dried fruit—especially prunes and figs—will solidify, forming crystals on the surface. This is okay. They're still edible, and delicious.

FRUITY FLAVOR

Unlike most commercial jams and jellies, 100% fruit spread contains no added sugars. Its sweetness comes from the sugar in the fruit itself. Treat yourself to a top-of-the-line brand. I like Crofter's Just Fruit Spread Organic Blackberry, which contains 10 calories, 2.6 grams carbs, and 2.6 grams sugar per 1 teaspoon. A less expensive alternative, but just as tasty, is Smucker's Simply Fruit Spreadable Fruit: 1 teaspoon contains 13 calories, 3.3 grams carbs, and 2.6 grams sugar.

One teaspoon of 100% spreadable fruit goes a long way toward sweetening up your menu. Here are a few ways to enjoy it.

- Mix it into fat-free plain yogurt.
- Stir it into plain cooked oats.
- Spread it on your daily refined-carb treat, such as an English muffin or a slice of whole grain toast.
- Whisk it into balsamic vinegar and olive oil—you've just made your own fruit vinaigrette, without a ton of added sugar.

As I mentioned earlier, fruit juice is pure sugar without any fiber to slow its journey through your digestive system, so I don't want you to be drinking it by the glassful. But juice helps tenderize meat and fish in a marinade, cooks down into a delicious sauce, and adds some brightness to a salad dressing. We use fruit juice in these ways, and the most you'll be taking in is 1/4 cup, which has around 1 teaspoon of sugar.

Days 19–25

Goals for Days 19 through 25

- **Have breakfast every morning.**

- **Mix and match the lunch and dinner options.** You can keep eating any of the Phase 1 or Phase 2 quick and easy meals or recipes, as well as incorporating the new options in this phase.

- **Have one serving of a processed whole grain product, if you like.** In this phase, your options are whole grain pasta, English muffin, bagel, bread, pita, tortilla, or burger bun. I stress the word *option*—you don't have to have a processed grain product every day.

- **Include one meal or snack that contains a natural sweetener per day, if you want to.** Like processed grain products, natural sweeteners are optional.

- **Have fruit up to three times a day.**

- **Don't forget to snack!**

- **Avoid the following foods: white flour and products made with it, white rice, and fruit juice as a beverage.**

- **Set your daily intention.**

LIVING SUGAR SMART IN PHASE 3

By now, we hope, you're in the swing of the plan and loving the many perks of a low-sugar lifestyle—weight loss, more restful sleep, glowing skin, and energy to burn. While you may have to manage the odd sugar craving, they should be fewer and farther between—and you should have plenty of ways to not only squelch them but head them off entirely. To help keep you moving along the path to sugar freedom, we're offering some new ways to please your palate, rest up, slow down, and replace emotionally driven urges for sugar with healthy alternatives. Continue to use the Cravings Crushers, the Sweet Freedom strategies, and the other tips from earlier phases, too!

Mix Up Some More Fabulous Flavored Waters

Now that you're free to enjoy the natural sweetness of fruit, team it with water for a healthy replacement for diet sodas or sweetened teas and juices. You'll never miss the sugar, because it's already there—in small amounts and from nature. As you did with the flavored waters in Chapter 7 (which, of course, you can keep drinking if you like), put the ingredients in a 2-quart jar, muddle with a wooden spoon or spatula, cover with 6 cups of ice, fill the jar with water, and stir. Pop it in the refrigerator for 2 hours to chill and let those luscious flavors mingle. Strain before drinking. Each recipe makes 2 quarts and will keep in the refrigerator for 2 or 3 days.

Berry-Basil Blast

8 fresh basil leaves
3 cups strawberries, halved

Scrunch the basil leaves to release their flavor. Combine with the berries.

Just Peachy

2 vanilla beans
6 peaches, pitted and sliced

Gently crush the beans and stir into the peaches.

Pear-Fect Ginger

10 slices fresh ginger
5 pears, cored and sliced

Stir the ginger and pears together.

Restore with Rhodiola

When stress drains your last drop of strength, consider trying an herbal ally: rhodiola, prized for its ability to help people modulate the stress response. Rhodiola is an adaptogen, a compound that helps the body acclimate to stress. A study published in the *Journal of Alternative and Complementary Medicine* showed that taking rhodiola reduces feelings of anxiety, depression, and fatigue. If you choose to try it, start with 200 milligrams a day. One caveat: This herb can overstimulate some people and lead to insomnia and irritability, problems that you definitely don't need when you're already under stress. So use it only if you feel exhausted and need a lift, and check with your doctor first.

Move with Nature

Days 19–25

You're a type-A desk jockey with a gym membership who just can't break away from meetings. And you've tried eyes-closed meditation, thank you very much, but you find it hard to sit still long enough to reap its benefits. If this sounds familiar, take a different approach: Spend some time outdoors. Studies show that it confers some of the same benefits as meditation.

A review of 11 studies involving 833 people, published in the journal *Environmental Science and Technology,* found that exercising in natural environments was associated with feeling more revitalized and positive, and less stressed, angry, and depressed, compared to exercising indoors. There's even evidence that exercising outside may feel easier (a definite perk!). Whether you're running, walking, or biking outdoors, lift up your eyes and engage your senses, drinking in every sensation—the breeze on your face, the crunch of those leaves, the chirp of birds. That's meditation, too!

Stretch Before You Sleep

Yoga postures, or asanas, were originally designed to calm the body and quiet the mind, preparing the yogi for meditation. The deepest meditative state, or *yoga nidra,* is known as "sleepless sleep"—where the mind is conscious of its surroundings, but the body is fully relaxed. I don't expect you to become a yogi, but turning off your mind and powering down your body before bed can lull you into a satisfying sleep. And as you know, people who sleep well lose more weight and don't get as many cravings.

You can always do our relaxing yoga routine in Chapter 12, but when you want a more focused option, dim the lights, hit the carpet, and assume the bridge pose. Lie on your back with knees bent, heels hip-width apart and parallel, close to your butt. Lift your hips up off the floor, pushing your pelvis toward the ceiling. Arch up onto your shoulders, then lace your palms together underneath your body and press your arms into the floor or mat. Hold the pose while taking 10 to 15 long, slow breaths.

Let It RAIN

Food cravings have a way of hitting when you're feeling squirrely. Scattered thoughts, overwhelming emotions, or negative chatter inside your head can conspire to make you give in to the siren song of sugar.

But a mindfulness practice called RAIN, developed by Tara Brach, a leading Western teacher of Buddhist meditation, can help you sit with those thoughts and feelings, rather than allow them to propel you toward sugar.

Each letter of RAIN spells out a positive way to engage churning feelings or negative thoughts. Use this technique to respond to cravings in a healthy way, rather than impulsively react to them.

R is for recognizing your thoughts, feelings, and sensations in the moment. What is happening now, and how can you be open to it? Can you slow down and articulate what you're thinking or feeling?

A is for accepting your thoughts and feelings exactly as they are, rather than judging them. When you accept that you are angry or sad or disappointed, those thoughts and emotions don't make you feel guilty or ashamed—and you don't have to smother them with food. Ask yourself, "What do these feelings want to tell me?"

I is for investigating your thoughts and feelings with nonjudgmental curiosity. Soothing self-talk, and tuning in to subtle changes in your body that accompany your thoughts and feelings, can help. ("I'm having the thought that I can't sit with this urge to eat. I notice that my mouth is watering.") Talk to yourself with kindness, as you would to a friend, rather than adopt a judgmental "Not again!" attitude.

N is for *not* identifying with your thoughts or feelings. They're not who you are. In fact, you're so much more than the thoughts and feelings that come and go. When you don't let them overwhelm you, it's easier to make conscious choices that don't depend on what you think or how you feel. How would it feel to make a conscious decision to eat, or not eat?

SUGAR SMART MENTOR

David L. Katz, MD, MPH

MAKE SUGAR DO DOUBLE DUTY. Enjoy sugar only in foods that really matter to you and that are also nutritious. Dark chocolate is a good example—it's good for you overall, but it certainly does contain added sugar.

REPROGRAM YOUR TASTE BUDS. Sweet is the only taste preference we're born with—it leads us to our mother's milk. The excess of sugar in modern food is a potent goad to appetite, exploiting this all-but-universal preference. But taste buds can be rehabilitated quite readily. The less sugar you eat in general, the less you need to feel satisfied and the less you tend to want. Simply by removing the Stealth Sugars in foods like jarred pasta sauces and salad dressings, you will likely start to prefer your food less sweet. Once you eliminate foods that contain Stealth Sugars, you can move on to beverages and desserts, where the sugar is more apparent.

FOCUS ON FLAVOR, NOT SWEETNESS. I prefer my desserts minimally sweetened. For example, when my wife bakes, she uses less than half the sugar a standard recipe calls for. I like dried fruit but not with added sugar. I don't understand how anyone would even think to sprinkle sugar over berries; they are plenty sweet enough direct from nature.

LEARN TO LOVE FOODS THAT LOVE YOU BACK. To keep my own sugar intake in check, I eat mostly natural, wholesome foods, getting intrinsic sugar in fruits and dairy foods. I don't drink soda, and I avoid eating foods that contain those Stealth Sugars. On any given day, I take in around 25 grams of added sugar or less, usually in dark chocolate, breakfast cereal, and, occasionally, my wife's cookies. We can all learn to love foods that love us back—we just have to get used to them as the norm. My family and I have done just that.

DAVID KATZ, MD, is the director of Yale University's Prevention Research Center, a clinical instructor in medicine at the Yale School of Medicine, editor-in-chief of the journal Childhood Obesity, founder and president of the nonprofit Turn the Tide Foundation, and medical director for the Integrative Medicine Center at Griffin Hospital in Derby, CT. Most recently, he is the author of Disease Proof: The Remarkable Truth About What Makes Us Well.

PHASE 3 QUICK & EASY MEALS

Breakfast

Canadian Bacon Apple-Cheddar Melt

Top half a whole wheat English muffin with 2 slices cooked Canadian bacon, half an apple, sliced, and 2 tablespoons shredded reduced-fat Cheddar cheese. Broil in a toaster oven or a regular oven for 3 minutes, or until the cheese is bubbly, then top with the other half of the muffin.

Nutrition per serving: 306 calories, 21 g protein, 40 g carbs, 6 g fiber, 15 g total sugar, 8 g fat, 3 g saturated fat, 1,055 mg sodium

Blueberry and Honey Yogurt Parfait

Layer ⅓ cup 0% plain Greek yogurt with ½ cup blueberries, 1 tablespoon sliced almonds, and 1 teaspoon honey. Repeat with the same amounts of yogurt, blueberries, almonds, and honey to complete the parfait.

Nutrition per serving: 308 calories, 22 g protein, 37 g carbs, 5 g fiber, 27 g total sugar, 10 g fat, <1 g saturated fat, 64 mg sodium

Classic Smoked Salmon Bagel

Top half of a whole wheat bagel or 1 slice whole wheat toast with 2 tablespoons light (or reduced-fat) cream cheese mixed with 1 tablespoon scallions, 2 slices tomato, 2 thin slices red onion, and 2 ounces smoked salmon.

Nutrition per serving: 291 calories, 20 g protein, 35 g carbs, 6 g fiber, 3 g total sugar, 9 g fat, 4 g saturated fat, 1,500 mg sodium

PB&J Toast and Café au Lait

Toast 1 slice whole wheat bread. Spread with 1 tablespoon natural peanut butter and 2 teaspoons 100% fruit spread. Serve with a 16-ounce fat-free café au lait (½ fat-free milk or unsweetened soy milk, ½ coffee) or 8 ounces fat-free milk or unsweetened soy milk.

Nutrition per serving: 338 calories, 16 g protein, 46 g carbs, 4 g fiber, 20 g total sugar, 11 g fat, 2 g saturated fat, 322 mg sodium

Lunch and Dinner

Crunchy Turkey-Pear Salad Sandwich

Mix together 2 tablespoons 0% plain Greek yogurt, 1 teaspoon reduced-fat mayo, 1 teaspoon lemon juice, and ½ teaspoon Dijon mustard. Gently toss together 2 ounces cubed roasted turkey or chicken breast, ¼ cup chopped pear, 1 tablespoon finely chopped red onion, 1 tablespoon chopped toasted pecans or walnuts, 1 tablespoon finely chopped Brie, and the yogurt mixture. Serve between 2 slices of lightly toasted whole wheat bread.

Nutrition per serving: 410 calories, 23 g protein, 50 g carbs, 10 g fiber, 10 g total sugar, 12 g fat, 3 g saturated fat, 359 mg sodium

Turkey Burger with Broccoli-Wheat Berry Toss

Stir ¼ teaspoon hot sauce (like Tabasco or Sriracha), ¼ teaspoon minced garlic, and 1 teaspoon chopped onion into 1 tablespoon 0% plain Greek yogurt. Heat ½ teaspoon olive oil in a nonstick skillet over medium heat. Add ½ cup onion and cook for 4 minutes, or until soft. Remove from the skillet. Add another 1 teaspoon olive oil to the skillet. Cook a 4-ounce turkey burger made from lean ground turkey breast for 4 minutes on each side, or until cooked through. Spread the yogurt mixture onto the bottom of a whole wheat hamburger bun and top with the burger, cooked onion, a slice of tomato, and the top of the bun. Serve with 1 cup steamed broccoli tossed with ⅓ cup cooked wheat berries, 1 teaspoon lemon juice, ⅛ teaspoon salt, and ¼ teaspoon minced garlic.

Nutrition per serving: 415 calories, 38 g protein, 45 g carbs, 8 g fiber, 6 g total sugar, 12 g fat, 2 g saturated fat, 553 mg sodium

Roast Beef, Swiss, and Arugula Sandwich

Spread 1 slice whole grain rye bread with 1 teaspoon Dijon mustard and top with 2 ounces sliced roast beef and 1-ounce slice Swiss cheese. Toss 1 cup arugula with 1 tablespoon balsamic vinegar. Place ¼ cup arugula on top of the cheese and top with another slice of bread. Serve the remaining ¾ cup arugula on the side.

Nutrition per serving: 411 calories, 32 g protein, 33 g carbs, 4 g fiber, 3 g total sugar, 16 g fat, 8 g saturated fat, 617 mg sodium

Loaded Shrimp Fajita Bowl with Brown Rice

Phase 3

Heat 2½ teaspoons olive oil in a non-stick skillet over medium-high heat. Cook 1 cup sliced bell peppers (any color) and ⅓ cup sliced onion for 5 minutes, or until soft. Add 3 ounces large shrimp and a pinch each of garlic powder, ground cumin, salt, and ground red pepper. Cook for 4 minutes, or until shrimp are pink. Remove from the heat and toss with 2 teaspoons lime juice and 2 tablespoons salsa. Serve over 1 cup brown rice topped with 1 tablespoon fat-free plain Greek yogurt, 1 tablespoon chopped black olives, and 1 tablespoon salsa.

Nutrition per serving: 410 calories, 24 g protein, 49 g carbs, 5 g fiber, 7 g total sugar, 14 g fat, 2 g saturated fat, 724 mg sodium

Halibut with Fennel and Citrus Vinaigrette and Roasted Potatoes

Cut a russet potato into wedges and toss with 1 teaspoon olive oil, ¼ teaspoon garlic powder, and ⅛ teaspoon each salt and pepper. Bake at 400°F for 20 minutes. Place 4 ounces halibut and 1 cup sliced fennel on a large sheet of foil. Drizzle with 2 teaspoons olive oil, 2 teaspoons lemon juice, and ⅛ teaspoon salt. Fold foil over and roll edges to seal the fish and fennel into a packet. Place the packet in the oven with the potatoes for the last 12 minutes of baking. Carefully remove the fish and fennel from the packet and serve with the potatoes.

Nutrition per serving: 420 calories, 27 g protein, 44 g carbs, 6 g fiber, 5 g total sugar, 15 g fat, 2 g saturated fat, 825 mg sodium

Rosemary Pork Tenderloin with Roasted Butternut Squash and Cauliflower

Toss 1½ cups peeled and cubed butter-nut squash with 1½ teaspoons olive oil, ⅛ teaspoon salt, and ¼ teaspoon garlic powder. Place on a baking sheet and bake at 425°F for 20 minutes. Stir, reduce the oven to 350°F, and add 1½ cups cauliflower florets to the bak-ing sheet. Bake for 20 minutes, or until the squash is soft and golden. Mean-while, mix together ⅛ teaspoon each salt, pepper, and garlic powder and 1 teaspoon dried rosemary and rub onto a 3-ounce piece of pork tenderloin. In an ovenproof skillet, heat 1 teaspoon olive oil over medium-high heat. Cook the pork for 1 minute on each side, then place the skillet in the oven with the veggies for 12 to 14 minutes, or until the meat reaches an internal temperature of 145°F. Toss the squash and cauliflower with ½ cup microwaved frozen corn ker-nels and serve with pork.

Nutrition per serving: 390 calories, 25 g protein, 47 g carbs, 10 g fiber, 11 g total sugar, 14 g fat, 2 g saturated fat, 692 mg sodium

Turkey, Roasted Pepper, and Avocado Roll-Up with Edamame

Mash ⅓ avocado and spread onto an 8" whole wheat tortilla. Top with 2 slices deli turkey, ⅓ cup roughly chopped roasted red pepper, and ⅓ cup shredded carrot. Roll up and serve alongside ½ cup edamame tossed with 1 teaspoon rice wine vinegar and a pinch of salt and black pepper.

Nutrition per serving: 409 calories, 32 g protein, 47 g carbs, 12 g fiber, 6 g total sugar, 12 g fat, 2 g saturated fat, 421 mg sodium

Artisan Bistro Grass-Fed Beef with Mushroom Sauce (Frozen Entrée)

Serve with a side of 2 cups microwaved frozen or fresh broccoli topped with 1½ tablespoons sliced almonds and 1 teaspoon lemon juice.

Nutrition per serving: 468 calories, 30 g protein, 102 g carbs, 6 g fiber, 6 g total sugar, 20 g fat, 4 g saturated fat, 619 mg sodium

Snacks (100 calories)

Pick one per day.

Banana-Pineapple Smoothie

Blend half a frozen sliced small banana with ¼ cup fresh, frozen, or canned-in-own-juice pineapple and ⅔ cup fat-free milk or unsweetened soy milk. Add a couple of ice cubes before blending for a thicker smoothie.

Nutrition per serving: 121 calories, 6 g protein, 25 g carbs, 2 g fiber, 19 g total sugar, <1 g fat, <1 g saturated fat, 69 mg sodium

Pick one per day.

Tuna Salad Cucumber Stackers

Mix 2 tablespoons drained and flaked albacore tuna with 1 teaspoon light mayo, 1 teaspoon lemon juice, and black pepper and dried dill to taste. Top 4 woven whole wheat crackers with the tuna salad and top each with 2 slices cucumber.

Nutrition per serving: 147 calories, 9 g protein, 15 g carbs, 2 g fiber, <1 g total sugar, 6 g fat, 1 g saturated fat, 271 mg sodium

Fruity Trail Mix

Combine 1 tablespoon chopped walnuts, 2 tablespoons raisins or chopped dried apricots, and ⅓ cup spoon-size shredded wheat cereal. Add ground cinnamon to taste.

Nutrition per serving: 158 calories, 3 g protein, 29 g carbs, 3 g fiber, 11 g total sugar, 5 g fat, <1 g saturated fat, 3 mg sodium

DAILY FOOD LOG

PHASE 3

Date:
Today's intention:

Place an X next to the meals and snacks you ate today.
You can mix and match your meals and snacks from Phases 1, 2, and 3. Boldface indicates an option added in this phase; an asterisk denotes a recipe that can be found in Chapter 11.

BREAKFAST

Hunger level ____

__ Apple-Cinnamon Oats with Walnuts
__ Apricot-Almond Breakfast Wrap
__ Banana Cream Pie Overnight Oats*
__ **Blueberry and Honey Yogurt Parfait**
__ Breakfast Quesadilla*
__ **Canadian Bacon Apple-Cheddar Melt**
__ Cashew-Coconut Muesli Yogurt
__ **Cinnamon-Apple Breakfast Polenta***
__ **Classic Smoked Salmon Bagel**
__ Crunchy Almond Yogurt
__ Crustless Mini Broccoli and Cheese Quiche*
__ Loaded Breakfast Potato
__ Mediterranean Scramble
__ Microwave Peanut Butter Oats
__ Mushroom-Quinoa Frittata*

__ On-the-Go Breakfast
__ **Orange–Vanilla Cream French Toast***
__ **PB&J Toast and Café au Lait**
__ Picnic Breakfast
__ Sausage-Potato Hash and Eggs*
__ Spicy Avocado Breakfast Bowl
__ Starbucks Spinach & Feta Breakfast Wrap
__ **Strawberry-Coconut Chia Breakfast Pudding***
__ Strawberry-Kiwi Crunch Yogurt
__ Turkey Sausage, Spinach, and Cheddar Wrap
__ **Whole Wheat Blueberry Protein Pancakes***

LUNCH AND DINNER

Hunger level _____

__ **Artisan Bistro Grass-Fed Beef with Mushroom Sauce (Frozen Entrée)**
__ **Asian Quinoa Salad***
__ Barley Risotto with Chicken and Asparagus*
__ Bento Box
__ **Beer BBQ Chicken Thighs with Corn and Tomato Salad***
__ Blue Cheese, Walnut, Chicken, and Quinoa Salad
__ Broiled Mustard Salmon with Roasted Broccoli and Quinoa
__ Build-Your-Own Meal
__ Chicken Sausage and Veggie Pita Pizza
__ Chipotle Burrito Bowl
__ Cool Cucumber, Tomato, Black Bean, and Barley Salad
__ **Crab Cakes with Garlic Kale***
__ Crunchy Sesame Chicken and Bulgur Bowl
__ **Crunchy Turkey-Pear Salad Sandwich**
__ Fast, Hearty Turkey Chili*
__ Fennel Slaw with Salmon and White Beans
__ Fiesta Egg Salad
__ Fish Tacos with Mango-Lime Salsa in Crispy Corn Tortillas*
__ Garlic-y Shrimp 'n' Grits
__ Grilled Shrimp Salad with Potatoes, Sunflower Seeds, and Goat Cheese
__ **Halibut with Fennel and Citrus Vinaigrette and Roasted Potatoes**
__ Hearty Lentil Sauté with Bulgur
__ **Loaded Shrimp Fajita Bowl with Brown Rice**
__ **Orange-Garlic Salmon with Kale and Barley***
__ Outback Steakhouse Victoria's 6-oz Filet

__ Panera Bread Chopped Chicken Cobb with Avocado
__ **Panko-Crusted Chicken Tenders with Honey-Mustard Dipping Sauce***
__ Penne with Meatballs*
__ **Poached Eggs with Fruity Wheat Berry Salad***
__ Pork Tenderloin with Roasted Pear-Cabbage Medley and Barley*
__ Potato, Pepper, and Chicken Sausage Sauté
__ **Roast Beef, Swiss, and Arugula Sandwich**
__ Roasted Veggie, Bulgur, and Chickpea Salad with Feta Dressing*
__ **Rosemary Pork Tenderloin with Roasted Butternut Squash and Cauliflower**
__ Spinach and Grapefruit Salad with Wheat Berries and Grilled Chicken
__ Starbucks Hearty Veggie & Brown Rice Salad Bowl
__ Steak and Roasted Baby Potatoes and Carrots
__ **Sugar Smart Asian Peanut Dressing***
__ **Sugar Smart BBQ Sauce***
__ Sugar Smart Marinara Sauce*
__ **Sugar Smart Teriyaki Sauce***
__ Tangy Mediterranean Tuna Salad
__ **Teriyaki Beef with Broccoli***
__ **Turkey Burger with Broccoli–Wheat Berry Toss**
__ **Turkey, Roasted Pepper, and Avocado Roll-Up with Edamame**
__ Turkey-Veggie Lasagna*
__ Vegetarian Stuffed Portobello*
__ Whole Wheat Tuna Pasta Salad over Mixed Greens

PHASE 3

SNACKS AND SIDES (100 CALORIES)

Hunger level ____

__ **Banana-Pineapple Smoothie**
__ Crudités and Hummus
__ Fruit and Protein Combo
What combo? _____

__ PB&J Yogurt
__ Turkey and Cheese Wrap

SNACKS, SIDES, AND DESSERTS (150 CALORIES)

Hunger level ____

__ 16-ounce Fat-Free Latte
__ **Banana–Chocolate Chip Bread Pudding***
__ Banana Coconut Roll
__ Berry-Veggie Smoothie*
__ Caprese
__ Cashew-Ginger Coconut Muesli
__ Cheesy Popcorn with Almonds
__ Chocolate-Cherry Smoothie*
__ Creamy Dark Chocolate–Banana-Coconut Pudding*
__ **Crunchy-Creamy Purple Slaw***
__ Crunchy Roasted Rosemary Chickpeas*
__ Easy Cinnamon-Apple Cobbler*
__ **Fruity Trail Mix**

__ **No-Bake Oatmeal Cookies***
__ PB Celery and Milk
__ Peachy Ginger All-Fruit Soft Serve*
__ Pear Wedges with Blue Cheese and Walnuts
__ Pumpkin Pie Trail Mix Popcorn
__ Roasted Fennel with Pine Nuts*
__ Roasted Lemon-Ginger Pears with Pecan Yogurt*
__ **Sugar Smart Energy Bars***
__ Tuna-Potato Wrap*
__ **Tuna Salad Cucumber Stackers**
__ Turkey, Cheese, and Veggies
__ **Watermelon and Feta Salad***
__ Yogurt-Covered Blueberries*

DAILY FOOD LOG *(cont.)*

Additional Foods:

Notes:

LISA DICKINSON

BEFORE

FOR LISA, MOST OF THE 20 TEASPOONS of sugar a day that she was downing came from sweetened beverages such as lemonade, iced tea, and coffee creamer. With four kids in the house, it wasn't a surprise that cookies and fudge pops were often available, and Lisa was indulging in them, too. "I always felt that I *needed* something sweet to eat right after a meal," she says.

Lisa's cravings were pretty intense on Phase 1 of the Sugar Smart Diet, and she was constantly reminded of what she was missing. "When my kids had cereal or fruit-flavored yogurt, they would say, 'You can't eat that!'" she says. To maintain control, she used positive self-talk. "When a craving hit, I'd tell myself that I could do this, that it would pass—and it did, usually in 10 to 15 minutes," she says. Within 4 days, her desire for sweets dramatically declined.

As she started to see results, her kids' reminders became more encouraging and motivated her. "After my first weigh-in, my oldest asked about my results. They kept me in check. I wanted them to see that I could stick with it. Aside from the weight loss, one of the biggest rewards of this plan is that I have more energy for bike rides and hikes with my kids."

Many of the healthy changes Lisa made while she was following the plan have become permanent habits. "I have no desire to return to my old way of eating," she says. She no longer drinks sweetened beverages or buys flavored yogurt, and she starts her day with peanut butter oatmeal instead of sugary cereals. Her family is benefiting, too. "The kids still get treats, but I'm more watchful. I make more stuff myself, and if a recipe has sugar, I cut it in half and add other healthy ingredients, like zucchini in brownies."

Overall, Lisa learned to limit her sugary foods to the ones she really wanted when she wanted them. "I like to have ice cream, but now it's an occasional treat. I use one of my kid's tiny cereal bowls, and it's enough."

6.2
POUNDS LOST

AGE:
38
ALL-OVER
INCHES LOST:
7.75

SUGAR SMART WISDOM
"You are stronger than sugar. You decide when and if you'll have it and when you won't. Don't let IT control you."

Phase 4: Days 26-32

HELLO, SUGAR!

You've now arrived at the phase of the Sugar Smart Diet that you'll follow for life. And—hallelujah!—it includes chocolate and ice cream.

In this phase, we reintroduce sugar simply for the pleasure of having sugar. At the beginning of this book, I told you that I didn't want to demonize sugar and that it wasn't my goal to have you banish it from your life forever. A little added sugar in your diet every day (if you want it) is perfectly fine. We define "a little" as no more than 6 teaspoons a day (24 grams) of added sugar (or 9 teaspoons for men). This does not include the sugar that's naturally present in whole foods. It's the sugar that gets added to processed foods and beverages and the sugar you use in cooking, sprinkle on food, or stir into beverages that you need to limit. Two small chocolate chip cookies have less *total* sugar than a medium orange (7 grams versus

9 grams), but all of the sugar in the cookies is added sugar and counts toward your 24-gram maximum, while none of the sugar in the orange does.

Until now, you've been eating less than 6 teaspoons of added sugar a day, so you know that a Sugar Smart diet can be delicious and satisfying. And my guess is that you don't even miss the Secret Sugars, which is where a good amount of our total sugar intake comes from. But you might like to have a sweet treat here or there. The good news is that you can and still stay within the 6-teaspoon daily limit. I show you how in this phase.

During these 7 days, I want you to follow the same eating strategy you did in Phase 3, but with one change: Add a treat. I've given you a list of dessert options that contain 100 to 150 calories and no more than 12 grams of added sugar. That's 3 teaspoons. From both a calorie and a sugar-intake perspective, this is a reasonable amount. It gives you a little something sweet to look forward to and leaves room for a few teaspoons of sugar to add to your morning coffee or in the packaged foods you eat. But it doesn't harm your health.

It pains me to waste my precious sugar on items like ketchup, so I carefully choose my packaged foods and limit those with added sugar. I want to have my 6 daily teaspoons where they matter most to me. And usually I pick a treat with some added nutritional value, such as the antioxidants in dark chocolate, healthy fats in a fruit and nut bar, whole grains in a granola bar, or calcium in ice cream. (The quick and easy desserts on pages 201–202 and the dessert recipes in Chapter 11 fall into that category.) But that's me. You can spend your 6 teaspoons any way you want.

For instance, maybe you'll choose to add a teaspoon of sugar (4 grams) to your coffee and drizzle a teaspoon of maple syrup (4 grams) on your oatmeal in the morning; have a hamburger on a bun (3 grams) with a tablespoon of ketchup (4 grams) at lunch; and three Twizzlers as your sweet treat (10 grams), for a total of 25 grams or just a smidgen over 6 teaspoons of sugar. That's perfectly okay. Staying slim, healthy, energetic, and sugar smart for life means being aware of where the sugar lurks in your diet and making informed choices. Phase 4 shows you how, step by step.

In this final phase, we also offer guidance on how to stick to a Sugar Smart Diet when you dine out and on special occasions—and what to do if you notice your sugar intake creeping up. And as you prepare to rejoin a sugary world, we offer advice for living the sweet life, for the rest of your life. So let's begin the final leg of your journey to sugar freedom.

RECONSIDERING SUGAR

When you began the Sugar Smart Diet, you probably felt a little trepidation. Would you be able to reset your sugar themostat? Could you really dial down your intake of Straight-Up Sugars, Secret Sugars, and Sugar Mimics; rebalance your metabolism; lose weight; and live to tell the tale? The answer is a resounding yes!

At this point, I bet you're noticing a lot of changes: Energy, up. Mood, brighter. Weight, down. Sugar cravings, crushed. And if you could look inside, you'd see your blood sugar and cholesterol levels have improved. More and more, you're experiencing the benefits of nutritional balance–more whole foods and fresh flavors, and significantly less sugar and refined starches. The pounds should be melting away, too. By the end of Phase 4, our test panelists lost up to 16 pounds, with their sugar bellies receding by as much as $3^3/_4$ inches, and 16 inches lost from belly, hips, legs, arms, and chest combined!

Now that those zero-sugar days are long past, and you can bring sugar back into your diet, you probably feel one of three ways: not really missing it (perhaps to your surprise), excited to be able to have treats again, or wondering whether you'll be able to reintroduce treats without eventually sliding back into old eating patterns. Because sugary foods have not been a part of your diet now for 3 weeks, you are in a perfect position to assess the previous role they played in your life and decide what part they will play in the future.

To do so, recall the sugar sources you identified as key on the first day of the Sugar Step-Down. How often do you think about them? Then have a small portion of one of them as you follow this version of the Sweet Freedom "Eat with Awareness" strategy from Chapter 7.

1. Look at your treat. Note your level of anticipation. Recall what you liked about it and how it used to make you feel when you ate it

(positive or negative). Compare those feelings to the way you've been feeling since it's been out of your diet. How do you think having the treat will change that? Are you looking forward to your first bite? What do you expect to feel after you eat it?

2. Take a bite. Notice the flavor and the texture. Does it taste the way you remembered it? Are you getting a rush of pleasure?

3. Eat the rest of your treat slowly, continuing to focus on flavor and texture. Do you like what you're eating? Did you miss it? Would you still say that this is one of your favorite treats?

4. After you're finished, take a few minutes to consider whether you feel the way you thought you would when you started eating. Did the treat live up to your expectations? Do you want more right away, or are you happy with the amount you had? Would you have been just as satisfied with something else?

5. Over the next hour or so, monitor your reactions to it carefully. Are you hungry sooner than you might have been otherwise? Do you feel cravings for that treat or another sugary food? Are you feeling headachy or a little tired? Or do you feel good physically and pleased that you treated yourself to something you love?

Try this exercise with a few different sugar sources during this week and see how your reactions vary. There are no right or wrong answers—the purpose is to help you become more aware of the effect sugar has on you. Before you started the Sugar Smart Diet, treating yourself with Straight-Up Sugars or Sugar Mimics may have been habit. You may have turned to food to soothe negative emotions, or you may have been caught up in a cycle of sugar highs and lows that drove you to reach for more sugar. But now you've broken the habit, found other ways to cope with stress, and stabilized your metabolism. Given all that, where does sugar fit in?

- If your key sugar sources are just as satisfying as you remembered them being, then you should have them—but in a reasonable way. If you can limit yourself to a small portion with 100 to 150 calories, then you can have one of them every day in place of the dessert options we list here. (If you want to have bigger serving sizes, wait until after Phase 4 and read the advice on page 194.)

- If your conclusion is that your key sugar sources no longer bring you as much pleasure, but you'd still like to have some treats in your life, then

Q: My grocery store has an entire aisle devoted to energy bars, and many of them tout their low sugar content on the label. Some contain fruit and nuts, but no added sugar. Is it okay to have one as a snack?

A: Yes, as long as you stick to a few guidelines. Choose one with 200 calories or less and at least 3 grams of fiber. Have it in place of your sugary treat for the day, or have it for one of your snacks and skip the other one. If a bar has added sugar but no fruit, choose one with 12 grams or less. If it contains a combination of fruit and added sugar, or has fruit but no added sugar, you can go up to 16 grams of sugar. The fruit is usually a puree of dried fruit, which on the Sugar Smart Diet counts as added sugar. But dried fruit does contain nutrients, and often these bars provide fiber, healthy fat, and protein in the form of nuts, which slows the breakdown of the sugar in your body. Here are some picks.

Cliff Mojo Peanut Butter Pretzel (1 bar), 190 calories, 9 g sugar, 2 g fiber

Kind Dark Chocolate Nuts and Sea Salt (1 bar), 200 calories, 5 g sugar, 7 g fiber

Kind Madagascar Vanilla Almond (1 bar), 210 calories, 4 g sugar, 5 g fiber

Larabar über Sticky Bun Sweet and Salty Fruit and Nut bar (1 bar), 220 calories, 7 g sugar, 3 g fiber

Luna Blueberry Bliss (1 bar), 180 calories, 13 g sugar*, 3 g fiber

Nature's Path Macaroon Crunch (2 bars), 200 calories, 8 g sugar, 3 g fiber

Nature's Path Trail Mixer Chewy Granola Bar (1 bar), 140 calories, 9 g sugar, 3 g fiber

*Some of the sugar in this product comes from fruit.

experiment with some of the quick and easy dessert options in this chapter or the dessert recipes in Chapter 11. They have a healthy bent, and that may be all you need now.

- If you discover that sugar overall has lost most of its allure for you, don't have it. No one has to eat sugar. Many of our test panelists found their perfect balance during either Phase 2 or 3. Robin said, "If you had told me when I started this plan that I'd be able to walk down the cookie aisle to get my kiddo Fig Newtons and crave absolutely nothing or that instead of longing for a Mounds bar, I now crave Sun Gold cherry tomatoes, I never would have believed it. But it's true!" And at the start of this phase, Myra said, "I haven't even looked at the menus, I'm so satisfied on Phase 3!" If you find out that you'd be happy without more dietary sweetness in your life, you can eat that way until you change your mind, if you even do.

- If you find that your favorite sugar sources trigger cravings, hunger, or other symptoms, consider replacing those foods with other sweets and carefully monitor your feelings and reactions. If any dessert-like food seems to have the same effect, you should stay on Phase 3 of the Sugar Smart Diet for another 2 weeks and then try again.

SMART SUGAR SWAPS

Now that you've determined the sugary indulgences you can't live without, it's time to eliminate items that waste precious teaspoons of sugar and identify alternatives that you enjoy just as much. This list of swaps and tips can help.

We've presented our swaps by category, so you can zip down the list and find the items most important to you. You'll find sugar swaps for beverages after this section. Prepare to discover new, better-for-you indulgences!

Grain Products

Sugar has no place in the bread aisle, but you'd never know it by how many grain products contain added grams.

Swap this . . .

▶ Arnold 100% Whole Wheat
(1 slice): 110 calories, 4 g sugar

▶ Quaker Instant Oatmeal
Maple & Brown Sugar (1 packet):
160 calories, 12 g sugar

▶ Kellogg's Raisin Bran
Crunch cereal (1 cup): 190
calories, 19 g sugar

▶ Bisquick Complete pancake &
waffle mix Simply Buttermilk
with Whole Grain (½ cup):
210 calories, 6 g sugar

. . . for this

▶ Food for Life Ezekiel 4:9 Flax
Sprouted Whole Grain Bread
(1 slice): 80 calories, 0 g sugar

▶ Trader Joe's Gluten-Free
Rolled Oats (½ cup uncooked):
150 calories, 1 g sugar

▶ Post Shredded Wheat cereal
(1 cup): 170 calories, 0 g sugar

▶ Bob's Red Mill Organic
7-Grain Pancake & Waffle mix
(⅓ cup): 190 calories, 2 g sugar

Condiments, Sauces, and Dressings

When it comes to your sugar allowance, waste not. Balsamic vinegar, pure olive oil, herbs, spices, hot sauce, salsa, and natural sweeteners add plenty of flavor without added sugars.

Swap this . . .

▶ Newman's Own Creamy
Balsamic dressing (1 tablespoon):
50 calories, 4 g sugar

▶ Bertolli Tomato & Basil
pasta sauce (½ cup):
70 calories, 12 g sugar

▶ Smuckers Strawberry Jam
(1 tablespoon): 50 calories,
12 g sugar

▶ La Choy Orange Ginger Sauce &
Marinade (1 tablespoon):
25 calories, 4 g sugar

. . . for this

▶ Newman's Own Creamy Caesar
dressing (1 tablespoon):
85 calories, 0 g sugar

▶ Monte Bene Tomato Basil
pasta sauce (½ cup):
40 calories, <1 g sugar

▶ Polaner All Fruit with Fiber,
Strawberry (1 tablespoon):
35 calories, 6 g sugar

▶ La Choy Stir-Fry Teriyaki Sauce
& Marinade (1 tablespoon):
10 calories, 1 g sugar

Sweet Treats

Skeptical? Just give them a try. One taste of the low-sugar indulgences on this list (we've sampled them all) and you'll never miss the sugar-laden items.

Swap this . . .	. . . for this
▶ Twix (1 package): 250 calories, 24 g sugar	▶ Dagoba Organic Chocolate Xocolatl dark chocolate bar 74% cacao (1 ounce): 140 calories, 7 g sugar
▶ Entenmann's Deluxe French Cheesecake (1 serving): 390 calories, 25 g sugar	▶ Yasso Frozen Greek Yogurt bars (1 coconut bar): 80 calories, 12 g sugar

The Healthiest Indulgence: Dark Chocolate

Good for the heart, good for the soul, maybe even good for your sugar belly! Dark chocolate, with its distinctive bittersweet taste and "top notes" of coffee, nuts, or cinnamon is an example of a better-for-you treat. Swap it for milk chocolate, and you'll consume significantly less sugar. But that's not the only reason we swoon for it: Although its flavor isn't traditionally sweet, its health benefits are.

Dark chocolate is rich in antioxidants called flavonoids, which give it its unique "bite" and are responsible for many of its health benefits. For example, flavonoids appear to benefit cardiovascular health by lowering blood pressure, improving blood flow to the brain and heart, and making blood less sticky, which reduces the risk of heart attack and stroke.

Moreover, compared to milk chocolate, dark chocolate promotes that I'm-full feeling known as satiety, lowers the desire to eat sweets, and reduces calorie intake, which may help with weight loss, a study published in *Nutrition & Diabetes* found. When researchers gave 16 participants 3½ ounces of either dark or milk chocolate and 2 hours later offered them pizza, those who consumed the dark chocolate ate 15 percent fewer calories from the pizza than those who had milk chocolate.

If you're used to milk chocolate, go dark gradually so you train your taste buds to appreciate the stronger taste. Look for a variety that has a 70 percent or higher cacao, or cocoa, content and lists cacao as its first ingredient.

Swap this . . .

▶ Premium ice cream, vanilla
(½ cup): 266 calories, 22 g sugar

▶ Jell-O vanilla pudding (½ cup):
110 calories, 17 g sugar

▶ Gummy worms (10 worms):
293 calories, 43.6 g sugar

▶ Starbucks Raspberry Swirl
Pound Cake (1 slice):
430 calories, 46 g sugar

. . . for this

▶ Creamies Ice Cream Bar (1 bar):
120 calories, 13 g sugar

▶ Julie's Organic Juliette Ice
Cream Sandwiches (1 bar):
100 calories, 6 g sugar

▶ Angie's Classic Sweet & Salty
Kettle Corn (2 cups): 140 calories,
8 g sugar

▶ Starbucks Almond Cookie
(1 cookie): 230 calories, 14 g sugar

Peanut Butter, Yogurt, and Miscellaneous

You won't miss the sugar in these swaps—the natural sugars in peanuts, yogurt, and fruit products are sweet enough on their own!

Swap this . . .

▶ JIF Peanut Butter
(2 tablespoons):
190 calories, 3 g sugar

▶ Stonyfield Organic Fat-Free
French Vanilla Yogurt (8 ounces):
170 calories, 33 g sugar

▶ Healthy Choice Modern Classics
Sweet & Sour Chicken:
390 calories 19 g sugar

▶ Mott's Original Applesauce
(sweetened, 4 ounces):
90 calories, 22 g sugar

▶ Del Monte Peach Chunks in
Heavy Syrup (½ cup):
100 calories, 23 g sugar

. . . for this

▶ Smucker's Organic Peanut
Butter (2 tablespoons):
210 calories, 1 g sugar

▶ Siggi's Icelandic Style Skyr
Strained Nonfat Yogurt,
Pomegranate & Passion Fruit
(5.3 ounces): 100 calories,
9 g sugar

▶ Smart Ones Bistro Selections
Slow Roasted Turkey Breast:
200 calories, <1 g sugar

▶ Mott's Original Natural
Applesauce (unsweetened,
4 ounces): 50 calories, 11 g sugar

▶ Dole Frozen Sliced Peaches
(¾ cup): 50 calories, 10 g sugar

Liquid Treats

Sweetened beverages such as sodas, sweetened teas and waters, and specialty coffee drinks count toward your daily added-sugar allotment. We count 100% fruit juice as an added sugar because juice has no fiber to slow the digestion of the sugar. While none of our swaps include artificial sweeteners, we recommend all-natural thirst quenchers like water, seltzer, green tea, black tea, and coffee. (You can put milk or cream and a teaspoon of honey or sugar in your coffee or tea, if you want.) If you haven't yet mixed up a pitcher of one of our flavored waters (Chapters 7 and 9) or tried our DIY flavored coffee (page 191), give them a try.

Swap this . . .

▶ Sprite (12 ounces): 140 calories, 38 g sugar

▶ Starbucks Hot Chocolate, made with fat-free milk and no whipped cream (8 ounces): 130 calories, 23 g sugar

▶ Snapple Green Tea (16 ounces): 120 calories, 30 g sugar

▶ Welch's Grape Juice (8 ounces): 140 calories, 36 g sugar

▶ Arizona Rx Energy (23 ounces): 345 calories, 83 g sugar

. . . for this

▶ 8 ounces of seltzer mixed with 4 ounces of 100% fruit juice: 55 calories, 11 g sugar (if made with orange juice)

▶ Homemade Chocolate Milk (page 202), served warm (8 ounces): 105 calories, 19 g sugar

▶ Honest Tea Jasmine Green Energy Tea (16 ounces): 34 calories, 10 g sugar

▶ R.W. Knudsen Family Just Cranberry juice (8 ounces): 70 calories, 9 g sugar

▶ Sweet Leaf Unsweet Tea, Lemon and Lime (16 ounces): 0 calories, 0 g sugar

Days 26-32

Goals for Days 26 through 32

- **Have breakfast every morning.**

- **Mix and match the lunch and dinner options.** All of our quick and easy meals and recipes (see Chapter 11) are on the table now. You'll find some new breakfast and lunch/dinner dishes added in this phase.

- **Have one serving of a processed grain product per day, if you like.** Sometimes you want a piece of crusty French bread, prefer regular pasta to whole grain, or want white rice with your take-out Chinese. In Phase 4, your daily processed grain product can be either regular or whole grain. However, I still want you to limit them to once a day. So if you have a sandwich at lunch, whether on a baguette or between two slices of whole wheat bread, don't have pasta (even if it is whole grain) at dinner. As you've learned, these Sugar Mimics can negatively affect blood sugar levels. To further reduce the impact of processed grain products, always pair them with lean protein, a bit of healthy fat, or fiber.

- **Include one meal or snack that contains a natural sweetener per day, if you want to.** Like processed grain products, natural sweeteners are optional.

- **Have one serving of fruit up to three times a day.**

- **Don't forget to snack!**

- **Have dessert!** This week and every week thereafter, if you want to, you can have a daily serving of sugary food that contains 100 to 150 calories and up to 12 grams of added sugar. Because of the effect on blood sugar levels, we consider a 6-ounce glass of 100% fruit juice to be a sugary treat.

- **Set your daily intention.**

LIVING SUGAR SMART IN PHASE 4

You're sure to be feeling as light in spirit as in body. Stress eating is out; mindful eating, daily relaxation time, and sound sleep are in. But you may need more ways to navigate tricky situations, so here is our last round of strategies. Try these or continue to use the ones you learned in previous phases.

THE SUGAR SMART GUIDE TO DINING OUT

Dining out has become an American way of life. We eat away from home an average of four times a week, according to the restaurant industry. The good news: If you stick to the template below, it's usually possible to order a meal that's low in added sugars anywhere, from diners to five-star restaurants. This is just an example of the foods you can choose; you don't have to order everything on the "menu."

One important tip: Dine mindfully. Mindful eating works at restaurants, too! In a small study published in the *Journal of Nutrition Education and Behavior*, older women who ate away from home at least three times a week, but who practiced mindful eating while dining out, lost almost 4 pounds in 6 weeks, even though they were only trying to maintain their weight. They also ate fewer calories and grams of fat per day, and found it easier to manage their weight.

THE SUGAR SMART DIET DINING-OUT MENU

BROTH-BASED SOUP OR STEAMED SEAFOOD
(steamed clams or shrimp cocktail, minus the cocktail sauce)

SALAD DRESSED WITH BALSAMIC VINEGAR AND OLIVE OIL
(skip the cheese, bacon bits, croutons, and creamy salad dressings)

GRILLED POULTRY OR FISH
(sans butter or fatty sauces)

GRILLED, ROASTED, OR STEAMED VEGGIES

A SMALL PORTION OF STARCH
*(a quantity of brown rice or grains that would fit
in the palm of your hand)*

FRUIT FOR DESSERT

(1 ALCOHOLIC BEVERAGE OPTIONAL)

SWAP COFFEE DRINKS FOR THIS

Specialty coffee shop drinks—like sugar-packed Frappuccinos and syrup-laced options—help grow sugar bellies, even if you don't add a scone to your coffee order. If you're hooked on coffee drinks, try our no-sugar, low-cal indulgence. At just 100 calories a serving, with zero sugar, it tastes decadent. (We used mocha-flavored coffee, but it tastes just as good made with vanilla- or hazelnut-flavored coffee or a regular brew.)

**1 cup strong mocha-flavored coffee
(cold or hot)
1¼ cups fat-free milk
½ teaspoon orange extract
unsweetened cocoa powder**

In a pitcher, combine the coffee, milk, and orange extract and stir. Serve hot or iced. Dust with cocoa powder before serving. Makes two 1.5-cup servings.

RELAX AND REFRESH

There's nothing like a hot bath to melt away tension or enjoy a little "me" time. According to *Prevention* advisory board member Tieraona Low Dog, MD, hot baths initially raise your heart rate and temperature. To dispel the heat, you perspire, which allows your body to rid itself of toxins. Then your blood vessels dilate and increase circulation, removing lactic acid from muscles, lowering blood pressure, and easing pain.

Ready to do some soaking? Here's Dr. Low Dog's recipe for a detox bath. Run a tub of hot water. Add 2 tablespoons of sea salt and 10 drops of one of the essential oils below, which you can buy at a natural foods store. Choose whichever suits your needs.

To ease tension: clary sage. The wonderful floral aroma relaxes you and lifts your spirits.

When you're feeling frazzled: lavender. This lovely floral fragrance helps ground and center you. It's perfect for those days when you're feeling anxious.

To calm yet clear your mind: sandalwood. Its warm, woodsy scent has been used for centuries to prepare the mind for meditation.

Check the water temperature for comfort, then soak for 20 to 30 minutes. If you're pregnant or have heart problems, talk to your doctor before taking a detox bath.

SLEEP PINK

You've likely heard of white noise, which is produced when the sounds of different frequencies are combined. It is often touted as a way to ease yourself into sleep. A study published in the *Journal of Theoretical Biology*, however, found that a noise with a much prettier name–pink noise–ushered in sleep even better.

Pink noise is a type of sound in which every octave carries the same power, or a perfectly consistent frequency. Think of rain falling on pavement or wind rustling the leaves on a tree. (That does sound relaxing!) It's called pink noise because light with a similar power spectrum would appear pink.

In the study, conducted to discover how pink noise would affect sleepers, a research team from China exposed 50 volunteers to either no noise or the pink variety during nighttime sleep and daytime naps while the participants' brain activity was monitored. A whopping 75 percent of the participants reported that they slept more restfully when the pink noise was on. When it came to brain activity, the amount of "stable sleep"–the most restful kind–increased 23 percent among the nighttime sleepers exposed to pink noise and more than 45 percent among nappers.

What's going on here? Sound plays a big role in brain activity and brain wave synchronization even while you're sleeping, the study notes. The steady drone of pink noise slows and regulates your brain waves, which is a hallmark of super-restful sleep. It's simple to "sleep pink"–just set up a fan that produces a steady, uninterrupted sound or use the rain forest setting on a noise machine.

REHEARSE STICKY EATING SITUATIONS— AND SOLVE THEM BEFOREHAND

It's inevitable that, at some point, you'll find yourself in a situation that challenges all that you know, or have learned, about making healthy choices. The holiday dinner at your in-laws'. An eating-related event. A conversation at home or at work that you know will be stressful or emotionally charged. How will you handle it?

How to Handle Parties

If you've struggled with overeating or an overactive sweet tooth in the past, any social event or celebration—from a simple dinner for two to a cocktail party or company picnic—may raise anxieties about food, eating with others, or socializing itself. I know, I've been there. Parties used to present dual temptations: all-you-can-eat foods from the sugar-heaven list and opportunities for anonymous eating. (Who's going to notice if you're scarfing handfuls of cookies?)

But if you're honest with yourself and prepare in advance both mentally (you can do it!) and physically (no empty stomachs allowed!), social eating doesn't have to derail your progress, even if it's led you to overeat in the past. The following low-sugar guidelines and emotional coping strategies can help. They're easy to remember, because they spell out the word SLIM. Review them before your next social event and remember them while you're there. More than likely, they'll help you conquer the impulse to swan-dive into the chocolate fountain.

S Savor flavor, not sugar. If you're dining out, follow the advice given on page 190. At other events, stick to whole foods as much as possible, skipping sweetened beverages, slow cooker fare, and store-bought pasta and macaroni salads. If you know the menu will offer mostly unhealthy options, eat one of your favorite meals from any of the phases before you go, and skip to the next letter on this list.

L Lavish your attention on the company. The key to making it through a special occasion is to keep your focus on the celebration, rather than the food. When you attend an event where food will be served, make it a point to talk to at least one person—your favorite aunt at a family reunion or a coworker who shares your interest in hiking or gardening. The more attention you give to others, the less you'll give to the food.

I Imbibe sensibly—stick to one drink. The stress of a social event, or the flaring of family tensions during the holidays, may tempt you to drink one more glass of wine than is wise. Keep your head. Overdoing it on alcohol can lower your inhibitions. That leaves you vulnerable to scarfing sugary treats at a party or ordering dessert when you hadn't planned to.

M Mind your thoughts and feelings. During the event, notice any thoughts and feelings that being there brings up. Do you feel overwhelmed or shy? Overjoyed and ready to party? Intense emotion, negative or positive, can lead to overeating. To help keep you centered, practice one of the emotional coping strategies you've learned, both before and during the event.

If you don't know, it can be helpful to use a technique called "coping ahead," developed by Marsha Linehan, PhD, a professor of psychology and an adjunct professor of psychiatry and behavioral sciences at the University of Washington. Coping ahead involves seeking awareness of potential obstacles and creating specific plans to help you deal with them. Unlike with worry, you're not going around in circles. You're creating a path to resolution.

Here's a simple, yet effective, exercise to practice this skill. You can use it to rehearse any situation in which you worry you may overeat.

1. Think of a situation in which you anticipate experiencing intense negative emotions.
2. Jot down your concerns about what may happen.
3. On a fresh page, write down a plan for ways you might cope ahead to manage your feelings and eating. What choices can you make both before and during the situation that would make you feel more confident and in control?

LIVING THE SUGAR SMART LIFE FOR GOOD: 6 GUIDELINES FOR DAYS 33 AND BEYOND

You've got strategies to crush cravings. Coping techniques to cool your emotional connection with sugar. Tips to sleep better, relax more, move daily, and enjoy life. As you prepare to strike out on your own, team the strategies you've been using throughout the plan with these big-picture strategies. Together, they'll help you stick to—and love—your sweet, Sugar Smart life!

1. CONTINUE TO SET AN INTENTION EVERY DAY

By now, I hope that setting an intention has become a habit, one that's had a real impact on your life. Don't give up doing that just because we've come to the end of the Sugar Smart Diet. In addition to helping you make your health a priority, intentions can steer you toward other goals and accomplishments.

My quiet time in the morning has made all difference in helping me stay energized, focused, and even serene through some tough times–including moving three kids, two cats, two mice, three fish, and a frog to a new city and a new house while holding down a busy job! Whether I use that time to day-dream, meditate, or just ruminate, it's all mine–an oasis of calm, where I turn down the volume on the competing demands on my energy and attention and suss out *my* personal priorities. When I set my daily intention, it's a pleasure to get out of bed to start the day. Hopefully, you've found that out for yourself!

2. MAKE BREAKFAST A MUST

Metabolism revver. Brain booster. Cravings crusher. Breakfast is all of those things. So whether you've lost the weight you want or are still working on it, continue to eat breakfast each day, and make sure it contains 15 to 20 grams of lean protein. Feel free to enjoy your favorite breakfasts from any phase, and stock your refrigerator, freezer, and pantry with cravings-crushing breakfasts like all-natural peanut butter, egg whites, low-fat ricotta cheese, and bags of frozen edamame.

3. FORGET ABOUT SUGAR GRAMS, ONCE A WEEK

It's your birthday or someone else's, and there is cake. You're visiting the town with the best ice cream shop on the planet. You're at a restaurant where the desserts are to die for. Or you just want a nice glass of lemonade on a hot summer day. I don't want you to concern yourself with parceling out a portion of the sugary treat that has exactly 150 calories and 12 grams of added sugar. Just have it–as long as you splurge only one time a week and skip your daily 150-calorie indulgence that day. The first few times, carefully monitor how you feel physically and emotionally afterward. Sometimes, the day after I've had an anything-goes meal is when I experience intense sugar cravings. Plan ahead, indulge, enjoy–and then clear your system of that sugar load by following a Phase 1 or 2 diet that day and perhaps even the next.

Sussing Out Added Sugars

Now that you're free to enjoy up to 6 teaspoons of added sugars (24 grams) a day (or 9 teaspoons for men) in any way your sugary little heart desires, you'll need to keep track of how much you're eating.

Sometimes, "sugar math" is easy. Stir a teaspoon of the sweet stuff into your coffee or drizzle a teaspoon of honey on your morning oatmeal, and you've consumed 4 grams of sugar, or one-sixth of your daily allotment. But as I've mentioned before, determining the amount of *added* sugars in packaged or prepared foods can be tricky. Food manufacturers aren't required to separate naturally occurring and added sugars on their labels. What they list is the product's *total* sugars, which can come from the sugars naturally in the food, added sugars, or both.

Sneaky! But not sneaky enough. Here's a quick-and-dirty way to estimate any food's added sugars.

- On the product's Nutrition Facts label, look for Total Sugars.
- If the product contains 0 grams of sugar (or a minimal amount, say up to 3 grams), you're in the clear.
- If the product contains sugar, consider all of it to be added unless the food contains a significant amount of fruit, milk, or yogurt, or "sweeter" vegetables such as beets, carrots, corn, green peas, sweet potatoes, and winter squash.
- Look at the product's ingredients list. Do you spot any form of added sugar? No? Then the sugar is naturally present in the food. Two examples: plain yogurt or unsweetened applesauce.
- If you do spot sugar or its aliases, it's sugar math time. Don't get nervous. Once you're familiar with how much natural sugar unsweetened foods contain, it's a snap to guesstimate how much added sugar the sweetened versions are packing.

For example, ½ cup of frozen corn has 4 grams of sugar but just one ingredient: corn. The same amount of canned cream-style corn contains 7 grams of sugar. Check the ingredients list—sure enough, sugar is listed. So you can figure that the canned variety has about 3 grams of added sugar. Or take unsweetened versus sweetened applesauce—12 grams of sugar for the unsweetened versus 25 grams per ½ cup for the sweetened (thanks to the addition of high fructose corn syrup). Do you love cream-style corn enough to spend almost a whole teaspoon of sugar on it? Do you want applesauce to supply nearly half your daily allowance of added sugar? Is it "spoon-worthy?" Only you can answer that. But thanks to sugar math, you've got a choice.

4. STAY AHEAD OF "SUGAR CREEP"

When people on diet plans relax their eating, the result is "sugar creep." A chocolate kiss here, a coffee drink there–eventually, their small nibbles and sips snowball, and they find themselves with a half-eaten tube of cookie dough in their hand, wondering how it happened.

What happened was not so much a relaxing of their eating. It's that they stopped eating with awareness. Little by little, the healthy habits they worked so hard to integrate into their lives slipped away, and old habits took over. It doesn't have to happen to you. Here are three simple but powerful ways to outsmart sugar creep. Stick to them and you'll continue to enjoy all of the pleasures of sugar, with none of the drawbacks.

Stick with the label-reading habit. That positive habit reinforces awareness, and it can help snap you back to reality when you're considering a treat that you may not really want and didn't plan to enjoy. Say, for example, your partner brings home a boxed raspberry cheese Danish. The label says that one serving packs 15 grams of sugar. That's just short of 4 teaspoons–most of your daily allotment if you're a woman! Do you really, really, *really* want that slice? Or would a few squares of dark chocolate or a slice of whole grain toast with 100% raspberry spread hit the spot just as well?

Plan your treats. For the most part, you should decide what you'll have as a treat on any particular day and stick to that. If you don't know what you'll be in the mood for, at least determine ahead of time *when* you'll have sugar. Are you going out to dinner and want dessert? Do you plan on working hard through the afternoon and think a 4 p.m. treat will be a nice break? The idea is to limit your spontaneous sugar indulgences as much as possible. Planning not only helps you manage your intake of sugar, but increases your enjoyment of it when you do indulge.

Take a daily mindful bite. Every day, give your full attention to the first bite of the sugary treat you've chosen. Gaze at it lovingly. Sigh over it. Give thanks for it, and give thought to its color, scent, temperature, and complexity of flavors. It's a way to pay respect to sugar and keep your awareness of its presence in your diet sharp. Sugar creep won't be able to gain the upper hand.

SUGAR SMART MENTOR

Ashley Koff, RD

SPACE OUT YOUR SUGAR. The health risk (including weight gain, fat accumulation, chronic inflammation, overly acidic digestive system) increases when either or both quality and quantity of added sugar are compromised. Should you have a latte with sweetened soy milk at the same time as a yogurt with honey or even add fruit to the honey yogurt to make a smoothie, the body is overwhelmed with too much "quick energy." It has to triage, if you will, aiming to send what it can to the cells and set aside (i.e., fat storage) what it doesn't. Not only can the extra sugar lead to weight gain, especially belly fat, but it feeds bad bacteria in your body, negatively impacting the body's immune function and digestive system. I like to teach clients that it's similar to getting a week's worth of work dumped on you first thing Monday morning as opposed to it being spaced out throughout the week. When you (or your body) are overwhelmed, stress and suboptimal performance are typically the ultimate outcomes.

SATISFY CRAVINGS NATURALLY. When I do get a sugar craving, I will always give into it with a quality source of carbohydrate—like a serving of dark chocolate or organic fruit—so that I don't allow that urge to build into something unmanageable. The human (emotional) brain doesn't like being told that it can't or even that it shouldn't have something. In fact, that can drive an even bigger obsession toward having it.

STAY BALANCED. If I notice that my desire for sugar is stronger than usual, I'll first try to identify why. Am I tired, emotional, stressed, dehydrated, or all of the above? To combat any of these, I rely on a magnesium supplement as well as food sources of magnesium (which include the cacao in quality dark chocolate) and look to nonfood fixes (baths, massage, workout). I also make sure that I am getting enough water and potassium so I stay adequately hydrated.

MONITOR YOUR REACTION TO SUGAR. When I overdo sugar or consume something abnormally sweet (for me)—think birthday cake icing, gelato, candy—there is a tendency for it to stay with me by way of a sugar craving for about 2 more days. So I monitor my consumption more closely on those subsequent days, make sure to get adequate sleep and exercise, and relax to prevent the craving from mounting a stronger offense.

ASHLEY KOFF, RD, *maintains an international private practice and is a coauthor of* Mom Energy *and the author of* Recipes for IBS. *She shares her message that better-quality food and supplement choices are the keys to optimal health with millions, regularly appearing on* The Dr. Oz Show, The Doctors, *and other TV programs, in magazines (she's* Prevention's *dietitian), on radio, and online at ashleykoffrd.com.*

5. HAVE A PLAN FOR BACKSLIDING

Day
33+

What if, despite your best intentions, sugar does creep up on you? Simply go back to Phase 1 for a week or two to reset your sugar thermostat. You can then either progress through the plan in the same way you just did or come straight back to Phase 4.

6. SAVOR LIFE AS MUCH AS SUGAR

We've been talking about savoring sweet foods—and when they're occasional treats, as they will be from now on, you certainly will! But there are other things to savor. Take a moment to think about your schedule. Does it include an activity that puts a curl in your toes, that gets you really stoked? We're not talking downtime in front of the tube. We're talking pleasure. The more you indulge in it in healthy ways, the less you'll look for it in sugar. And the more pleasure and joy and laughter you add to your life, the less you feel the need to derive pleasure from food.

Years ago, a boyfriend's mother told me her secret to a fulfilling life: She did something she really loved for 20 minutes every day. What a simple and great idea! This "20-minute rule" clicked with me, and I immediately made a list of nonfood pleasures that I could choose from as a reward. What I'm saying is, hang on to your Rewards Card. Treat yourself to one of its pleasures each day, and as you discover new ones, revise your card. And remember—the sweetness of life is in the moment, and pleasure-filled moments make a life. Sometimes, when I'm pressed for time (deadlines!), my "reward" is as simple as spritzing on some scent or blasting a Lady Gaga tune.

But there's another, lesser-known dimension to pleasure: savoring. To savor something is to enjoy it thoroughly, wringing every drop of pleasure from it. And research suggests it's the key to true happiness.

In a study published in the *Journal of Positive Psychology*, researchers had 101 women and men keep diaries for 30 days. They recorded "pleasant events" and how much they savored or squelched them. Savorers got more pleasure by stopping to focus on a good thing, telling someone else about it, or even screaming in delight. Wet-blanket types killed the joy by carping that it could have been better, they didn't deserve it, or it was almost over. Ultimately, savorers got the biggest happiness boost from pleasurable moments.

The skill set for good savoring is one part wild abandon (hooting, hollering, jumping up and down) and one part mature wisdom (the "smell the roses while you can" side). Whether you're one or the other, practicing the fine art of savoring can help you keep sugar in its rightful place in your life.

To reap the benefits of this little-known component of pleasure, embark on what the study's lead researcher calls "a savoring adventure." It could be a walk in the woods, a trip into a city, or cooking a meal you love. Then do three things:

- Before the experience, anticipate how wonderful it will be.
- During the experience, focus on the sensations and feelings you're having. Use all five senses. Be nonjudgmental. Express your emotions to whomever you're with or by writing them down later.
- Afterward, look back on the event. Share it with someone.

Whatever your savor-worthy activity, start planning it now. Sugar is one of life's pleasures, and there are plenty more to revel in!

PHASE 4 QUICK & EASY MEALS

Breakfast

Peaches 'n' Cream Waffles

Top 1 toasted whole grain toaster waffle (like Van's Whole Grain) with ½ cup 0% plain Greek yogurt, ½ cup fresh or frozen and thawed sliced peaches, and 2 tablespoons sunflower seeds.

Nutrition per serving: 294 calories, 19 g protein, 28 g carbs, 4 g fiber, 14 g total sugar, 13 g fat, 2 g saturated fat, 234 mg sodium

Nutty Choco-Banana Oatmeal

In a medium microwaveable bowl, combine 1 cup fat-free milk (or unsweetened soy milk), ⅓ cup rolled oats, ½ small ripe banana, mashed, and 1 tablespoon unsweetened cocoa powder. Microwave on high for 2 minutes, then stir. Microwave for 30 seconds, or until the oats are soft. Stir in 1 teaspoon maple syrup and 1 tablespoon walnuts.

Nutrition per serving: 314 calories, 15 g protein, 50 g carbs, 6 g fiber, 23 g total sugar, 8 g fat, 2 g saturated fat, 134 mg sodium

Creamy Ricotta, Basil, and Tomato Penne

Heat ½ teaspoon olive oil a nonstick skillet over medium-high heat. Add ¾ cup halved grape tomatoes and ¼ cup chopped onion and cook, stirring frequently, for 5 minutes, or until the tomatoes begin to pucker. Add 2 tablespoons chopped fresh basil leaves and 1 teaspoon minced garlic and cook for 1 minute. Stir in 1¼ cups cooked whole wheat (or regular) penne and ½ cup part-skim ricotta cheese and heat on low for 3 minutes, or until the cheese melts slightly.

Nutrition per serving: 450 calories, 25 g protein, 63 g carbs, 7 g fiber, 7 g total sugar, 13 g fat, 7 g saturated fat, 572 mg sodium

BBQ Tempeh and Corn Tacos

Cook 2 tablespoons chopped onion, ½ cup crumbled tempeh or tofu, and ¼ cup frozen and thawed corn kernels in 1 teaspoon olive oil for 6 minutes, or until the tofu is browned. Stir in 3 tablespoons Sugar Smart BBQ Sauce (page 234). Divide the mixture between two 6" corn tortillas and top each with 1 tablespoon finely chopped onion, ½ cup chopped spinach, 2 teaspoons 0% plain Greek yogurt, and 2 teaspoons chopped avocado.

Nutrition per serving: 427 calories, 23 g protein, 51 g carbs, 8 g fiber, 9 g total sugar, 18 g fat, 3 g saturated fat, 86 mg sodium

Desserts (100–150 calories)

Blueberry–Double Chocolate Ice Cream

Top ⅓ cup Dreyer's/Edy's Slow Churned chocolate ice cream with 2 teaspoons semisweet chocolate chips and ¼ cup blueberries.

Nutrition per serving: 116 calories, 2 g protein, 21 g carbs, 2 g fiber, 18 g total sugar, 4 g fat, 2 g saturated fat, 28 mg sodium

Chocolate-Cherry Walnut Turtle

Heat ⅓ ounce chopped dark chocolate (70% or more cacao) in the microwave on low until melted. Stir in 2 teaspoons walnuts and 1 tablespoon dried cherries. Spoon onto waxed paper and chill in the refrigerator for 10 minutes, or until hard.

Nutrition per serving: 102 calories, 2 g protein, 11 g carbs, 1 g fiber, 8 g total sugar, 7 g fat, 2 g saturated fat, 2 mg sodium

Balsamic Strawberries with Pistachios and Chocolate

Toss ½ cup sliced strawberries with 1 teaspoon balsamic vinegar. Let sit for at least 10 minutes, then add 2 teaspoons pistachios and 2 teaspoons semisweet chocolate chips. (Note: The balsamic vinegar may be omitted.)

Nutrition per serving: 113 calories, 2 g protein, 19 g carbs, 4 g fiber, 12 g total sugar, 5 g fat, 2 g saturated fat, 24 mg sodium

Microwave S'more

Top 1 graham cracker square with 1 thin square (about ⅓ ounce) of dark chocolate (70% or more cacao) and 1 marshmallow. Heat in the microwave for 25 seconds, or until the chocolate is slightly melted and the marshmallow is puffy.

Nutrition per serving: 93 calories, <1 g protein, 16 g carbs, <1 g fiber, 10 g total sugar, 4 g fat, 2 g saturated fat, 49 mg sodium

Maple-Almond Ricotta Whip

Whisk together ¼ cup part-skim ricotta cheese, 1 teaspoon maple syrup, ground cinnamon to taste, ¼ teaspoon vanilla extract, and 1 teaspoon sliced almonds.

Nutrition per serving: 114 calories, 7 g protein, 8 g carbs, <1 g fiber, 5 g total sugar, 6 g fat, 3 g saturated fat, 78 mg sodium

Banana Split

Top ¼ cup Dreyer's/Edy's Slow Churned vanilla or chocolate ice cream with ¼ banana, sliced, and 1 teaspoon chocolate syrup.

Nutrition per serving: 108 calories, 2 g protein, 21 g carbs, <1 g fiber, 15 g total sugar, 2 g fat, 1 g saturated fat, 33 mg sodium

Homemade Chocolate Milk

Whisk together 2 teaspoons unsweetened cocoa powder, 2 teaspoons maple syrup, and ¾ cup fat-free milk (or unsweetened soy milk) until smooth. Add 3 to 4 ice cubes to chill.

Nutrition per serving: 105 calories, 7 g protein, 20 g carbs, 1 g fiber, 19 g total sugar, <1 g fat, <1 g saturated fat, 80 mg sodium

Hershey's Kisses (6)

Nutrition per serving: 100 calories, 12 g sugar

Honey Maid Graham Crackers (2 sheets)

Nutrition per serving: 130 calories, 8 g sugar

Lindt Excellence 70% Cocoa (2 squares)

Nutrition per serving: 125 calories, 6 g sugar

Lindt Excellence 85% Cocoa (2 squares)

Nutrition per serving: 115 calories, 3 g sugar

Barnum's Animals Crackers (8 pieces)

Nutrition per serving: 120 calories, 7 g sugar

Carr's Ginger Lemon Cremes (1)

Nutrition per serving: 70 calories, 6 g sugar

Pepperidge Farm Milano Cookies (1)

Nutrition per serving: 60 calories, 4 g sugar

Pepperidge Farm Nantucket Cookies (1)

Nutrition per serving: 130 calories, 8 g sugar

Oreos (2)

Nutrition per serving: 106 calories, 9 g sugar

DAILY FOOD LOG

PHASE 4

Date:

Today's intention:

Place an X next to any meals and snacks you ate today.
You can mix and match your meals and snacks from Phases 1, 2, 3, and 4. Boldface indicates an option added in this phase; an asterisk denotes a recipe that can be found in Chapter 11.

BREAKFAST

Hunger level _____

__ Apple-Cinnamon Oats with Walnuts
__ Apricot-Almond Breakfast Wrap
__ Banana Cream Pie Overnight Oats*
__ Blueberry and Honey Yogurt Parfait
__ Breakfast Quesadilla*
__ Canadian Bacon Apple-Cheddar Melt
__ Cashew-Coconut Muesli Yogurt
__ Cinnamon-Apple Breakfast Polenta*
__ Classic Smoked Salmon Bagel
__ Crunchy Almond Yogurt
__ Crustless Mini Broccoli and Cheese Quiche*
__ Loaded Breakfast Potato
__ Mediterranean Scramble
__ Microwave Peanut Butter Oats
__ Mushroom-Quinoa Frittata*
__ **Nutty Choco-Banana Oatmeal**
__ On-the-Go Breakfast

__ Orange–Vanilla Cream French Toast*
__ PB&J Toast and Café au Lait
__ **Peaches 'n' Cream Waffles**
__ Picnic Breakfast
__ **Power Granola***
__ Sausage-Potato Hash and Eggs*
__ Spicy Avocado Breakfast Bowl
__ Starbucks Spinach & Feta Breakfast Wrap
__ Strawberry-Coconut Chia Breakfast Pudding*
__ Strawberry-Kiwi Crunch Yogurt
__ Turkey Sausage, Spinach, and Cheddar Wrap
__ Whole Wheat Blueberry Protein Pancakes*

PHASE 4

LUNCH AND DINNER

Hunger level ____

__ Artisan Bistro Grass-Fed Beef with Mushroom Sauce (Frozen Entrée)

__ Asian Quinoa Salad*

__ Barley Risotto with Chicken and Asparagus*

__ **BBQ Tempeh and Corn Tacos**

__ Beer BBQ Chicken Thighs with Corn and Tomato Salad*

__ Bento Box

__ Blue Cheese, Walnut, Chicken, and Quinoa Salad

__ Broiled Mustard Salmon with Roasted Broccoli and Quinoa

__ Build-Your-Own Meal

__ Chicken Sausage and Veggie Pita Pizza

__ Chipotle Burrito Bowl

__ Cool Cucumber, Tomato, Black Bean, and Barley Salad

__ Crab Cakes with Garlic Kale*

__ **Creamy Ricotta, Basil, and Tomato Penne**

__ Crunchy Sesame Chicken and Bulgur Bowl

__ Crunchy Turkey-Pear Salad Sandwich

__ Fast, Hearty Turkey Chili*

__ Fennel Slaw with Salmon and White Beans

__ Fiesta Egg Salad

__ Fish Tacos with Mango-Lime Salsa in Crispy Corn Tortillas*

__ Garlic-y Shrimp 'n' Grits

__ Grilled Shrimp Salad with Potato, Sunflower Seeds, and Goat Cheese

__ Halibut with Fennel and Citrus Vinaigrette and Roasted Potatoes

__ Hearty Lentil Sauté with Bulgur

__ Loaded Shrimp Fajita Bowl with Brown Rice

__ Orange-Garlic Salmon with Kale and Barley*

__ Outback Steakhouse Victoria's 6-oz Filet

__ Panera Bread Chopped Chicken Cobb with Avocado

__ Panko-Crusted Chicken Tenders with Honey-Mustard Dipping Sauce*

__ Penne with Meatballs*

__ Poached Eggs with Fruity Wheat Berry Salad*

__ Pork Tenderloin with Roasted Pear-Cabbage Medley and Barley*

__ Potato, Pepper, and Chicken Sausage Sauté

__ Roast Beef, Swiss, and Arugula Sandwich

__ Roasted Veggie, Bulgur, and Chickpea Salad with Feta Dressing*

__ Rosemary Pork Tenderloin with Roasted Butternut Squash and Cauliflower

__ Spinach and Grapefruit Salad with Wheat Berries and Grilled Chicken

__ Starbucks Hearty Veggie & Brown Rice Salad Bowl

__ Steak and Roasted Baby Potatoes and Carrots

__ Sugar Smart Asian Peanut Dressing*

__ Sugar Smart BBQ Sauce*

__ Sugar Smart Marinara Sauce*

__ Sugar Smart Teriyaki Sauce*

__ Tangy Mediterranean Tuna Salad

__ Teriyaki Beef with Broccoli*

__ Turkey Burger with Broccoli–Wheat Berry Toss

PHASE 4

LUNCH AND DINNER *(cont.)*

__ Turkey, Roasted Pepper, and Avocado Roll-Up with Edamame
__ Turkey-Veggie Lasagna*

__ Vegetarian Stuffed Portobello*
__ Whole Wheat Tuna Pasta Salad over Mixed Greens

SNACKS (100 CALORIES)

Hunger level _____

__ Banana-Pineapple Smoothie
__ Crudités and Hummus
__ Fruit and Protein Combo
What combo? _____

__ PB&J Yogurt
__ Turkey and Cheese Wrap

SNACKS, SIDES, AND DESSERTS (150 CALORIES)

Hunger level _____

__ 16-Ounce Fat-Free Latte
__ **Balsamic Strawberries with Pistachios and Chocolate**
__ Banana–Chocolate Chip Bread Pudding*
__ Banana-Coconut Roll
__ **Banana Split**
__ **Barnum's Animals Crackers, 8 pieces**
__ Berry-Veggie Smoothie*
__ **Blueberry–Double Chocolate Ice Cream**
__ Caprese
__ **Carr's Ginger Lemon Cremes, 1 cookie**
__ Cashew-Ginger Coconut Muesli
__ Cheesy Popcorn with Almonds
__ Chocolate-Cherry Smoothie*
__ **Chocolate-Cherry Walnut Turtle**
__ **Chocolate Clouds with Berries***
__ **Cranberry-Walnut Wild Rice Pilaf***
__ Creamy Dark Chocolate–Banana-Coconut Pudding*

__ Crunchy-Creamy Purple Slaw*
__ Crunchy Roasted Rosemary Chickpeas*
__ Easy Cinnamon-Apple Cobbler*
__ Fruity Trail Mix
__ **Hershey's Kisses, 6**
__ **Homemade Chocolate Milk**
__ **Honey Maid Graham Crackers, 2 sheets**
__ Lindt Excellence 70% Cocoa, 2 squares
__ Lindt Excellence 85% Cocoa, 2 squares
__ **Microwave S'more**
__ **Maple-Almond Ricotta Whip**
__ **Mini Banana Cream Pie***
__ **Mini Berry Turnovers***
__ No-Bake Oatmeal Cookies*
__ **Oreos, 2**
__ PB Celery and Milk
__ Peachy Ginger All-Fruit Soft Serve*

(continued)

DAILY FOOD LOG *(cont.)*

SNACKS, SIDES, AND DESSERTS (150 CALORIES) *(cont.)*

__ Pear Wedges with Blue Cheese and Walnuts
__ **Pepperidge Farm Milano Cookies, 1**
__ **Pepperidge Farm Nantucket Cookies, 1**
__ **Pinto Bean Brownies***
__ Pumpkin Pie Trail Mix Popcorn
__ Roasted Fennel with Pine Nuts*
__ Roasted Lemon-Ginger Pears with Pecan Yogurt*

__ **Strawberry Cheesecake Bites***
__ Sugar Smart Energy Bars*
__ Tuna-Potato Wrap*
__ Tuna Salad Cucumber Stackers
__ Turkey, Cheese, and Veggies
__ Watermelon and Feta Salad*
__ Yogurt-Covered Blueberries*

Additional Foods:

Notes:

BEFORE

SCOTT LIEVENDAG
JESSICA LIEVENDAG

Scott and Jessica, who have been married for 21 years, were used to being a team. The Sugar Smart Diet gave them a chance to join forces in a new way, and they discovered that, like most things, getting healthy is easier when you do it together.

In the past, Jessica had lost weight on high-protein diets and point-counting plans, but it was always difficult. "I was in a better frame of mind this time because we were both doing it," she says. This was particularly helpful when they both had to pass on cake and champagne at several celebrations during the first phases of the plan. "I was more positive instead of being resentful that I was the only one on a diet."

For Scott, who usually turned to exercise programs like P90X and some portion control to lose weight, this was the first "diet" that he'd ever tried, and he found the support essential. "When you do stuff together, you encourage each other and you're more accountable," he says.

The team approach worked well for cooking, too. The Lievendags traded their familiar dishes for new recipes and new foods like quinoa and bulgur. To speed up meal prep, "we tag-teamed it," says Jessica. Scott did the planning and got dinner started since he often worked from home. Then, he'd text Jessica shopping lists of last-minute items he needed or food for the next day's meals, and she'd stop at the grocery store on her way home. Now they prepare foods like quinoa ahead of time to have on hand for quick meals. One of their favorites is to stir-fry vegetables and then add quinoa. "It's like fried rice," Scott says.

The Sugar Smart Diet helped the whole Lievendag family. "My daughter loves hummus and the other day I noticed that she was eating it with carrots instead pita chips," says Jessica. Scott has seen a change in their son's mood. "He's more compliant when we ask him to do something instead of talking back and having a bad

11.2
POUNDS LOST

Scott
AGE:
48

ALL-OVER
INCHES LOST:
10

SUGAR SMART WISDOM:
"Get some exercise each day—even if it's working in the yard. And don't be too hard on yourself in the beginning if it's challenging. The exercises get easier the more you do them."

attitude." He attributes the improvement to there being fewer sugary snacks in the house.

Scott and Jessica used to skip breakfast and feel famished in the afternoon, but now a hearty, filling breakfast—like the Loaded Breakfast Potato (page 127), one of Scott's favorites—is on the menu every morning. The Bento Box (page 146) is Jessica's go-to for lunch. "It makes eating easier since I have only 10 to 15 minutes between clients to eat," says Jessica, who is a counselor. "I nibble on it throughout the day."

Eating more regularly and choosing healthier options has also curbed their post-dinner snacking, which was usually ice cream. Scott is also making better choices when he travels for work. "I'm much more aware of the types of foods I want to eat," Scott says. "I'm having more salads and fish with vegetables. Before I'd have pizza and sandwiches."

Along with shedding pounds and inches, Scott lowered his blood pressure a total of 30 points to a very healthy 108/52. And his already healthy fasting glucose level dropped 17 points. "I have more endurance now," he says. "I shoveled 3 yards of dirt for an hour and a half the other day while I was working in the garden. It was easy, and I didn't feel sore."

Jessica, who had previously lost about 6 pounds by increasing her exercise, finally got off her 2-month long plateau. "My clothes are fitting better and that gives me the incentive to keep eating better," she says. She didn't even mind that the kids ate the piece of wedding cake that she had been saving in the freezer. "I wouldn't have eaten it. I didn't want to ruin what I'd accomplished."

4.8
POUNDS LOST

Jessica

AGE:
48

ALL-OVER
INCHES LOST:
9.5

SUGAR SMART WISDOM:
"Link your workouts to something you enjoy. I was addicted to Downton Abbey *on* NetFlix, *but I would only allow myself to watch it if I was walking on the treadmill. One day, I walked and watched for more than an hour."*

THE SUGAR SMART DIET RECIPES

"These recipes are *amazing*!" That's the feedback we got from Robyn, one of our Sugar Smart Diet test panelists. Another tester, Colleen, confided, "My husband is always a bit worried when I go off on one of my 'tangents,' as he calls them, but he looked through the recipes with me and said they looked really good!"

Hearing that kind of response from Robyn, Colleen, and many other test panelists made me very happy because I wanted these recipes to be delicious and convenient. I know that I never want to cook one way for myself and another for my husband and kids, and I know that I'm not willing to sacrifice flavorful food, even in the name of health, so I would never expect you to either!

These dishes are as well suited to company as they are to family meals—and many of them take 30 minutes or less to make!

You'll find 50 terrific meals, snacks, and yes, desserts, in this chapter. They're organized by phase, and, as with the quick and easy meals in Chapters 6–10, you can always choose dishes from the phase you are currently following as well as the previous phases. Because I wanted to give you lots of options, the majority of these recipes fit into Phases 1 and 2. Enjoy these flavorful dishes!

BREAKFAST

Mushroom-Quinoa Frittata

Makes 4 servings
PREP TIME: 10 minutes ● **TOTAL TIME:** 30 minutes

4 eggs
4 egg whites
2 tablespoons water
2 teaspoons olive oil
½ cup chopped onion
1 cup quartered
  mushrooms
1 cup chopped zucchini
1 tablespoon dried
  oregano
½ teaspoon salt
½ teaspoon freshly
  ground black pepper
3 cups cooked quinoa
4 tablespoons grated
  Parmesan cheese

1. Whisk together the eggs, egg whites, and water.

2. Heat the oil in an ovenproof skillet over medium-high heat. Add the onion, mushrooms, and zucchini and cook, stirring frequently, for 6 minutes, or until soft and golden. Add the oregano, salt, pepper, and quinoa and cook for 1 minute.

3. Add the eggs and cheese to the skillet and gently stir to just incorporate the egg. Cook over medium-high heat for 8 minutes, or until the eggs are firm.

4. Transfer the skillet to the broiler and broil on high for 3 minutes, or until the top is golden brown.

Nutrition per serving: 311 calories, 19 g protein, 34 g carbs, 5 g fiber, 4 g total sugar, 11 g fat, 3 g saturated fat, 514 mg sodium

Sausage-Potato Hash and Eggs

Makes 4 servings
PREP TIME: 5 minutes ● **TOTAL TIME:** 35 minutes

4 teaspoons olive oil
2 russet potatoes, cubed
½ yellow onion, finely
   chopped
1 bell pepper, finely
   chopped
4 cooked turkey sausage
   links, crumbled
4 eggs

1. Heat the oil in a large skillet over medium-high heat. Add the potatoes and cook, stirring every few minutes, for 15 to 20 minutes, or until soft. Add the onion and pepper and cook for 5 minutes. Add the sausage and cook for 4 minutes, or until warmed through.

2. Coat another large skillet with cooking spray and heat over medium-high heat. Add the eggs and cook to desired doneness, about 5 minutes for over easy. On each of 4 plates, place 1 egg and 1½ cups of the hash.

Nutrition per serving: 317 calories, 14 g protein, 40 g carbs, 4 g fiber, 4 g total sugar, 12 g fat, 2.8 g saturated fat, 205 mg sodium

Crustless Mini Broccoli and Cheese Quiche

Makes 12 mini quiches
PREP TIME: 10 minutes ● **TOTAL TIME:** 40 minutes + cooling time

1 tablespoon olive oil
2 cups chopped broccoli
   florets
½ cup chopped red bell
   pepper
1 can (12 ounces) low-fat
   2% evaporated milk
4 eggs
2 egg whites
⅔ cup cooked quinoa
2 cups shredded
   reduced-fat Cheddar
   cheese
¼ teaspoon salt
¼ teaspoon freshly
   ground black pepper

1. Preheat the oven to 350°F. Heat the oil in a medium skillet over medium-high heat. Add the broccoli and pepper and cook, stirring frequently, for 6 minutes, or until the broccoli is slightly tender. Remove from the skillet and set aside.

2. In a large bowl, whisk together the milk, eggs, and egg whites. Gently stir in the quinoa. Stir in the broccoli mixture, cheese, salt, and pepper.

3. Coat a 12-cup muffin tin with cooking spray and pour about ¼ to ⅓ cup of the mixture into each muffin cup. Bake for 25 minutes, or until the eggs are firm and a fork inserted in the center comes out clean. Let cool for 15 minutes, then remove from the tin. Refrigerate for up to 3 days or freeze for up to 2 months.

Nutrition per serving (2 mini quiches): 271 calories, 22 g protein, 15 g carbs, 2 g fiber, 8 g total sugar, 14 g fat, 6 g saturated fat, 511 mg sodium

Note: You can serve 1 mini quiche as a snack.

Breakfast Quesadilla

Makes 4 servings
PREP TIME: 5 minutes ● **TOTAL TIME:** 15 minutes

4 eggs
4 egg whites
2 tablespoons water
4 teaspoons olive oil
4 whole wheat tortillas
  (8" diameter)
½ cup shredded reduced-
  fat Cheddar cheese
4 tablespoons
  no-sugar-added salsa

1. Preheat the broiler.

2. In a medium bowl, whisk the eggs, egg whites, and water. Heat the oil in a medium skillet over medium-high heat. Add the eggs and cook, stirring gently every 30 to 40 seconds, for 5 minutes, or until set but not dry. Remove from the heat.

3. Coat a baking sheet with cooking spray.

4. Place one-quarter of the egg mixture on each tortilla and top each with 2 tablespoons cheese and 1 tablespoon salsa. Fold the tortillas in half and place on the baking sheet. Broil for 2 minutes on each side, or until golden and crispy.

Nutrition per serving: 291 calories, 18 g protein, 31 g carbs, 4 g fiber, 1.5 g total sugar, 12 g fat, 4 g saturated fat, 591 mg sodium

Banana Cream Pie Overnight Oats

Makes 1 serving
PREP TIME: 5 minutes ● **TOTAL TIME:** 5 minutes + chilling time

½ medium, very ripe
  banana
2 teaspoons almond
  butter
½ teaspoon vanilla
  extract
½ cup fat-free milk or
  unsweetened soy milk
½ cup fat-free plain
  yogurt
⅓ cup rolled oats

1. In a medium bowl, mash the banana with the almond butter and vanilla until smooth.

2. In a separate bowl, stir the milk and yogurt into the oats and soak for 5 minutes. Pour into the banana mixture and stir until incorporated.

3. Cover and let sit overnight in the refrigerator. In the morning, stir and enjoy. Or, if you prefer warm oats, microwave on high for 2 minutes, stirring every 30 seconds.

Nutrition per serving: 336 calories, 17 g protein, 50 g carbs, 5 g fiber, 24 g total sugar, 8 g fat, 1 g saturated fat, 172 mg sodium

Note: This recipe can be doubled, tripled, or even quadrupled.

Cinnamon-Apple Breakfast Polenta

Makes 4 servings

PREP TIME: 5 minutes ● **TOTAL TIME:** 25 minutes

4½ cups fat-free milk
1 cup coarsely ground cornmeal
2 teaspoons vanilla extract
2 teaspoons ground cinnamon, divided
½ cup plus 2 tablespoons toasted sliced almonds
1 teaspoon canola oil
1 large apple, thinly sliced
2 teaspoons maple syrup

1. Bring the milk to a boil in a large saucepan and whisk in the cornmeal. Lower the heat and simmer, stirring, for 5 to 10 minutes or until thickened. Stir in the vanilla, 1 teaspoon of the cinnamon, and ¼ cup of the almonds.

2. Heat the oil in a small skillet over medium-high heat. Add the apple and cook, stirring frequently, for 5 minutes, or until golden and soft. Stir in the remaining ¼ cup plus 2 tablespoons almonds, maple syrup, and the remaining 1 teaspoon cinnamon.

3. Divide the cornmeal among 4 bowls and swirl one-quarter of the apple mixture into each.

Nutrition per serving (1⅓ cups): 336 calories, 15 g protein, 50 g carbs, 5 g fiber, 22 g total sugar, 10 g fat, 1 g saturated fat, 127 mg sodium

Strawberry-Coconut Chia Breakfast Pudding

Makes 4 servings

PREP TIME: 5 minutes ● **TOTAL TIME:** 5 minutes + chilling time

4 cups fat-free milk or unsweetened soy milk
¾ cup chia seeds
⅓ cup unsweetened dried coconut flakes
4 teaspoons maple syrup
3 cups chopped strawberries, divided
4 teaspoons sliced almonds, divided

1. In a large bowl, stir together the milk, chia seeds, coconut, maple syrup, and 2 cups of the strawberries. Cover with plastic wrap and refrigerate for at least 4 hours or overnight, until the mixture is the texture of thin oatmeal.

2. Scoop the strawberry mixture into 4 serving bowls. Top each with 1 teaspoon chopped almonds and ¼ cup strawberries.

Nutrition per serving (1¼ cups): 329 calories, 15 g protein, 40 g carbs, 14 g fiber, 23 g total sugar, 14 g fat, 4 g saturated fat, 111 mg sodium

Whole Wheat Blueberry Protein Pancakes

Makes 4 servings

PREP TIME: 10 minutes ● **TOTAL TIME:** 20 minutes

1 cup fat-free milk
1 tablespoon white vinegar
1 cup whole wheat flour
½ teaspoon baking powder
¼ teaspoon baking soda
¼ teaspoon salt
1 tablespoon maple syrup, divided
1 cup fresh or frozen and thawed blueberries
1 egg
1 tablespoon butter, melted
10 tablespoons 0% plain Greek yogurt, divided

1. In a small bowl, combine the milk and vinegar.

2. In a large bowl, whisk the flour, baking powder, baking soda, salt, and 1 teaspoon of the maple syrup. Gently stir in the blueberries to coat them with the flour mixture.

3. In a medium bowl, whisk together the egg, milk mixture, butter, and 2 tablespoons of the yogurt for 1 minute, or until smooth. Add to the blueberry mixture and stir gently to combine, until there are no dry flour patches but the batter is still slightly clumpy. Do not overmix.

4. Coat a nonstick griddle with cooking spray and heat to 375°F or heat over medium-high heat. (Or heat a large skillet coated with cooking spray over medium-high heat.) Working in batches, depending on the size of the skillet, scoop the batter onto the griddle to form 4" circles. Cook on one side for 2 to 3 minutes, or until bubbles begin to form on the surface. Flip and cook for 2 minutes, or until the pancakes are firm.

5. Divide the pancakes among 4 plates. Top each serving with 2 tablespoons yogurt and ½ teaspoon maple syrup.

Nutrition per serving (2 pancakes with toppings): 324 calories, 16 g protein, 57 g carbs, 7 g fiber, 11 g total sugar, 6 g fat, 3 g saturated fat, 283 mg sodium

Orange-Vanilla Cream French Toast

Makes 4 servings

PREP TIME: 5 minutes ● **TOTAL TIME:** 20 minutes + chilling time

6 egg whites
2 teaspoons grated
    orange peel
1 cup fat-free milk
3½ teaspoons vanilla
    extract, divided
1¼ cups orange juice,
    divided
4 slices whole grain
    bread
4 teaspoons maple syrup
2 tablespoons canola oil
1 cup 0% plain
    Greek yogurt

1. In a large bowl, whisk together the egg whites, orange peel, milk, 2 teaspoons of the vanilla extract, and ¼ cup of the orange juice until thoroughly mixed.

2. Slice each piece of bread in half diagonally. Soak the bread in the egg mixture and cover the bowl in plastic wrap. Refrigerate for 1 hour (or overnight), turning halfway through to ensure the egg soaks into both sides of the bread.

3. In a small saucepan, combine the maple syrup and the remaining 1 cup orange juice and 1½ teaspoons vanilla. Simmer, stirring every 30 seconds, for 10 minutes, or until the mixture has reduced by one-third.

4. Heat the oil in a large skillet over medium-high heat. Add the soaked slices of bread and cook for 2½ minutes on each side. On each of 4 plates, place 2 halves, top each half with 2 tablespoons yogurt, and drizzle with 2 tablespoons of the orange juice mixture.

Nutrition per serving (2 halves with toppings): 296 calories, 14 g protein, 38 g carbs, 4 g fiber, 19 g total sugar, 9 g fat, 1 g saturated fat, 235 mg sodium

PHASE 4

Power Granola

Makes 14 servings

PREP TIME: 10 minutes ● **TOTAL TIME:** 55 minutes

2 cups rolled oats
¾ cup sliced almonds
½ cup chopped pecans
½ cup pumpkin seeds
½ cup shredded
 unsweetened coconut
½ cup dried cranberries
1 teaspoon ground
 cinnamon
¼ teaspoon ground
 nutmeg
1 teaspoon sea salt
4 tablespoons maple
 syrup
2 tablespoons natural
 peanut butter
1 tablespoon coconut oil
1 tablespoon canola oil
½ teaspoon vanilla
 extract

1. Preheat the oven to 300°F. Line a baking sheet with parchment paper or a nonstick mat.

2. In a large mixing bowl, stir together the oats, almonds, pecans, pumpkin seeds, coconut, dried cranberries, cinnamon, nutmeg, and salt until fully combined.

3. In a medium saucepan over medium heat, stir together the maple syrup, peanut butter, coconut oil, canola oil, and vanilla. Bring to a boil, then reduce the heat to a simmer and cook, stirring frequently, for 3 minutes, or until it has a smooth, uniform consistency.

4. Pour the syrup mixture over the oats mixture and stir well, until all of the ingredients are thoroughly combined and there are no dry oats.

5. Spread the granola mixture onto the baking sheet. Bake for 45 minutes, stirring every 15 minutes to ensure even crispness.

Note: Serve ⅓ cup granola with 6 ounces 0% plain Greek yogurt for a simple and Sugar Smart Diet–approved breakfast.

Nutrition per serving (⅓ cup granola): 202 calories, 5 g protein, 19 g carbs, 2 g fiber, 7 g total sugar, 13 g fat, 4 g saturated fat, 170 mg sodium

LUNCHES AND DINNERS

PHASE 1

Barley Risotto with Chicken and Asparagus

Makes 4 servings
PREP TIME: 10 minutes ● **TOTAL TIME:** 45 minutes

3 tablespoons lemon
  juice
¼ teaspoon salt
1 clove garlic, minced
4 teaspoons olive oil,
  divided
1 pound boneless,
  skinless chicken
  thighs
1 pound asparagus,
  ends trimmed
5 cups low-sodium
  chicken or vegetable
  broth
1 large yellow onion,
  finely chopped
1 shallot, finely chopped
1 tablespoon chopped
  fresh sage leaves or
  2 teaspoons dried
¼ teaspoon freshly
  ground black pepper
1 cup pearled barley

1. Preheat the oven to 400°F. Line a baking sheet with foil.

2. In a medium bowl, whisk together the lemon juice, salt, garlic, and 1 teaspoon of the oil. Add the chicken and asparagus and toss with the dressing.

3. Place the chicken on the baking sheet and bake for 20 to 25 minutes, or until the internal temperature is 165°F. Add the asparagus to the baking sheet during the final 10 minutes of cooking.

4. Meanwhile, pour the broth into a medium sauce-pan and cook over medium heat for 5 minutes, or until steaming. Remove from the heat.

5. Heat the remaining 3 teaspoons oil in a large sauce-pan over medium-high heat. Add the onion and cook, stirring frequently, for 5 minutes, or until soft. Add the shallot and cook for 2 minutes. Add the sage and black pepper and cook for 1 minute. Reduce the heat slightly, add the barley, and cook, stirring, for 1 minute.

6. Add 1 cup of the broth to the barley mixture and cook, stirring, for 4 minutes, or until all the liquid is absorbed. Add another ½ cup broth to the mixture and cook, stirring, for 3 minutes, or until absorbed. Continue this process with the remaining broth until all of it is absorbed and the barley is tender and creamy, about 20 more minutes.

7. Remove from the heat, cover, and let sit for 5 min-utes. Serve the barley risotto topped with the chicken and asparagus.

Nutrition per serving (4 ounces chicken, ¾ cup barley, 5 spears asparagus):
467 calories, 37 g protein, 48 g carbs, 12 g fiber, 6 g total sugar,
16 g fat, 4 g saturated fat, 451 mg sodium

Fast, Hearty Turkey Chili

Makes 4 servings

PREP TIME: 5 minutes ● **TOTAL TIME:** 20 minutes

2 tablespoons
+ 2 teaspoons
extra-virgin olive oil
1 cup finely chopped
onion
8 ounces ground turkey
breast
2 cups reduced-sodium
canned tomatoes
1 cup reduced-sodium
chicken broth
1 cup no-salt-added
tomato paste
2⅔ cups canned kidney
beans, rinsed and
drained
3 teaspoons chili powder
½ teaspoon ground
cumin
¼ cup chopped scallions

1. In a large skillet, heat the oil over medium-high heat. Add the onion and turkey and cook, stirring frequently, for 5 minutes, or until the turkey is cooked through and broken apart and the onion is tender.

2. Add the tomatoes, broth, tomato paste, kidney beans, chili powder, and cumin and simmer for 10 minutes. Serve topped with the scallions.

Nutrition per serving (1 cup): 445 calories, 31 g protein, 61 g carbs, 14 g fiber, 19 g total sugar, 12 g fat, 2 g saturated fat, 438 mg sodium

Vegetarian Stuffed Portobello

Makes 4 servings

PREP TIME: 15 minutes ● **TOTAL TIME:** 40 minutes

4 portobello mushroom
   caps
2 tablespoons olive oil,
   divided
⅓ cup toasted pine nuts
½ block extra-firm tofu,
   drained and cubed
½ cup finely chopped
   onion
2 cloves garlic, minced
2 tomatoes, chopped
2 cups chopped fresh
   spinach
1 teaspoon dried basil
2¼ cups cooked brown
   rice (may use cooked
   frozen or
   microwaveable rice)
1 egg white, lightly
   beaten
¼ teaspoon freshly
   ground black pepper
2 tablespoons shredded
   Parmesan cheese
¾ cup shredded part-
   skim mozzarella
   cheese, divided
3 tablespoons chopped
   fresh basil

1. Preheat the oven to 375°F. Coat a baking sheet with cooking spray.

2. Trim the stem from each mushroom and wipe clean. Using 1 tablespoon of the oil, brush the outside top of each mushroom.

3. Toast the pine nuts in a medium skillet over medium heat for 3 to 4 minutes, or until they become fragrant. Remove from the skillet.

4. Heat the remaining 1 tablespoon oil in the same skillet over medium-high heat. Add the tofu, onion, and garlic and cook, stirring frequently, for 3 to 4 minutes, or until the onion is tender and tofu is browned. Add the tomatoes, spinach, and dried basil. Cook, stirring frequently, for 2 to 3 minutes.

5. Remove from the heat. Stir in the rice, egg white, pepper, Parmesan, and ⅓ cup of the mozzarella. Spoon one-quarter of the rice mixture into each mushroom cap. Top each evenly with the remaining mozzarella and the fresh basil. Place the mushroom caps, stuffing side up, on the baking sheet. Bake for 15 minutes, or until the mushrooms are tender and the cheese is bubbly.

Nutrition per serving (1 stuffed mushroom cap): 395 calories, 19 g protein, 34 g carbs, 5 g fiber, 6 g total sugar, 22 g fat, 5 g saturated fat, 483 mg sodium

PHASE 1

Roasted Veggie, Bulgur, and Chickpea Salad with Feta Dressing

Makes 4 servings
PREP TIME: 5 minutes ● **TOTAL TIME:** 25 minutes

2 cups low-sodium chicken or vegetable broth
1 cup dry bulgur
4 bell peppers, each sliced into 8 pieces
1 large yellow onion, cut into chunks
2 tablespoons + 2 teaspoons olive oil, divided
2⅔ cups rinsed and drained canned chickpeas
2 tablespoons + 2 teaspoons red wine vinegar
2 tablespoons + 2 teaspoons lemon juice
2 teaspoons minced garlic
1 teaspoon dried oregano
½ cup crumbled feta cheese

1. Preheat the oven to 400°F.

2. In a medium saucepan, bring the broth to a boil. Add the bulgur, cover, and remove from the heat. Allow to sit for 20 minutes, or until all the liquid is absorbed.

3. Toss the bell peppers and onion with 4 teaspoons of the oil and place on a baking sheet. Bake for 10 minutes, then turn the peppers and onion and add the chickpeas. Bake for 10 minutes, or until the onion is golden and both onion and peppers are soft.

4. In a small bowl, whisk together the vinegar, lemon juice, garlic, oregano, feta, and the remaining 4 teaspoons oil. Toss the chickpea and veggie mixture with the bulgur and drizzle with the dressing.

Nutrition per serving (about 2½ cups): 461 calories, 18 g protein, 63 g carbs, 9 g fiber, 7 g total sugar, 17 g fat, 5 g saturated fat, 471 mg sodium

Fish Tacos with Mango-Lime Salsa in Crispy Corn Tortillas

Makes 4 servings
PREP TIME: 15 minutes ● **TOTAL TIME:** 30 minutes

1 mango, chopped
½ cup chopped red onion
2 teaspoons finely
   chopped jalapeño
   pepper (wear plastic
   gloves when handling)
1 tablespoon lime juice
½ teaspoon garlic
   powder, divided
½ teaspoon salt, divided
¼ teaspoon chili powder
¼ teaspoon ground
   cumin
¾ pound cod fillets
2 teaspoons olive oil
8 corn tortillas
   (6" diameter)
1 cup shredded Mexican
   blend cheese
½ cup 0% plain
   Greek yogurt

1. Preheat the oven to 425°F. Line a baking sheet with foil.

2. In a medium bowl, combine the mango, onion, chile pepper, lime juice, ¼ teaspoon of the garlic powder, and ¼ teaspoon of the salt. Cover with plastic wrap and set aside.

3. In a small bowl, mix together the chili powder, cumin, and the remaining ¼ teaspoon garlic powder and ¼ teaspoon salt.

4. Drizzle the cod with the oil, rub with the spice mixture, and place on the baking sheet. Bake for 15 minutes. During the last 9 minutes of baking, coat the tortillas lightly on both sides with cooking spray and place in the oven with the fish. Hang each tortilla over 2 rungs of the oven rack so they become crisp.

5. Break the cod into small pieces with a fork. Fill each corn tortilla shell with a scant ¼ cup cod pieces, 2 tablespoons cheese, 3 tablespoons mango salsa, and 1 tablespoon yogurt.

Nutrition per serving (2 tacos): 432 calories, 33 g protein, 35 g carbs, 3 g fiber, 11 g total sugar, 19 g fat, 9 g saturated fat, 995 mg sodium

Pork Tenderloin with Roasted Pear-Cabbage Medley and Barley

Makes 4 servings

PREP TIME: 15 minutes ● **TOTAL TIME:** 55 minutes

2¾ cups low-sodium chicken broth

1 cup pearled barley

¼ teaspoon ground cinnamon

½ teaspoon paprika

1 teaspoon garlic powder

¼ teaspoon freshly ground black pepper

½ teaspoon salt, divided

¼ large cabbage, thinly sliced

1 large pear, sliced

½ teaspoon caraway seeds

4 teaspoons olive oil, divided

1–1¼ pounds pork tenderloin

1. Preheat the oven to 425°F.

2. In a medium saucepan, bring the broth and barley to a boil. Reduce the heat to a simmer and cook for 40 minutes, or until all the liquid is absorbed and the barley is tender.

3. In a small bowl, mix together the cinnamon, paprika, garlic powder, pepper, and ¼ teaspoon of the salt.

4. In a medium bowl, toss the cabbage and pear with the caraway seeds, 2 teaspoons of the oil, and the remaining ¼ teaspoon salt and place in a medium baking dish. Rub the pork loin with the remaining 2 teaspoons oil followed by the spice mixture and place in the baking dish beside the cabbage mixture.

5. Cook for 25 minutes, or until a thermometer inserted in the center of the pork reaches 140°F and the juices run clear. Remove from the oven and let stand for 5 minutes, or until the temperature registers 145°F. Serve the pork and cabbage mixture over the barley.

Nutrition per serving (⅔ cup barley, 5 ounces pork, 1½ cups cabbage-pear mix):
432 calories, 40 g protein, 49 g carbs, 12 g fiber, 8 g total sugar, 10 g fat, 2 g saturated fat, 435 mg sodium

Penne with Meatballs

Makes 4 servings

PREP TIME: 10 minutes ● **TOTAL TIME:** 35 minutes

4 teaspoons olive oil, divided
½ large yellow onion, finely chopped
½ green zucchini, finely chopped
1 carrot, grated
2 cloves garlic, minced
¼ teaspoon chili powder
¼ teaspoon salt
¼ teaspoon freshly ground black pepper
½ cup whole wheat bread crumbs
1 pound lean ground beef
2 cups whole wheat penne
2 cups Sugar Smart Marinara Sauce (page 234) or jarred no-sugar-added marinara sauce

1. Heat 2 teaspoons of the oil in a medium skillet over medium-high heat. Add the onion and cook, stirring frequently, for 3 minutes, or until soft. Add the zucchini and cook for 3 minutes. Add the carrot and cook for 3 minutes. Stir in the garlic, chili powder, salt, and pepper. Remove from the heat.

2. In a large bowl, stir the onion mixture and bread crumbs into the beef until fully incorporated. Divide the mixture into 16 pieces, rolling each into a small ball. Heat the remaining 2 teaspoons olive oil in a large skillet over medium heat. Cook the meatballs for 5 minutes. Flip and cook for 5 minutes. Turn the meatballs on their side and cook for 2 minutes. Flip to the opposite side and cook for 2 minutes.

3. Bring a medium pot of water to a boil and add the penne. Cook al dente according to package directions. Drain. Serve the meatballs with the marinara sauce over the pasta.

Nutrition per serving (4 meatballs, 1½ cups pasta, ½ cup marinara): 463 calories, 34 g protein, 53 g carbs, 10 g fiber, 10 g total sugar, 13 g fat, 4 g saturated fat, 687 mg sodium

PHASE 2

Turkey Veggie Lasagna

Makes 6 servings

PREP TIME: 15 minutes ● **TOTAL TIME:** 1 hour 20 minutes

2 teaspoons olive oil, divided

2 cloves garlic, minced

8 ounces ground turkey breast

2 cups chopped cremini (baby bella) mushrooms

4 cups Sugar Smart Marinara Sauce (page 234) or jarred no-sugar-added marinara sauce

1 container (15 ounces) part-skim ricotta cheese

1 package (10 ounces) frozen chopped spinach, thawed and squeezed dry

1 tablespoon chopped fresh basil

1 egg, lightly beaten

¼ teaspoon freshly ground black pepper

¼ teaspoon ground nutmeg

9 whole grain lasagna noodles, cooked al dente according to package directions

1 cup shredded part-skim mozzarella cheese

¼ cup grated Parmesan cheese

1. Preheat the oven to 350°F.

2. Heat 1 teaspoon of the oil in a large skillet over medium-high heat and add the garlic. Add the turkey and cook, breaking up the turkey into small pieces using a spoon or spatula, for 5 minutes, or until no longer pink on the outside. Transfer the turkey to a plate.

3. Heat the remaining 1 teaspoon oil in the same skillet. Add the mushrooms and cook for 5 minutes, or until they begin to release their liquid and become browned. Transfer the mushrooms to a bowl. Add the turkey back to the skillet, along with marinara sauce. Let simmer for 3 minutes, or until hot.

4. In a medium bowl, mix together the ricotta, spinach, basil, egg, pepper, and nutmeg.

5. Spread ½ cup marinara mixture on the bottom of a 13" × 9" baking dish. Top with a layer of 3 lasagna noodles. They can be slightly overlapping. Spread one-half of the ricotta mixture over the top of the noodles. Then add one-third of the mushrooms, one-third of the remaining sauce, and one-third of the mozzarella. Repeat the same layer once more, starting with the noodles, then top with the final one-half of ricotta, and one-third of the mushrooms, sauce, and mozzarella.

6. Bake, covered with aluminum foil, for 40 minutes. Uncover and bake for 10 minutes, or until the cheese is bubbly and browned on the top.

Nutrition per serving (one 4" × 5" slice): 460 calories, 32 g protein, 46 g carbs, 7 g fiber, 11 g total sugar, 18 g fat, 8 g saturated fat, 702 mg sodium

PHASE 3

Teriyaki Beef with Broccoli

Makes 4 servings

PREP TIME: 10 minutes ● **TOTAL TIME:** 50 minutes + marinating time

¼ cup Sugar Smart
Teriyaki Sauce
(page 235)

12 ounces flank steak,
sliced into thin strips
across the grain

2½ cups low-sodium
chicken or vegetable
broth

1 cup brown rice

2 teaspoons canola oil

½ yellow onion, sliced

1 red bell pepper, sliced

3 cups broccoli florets

2 teaspoons cornstarch

¼ teaspoon red-pepper
flakes

2 tablespoons toasted
sesame seeds

1. In a large bowl, pour the teriyaki sauce over the beef and toss to coat. Store, covered with plastic wrap, in the refrigerator for 1 hour or overnight.

2. In a large saucepan, bring the broth and rice to a boil. Reduce the heat to low and simmer, covered, for 40 minutes, or until all the water is absorbed.

3. Heat the oil in a large skillet over medium-high heat. Add the onion, pepper, and broccoli and cook for 4 minutes, or until the onion softens and the broccoli turns bright green. Transfer to a bowl.

4. Drain the beef, reserving the excess sauce. Toss the beef with the cornstarch and cook in the same skillet over high heat for 2 to 3 minutes, or until browned. Add the vegetables, pepper flakes, and reserved sauce to the skillet and cook for 2 minutes. Serve over the rice, sprinkled with the sesame seeds.

Nutrition per serving (1½ cups beef mixture, ¾ cup rice): 462 calories, 28 g protein, 49 g carbs, 5 g fiber, 5 g total sugar, 18 g fat, 6 g saturated fat, 385 mg sodium

PHASE 3

Beer BBQ Chicken Thighs with Corn and Tomato Salad

Makes 4 servings

PREP TIME: 10 minutes ● **TOTAL TIME:** 1 hour

1 pound boneless, skinless chicken thighs
½ teaspoon salt
½ teaspoon freshly ground black pepper
2 tablespoons + 1 teaspoon olive oil, divided
¾ cup Sugar Smart BBQ Sauce (page 234)
¾ cup beer (any kind)
2 cloves garlic, minced or crushed
1½ cups frozen corn, thawed
1½ cups chopped tomatoes
½ cup sliced scallions, white and green parts
¼ cup chopped fresh cilantro
1 tablespoon white wine vinegar
2 teaspoons lime juice
1 teaspoon honey
¾ cup brown rice
1 teaspoon grated lemon peel
1¾ cups water

1. Season the chicken on both sides with the salt and pepper. Heat 1 tablespoon of the oil in a large Dutch oven over medium-high heat and cook the chicken for 3 minutes on each side, or until browned. Remove the chicken and set on a plate.

2. Add the barbecue sauce, beer, and garlic to the pot. Bring to a light boil, then reduce the heat to low, add the chicken, and let simmer for 35 minutes.

3. Meanwhile, in a medium bowl, combine the corn, tomatoes, scallions, and cilantro. In a small bowl, whisk together the vinegar, lime juice, honey, and 2 teaspoons of the oil. Fold the dressing into the corn mixture. Season with salt and pepper to taste.

4. Heat the remaining 2 teaspoons oil in a medium saucepan over medium heat. Add the rice and lemon peel and cook, stirring to coat the rice, for 2 minutes. Add the water, bring to a boil, then reduce the heat, cover, and simmer for 45 minutes, or until the liquid is absorbed.

5. Using tongs, remove the chicken from the pot and set aside. Bring the remaining sauce to a light boil again, then reduce the heat and simmer for 3 minutes, allowing the sauce to thicken.

6. Heat an indoor or outdoor grill to medium-high. Brush the chicken on both sides with the sauce from the pot. Grill the chicken for 2 to 3 minutes on each side, or until there are grill marks. Serve the chicken over the rice, with the corn and tomato salad on the side.

Nutrition per serving (4 ounces chicken, ¾ cup corn and tomato salad, ⅔ cup rice): 470 calories, 29 g protein, 54 g carbs, 7 g fiber, 12 g total sugar, 15 g fat, 2 g saturated fat, 440 mg sodium

PHASE 3

Panko-Crusted Chicken Tenders with Honey-Mustard Dipping Sauce

Makes 6 servings
PREP TIME: 15 minutes ● **TOTAL TIME:** 35 minutes

¼ cup whole wheat flour
1 egg, lightly beaten
¼ cup Dijon mustard, divided
1 cup whole wheat panko (bread crumbs)
½ cup unsweetened coconut flakes
½ teaspoon salt
½ teaspoon freshly ground black pepper
1 pound boneless, skinless chicken breast tenders, cut in half widthwise into 2" to 3" pieces
1 tablespoon honey
⅓ cup 0% plain Greek yogurt
½ teaspoon dried rosemary

1. Preheat the oven to 375°F.

2. Pour the flour in a wide, shallow bowl. Whisk together the egg and 1 teaspoon of the mustard in another shallow bowl. Fill a third shallow bowl with the panko, coconut, salt, and pepper.

3. Dredge each piece of chicken in the flour, coating lightly and evenly. Dip the floured chicken in the egg mixture, shaking off the excess, then dip it into the panko mixture, lightly pressing the chicken into the panko until evenly coated.

4. Coat each side of the breaded chicken with cooking spray. Place on a wire baking rack over a baking sheet. Bake for 15 to 20 minutes, or until no longer pink and the juices run clear.

5. In a small bowl, stir together the honey, yogurt, rosemary, and the remaining mustard. Serve the chicken tenders with the honey-mustard mixture as the dipping sauce or drizzled on top.

Nutrition per serving (about 4 tenders with 1½ tablespoons dipping sauce):
313 calories, 15 g protein, 27 g carbs, 4 g fiber, 4 g total sugar, 17 g fat, 6 g saturated fat, 695 mg sodium

For a Sugar Smart dinner: Pair 1 serving of the chicken tenders with 1½ tablespoons of the dipping sauce, ½ cup whole grain, and 1 cup steamed vegetables with 1 teaspoon olive oil, or a green salad with 1 tablespoon balsamic vinaigrette.

PHASE 3

Orange-Garlic Salmon with Kale and Barley

Makes 4 servings
PREP TIME: 10 minutes ● **TOTAL TIME:** 45 minutes

1 cup pearled barley
4 wild salmon or halibut fillets (4 ounces each)
⅛ teaspoon kosher salt
⅛ teaspoon freshly ground black pepper
2 tablespoons + 2 teaspoons extra-virgin olive oil, divided
6 cups kale, roughly chopped
½ cup chopped sweet onion
4 teaspoons minced garlic
4 teaspoons minced ginger
¼ cup dry white wine
1 cup orange juice
2 teaspoons maple syrup
2 teaspoons reduced-sodium soy sauce

1. Cook the barley according to package directions.

2. Sprinkle each salmon fillet evenly on both sides with the salt and pepper. Heat 4 teaspoons of the oil in a large skillet over medium-high heat. Add the salmon and kale and cook for 2 to 3 minutes. Turn the fillets and continue cooking for 2 to 3 minutes, or until the fish flakes easily with a fork. Transfer the salmon and kale to a plate.

3. Heat the remaining 4 teaspoons oil in the same skillet. Add the onion, garlic, and ginger and cook for 30 seconds, or until fragrant but not browned. Add the wine and cook for 3 minutes, or until the liquid is almost evaporated. Add the orange juice, maple syrup, and soy sauce. Bring to a boil, then lower the heat and simmer for 1 minute.

4. Return the salmon and kale to the skillet, spoon the sauce over all to coat, and heat through for 1 minute. Transfer to plates with one-quarter of the barley, spoon any remaining juices over the salmon and barley, and serve.

Nutrition per serving (1 salmon fillet, ¾ cup barley, ¾ cup kale): 469 calories, 28 g protein, 53 g carbs, 10 g fiber, 8 g total sugar, 17 g fat, 2 g saturated fat, 464 mg sodium

Crab Cakes with Garlic Kale

Makes 4 servings
PREP TIME: 10 minutes ● **TOTAL TIME:** 25 minutes

4 cans (6 ounces each) lump crabmeat, drained
½ cup finely chopped red onion
2 tablespoons Sugar Smart BBQ Sauce (page 234)
2 eggs, lightly beaten
⅔ cup whole wheat bread crumbs
4 teaspoons olive oil, divided
½ large yellow onion, sliced
4 cloves garlic, minced
8 cups kale
1½ cups canned white beans, rinsed and drained

1. In a medium bowl, mix the crabmeat, onion, barbecue sauce, and eggs until well combined. Stir in the bread crumbs until the mixture forms a loose ball. Divide into 8 patties.

2. Heat 2 teaspoons of the oil in a large skillet over medium-high heat. Add the patties and cook for 4 minutes on each side, or until golden brown and cooked through.

3. Heat the remaining 2 teaspoons oil in a medium skillet over medium-high heat. Add the onion and cook for 3 minutes, or until soft. Add the garlic, kale, and beans and cook for 3 minutes, or until the kale is wilted. Serve the crab cakes over the kale mixture.

Nutrition per serving (2 crab cakes and 1½ cups greens): 456 calories, 44 g protein, 48 g carbs, 9 g fiber, 4 g total sugar, 11 g fat, 2 g saturated fat, 644 mg sodium

Poached Eggs with Fruity Wheat Berry Salad

Makes 4 servings

PREP TIME: 15 minutes ● **TOTAL TIME:** 1 hour 5 minutes

8 cups baby spinach leaves, chopped

2 cups chopped cucumber

2 cups chopped carrot

¾ cup wheat berries

1 apple, chopped

⅓ cup sliced almonds

3 tablespoons + 1 teaspoon olive oil

¼ cup white wine vinegar

1 tablespoon orange juice

2 teaspoons Dijon mustard

Salt and freshly ground black pepper

1 teaspoon white vinegar (or any other type)

4 eggs

1. In a large salad bowl, combine the spinach, cucumber, and carrot.

2. Bring 2¼ cups water to a boil in a medium pot. Add the wheat berries, reduce the heat to low, and simmer for 45 to 50 minutes, or until chewy but tender. Check for doneness about 30 minutes into the cooking time, then every 10 minutes afterward. (Cooking time varies depending on the age and type of wheat berries.)

3. Combine the wheat berries with the apple, almonds, and the 1 teaspoon oil. Then add to the spinach mixture.

4. In a small bowl, whisk together the vinegar, orange juice, and mustard until evenly mixed. Season with salt and pepper to taste. Slowly whisk in the 3 tablespoons oil until the dressing is uniform.

5. Fill a large, shallow saucepan or skillet three-quarters full with water. Heat over high heat until the water is steaming but not quite boiling. Add the vinegar (this will help the egg whites stay together) and stir the water with a spoon in one direction until it's swirling quickly. Crack an egg into a ladle or a small cup, and gently lower it into the moving water. Repeat with the remaining eggs. Turn the heat off, cover, and let the eggs cook until the yolks are cooked to preferred doneness, 7 to 8 minutes for over easy. Remove the eggs with a slotted spoon.

6. Divide the salad evenly into 4 salad bowls, top each with an egg, and drizzle with the dressing.

Nutrition per serving (3 cups salad): 437 calories, 18 g protein, 44 g carbs, 11 g fiber, 10 g total sugar, 23 g fat, 4 g saturated fat, 316 mg sodium

Note: Make a large batch of wheat berries ahead of time, then use in this recipe and in other dishes throughout the week. If using cooked wheat berries for this recipe, use 2 cups instead of the ¾ cup uncooked. This will reduce the recipe's cook time to 10 minutes and the total time to 25 minutes.

Asian Quinoa Salad

Makes 4 servings

PREP TIME: 10 minutes ● **TOTAL TIME:** 35 minutes

1 cup quinoa
2 cups water
¾ pound cooked skinless
   chicken breast,
   shredded or cubed
   (about 2¼ cups)
1 cup shredded red
   cabbage
1 cup shelled and cooked
   edamame
1 cup chopped cucumber
1 red bell pepper, finely
   chopped
¾ cup shredded carrot
¼ cup chopped cilantro
½ cup Sugar Smart
   Asian Peanut Dressing
   (page 235)

1. In a medium saucepan, add the quinoa and water. Bring to a boil, then reduce to low and simmer for 13 to 15 minutes, or until the liquid is absorbed and the quinoa is soft. Spread the quinoa out on a baking sheet and allow to cool to room temperature, about 10 minutes.

2. In a large bowl, combine the chicken, cabbage, edamame, cucumber, pepper, carrot, and cilantro. Add the quinoa to the bowl. Toss the salad with the dressing to coat, and serve. Or refrigerate the salad overnight without dressing and add the dressing when ready to serve.

Nutrition per serving (2 cups salad, 2 tablespoons dressing): 481 calories, 38 g protein, 40 g carbs, 7 g fiber, 7 g total sugar, 19 g fat, 2 g saturated fat, 201 mg sodium

Sugar Smart Marinara Sauce

Makes 5 cups
PREP TIME: 10 minutes ● **TOTAL TIME:** 40 minutes

1 tablespoon olive oil
1 large onion, finely
    chopped
5 cloves garlic, minced
2 carrots, finely chopped
1 can (28 ounces)
    crushed tomatoes
1 can (14.5 ounces)
    crushed tomatoes
1½ teaspoons dried basil
1 bay leaf
Pinch of crushed red-
    pepper flakes
Freshly ground black
    pepper

1. Heat the oil in a large skillet with deep sides over medium-high heat. Add the onion and cook for 5 minutes, or until translucent. Add the garlic and carrots and cook for 5 minutes.

2. Add both cans of tomatoes, the basil, bay leaf, pepper flakes, and black pepper to taste. Bring the sauce to a boil, then reduce the heat to low and let simmer for 20 minutes. Remove the bay leaf. Use the sauce right away, or it can be refrigerated in a sealed container for up to 3 days or frozen for up to 2 months.

Nutrition per serving (½ cup): 70 calories, 2 g protein, 12 g carbs, 3 g fiber, 7 g total sugar, 1 g fat, 0 g saturated fat, 320 mg sodium

Sugar Smart BBQ Sauce

Makes 1 cup
PREP TIME: 5 minutes ● **TOTAL TIME:** 25 minutes

1 cup no-sugar-added
    tomato sauce
1 tablespoon cider
    vinegar
1 tablespoon +
    1 teaspoon maple
    syrup
1½ teaspoons garlic
    powder
4 teaspoons smoked
    paprika
1½ teaspoons chili
    powder
¼ teaspoon freshly
    ground black pepper
¼ teaspoon salt
Pinch of ground
    cinnamon

In a small saucepan, combine the tomato sauce, vinegar, maple syrup, garlic powder, paprika, chili powder, pepper, salt, and cinnamon. Stir well. Cook over low heat, stirring, for 15 to 20 minutes, or until the mixture thickens and the color deepens. Store in an airtight container in the refrigerator for up to 10 days.

Nutrition per serving (1 tablespoon): 12 calories, <1 g protein, 3 g carbs, <1 g fiber, 3 g total sugar, <1 g fat, 0 g saturated fat, 143 mg sodium

Sugar Smart Teriyaki Sauce

Makes 1 cup
PREP TIME: 1 minute ● **TOTAL TIME:** 5 minutes

½ cup reduced-sodium
soy sauce
⅓ cup water
1 tablespoon honey
2 teaspoons minced
garlic
1 tablespoon grated
ginger
½ teaspoon sesame oil

In a small saucepan over medium-high heat, combine the soy sauce, water, honey, garlic, ginger, and oil. Bring to a boil, stirring constantly, then reduce the heat to low and simmer for 4 minutes. Store in a tightly covered container in the refrigerator for up to 1 week.

Nutrition per serving (1 tablespoon): 10 calories, 0 g protein, 2 g carbs, 0 g fiber, 1 g total sugar, 0 g fat, 0 g saturated fat, 266 mg sodium

Sugar Smart Asian Peanut Dressing

Makes ⅔ cup
PREP TIME: 10 minutes ● **TOTAL TIME:** 10 minutes

¼ cup unseasoned rice
vinegar
1 tablespoon light or
reduced-sodium soy
sauce
1 tablespoon natural
peanut butter
1 tablespoon honey
1 teaspoon minced garlic
1 teaspoon grated ginger
(optional)
½ teaspoon spicy red-
pepper sauce, like
Sriracha sauce
(optional)
3 tablespoons canola oil
1 teaspoon toasted
sesame oil

In a medium bowl, whisk together the vinegar, soy sauce, peanut butter, honey, garlic, ginger (if using), pepper sauce (if using), and the oils. Store in a tightly covered container in the refrigerator for up to 1 week. Use on salads, in grain or pasta dishes, or on poultry or meat dishes.

Nutrition per serving (1 tablespoon): 60 calories, 1 g protein, 2 g carbs, 0 g fiber, 2 g total sugar, < 5 g fat, <1 g saturated fat, 56 mg sodium

SNACKS & SIDES

Crunchy Roasted Rosemary Chickpeas

Makes 4 servings
PREP TIME: 5 minutes ● **TOTAL TIME:** 30 minutes

1 can (15 ounces) chickpeas, rinsed and drained
1½ tablespoons olive oil
¼ teaspoon garlic powder
1½ teaspoons dried rosemary
¼ teaspoon salt

1. Preheat the oven to 400°F.

2. Spread the chickpeas on a paper towel in a single layer. Place another paper towel on top and gently dab to remove excess water. Transfer the chickpeas to a baking sheet. Pour the oil on the chickpeas, tossing with your hands to ensure that all chickpeas are coated in oil. Spread chickpeas into a single layer.

3. Bake for 15 minutes. Stir and place back in the oven for 5 to 10 minutes, or until golden and crisp. Toss the chickpeas with the garlic powder, rosemary, and salt.

Nutrition per serving (⅓ cup): 130 calories, 4 g protein, 14 g carbs, <1 g fiber, 0 g total sugar, 7 g fat, 1 g saturated fat, 267 mg sodium

Roasted Fennel with Pine Nuts

Makes 4 servings
PREP TIME: 5 minutes ● **TOTAL TIME:** 35 minutes

4 bulbs fennel
2 tablespoons olive oil
½ teaspoon salt
¼ teaspoon freshly ground pepper
¼ cup pine nuts

1. Preheat the oven to 400°F.

2. Slice the root end off the fennel bulbs and discard. Slice the frond end off the bulbs, from the light green part. Reserve ½ cup of the fronds. Slice the remaining fennel bulb into ½" slices, then cut the slices in half.

3. Toss the fennel chunks with the oil, salt, and pepper. Spread the fennel in a single layer on a baking sheet and bake, stirring once halfway through, for 25 to 30 minutes, or until tender and golden. During the last 5 minutes of baking, add the pine nuts and reserved fronds.

Nutrition per serving (1½ cups): 154 calories, 3 g protein, 8 g carbs, 4 g fiber, 4 g total sugar, 13 g fat, 1 g saturated fat, 472 mg sodium

Tuna-Potato Wrap

Makes 4 wraps

PREP TIME: 15 minutes ● **TOTAL TIME:** 35 minutes

1 large Yukon Gold or red potato, peeled and chopped

2 cloves garlic, minced

3 tablespoons reduced-fat mayonnaise

2 tablespoons cider vinegar

½ teaspoon salt

¼ teaspoon freshly ground black pepper

2 cans (5 ounces each) albacore tuna, drained and flaked

1 carrot, finely chopped

½ large yellow onion, finely chopped

4 large romaine lettuce leaves

1. Place the potato in a large saucepan of water and bring to a simmer. Cook for 20 minutes, or until tender. Drain and let cool.

2. In a small bowl, whisk together the garlic, mayonnaise, vinegar, salt, and pepper.

3. In a large bowl, stir together the tuna, carrot, and onion. Add the potatoes and toss lightly. Gently stir in the mayonnaise mixture until the potato chunks are coated and mixed thoroughly with the tuna.

4. Remove the stem from each lettuce leaf and place on a plate. Put ¾ cup of the potato mixture in the center of each leaf. Fold the two ends of the lettuce leaf onto the potato mixture and then roll the sides up, like a burrito.

Nutrition per serving (1 wrap): 159 calories, 15 g protein, 15 g carbs, 2 g fiber, 3 g total sugar, 4 g fat, 1 g saturated fat, 396 mg sodium

Note: You can make the filling ahead of time and store it in the refrigerator for up to 3 days. Fill the lettuce leaves right before serving.

Berry-Veggie Smoothie

Makes 1 serving

PREP TIME: 5 minutes ● **TOTAL TIME:** 5 minutes

1 cup fat-free milk

⅓ cup fresh or frozen blueberries

½ small banana, frozen in pieces

1 cup raw baby spinach leaves

3–4 ice cubes

In a blender, combine (in this order) the milk, blueberries, banana, spinach, and ice cubes. Blend for 1 minute, or until smooth.

Nutrition per serving: 165 calories, 10 g protein, 32 g carbs, 3 g fiber, 23 g total sugar, 1 g fat, 0 g saturated fat, 153 mg sodium

Chocolate-Cherry Smoothie

Makes 2 servings
PREP TIME: 2 minutes ● **TOTAL TIME:** 2 minutes

1 cup fat-free milk
1 large banana
1 cup fresh or frozen
 unsweetened pitted
 cherries
4 teaspoons cocoa
 powder
1 cup ice

In a blender, combine the milk, banana, cherries, cocoa powder, and ice. Blend on high for 1 minute, or until smooth.

Nutrition per serving: 159 calories, 6 g protein, 36 g carbs, 5 g fiber, 25 g total sugar, 1 g fat, <1 g saturated fat, 53 mg sodium

Watermelon and Feta Salad

Makes 4 servings
PREP TIME: 10 minutes ● **TOTAL TIME:** 10 minutes

2 tablespoons lime juice
2 tablespoons orange
 juice
1 tablespoon minced
 shallots
¼ teaspoon salt
2½ tablespoons olive oil
3 cups arugula, washed
 and dried
2 cups seedless
 watermelon, cut into
 1" cubes
¼ cup chopped fresh
 mint leaves
3 ounces feta cheese,
 crumbled or cut into
 small cubes

1. In a medium bowl, whisk the lime juice, orange juice, shallots, and salt. Gradually whisk in the oil.

2. In a large salad bowl, combine the arugula, watermelon, mint, and feta. Pour the dressing over the salad and toss gently to coat. Serve immediately, or leave off the dressing, cover, and refrigerate for up to 2 days.

Nutrition per serving (1¼ cups): 165 calories, 4 g protein, 9 g carbs, <1 g fiber, 7 total sugar, 13 g fat, 4 g saturated fat, 389 mg sodium

Note: Have this as a snack (1 cup counts as a 150-calorie snack), or serve it as a starter salad or a side dish with chicken or fish.

Crunchy-Creamy Purple Slaw

Makes 4 servings
PREP TIME: 4 minutes ● **TOTAL TIME:** 4 minutes

4 tablespoons 0% plain
    Greek yogurt
2 tablespoons cider
    vinegar
2 tablespoons + 2
    teaspoons apple juice
4 cups thinly sliced
    purple cabbage
½ cup chopped apple
¼ cup toasted, salted
    sunflower seeds

In a large bowl, whisk together the yogurt, vinegar, and juice until smooth. Add the cabbage, apple, and sunflower seeds and toss well.

Nutrition per serving (about 1½ cups): 94 calories, 4 g protein, 12 g carbs, 3 g fiber, 7 g total sugar, 4 g fat, <1 g saturated fat, 55 mg sodium

Sugar Smart Energy Bars

Makes 6 bars
PREP TIME: 10 minutes ● **TOTAL TIME:** 10 minutes

½ cup + 1 tablespoon
    rolled oats
¼ teaspoon ground
    cinnamon
2 tablespoons chopped
    dried apricots
1 tablespoon chopped
    almonds
1 tablespoon roasted
    unsalted sunflower
    seeds
⅓ cup creamy peanut
    butter
2 tablespoons honey
2 teaspoons vanilla
    extract

1. In a large bowl, stir together the oats, cinnamon, apricots, almonds, and sunflower seeds until fully combined.

2. In a small microwaveable container, stir together the peanut butter, honey, and vanilla. Microwave on high for 20 seconds. Stir and microwave for 10 seconds, or until soft. If the mixture is still not a spreadable consistency, microwave in 10-second increments until smooth.

3. Stir the peanut butter mixture into the oat mixture, fully coating the oats. Use your hands to gently knead the mixture until it sticks together.

4. Divide the mixture in half. Divide each of those pieces into three. Roll each into a ball and gently press into a small rectangle. Store in a sealed container in the refrigerator for up to 1 week.

Nutrition per serving (1 bar): 159 calories, 5 g protein, 16 g carbs, 2 g fiber, 9 g total sugar, 9 g fat, 2 g saturated fat, 73 mg sodium

Cranberry-Walnut Wild Rice Pilaf

Makes 4 servings

PREP TIME: 5 minutes ● **TOTAL TIME:** 50 minutes

1 teaspoon butter
1 teaspoon olive oil
½ cup chopped onion
¾ cup wild rice
3 tablespoons dried
    cranberries
2¼ cups low-sodium
    chicken broth
11 walnut halves
¼ cup chopped scallions
Sea salt and freshly
    ground black pepper

1. Preheat the oven to 400°F.

2. Heat the butter and olive oil in a 1½- to 2-quart pot over medium heat. Add the onion and cook for 3 to 4 minutes, or until translucent. Add the rice and cranberries and cook, stirring well to coat, for 2 minutes. Add the broth and bring the mixture to a boil over high heat. Reduce the heat to low, cover, and simmer for 40 to 45 minutes, or until the liquid is absorbed and the rice is tender.

3. Arrange the walnuts on a baking sheet and toast for 6 minutes, or until browned and fragrant. Roughly chop the walnuts.

4. Add the walnuts and scallions to the rice. Season with salt and pepper to taste.

Nutrition per serving (about ½ cup): 208 calories, 8 g protein, 31 g carbs, 3 g fiber, 5 total sugar, 7 g fat, 1 g saturated fat, 45 mg sodium

Note: Serve as a side dish along with 4 ounces of lean protein and 1 cup of vegetables. For a vegetarian meal, double the serving, or add ¾ cup beans, such as chickpeas or white beans, to a single serving and serve with a vegetable or salad.

DESSERTS

Peachy Ginger All-Fruit Soft Serve

Makes 2 servings
PREP TIME: 3 minutes ● **TOTAL TIME:** 3 minutes

1 large, very ripe banana, sliced and frozen
1⅓ cups frozen peaches, slightly thawed
¼ teaspoon powdered ginger

In a food processor or blender, combine the banana, peaches, and ginger. Process or blend for 1 minute. Scrape down the sides and stir. Continue to blend in 20-second increments until smooth but firm.

Nutrition per serving (¾ cup): 102 calories, 2 g protein, 26 g carbs, 3 g fiber, 17 g total sugar, <1 g fat, 0 g saturated fat, 1 mg sodium

Easy Cinnamon-Apple Cobbler

Makes 4 servings
PREP TIME: 5 minutes ● **TOTAL TIME:** 25 minutes

2 firm apples, such as Pink Lady or Honeycrisp, chopped into ½" pieces
1 teaspoon vanilla extract
½ teaspoon ground cinnamon, divided
¼ cup rolled oats
⅓ cup chopped walnuts
1 tablespoon unsalted butter

1. Coat a medium skillet with cooking spray and heat over medium heat. Cook the apples, stirring frequently, for 15 minutes, or until soft and golden brown on all sides.

2. Transfer the apples to a medium bowl and gently toss with the vanilla and ¼ teaspoon of the cinnamon.

3. Stir the oats and walnuts together in a small bowl. Add the butter to the same skillet you used for the apples. Place over medium heat and add the oat mixture. Cook, stirring frequently, for 2 to 3 minutes, or until browned. Stir in the remaining ¼ teaspoon cinnamon and transfer to a small bowl.

4. Divide the apple mixture among 4 small bowls. Top each with one-quarter of the oat mixture. Microwave each bowl on medium power for 1 minute. Let rest for 1 minute before serving.

Nutrition per serving (⅓ cup apple mixture with a heaping tablespoon oat mixture): 142 calories, 2 g protein, 15 g carbs, 3 g fiber, 8 g total sugar, 9 g fat, 2 g saturated fat, 2 mg sodium

PHASE 2

Roasted Lemon-Ginger Pears with Pecan Yogurt

Makes 4 servings

PREP TIME: 5 minutes ● **TOTAL TIME:** 40 minutes

2 ripe, firm pears, such as Bosc

4 teaspoons butter, divided

¼ teaspoon ground cinnamon

1 teaspoon vanilla extract

1 tablespoon lemon juice

½ teaspoon powdered ginger, divided

6 ounces 0% plain Greek yogurt

¼ cup chopped pecans

1. Preheat the oven to 375°F.

2. Core the pears and cut in half lengthwise. Arrange the pear halves, cut side up, in a baking dish. Place 1 teaspoon butter in the center of each pear half. In a small bowl, stir together the cinnamon, vanilla, lemon juice, and ¼ teaspoon of the ginger. Drizzle the mixture over the top of the pear halves. Add 2 tablespoons water to the baking dish.

3. Bake for 20 minutes, spooning the juices from the pan over the pear halves occasionally. If the juices begin to dry up, add water, 1 tablespoon at a time, as needed. Gently turn the pears so that the cut side is down and bake for 15 minutes, or until the pears are tender and caramelized.

4. Mix the remaining ¼ teaspoon of the ginger into the yogurt.

5. Add the pecans to a small skillet over medium heat. Cook for 3 minutes, or until fragrant. Remove from the heat.

6. Remove the pears from the oven. Top each pear half with a large dollop of yogurt and the pecans. Spoon any additional liquid from the dish over the top of each serving.

Nutrition per serving (½ pear topped with 3 tablespoons yogurt and 1 tablespoon pecans): 158 calories, 5 g protein, 16 g carbs, 4 g fiber, 10 g total sugar, 9 g fat, 3 g saturated fat, 44 mg sodium

Yogurt-Covered Blueberries

Makes 2 servings
PREP TIME: 15 minutes ● **TOTAL TIME:** 15 minutes + freezing time

6 ounces 0% plain
    Greek yogurt
1 teaspoon vanilla
    extract
2 cups fresh blueberries,
    divided

1. Cover a large baking sheet or 2 large flat plates with aluminum foil or parchment paper.

2. In a blender, combine the yogurt, vanilla, and ⅓ cup of the blueberries. Blend until smooth. Pour into a bowl.

3. Using a toothpick or your fingers, dip the remaining blueberries into the yogurt, coating each one thoroughly. Place each on the baking sheet and freeze for 1 hour, or until the yogurt has hardened.

4. Transfer the blueberries to a sealed container or resealable plastic bag. Store in the freezer until ready to eat.

Nutrition per serving (approximately 1 cup): 141 calories, 10 g protein, 25 g carbs, 4 g fiber, 18 g total sugar, 1 g fat, 0 g saturated fat, 32 mg sodium

Creamy Dark Chocolate-Banana-Coconut Pudding

Makes 4 servings
PREP TIME: 7 minutes ● **TOTAL TIME:** 7 minutes

3 very ripe bananas
¼ cup + 1 tablespoon
    unsweetened cocoa
    powder
1 cup 0% plain
    Greek yogurt
1 teaspoon vanilla
    extract
3 tablespoons
    unsweetened coconut
    flakes, divided

1. Mash the bananas with a fork in a medium bowl until smooth and creamy. If desired, use a hand blender to puree them.

2. Add the cocoa powder, yogurt, vanilla, and 1 tablespoon of the coconut to the bananas. Using a fork, stir vigorously for 3 minutes, or until all of the ingredients are well combined.

3. Divide the pudding into 4 small bowls or ramekins. Sprinkle each bowl evenly with the remaining coconut flakes. Serve cold.

Nutrition per serving (½ cup): 154 calories, 8 g protein, 27 g carbs, 5 g fiber, 13 g total sugar, 4 g fat, 3 g saturated fat, 27 mg sodium

Notes: May also be frozen in ice-pop molds and eaten as a frozen dessert. An equal amount of nuts or seeds can be substituted for the coconut flakes.

PHASE 3

No-Bake Oatmeal Cookies

Makes 6 cookies

PREP TIME: 10 minutes ● **TOTAL TIME:** 10 minutes

¾ cup rolled oats
½ teaspoon ground cinnamon
2 tablespoons raisins, chopped
1 tablespoon chopped walnuts
¼ cup unsweetened shredded coconut
¼ cup salted almond butter
2 tablespoons maple syrup

1. In a medium bowl, coat the oats with the cinnamon, mixing well. Stir in the raisins, walnuts, and coconut until they're evenly distributed.

2. In a small microwaveable container, combine the almond butter and syrup. Microwave on high for 20 seconds. Stir and microwave for 10 seconds, or until soft. If the mixture is still not a spreadable consistency, microwave in 10-second increments until smooth.

3. Pour the almond butter mixture over the oats and stir until all of the oats are coated. Using your hands, press the mixture into a patty. Divide into 6 pieces, rolling each into a ball and then gently pressing into a flattened circle. Store in a sealed container in the refrigerator for up to 1 week.

Nutrition per serving (1 cookie): 159 calories, 4 g protein, 17 g carbs, 3 g fiber, 7 g total sugar, 9 g fat, 3 g saturated fat, 26 mg sodium

Note: You can use an equal amount of natural peanut butter in place of the almond butter if you prefer.

Banana-Chocolate Chip Bread Pudding

Makes 12 servings

PREP TIME: 15 minutes ● **TOTAL TIME:** 1 hour 10 minutes + cooling time

8 slices hearty whole wheat bread, torn into 1" pieces
3 ripe bananas
1¾ cups 1% milk
6 ounces 0% plain Greek yogurt
1 egg
3 egg whites
½ cup maple syrup
1½ teaspoons vanilla extract
1 teaspoon ground cinnamon
¼ teaspoon ground nutmeg
¼ teaspoon salt
⅓ cup dark chocolate chips
¼ cup chopped walnuts

1. Preheat the oven to 350°F. Coat a 13" × 9" baking dish with cooking spray.

2. Add the bread pieces to the baking dish.

3. Mash 2 of the bananas in a small bowl until smooth.

4. In a large bowl, whisk together the milk, yogurt, eggs, egg whites, maple syrup, vanilla, cinnamon, nutmeg, and salt for 3 to 4 minutes, or until smooth and the yogurt is fully incorporated. Stir in the mashed bananas and whisk until well combined. Slice the third banana and gently stir into the batter.

5. Pour the mixture over the bread in the baking dish. Sprinkle the chocolate chips and walnuts throughout, letting some fall to the bottom and some stay on top.

6. Bake for 55 minutes, or until a knife inserted in the center comes out clean. Let sit for about 10 minutes before serving.

Nutrition per serving (2" × 2" piece): 174 calories, 7 g protein, 28 g carbs, 2 g fiber, 18 g total sugar, 5 g fat, 2 g saturated fat, 166 mg sodium

Chocolate Clouds with Berries

Makes 8 clouds

PREP TIME: 10 minutes ● **TOTAL TIME:** 10 minutes + freezing time

1 cup heavy whipping cream

2 tablespoons confectioners' sugar

2 tablespoons cocoa powder

1 teaspoon vanilla extract

6 cups sliced strawberries

1. Cover a large plate or baking sheet with parchment paper or aluminum foil.

2. Whip the cream in a medium bowl using a hand mixer with the whisk attachment, or a regular mixer, for 2 minutes, or until soft peaks begin to form. Add the sugar, cocoa powder, and vanilla and mix for 30 seconds to 1 minute, or until combined.

3. Pour the mixture into a pastry bag or a plastic freezer bag with the corner snipped off. Swirl 8 dollops of cream onto the plate or baking sheet. Freeze for 3 hours.

4. Serve over the strawberries, or transfer to an airtight container and store in the freezer for up to 1 month.

Nutrition per serving (1 cloud and ¾ cup berries): 154 calories, 2 g protein, 13 g carbs, 3 g fiber, 8 g total sugar, 11 g fat, 7 g saturated fat, 13 mg sodium

Strawberry Cheesecake Bites

Makes 4 servings

PREP TIME: 15 minutes ● **TOTAL TIME:** 15 minutes

16 strawberries

4 ounces light cream cheese

4 ounces 0% plain Greek yogurt

4 tablespoons confectioners' sugar

1 teaspoon vanilla extract

¼ cup crushed graham cracker crumbs

1. Hollow out each strawberry using a paring knife or strawberry corer.

2. Using a blender or mixer, mix the cream cheese, yogurt, sugar, and vanilla together for 2 minutes, or until well combined.

3. Pour the mixture into a plastic freezer bag. Snip off one corner and pipe about 1 tablespoon of filling into each strawberry.

4. Dip the top of each strawberry in the graham cracker crumbs.

Nutrition per serving (4 strawberries): 166 calories, 7 g protein, 21 g carbs, 2 g fiber, 14 g total sugar, 6 g fat, 3 g saturated fat, 132 mg sodium

Pinto Bean Brownies

Makes 20 brownies

PREP TIME: 15 minutes ● **TOTAL TIME:** 50 minutes

½ cup whole wheat flour

¾ cup granulated sugar

¾ cup unsweetened cocoa

⅓ cup firmly packed dark brown sugar

½ teaspoon baking powder

1 teaspoon instant coffee (optional)

⅛ teaspoon salt

¾ cup dark chocolate chips (60% cacao or higher), divided

1 can (15 ounces) pinto beans, rinsed and drained

⅓ cup fat-free milk

3 tablespoons canola or coconut oil

1 tablespoon vanilla extract

4 egg whites, lightly beaten

1. Preheat the oven to 350°F. Coat a 9" × 9" baking pan with cooking spray.

2. In a large bowl, combine the flour, granulated sugar, cocoa, brown sugar, baking powder, coffee (if using), and salt and whisk to fully combine.

3. Place ½ cup of the chocolate chips in a small microwaveable bowl. Microwave on medium power for 30 seconds. Stir and repeat in 30-second increments for 2 minutes total, or until fully melted and smooth.

4. In a blender or food processor, combine the beans, milk, oil, vanilla, egg whites, and the melted chocolate. Blend or process for 1 minute, or until smooth. Add to the flour mixture and stir until smooth. Gently stir in the remaining ¼ cup chocolate chips.

5. Pour the batter into the baking pan. Bake for 30 to 35 minutes, or until the brownies are firm and don't jiggle in the center when nudged.

Nutrition per serving (one 2" × 2" brownie): 150 calories, 3 g protein, 23 g carbs, 2 g fiber, 14 g total sugar, 6 g fat, 2 g saturated fat, 59 mg sodium

Notes: You can use unsweetened almond, coconut, hemp, rice, or soy milk in place of the fat-free milk, if you prefer.

PHASE 4

Mini Banana Cream Pie

Makes 4 servings

PREP TIME: 5 minutes ● **TOTAL TIME:** 15 minutes

¼ cup rolled oats
¼ cup walnuts
Pinch of ground
    cinnamon
1 tablespoon honey
¼ cup heavy cream
1 teaspoon sugar
1 banana, sliced

1. Preheat the oven to 300°F.

2. In a blender, combine the oats, walnuts, and cinnamon. Pulse about 10 times until the mixture resembles fine crumbs. Add the honey and pulse about 5 more times until the mixture comes together into a smooth ball.

3. Divide the mixture into 4 pieces. Press each piece into the bottom of a 6-cup nonstick muffin tin, extending the mixture about ¼" up the side of each tin. Bake for 5 minutes, or until golden. Remove from the oven and slip each crust out onto a cooling rack. Cool for 5 minutes.

4. Whip the cream in a medium bowl using a whisk attachment of a mixer, until soft peaks form. Add the sugar and whip again until stiff peaks form. Place one-quarter of the sliced banana and 1 tablespoon of the whipped cream onto each crust.

Nutrition per serving (1 mini pie): 162 calories, 2 g protein, 18 g carbs, 2 g fiber, 10 g total sugar, 10 g fat, 4 g saturated fat, 7 mg sodium

PHASE 4

Mini Berry Turnovers

Makes 4 servings

PREP TIME: 15 minutes ● **TOTAL TIME:** 25 minutes

½ cup mixed berries, frozen and thawed, drained
1 tablespoon maple syrup
1 tablespoon sugar
¼ teaspoon ground cinnamon
20 (3") wonton wrappers
2 teaspoons butter, melted

1. Preheat the oven to 350°F. Line a large baking sheet with parchment paper.

2. Gently mash the berries with a fork. Mix with the maple syrup. Drain the excess liquid from the berry mixture into a small dish.

3. In a small bowl, mix the sugar and cinnamon.

4. Place a wonton wrapper on a cutting board. Dip your finger in water and gently run it along the perimeter of the wonton wrapper. Place a scant teaspoon of berry mixture in the center of the wrapper and fold two diagonal corners toward each other to form a triangle. Press the edges together to seal in the fruit mixture and transfer to the baking sheet. Continue this process with the remaining 19 wrappers.

5. Brush each filled wonton with butter and sprinkle with a generous pinch of the cinnamon mixture.

6. Bake for 10 minutes, or until the edges are crispy and golden. Serve with the reserved berry juice as a dipping sauce or drizzle.

Nutrition per serving (5 wontons and 1½ teaspoons berry juice): 168 calories, 4 g protein, 32 g carbs, 1 g fiber, 7 g total sugar, 3 g fat, 1 g saturated fat, 230 mg sodium

THE SUGAR SMART WORKOUT

On the path to the sweet life, as you shed your sugar belly, you're bound to find that some of your old ideas melt away, too. One idea that is past its shelf life is that exercise is hard, boring, sweaty drudgery and less rewarding than scarfing cookie dough from the tube.

If that sentiment about sums it up for you, I understand. Like you, I lived through the feel-the-burn, no-pain-no-gain 1980s and 1990s—the Dark Buns of Steel Age of Exercise, you might say. But if you can be open to a new way of thinking about exercise, you just might develop an entirely new perspective. In a life of chronic stress and constant doing for others, exercise is your time to turn off your smartphone, walk away from the everyday demands of life, and do *you*. You're off the clock, free to ponder life's eternal mysteries or work out everyday vexations or marvel at the elegant machinery that is your body–and, believe it or not, grab a sweet hit of joy.

Essayist and literary critic C. S. Lewis observed, "We are not bodies with souls, but rather souls with bodies." Exercise is a way to bring them together. In a very real sense, people who exercise regularly–whether they walk, run, Zumba, or do yoga–are tending their lives along with their bodies. We all know someone who raves about how their daily walk or run or gym time has changed their life. If you open your mind to the rewards of exercise that don't involve the scale, and seek pleasure in moving your body, that someone can be you.

The rewards of the Sugar Smart Workout will show on the outside in ways you and your doctor can see and measure: a slimmer body, a flatter belly, better blood sugar control, and a reduced risk of diabetes and heart disease (or better control of these conditions if you already have them). But the extra perks of regular exercise–a more sparkly outlook on life, energy to burn, self-confidence, an increased appetite for pleasure–radiate outward and inform your whole life. It's no exaggeration to say that a strong, fit, vital body is your ticket to a life of pleasure, fulfillment, even adventure and a sense of accomplishment. Gayle, one of our test panelists, walked a half marathon (13.1 miles) while she was following the Sugar Smart Diet–and finished in just over $3\frac{1}{2}$ hours. "That was a personal best for me," she says, "I was so proud of myself."

FOR SPEEDY RESULTS, JUST ADD EXERCISE

Truth be told, if you followed the Sugar Smart Diet without working out, you would still lose weight and reset your sugar thermostat. But when it comes to controlling sugar cravings and blood sugar levels, you just can't beat the effects of exercise. You will simply see faster, better results, as the research shows.

- If your main goal is to shrink your belly, you should know that exercise targets visceral fat better than diet alone. A study of 209 women and men on low-calorie diets, published in the *International Journal of Obesity*, found that those who exercised lost 30 percent more belly fat than those who didn't.

- If you struggle to stick to a diet, exercise appears to suppress the desire to eat by giving your brain a healthier option. A study of 30 people, published in the *Journal of Applied Physiology*, found that a single bout of exercise reduced the response of nerve cells in the brain's reward regions.
- If you have diabetes, exercise has been found to reduce the need for diabetes medications. In one study published in *Diabetes Care*, people with diabetes lifted weights for 35 minutes, three times a week. In 4 months, 72 percent were able to reduce their dose of diabetes medications.
- Exercise also helps you keep the weight off once you lose it. Data from the National Weight Control Registry, a long-running study of people who have lost at least 30 pounds and kept them off for one year or longer, shows that 90 percent of people who have maintained their weight loss cite exercise as one of their strategies.

Those are compelling findings—and if you like to walk, you're in luck. Recent research into the effects of walking on health have yielded similarly spectacular conclusions.

- Brisk walking can lower the risk of high blood pressure, high cholesterol, and diabetes.
- A long, brisk morning walk can rein in appetite and reduce cravings all day.
- A 15-minute stroll after meals can head off undesirable post-meal blood sugar spikes.

Amazing! I knew we had to work these findings into the Sugar Smart exercise plan. So I reached out to Michele Stanten, *Prevention*'s former fitness director, walking coach, and certified trainer. Michele developed a fun and flexible workout that's as simple as it is effective.

My main goal is to get you moving. If you already have a workout routine you enjoy, that's terrific. If you'd prefer to stick with your walking-only routine, that's good too. But I encourage you to take a close look at Michele's plan. It's designed to help you burn fat, build muscle, and beat stress. All three elements will help shrink your sugar belly and lower your blood sugar levels. But Michele keeps it real, too. No need for pricey equipment, special clothing, or even a gym membership. And although I'm asking you to devote 45 minutes, 6 days a week, to exercise, you can break it up into 15-minute chunks throughout the day. So give it a shot! The way I see it, you have nothing to lose except more belly.

THE SUGAR SMART WORKOUT BASICS

The Sugar Smart Workout is built around three main components. Cardiovascular exercise, or *cardio,* conditions your heart and lungs as it burns calories and blasts fat. *Strength training* builds calorie-burning muscle and boosts your body's sensitivity to insulin as it strengthens your bones. *Easy yoga* improves flexibility, and, unlike other forms of stretching, can help build muscle while both relaxing and invigorating your body. It also helps keep stress in check, which in turn makes people prone to emotional eating less likely to reach for sugar.

Team up these different forms of exercise, all with multiple benefits, and the results speak for themselves: a stronger, slimmer, healthier body. Muscles use glucose as fuel, so any type of physical activity can reduce blood sugar levels. Exercise also helps the body use insulin more efficiently, which in turn helps the body use more glucose. And improved response to insulin means fewer blood sugar spikes that encourage your body to pack away extra fat.

Why Do Cardio?

Activities that raise your heart rate, like brisk walking, running, swimming, Zumba, and dancing, help melt the just-under-the-skin fluff that pads your hips, thighs, butt, chest, arms, and back. Cardio keeps a sugar belly gone, too: Just 80 minutes a week slowed weight gain in 97 overweight women and stopped them from regaining visceral fat a year after weight loss, according to study in the journal *Obesity.*

Anything that keeps you moving counts as cardio. You can walk outside or use the stationary bike, treadmill, or elliptical trainer you have at home or at your gym. You can ride your bicycle. Swim. Take up fencing. Join a ballet or

Walk This Way

Of course you know how to walk. But when you walk for fitness, using proper form can increase your speed, which will maximize your calorie burn. Each time you step outside, practice this checklist of proper techniques. If you're walking on a treadmill, the same techniques apply.

Lower Body

- Many people trying to walk briskly take overly long strides, which can actually slow you down. Instead, take shorter, quicker steps, rolling from heel to toes and pushing off with your toes.
- Keep your torso upright. Leaning too far forward or back will slow you down.
- It's okay for your waist to twist as you walk. Trying to reduce the movement of your hips will slow you down.

Upper Body

- Keep your head upright, your eyes straight ahead, and your shoulders and neck relaxed.
- Keep your elbows at 90 degrees and your hands relaxed.
- Swing your arms forward and back, and keep them close to your body.
- To increase your pace, speed up your arm swing. Your legs will follow!

tap-dancing class. Dance in your living room to the Beatles, Bruno Mars, or Beyoncé. Take a Zumba or a Spinning class. Do an exercise DVD. Cross-country ski. Hike in the woods. The options are endless.

The Benefits of Strength Training

You, lift weights? Absolutely! There's no need to strain or grunt. Nor will you Hulk up, no matter how hard you work out, because women don't have enough of the hormones needed to build man-size muscles. What strength training will give you is a revved-up metabolism. After around age 35, if you're not building or maintaining muscle, you're losing it–and that can affect both your blood sugar and your weight in not-so-positive ways. Strength training can counteract the gradual age-related decline in muscle.

Every pound of muscle you add boosts your resting metabolic rate, or RMR, because muscle is more metabolically active than fat (i.e., requires more energy). That means you burn calories when you're doing absolutely nothing. Because muscle is denser and more compact than fat, it's possible to end up a few pounds heavier but wearing smaller sizes!

More muscle also means better blood sugar control and a reduced risk of type 2 diabetes. In a study of 30,022 men published in *JAMA Internal Medicine*, those who did even small amounts of strength training regularly saw a

Strength-Training Basics

If you're new to strength training, the process can seem a bit intimidating. But it's simpler than you think. These guidelines, which cover proper form and breathing techniques, can help you learn the ropes. Keep in mind that it's normal to experience slight muscle soreness or fatigue. It should fade after a week or two.

- The word *rep* is short for repetition. Each time you lift and lower a dumbbell, or roll your upper body up off the floor and then lower it back down, you've completed one repetition. A specific number of repetitions is called a set.
- The amount of weight you start with depends on how fit you are. But most people underestimate their strength and fitness level. If you can breeze through a set without fatigue, your weights are too light. The last rep should feel hard. If you can barely get through the last few reps of an exercise, though, you need a lighter weight. You may need different weight amounts for different exercises.
- Perform the moves slowly and with focus. Take 3 seconds to lift or push a weight into place, hold the position for 1 second, and take another 3 seconds to return to your starting position.
- Don't hold your breath. This can cause changes in blood pressure, especially for people with heart disease. Rather, inhale slowly through your nose and exhale slowly through your mouth.
- Exhale as you lift or push, and inhale as you relax.
- Use smooth, steady movements. To prevent injury, don't jerk or thrust weights into position, and avoid "locking" your knees and elbows.
- Don't perform the same strength routine 2 days in a row. Alternate the Total Body Toner and the Sugar Belly Blaster so that your muscles have time to repair themselves.

25 percent reduction in risk. By building your muscles, you're building added protection against diabetes and the host of health-threatening conditions that come along with it.

Michele has created two strength-training routines: the Total Body Toner and the Sugar Belly Blaster, and you'll alternate between the two. The Total Body Toner shapes and strengthens your muscles from head to toe in just four moves. You target multiple body parts—like your arms and legs simultaneously—and you go through the moves deliberately but quickly, doing the four moves once all the way through and then repeating the series two more times. This is a better fat-blasting strategy than doing three sets of one move before going on to the next. And I saved the best part for last: You can do it anywhere, and you're done in 15 minutes.

The crunch is dead! Long live core training! The Sugar Belly Blaster consists of five moves that not only flatten your belly, but go beyond your abs to tone and tighten your entire core, which includes the muscles of your back, sides, pelvis, and butt. Core training helps you develop what exercise physiologists call functional fitness—the ability to sail through everyday tasks without injury or discomfort. Your core comes into play every time you move, whether you're taking a basket of laundry upstairs, carrying groceries into the house, or washing your car. When you exercise your core, you also tone your abs, keep your lower back strong, and improve your posture. Like the Total Body Toner, it's something you can do anywhere in a fast 15 minutes.

Yoga for Muscles, Mind, and Belly

When you're writing a book about sugar, people seem to feel the need to confess their "sugar sins." One of my coworkers, a paragon of healthy eating, admitted that she plows through package after package of "kid candy"–gummy bears, Smarties, Twizzlers–when she's on deadline. Friends have told me that they soothe themselves after a hectic day by plopping down in front of the TV with a pint of ice cream, a bag of cookies, or a bar (or two) of chocolate. When you understand what's happening biologically, it really doesn't come as any surprise that we tend to reach for sugar (and fat) when we're under pressure.

Stress raises your body's production of the hormones adrenaline and corti-sol. These hormones prepare your body to react to a threat: to fight or flee. Your heartbeat increases, your digestive system slows down so more blood and oxygen flow to your muscles, your vision becomes acute—and your insulin levels rise, triggering the body to store fat rather than burn it, in case you need extra energy in the future. So with all that going on, your appetite increases, specifically for sugar and fatty foods, which of course are concentrated sources of energy.

Putting It All Together

These sample weekly schedules show you how you can mix up the workouts.

Single workout sessions

Day 1	Day 2	Day 3	Day 4	Day 5	Day 6	Day 7
45 min cardio	30 min cardio & Total Body Toner	45 min cardio	30 min cardio & Sugar Belly Blaster	30 min cardio & Total Body Toner	15 min cardio, Sugar Belly Blaster & Energizing Yoga	Rest

Three short workout sessions a day

	Day 1	Day 2	Day 3	Day 4	Day 5	Day 6	Day 7
Morning	15 min cardio	15 min cardio	15 min cardio	Rest	15 min cardio	15 min cardio	Energizing Yoga
Afternoon	15 min cardio	15 min cardio	15 min cardio	Rest	15 min cardio	15 min cardio	Sugar Belly Blaster
Evening	15 min cardio	Total Body Toner	Sugar Belly Blaster	Rest	Total Body Toner	Relaxing Yoga	15 min cardio

Combination of single and short workout sessions

	Day 1	Day 2	Day 3	Day 4	Day 5	Day 6	Day 7
Morning	30 min cardio & Sugar Belly Blaster	15 min cardio	15 min cardio	Rest	30 min cardio & Total Body Toner	30 min cardio	Energizing Yoga
Afternoon		15 min cardio	15 min cardio	Rest			15 min cardio
Evening		Total Body Toner	Sugar Belly Blaster	Rest		Relaxing Yoga	15 min cardio

What's more, cortisol triggers the storage of belly fat. That's because belly fat is the first fat your body draws on for fuel when it's needed. So if you're under fire, it makes sense that your body would want to make sure you have some fat in reserve for the future. If the stress response happens occasionally, like when you need to run from an attacker, jump out of the way of an oncoming car, or escape a burning building, no big deal. But when stress is chronic, you end up in a cycle of cravings, eating, and belly fat storage.

Here's where a relaxing mind-body exercise like yoga can help. The deep breathing, muscle relaxation, and focus involved help to shut down the stress response. That's why Michele and I thought it was so important to include yoga routines in the Sugar Smart Workout. Do them regularly and they can train your brain to respond less frantically to day-to-day pressure. As with our strength routines, we have two yoga options for you. **Energizing Yoga** improves circulation and wakes up your brain and body. It helps you feel calm, strong, and ready for action. **Relaxing Yoga** is more peaceful and is perfect for unwinding after a long or tough day.

THE SUGAR SMART WORKOUT: WHAT TO DO

You'll be combining cardio, strength training, and yoga into workout sessions that total 45 minutes of exercise a day, 6 days a week. The most important thing is that you get your workouts in, but if you want to fine-tune your results, you might want to think about the timing of your sessions. Studies have shown that longer morning workouts can help control cravings and appetite, while a 15-minute exercise session performed about 30 minutes after each meal (breakfast, lunch, and dinner) has a more favorable impact on blood sugar levels.

Option #1: Work Out in the Morning, Curb Appetite All Day

Those daily protein-packed breakfasts should be putting a huge dent in your sugar cravings. However, if you always feel hungry no matter how filling your meal, add a brisk 45-minute walk or a 30-minute walk paired with a 15-minute strength or yoga session to your morning routine. It may help rein in your appetite for the rest of the day.

In a study published in the journal *Medicine & Science in Sports & Exercise*, researchers wanted to examine the effect of a single exercise session on what scientists call "food motivation" and what everyone else calls "the desire to eat." So over two separate days, they measured the neural activity in the brains of 18 average-weight and 17 overweight women as they viewed images of food on computer screens. (Neurons in the brain do things like "talk" to each other and process information. Those things are called neural activity, and that's what the team was measuring.)

On the first day, the women walked briskly on treadmills for 45 minutes. Immediately afterward, electrodes were attached to their scalps, and an EEG machine measured their neural activity while they looked at pictures of food and flowers. (The flower pictures served as a control.)

The same experiment was conducted a week later at the same time of the morning, but without the vigorous walk. The women logged what they ate and how much they moved, on both days.

The results? The areas of the women's brains related to attention and emotion were less "turned on" by the pictures of food after they walked, the researchers found. In other words, they had less interest in food following a workout. And in case you were wondering, the logs the women kept revealed that exercise *didn't* lead to overeating later in the day. While more research is needed to determine how long a reduced interest in food can last after exercise, the findings seem to stand the "exercise makes you hungrier" claim on its head.

Option #2: Exercise after Meals, Manage Blood Sugar All Day

Does your after-dinner "nightcap" consist of curling up on the couch and firing up Netflix? That's totally understandable, but taking a 15-minute post-meal walk or doing some strength moves while you watch TV—especially after your evening meal—can help regulate your blood sugar and reduce your risk of type 2 diabetes, research has found.

In the study, published in the journal *Diabetes Care*, 10 healthy seniors spent three 48-hour spans in a lab. During each session, participants ate the same foods and followed one of three exercise routines: They either walked at an easy-to-moderate pace on a treadmill for 15 minutes after each meal, walked 45 minutes in the morning, or walked 45 minutes in the afternoon. In each of the three scenarios, the participants' blood sugar levels were tracked 24/7 with "continuous glucose monitoring," in which a tiny sensor inserted under the skin kept track of glucose levels.

Walking Is as Good as Running to Ward Off Diabetes

Think running has the edge over walking when it comes to lowering chronic disease risk? Think again. Brisk walking reduces the risk of diabetes and other major chronic diseases as well as running does, according to a study published in the journal *Arteriosclerosis, Thrombosis, and Vascular Biology*.

Researchers at Lawrence Berkeley National Laboratory in Berkeley, California, collected data from the National Runners' Health Study and the National Walkers' Health Study, which included 33,060 runners and 15,945 walkers, mostly in their forties and fifties.

What they found: The same energy used for moderate-intensity walking and high-intensity running resulted in similar risk reductions for diabetes, high blood pressure, high cholesterol, and heart disease overall, over the study's 6 years. Unlike previous studies, the researchers assessed walking and running expenditure by distance, not by time. This means that the farther the runners ran and the walkers walked, the more their health benefits increased. If the amount of energy expended was the same between the two groups, then the health benefits were comparable.

Look at the data the study crunched, and you can see that walking walks away a winner:

- Diabetes: Running lowered the risk by 12.1 percent; walking, by 12.3 percent.
- High blood pressure: Running reduced the risk by 4.2 percent; walking, by 7.2 percent.
- High cholesterol: Running reduced the risk by 4.3 percent; walking, by 7 percent.
- Heart disease: Running decreased the risk by 4.5 percent; walking, by 9.3 percent.

The short post-meal walks were more effective at regulating blood sugar levels for up to 24 hours, the study found. This is key, because typically, your body can handle the normal blood sugar fluctuations that occur about 30 minutes after you eat. But as you get older (or if you're inactive throughout the day), your body doesn't react as efficiently, which leads to prolonged high blood sugar levels. The same thing happens if you are insulin sensitive or if you have diabetes. Over time, as you've learned, chronically high blood sugar can heighten your risk of getting type 2 diabetes and heart disease.

The study found that the most effective time to go for a postmeal walk was after dinner. The exaggerated rise in blood sugar after this meal–often the largest of the day–can last well into the night and early morning. This was curbed significantly as soon as the volunteers hit the treadmill. So, if you can only wedge one of the three "bursts" into your day, make it the evening one.

What if you want to control appetite and lower your blood sugar level? You can mix and match your workout routine on different days.

TOTAL BODY TONER

Perform this routine at least twice a week. Do each exercise for the recommended number of reps, then repeat the series of exercises two more times. Use a weight that leaves you feeling fatigued at the end of each exercise. You can use a different amount of weight for different exercises, if needed. If you become tired on the second time through the series of exercises, you may need to decrease the weight for your last go-round.

● Chest Pump

Lie on your back with your knees bent, feet flat on the floor. Hold the dumbbells by your shoulders, elbows pointing out to the sides **[A]**. Straighten your arms and press the dumbbells up over your chest **[B]**. When your arms are fully extended, lift your shoulders off the floor to press the dumbbells a little higher **[C]**. Hold for a second. Lower your shoulders, keeping your arms straight, then bend your arms to return to the start position. Do 10 times.

Make it easier: *Skip the shoulder lift.*

● Side Lunge with a Curl and Press

Stand with your feet together and hold the dumbbells by your shoulders, arms bent and elbows pointing down **[A]**. Step your left foot out to the side and bend your left leg to sit back while keeping the right leg straight. As you lunge, extend your arms and lower the dumbbells **[B]**. Press into your left foot and straighten your leg to stand up. As you do that, bend your elbows and curl the dumbbells toward your shoulders, then press them overhead as you bring your feet back together **[C]**. Do 10 times, then repeat the lunge on the opposite side.

Make it easier: *Break up the exercise into two separate moves: Do the side lunges, only going as low as is comfortable for your knees. Then stand with your feet about hip-width apart and perform a biceps curl followed by an overhead press.*

Hinge and Row

Stand with your feet about hip-width apart, holding the dumbbells with your arms at your sides. Keeping your abs tight and your chest lifted, bend at the hips and slowly lower until your torso is about parallel to the floor and the dumbbells hang beneath your shoulders **[A]**. Don't round your back. Bend your elbows and pull the dumbbells up toward your rib cage **[B]**. Lower the dumbbells and then stand back up. Do 10 times.

Make it easier: *Do single-arm rows with a chair. Holding one dumbbell, bend forward and place your free hand on the seat of a chair, then perform rows with the opposite arm.*

● Upswing

Stand with your feet about hip-width apart and hold a dumbbell down in front of you with both hands. Bend your hips and knees and sit back into a squat, lowering the dumbbell to the outside of your left leg **[A]**. As you stand up, raise the dumbbell diagonally across your body, keeping your arms extended, and rotate your torso to the right **[B]**. Do 10 times, then repeat, swinging your arms in the opposite direction.

A

B

SUGAR BELLY BLASTER

Do this series of exercises in order 2 times through. Rest and/or stretch for 30 to 60 seconds between exercises. Do this routine at least twice a week.

● Pelvic Tilts

Lie faceup on the floor with your knees bent and feet flat on the floor **[A]**. Pull your navel toward your spine and curl your tailbone up toward the ceiling, lifting your hips slightly off the floor **[B]**. Hold for a second, then release **[C]**. Do 20 times.

> This is a deep, subtle move. You aren't looking for a lot of lift, but rather full contact of your lower back to the mat.

● Shifting Plank

Hold a pushup position, balancing on the balls of your feet and toes and your palms, hands directly beneath your shoulders **[A]**. Shift your weight forward **[B]**, to the left, and to the right **[C]**, without moving your hands. Hold each position for up to a count of 5 and return to center in between each shift. Do 3 times.

Make it easier: *Hold the plank without shifting.*

Up the challenge: *Raise one foot off the floor and then shift.*

● Bicycle

Lie faceup on the floor with your knees bent, feet flat on the floor, and hands behind your head. Raise your head and shoulders off the floor and twist to the right, bringing your right knee in toward your left elbow and extending your left leg at about a 45-degree angle. Lower and switch sides, twisting to the left and bringing your left knee and right elbow toward each other. Do 20 times, alternating sides. Each side counts as 1 rep.

Make it easier: *Lift only one leg while keeping the other foot on the floor.*

Up the challenge: *Lower your extended leg so it is closer to the floor.*

● Seated Balance

Sit with your legs bent, feet on the floor, and grasp your hands behind your thighs. Shift your weight back onto your sitz bones as you raise your feet off the floor so your calves are parallel to the floor. Once you've found your point of balance, extend your arms out in front of you. Keep your chest lifted and don't round your back. Hold for 1 minute. If needed, you can bring your legs down and take a break. Then hold again until your holding time adds up to 1 minute.

Make it easier: *Lift your feet only a few inches off the floor. You can even keep the tips of your toes on the floor, if needed.*

Up the challenge: *Straighten your legs so your toes are pointing toward the ceiling.*

● Standing Balance

Balancing on one leg, swing your arms forward and back as vigorously as possible **[A]**. Next, alternate reaching one arm up overhead and lean to that side **[B]**. Then rotate your torso from side to side **[C]**. Do each of these moves 20 times, alternating arms. Each swing or twist counts as 1 rep. Switch legs and repeat. Finally, extend your arms overhead and diagonally to the left **[D]**, and pull your arms and right leg toward each other and then apart **[E]**. Do 10 times, then switch legs.

Make it easier: *Take a break, putting your foot down in between moves.*

Up the challenge: *Stand on a pillow as you perform the moves.*

● Mountain

Stand tall with your feet together, toes forward, and arms at your sides, palms in. Lift your chest and drop your shoulders back and down. Breathe deeply for 1 minute, pressing your feet into the floor and reaching the crown of your head toward the ceiling.

● Arm Circles

Inhale and raise your arms out to the sides, palms up, and circle them overhead. Exhale and lower them back to your sides. Repeat Arm Circles 4 more times, but don't lower your arms on the final time through. Instead move into Forward Bend.

● Forward Bend

Exhale and reach your arms out in front of you, palms down, as you bend forward from your hips, keeping your back flat and chest lifted as you lower until you're about parallel to the floor. Then round your back and place your hands on your thighs, shins, feet, or floor—whatever is most comfortable **[A]**. Bend your knees slightly if you feel any strain. Inhale as you flatten your back and lift your head and chest up to look forward **[B]**. Exhale and round your back to look at your legs. Inhale to stand up, circling your arms out to the sides and overhead, and then down to your sides.

Repeat Arm Circles and Forward Bend together 4 more times, but don't stand up on the final time through. Instead move into Plank.

● Plank

Inhale and bend your knees and place your hands on the floor alongside your feet. Step your feet back one at a time and balance on your hands, your toes, and the balls of your feet. Your hands should be directly beneath your shoulders. Your heels, ankles, butt, spine, shoulders, neck, and head should all be in line.

● Upward-Facing Dog

Exhale and bend your elbows back, keeping your arms close to your body, and slowly lower yourself to the floor, like you're doing a pushup **[A]**. With your toes pointed and palms on the floor in front of your shoulders, inhale and gently lift your upper body off the floor as far as comfortably possible, opening up your chest and pressing the tops of your feet into the floor **[B]**. Use your back muscles, not your hands, to lift.

A

B

Downward-Facing Dog

As you exhale, flip your feet so you're on your toes and the balls of your feet. Lift your hips toward the ceiling and press back into an inverted V position. Hold for 5 breaths. On your next breath, walk your feet toward your hands, moving into a Forward Bend. Inhale and flatten your back, lifting your head and chest up as you look forward. Exhale and round your back, looking at your legs. Inhale to stand up, circling your arms out to the sides and overhead, and then down to your sides into Mountain pose.

Repeat the poses from Mountain through Downward-Facing Dog 4 more times (but without the repeats above). Remain in Downward-Facing Dog on the final time through. Then move into Crescent Lunge.

Crescent Lunge

Inhale and lift your left leg behind you. As you exhale, swing it forward, stepping your left foot in between your hands. Inhale and bend your left knee, keeping it directly over your ankle, and raise your arms overhead. Toes point forward and your right heel is lifted off the floor.

● Warrior 2

Exhale and lower your arms, turning your body toward the right, lowering your right heel, and angling your right toes toward the back right corner of the mat. Reach your arms out to the sides from your fingertips, looking toward your left hand.

● Reverse Warrior

As you exhale, circle your right arm, placing your right hand on your right leg, and raise your left arm overhead, looking toward your left hand. Circle both hands down onto the floor on either side of your left foot. Step your left foot back into Plank pose.

Repeat the poses from Plank (without the repeats), but lift your right leg when you are in Downward-Facing Dog in order to perform Crescent Lunge on the opposite side. Then from Plank, do Upward- and Downward-Facing Dogs again, return to the Forward Bend, and finish in Mountain pose, breathing deeply for at least a minute.

Seated Twists & Bends

Sit cross-legged with your hands out to your sides and your fingertips lightly touching the floor. Inhale and raise your arms overhead. As you exhale, twist to the left and lower your arms so the right one is in front of you (in the 12 o'clock position, if you were sitting on a clock) and the left one slightly behind you (in the 7 to 8 o'clock position) **[A]**. Repeat twisting to the opposite side. Do 20 total, alternating sides. Face forward and recross your legs so the opposite one is in front. Reach your left arm up overhead and bend to the right as you inhale **[B]**, then return to start position as you exhale. Repeat to the opposite side. Do 20 total, alternating sides. Walk your hands out in front of you and fold over your legs as far as comfortable **[C]**. Hold for 8 deep breaths. Walk your hands back in and sit up. Then recross your legs and repeat.

● Cat Cow Stretches

Shift forward so you are on all fours with your hands beneath your shoulders, your knees beneath your hips, and your head in line with your spine. Inhale and lift your chest and tailbone toward the ceiling to arch your back **[A]**. Exhale and round your back, tucking your tailbone and dropping your chin toward your chest **[B]**. As you inhale, sit back onto your heels, stretching your hips back and your arms forward **[C]**. Come back up to the start position as you exhale. Do 10 times. Next, raise your right arm straight up to the ceiling, looking at your hand. Then sweep your arm down under your body and behind your left arm so your head and shoulder rest on the mat **[D]**. Hold for 3 to 5 breaths. Come back up and repeat with your left arm.

● Knee Hugs

Lie faceup on the floor and pull one leg into your chest, feeling the stretch in your back. You can lift your head off the floor and toward your knee for a deep stretch. Hold for 8 deep breaths. Release your leg and repeat with the opposite leg. Then pull both knees into your chest. Hold each position for 8 deep breaths.

● Corpse Pose

Lie faceup on the floor with your arms extended and slightly angled away from your body, palms up. Your legs should be at a comfortable distance apart and relaxed so your feet roll out. Close your eyes and focus on your breathing for at least 3 minutes. You can put on some relaxing music or focus on a positive phrase such as "I am getting healthy" to enhance the effects. Feel free to remain in this pose as long as you like.

APPENDIX A

Dining Out the Sugar Smart Way

A milkshake stuffed with *an entire slice* of apple pie, which packs more than 2 days' worth of sugar (13 teaspoons). A breakfast platter of deep-fried steak, pancakes, hash browns, eggs, gravy, and syrup, swimming in 11 teaspoons of the sweet stuff.

They don't make jeans big enough for sugar-soaked fare like this. (We won't even get into the calories, fat, refined carbs, and sodium.) Yet that's what's on the menu at some of the nation's top restaurant chains.

From page 1, we've told the hard truth: You can't change the glut of sugar in the American food supply–or in its restaurants. What you *can* do: Get sugar smart. Make healthy choices that lower your sugar intake, protect your health, and shrink your sugar belly, even if you dine out frequently.

The bad news first: Chain restaurants and fast-food joints don't make it easy to eat sugar smart. A study published in the *American Journal of Preventive Medicine* found that the nutritional quality of meals at McDonald's and other fast-food chains has risen by only 3 points in 14 years. That is, their overall score on the USDA's Healthy Eating Index, which measures healthy eating on a 100-point scale, has inched from 45 to 48.

An overall score of 48 out of 100? That's a big, fat F. And that diet score is even lower than the average American's score of 55, which is nothing to brag about, either.

Now for the good news: You can improve your personal healthy eating score. Today. Large chains are mandated to make nutrition information available to the public, which often causes them to rethink their menus. This means healthier options and smaller portions. Even better news: While most chain restaurants contain plenty of sugar bombs, many offer healthy options for the sugar smart.

Still, hidden sugars in restaurant foods can be difficult to detect. So this appendix does the work for you: It reveals the best—and worst—menu options at more than two dozen popular restaurants and pizza chains. Each restaurant listing features five Sugar Bombs (some of the highest-sugar items on the menu) and comparable Smarter Choices (featuring some of the lower-sugar options). Each Sugar Bomb listing is arranged by highest sugar content to lowest, while the Smarter Choices are ordered from least amount of sugar to most. There's also a section on how to choose low-sugar items when you head out for Italian, Chinese, or other ethnic cuisine. (For more sugar-smart dietary options, check out "Grocery Shopping the Sugar Smart Way" on page 300.)

Ordering lower-sugar options when you dine out just got a whole lot easier. Let's begin with the ground rules of sugar-smart eating.

STICK TO THE BASICS FOR SUGAR SMART SUCCESS

On the Sugar Smart Diet, you lower your consumption of added sugars, not your expectations of dining out deliciously. The following strategies can ensure that you enjoy a special meal without undoing your progress (or the button on your jeans).

Plan for indulgences. If you're dying for a piece of cheesecake from your favorite restaurant, follow Phase 1 the day before your meal and bank your sugar allotment. The same recommendation applies when you know you'll want a slice of cake at a wedding or a relative's irresistible holiday dish.

Order before you go. Most restaurants have Web sites and post their menus online. Review the menu, make your low-sugar selections, and "order" before you go.

Once seated, don't open the menu. Just rattle off your order. If you can ask for a party or holiday menu in advance, adopt a similar strategy. This way, you're not overwhelmed by the choices on the table or at the buffet.

Choose low-fat options. For flavor with less fat, order seafood, skinless poultry, lean meat, and even veggies grilled, broiled, baked, steamed, or poached. Also, request that the chef reduce or eliminate any butter or oil used to prepare your entrée. And remember that trick about requesting fatty salad dressings on the side and dipping only the tines of your fork into the dressing? You can use the same trick with gravy or sauces, too. Or simply request your entrée without them.

Box before you eat. Restaurants will typically honor requests that lower the added sugars in their side dishes and entrées. But because restaurant portions are notoriously huge, you'll probably still need to practice portion control. Even whole foods contain calories, and if you eat too much, you're likely to consume unnecessary calories. So practice proactive portion control: Ask your waiter to serve just half of your meal, and box up the other half to take home.

Tote your own dressing. Across the board, the salad dressings at most restaurants can turn even a grilled-chicken salad into a sugar bomb. (Remember, low-calorie or low-fat salad dressings are typically loaded with sugar!) If you opt for a dinner-size salad, either stick to a basic oil-and-vinegar dressing or–if you're brave–bring along your favorite low-sugar bottled dressing. Chances are, neither your server nor the other patrons will bat an eyelash.

SUGAR BOMBS AND SMARTER CHOICES AT 25 FAVORITE EATERIES

Hungry? Get ready to enjoy a healthy, low-sugar meal at one of your favorite fast-food or chain restaurants–without feeling hungry or deprived. To maximize deliciousness and minimize sugar, keep a few things in mind.

1. You already know that most desserts and beverages like sodas, shakes, and smoothies are sugar bombs, but we still listed a few to show you exactly how much sugar they contain.
2. All items listed are the smallest sizes available (except where noted).
3. At big chain restaurants, appetizers are guilty until proven innocent.

ARBY'S

Sugar Bombs

Cherry Turnover: 390 calories, 2 g fiber, 40 g sugars

Arby-Q: 400 calories, 2 g fiber, 23 g sugars

Market Fresh Roast Turkey, Ranch, and Bacon Sandwich: 800 calories, 5 g fiber, 18 g sugars

Market Fresh Roast Turkey and Swiss Sandwich: 700 calories, 5 g fiber, 18 g sugars

French Toast Sticks: 350 calories, 2 g fiber, 16 g sugars

Smarter Choices

Ham, Egg, and Cheese Wrap: 420 calories, 2 g fiber, 1 g sugars

French Dip and Swiss with Au Jus: 540 calories, 2 g fiber, 3 g sugars

Angus Three Cheese and Bacon: 630 calories, 2 g fiber, 4 g sugars

Chopped Farmhouse Salad—Roast Turkey (with Light Italian Dressing): 250 calories, 3 g fiber, 6 g sugars

Roast Beef Classic: 360 calories, 1 g fiber, 6 g sugars

AU BON PAIN

Sugar Bombs

Blueberry Yogurt and Wild Blueberry Parfait: 410 calories, 4 g fiber, 53 g sugars

Turkey Cranberry Brie Sandwich: 720 calories, 12 g fiber, 38 g sugars

Low-Fat Berry Yogurt Muffin: 300 calories, 2 g fiber, 32 g sugars

Turkey, Apple, Brie, and Spinach Salad with Fat-Free Raspberry Dressing: 480 calories, 8 g fiber, 27 g sugars

Tomato Basil Bisque (medium): 240 calories, 2 g fiber, 17 g sugars

Smarter Choices

Whole Wheat Skinny Bagel: 90 calories, 6 g fiber, 1 g sugars

Tuscan Grilled Cheese Sandwich: 620 calories, 2 g fiber, 2 g sugars

Chicken Gumbo Soup (medium): 190 calories, 2 g fiber, 2 g sugars

Caesar Asiago Salad: 180 calories, 4 g fiber, 3 g sugars

Chocolate and Crème Torsade: 230 calories, 2 g fiber, 10 g sugars

BOSTON MARKET

Sugar Bombs

Sweet Potato Casserole: 450 calories, 4 g fiber, 59 g sugars

Cinnamon Apples: 240 calories, 4 g fiber, 49 g sugars

St. Louis Style BBQ Ribs (¼ rack): 590 calories, 1 g fiber, 29 g sugars

Pulled BBQ Chicken Sandwich: 620 calories, 4 g fiber, 24 g sugars

Pastry-Top Chicken or Turkey Pot Pie: 800/820 calories, 5 g fiber, 7 g sugars

Smarter Choices

Turkey Breast (regular): 200 calories, 0 g fiber, 0 g sugars

Rotisserie Chicken (¼ white, skinless): 220 calories, 0 g fiber, 0 g sugars

Garlic Dill New Potatoes: 100 calories, 2 g fiber, 1 g sugars

Roast Beef Brisket (regular): 230 calories, 0 g fiber, 1 g sugars

Fresh Steamed Vegetables: 80 calories, 3 g fiber, 3 g sugars

BURGER KING

Sugar Bombs

Vanilla Milk Shake (medium): 730 calories, 0 g fiber, 110 g sugars

Brownie Sundae: 530 calories, 2 g fiber, 70 g sugars

BK Ultimate Breakfast Platter: 1,450 calories, 5 g fiber, 41 g sugars

Tendercrisp Chicken, Apple, and Cranberry Garden Fresh Salad with Dressing: 700 calories, 5 g fiber, 37 g sugars

Whopper Sandwich with Cheese: 710 calories, 3 g fiber, 14 g sugars

Smarter Choices

Ranch Grilled Chicken Wrap: 350 calories, 1 g fiber, 1 g sugars

BK Breakfast Muffin Sandwich—Egg and Cheese: 220 calories, 1 g fiber, 2 g sugars

Whopper Jr. Sandwich with Cheese: 380 calories, 2 g fiber, 6 g sugars

2% Latte (medium): 180 calories, 0 g fiber, 12 g sugars

Soft Serve Cup: 140 calories, 0 g fiber, 19 g sugars

CARRABBA'S

Sugar Bombs

Lasagne: 756 calories, 7 g fiber, 18 g sugars

Seasonal Salad—Citrus Arugula Salad with Sirloin, Salmon, Shrimp, or Chicken: 517–857 calories, 16 g fiber, 15 g sugars

Italian Classics: 699 calories, 7 g fiber, 13 g sugars

Mozzarella Marinara Appetizer: 563 calories, 5 g fiber, 8 g sugars

Fire-Roasted Tomato Basil Soup: 246 calories, 2 g fiber, 8 g sugars

Smarter Choices

Grilled Chicken: 179 calories, 0 g fiber, 0 g sugars

Minestrone Soup: 118 calories, 5 g fiber, 0 g sugars

Grilled Salmon: 478 calories, 0 g fiber, 1 g sugars

Caesar Salad (side): 297 calories, 2 g fiber, 1 g sugars

Crab Cakes: 254 calories, 2 g fiber, 2 g sugars

CHILI'S

Sugar Bombs

Caribbean Salad with Grilled Chicken: 700 calories, 8 g fiber, 67 g sugars

Crispy Honey-Chipotle Chicken Crispers: 1,700 calories, 13 g fiber, 57 g sugars

Original Ribs: 1,630 calories, 8 g fiber, 47 g sugars

Triple Dipper Boneless Honey-Chipotle Wings: 670 calories, 2 g fiber, 34 g sugars

Crispy Chicken Tacos: 1,510 calories, 12 g fiber, 33 g sugars

Smarter Choices

Classic Sirloin (6 oz): 320 calories, 0 g fiber, 0 g sugars

Rice and Black Beans: 290 calories, 7 g fiber, 2 g sugars

Spicy Garlic and Lime Shrimp (6 shrimp): 170 calories, 1 g fiber, 3 g sugars

Black Bean Burger Only: 170 calories, 7 g fiber, 3 g sugars

Grilled Chicken Salad: 430 calories, 5 g fiber, 9 g sugars

"Where's My Favorite Restaurant?"

You may be wondering why this appendix doesn't list some of your favorite restaurant chains—places like Applebee's, Olive Garden, and TGI Fridays. We tried, but the chains below either don't include sugar values in their online menus or don't offer online nutrition information for their menu items at all. (We even contacted their media people, but no luck.)

These restaurants include:

- Applebee's
- Baja Fresh
- The Cheesecake Factory
- Cracker Barrel
- Olive Garden
- Red Lobster
- Ruby Tuesday
- Texas Roadhouse
- TGI Fridays

Take heart: You don't have to avoid these restaurants. Simply follow the menu on page 190 to order a meal that fits the guidelines of the Sugar Smart Diet. Or use the interactive nutrition calculators offered by some restaurant chains, like Chipotle Mexican Grill and Red Robin. They're fun to use, and more important, they teach you how to make sugar-smart choices.

For example, Red Robin's online "Customizer" allows you to plug in the items on the menu you'd like to eat; then, the application calculates nutrition values and allows you to add or omit ingredients. For example, a Simply Grilled Chicken Salad contains 539 calories, 8 grams of sugar, 6 grams of fiber, and 46 grams of protein. Omit the cheese, and your meal lightens up to 428 calories, with no changes to fiber and sugar.

Using Chipotle's calculator, you can build your own taco, burrito, burrito bowl, or salad, and it's entirely possible to build a healthy meal. For example, a taco on a soft corn tortilla with chicken, fajita veggies, and salsa contains 440 calories, 6 grams of sugar, and 5 grams of fiber. *Muy delicioso!*

DENNY'S

Sugar Bombs

Banana Pecan Pancake Breakfast with Maple-Flavored Syrup (2 oz):
850 calories, 10 g fiber, 102 g sugars

Caramel Apple Crisp: 740 calories, 5 g fiber, 89 g sugars

Strawberry Mango Pucker: 220 calories, 1 g fiber, 52 g sugars

Smarter Choices

Senior Belgian Waffle Slam with Egg:
520 calories, 1 g fiber, 1 g sugars

Caesar Salad with Dressing: 450 calories, 4 g fiber, 2 g sugars

Fit Fare Sirloin Steak with Whole Grain Rice and Steamed Zucchini and Squash:
530 calories, 5 g fiber, 2 g sugars

DENNY'S (*cont.*)

Sugar Bombs

Cranberry Apple Chicken Salad with Balsamic Vinaigrette: 450 calories, 5 g fiber, 36 g sugars

Grilled Chicken Breast on a Whole Wheat Bun with BBQ Sauce: 445 calories, 3 g fiber, 22 g sugars

Smarter Choices

Country-Fried Steak and Eggs with Hash Browns: 690 calories, 4 g fiber, 2 g sugars

Hearty Wheat Pancakes with Turkey Bacon Strips (2 pancakes, 2 strips): 360 calories, 8 g fiber, 4 g sugars

DUNKIN' DONUTS

Sugar Bombs

Vanilla Bean Coolatta: 630 calories, 0 g fiber, 130 g sugars

Frozen Caramel Coffee Coolatta with Milk: 550 calories, 0 g fiber, 107 g sugars

Blueberry Crumb Donut: 500 calories, 2 g fiber, 52 g sugars

Blueberry Muffin: 460 calories, 2 g fiber, 44 g sugars

Oatmeal Raisin Cookie: 290 calories, 3 g fiber, 38 g sugars

Smarter Choices

Bacon, Egg, and Cheese on an English Muffin: 290 calories, 7 g fiber, 2 g sugars

Sugared Cocoa Donut: 200 calories, 2 g fiber, 4 g sugars

Caramel Latte Lite (medium): 120 calories, 0 g fiber, 15 g sugars

Cheese Danish: 330 calories, 1 g fiber, 17 g sugars

Honey Bran Raisin Muffin: 440 calories, 4 g fiber, 40 g sugars

FRIENDLY'S

Sugar Bombs

Caramel Fudge Oreo Brownie Sundae: 1,410 calories, 2 g fiber, 124 g sugars

Jim Dandy Sundae with Strawberry Topping: 1,090 calories, 2 g fiber, 121 g sugars

Chocolate Chip Pancakes with Sausage: 1,410 calories, 2 g fiber, 104 g sugars

Fribble Shake—Vanilla: 780 calories, 0 g fiber, 92 g sugars

Honey BBQ Chicken Strips (5 strips): 1,580 calories, 5 g fiber, 73 g sugars

Smarter Choices

Build Your Own Omelette (3 eggbeaters, American cheese, onions and peppers, and bacon): 340 calories, 1 g fiber, 4 g sugars

The Original Set Up Burger: 970 calories, 4 g fiber, 4 g sugars

Happy Ending Hot Fudge Sundae: 330 calories, 1 g fiber, 30 g sugars

Nutty Caramel Waffle Sundae: 720 calories, 3 g fiber, 53 g sugars

Ice Cream Soda—Coffee: 730 calories, 0 g fiber, 59 g sugars

IHOP

Sugar Bombs

Cinn-A-Stack French Toast: 940 calories, 9 g fiber, 62 g sugars

Whole Wheat Pancakes with Blueberries (4 pancakes): 600 calories, 10 g fiber, 41 g sugars

Berry Berry Brioche French Toast: 770 calories, 6 g fiber, 40 g sugars

Sirloin Steak Tips Dinner: 790 calories, 4 g fiber, 29 g sugars

Crispy Chicken Salad with Grilled Chicken: 1,280 calories, 7 g fiber, 28 g sugars

Smarter Choices

Double BLT Sandwich (half): 410 calories, 2 g fiber, 3 g sugars

Take 2 Combo! House Salad with Reduced-Fat Italian Dressing and Chicken Tortilla Soup: 295 calories, 6 g fiber, 9 g sugars

Simple & Fit Grilled Balsamic-Glazed Chicken: 440 calories, 8 g fiber, 13 g sugars

Original Buttermilk Pancakes (3 pancakes): 470 calories, 4 g fiber, 13 g sugars

Simple & Fit Vegetable Omelette with Spinach, Mushrooms, and Tomatoes with Mixed Fruit: 310 calories, 5 g fiber, 16 g sugars

JAMBA JUICE

Sugar Bombs

Peanut Butter Moo'd Smoothie (original 24 oz): 770 calories, 5 g fiber, 109 g sugars

Strawberry Surf Rider Smoothie (original 24 oz): 430 calories, 4 g fiber, 93 g sugars

Mega Mango Smoothie (original 24 oz): 340 calories, 5 g fiber, 78 g sugars

Chunky Strawberry Topper, Fruit and Yogurt Parfait: 520 calories, 9 g fiber, 50 g sugars

Thai-Style Chicken and Sweet Chili Mini Wrap: 250 calories, 9 g fiber, 9 g sugars

Smarter Choices

Spinach 'n Cheese Breakfast Wrap: 240 calories, 3 g fiber, 1 g sugars

Berry Agave Bar: 220 calories, 3 g fiber, 8 g sugars

Make It Light Caribbean Passion Smoothie (original 24 oz): 220 calories, 3 g fiber, 42 g sugars

Berry Blend Smoothie (original 24 oz): 390 calories, 8 g fiber, 54 g sugars

Matcha Green Tea Blast Smoothie (original 24 oz): 420 calories, 2 g fiber, 82 g sugars

MCDONALD'S

Sugar Bombs

Strawberry McCafé Shake (16 oz): 690 calories, 0 g fiber, 100 g sugars

Snack-Size McFlurry with Rolo: 510 calories, 1 g fiber, 63 g sugars

Fruit and Maple Oatmeal: 290 calories, 5 g fiber, 32 g sugars

Premium Southwest Salad with Crispy Chicken: 450 calories, 7 g fiber, 13 g sugars

Bacon and Cheese Quarter Pounder: 600 calories, 3 g fiber, 12 g sugars

Smarter Choices

Sausage McMuffin with Egg: 450 calories, 4 g fiber, 2 g sugars

Premium McWrap Chicken and Bacon (grilled): 460 calories, 3 g fiber, 4 g sugars

Kiddie Cone: 45 calories, 0 g fiber, 6 g sugars

Hamburger: 250 calories, 2 g fiber, 6 g sugars

McCafé Latte (medium): 210 calories, 1 g fiber, 15 g sugars

OUTBACK STEAKHOUSE

Sugar Bombs

Chocolate Thunder from Down Under (serves 4): 1,574 calories, 6 g fiber, 130 g sugars

Sweet Potato with Brown Sugar: 364 calories, 9 g fiber, 25 g sugars

Steakhouse Salad: 914 calories, 5 g fiber, 22 g sugars

Seared Ahi Tuna Appetizer (regular, serves 4): 469 calories, 3 g fiber, 17 g sugars

Wood-Fire Grilled Pork Chop: 383 calories, 0 g fiber, 15 g sugars

Smarter Choices

Victoria's 8-oz Filet: 301 calories, 0 g fiber, 0 g sugars

Grilled Shrimp on the Barbie Appetizer (serves 2): 325 calories, 3 g fiber, 3 g sugars

Caesar Salad Shrimp: 560 calories, 6 g fiber, 4 g sugars

Dressed Baked Potato (with sour cream): 267 calories, 7 g fiber, 7 g sugars

Classic Cheesecake (serves 2): 334 calories, 0 g fiber, 21 g sugars

PANERA BREAD

Sugar Bombs

Caramel Frozen Drink: 560 calories, 0 g fiber, 76 g sugars

Cobblestone Sweet Rolls: 640 calories, 4 g fiber, 62 g sugars

Strawberry Granola Parfait: 310 calories, 3 g fiber, 30 g sugars

Fuji Apple Salad with Chicken (full size): 550 calories, 6 g fiber, 21 g sugars

All Natural Bistro French Onion Soup Topped with Croutons and Gruyere (bowl): 320 calories, 1 g fiber, 14 g sugars

Smarter Choices

Acai Berry Green Tea (21 oz): 0 calories, 0 g fiber, 0 g sugars

Broccoli Cheddar Soup (bowl): 330 calories, 8 g fiber, 0 g sugars

Breakfast Power Sandwich: 340 calories, 4 g fiber, 3 g sugars

Chopped Chicken Cobb Salad with Avocado (full size): 650 calories, 6 g fiber, 3 g sugars

French Croissant: 300 calories, 1 g fiber, 5 g sugars

PAPA JOHN'S

Sugar Bombs

Applepie (4 sticks): 480 calories, 2 g fiber, 43 g sugars

Hawaiian BBQ Chicken Pizza (1 slice): 240 calories, 1 g fiber, 8 g sugars

Parmesan Breadsticks (2 sticks): 340 calories, 2 g fiber, 5 g sugars

Honey Chipotle Wings (2 wings): 190 calories, 0 g fiber, 5 g sugars

Cheesesticks (4 sticks): 370 calories, 2 g fiber, 4 g sugars

Smarter Choices

Papa's Chicken Poppers (5 poppers): 100 calories, 0 g fiber, 0 g sugars

Spicy Buffalo Wings (2 wings): 170 calories, 0 g fiber, 1 g sugars

BBQ Wings (2 wings): 190 calories, 0 g fiber, 2 g sugars

Cheese Pizza, Pizza for One (1 slice): 180 calories, 1 g fiber, 3 g sugars

Pepperoni Pizza, Pizza for One (1 slice): 210 calories, 1 g fiber, 3 g sugars

PIZZA HUT

Sugar Bombs

Cinnamon Sticks with White Icing Dipping Cup (2 pieces): 330 calories, 1 g fiber, 46 g sugars

Crispy Bone In Wings, Honey BBQ (2 pieces): 270 calories, 1 g fiber, 13 g sugars

Crispy Bone In Wings, Spicy Asian (2 pieces): 260 calories, 1 g fiber, 13 g sugars

6" Personal Pan Pizza, Supreme: 730 calories, 4 g fiber, 8 g sugars

6" Personal Pan Pizza, Meat Lover's: 850 calories, 4 g fiber, 7 g sugars

Smarter Choices

Baked Hot Wings (2 pieces): 100 calories, 0 g fiber, 0 g sugars

12" Medium Hand-Tossed Pizza, Cheese (1 slice): 200 calories, 1 g fiber, 1 g sugars

12" Medium Hand-Tossed Pizza, Pepperoni (1 slice): 210 calories, 1 g fiber, 1 g sugars

12" Medium Pan Pizza, Cheese (1 slice): 240 calories, 1 g fiber, 2 g sugars

12" Medium Pan Pizza, Pepperoni (1 slice): 260 calories, 1 g fiber, 2 g sugars

QUIZNOS

Sugar Bombs

Harvest Chicken Salad: 300 calories, 2 g fiber, 19 g sugars

Honey Bacon Club: 540 calories, 2 g fiber, 14 g sugars

Bourbon Steak Sub: 660 calories, 2 g fiber, 13 g sugars

Honey Bourbon Chicken Sub: 360 calories, 2 g fiber, 13 g sugars

Black Angus Sub: 550 calories, 2 g fiber, 12 g sugars

Smarter Choices

Cobb Salad: 380 calories, 1 g fiber, 3 g sugars

Basil Pesto Chicken Sub: 370 calories, 3 g fiber, 5 g sugars

Greek Chicken Flatbread: 420 calories, 3 g fiber, 5 g sugars

Sonoma Turkey Sub: 440 calories, 3 g fiber, 5 g sugars

Veggie Guacamole Sub: 450 calories, 3 g fiber, 5 g sugars

SMOKEY BONES BAR AND FIRE GRILL

Sugar Bombs

Pretzel Bones Appetizer: 1,270 calories, 8 g fiber, 138 g sugars

Nutty Chicken Salad: 970 calories, 9 g fiber, 80 g sugars

Baby Back Ribs (house rack): 1,990 calories, 1 g fiber, 68 g sugars

Sweet Potato Stix: 790 calories, 13 g fiber, 54 g sugars

Smokehouse Burger: 1,300 calories, 4 g fiber, 26 g sugars

Smarter Choices

Fresh Steamed Broccoli: 70 calories, 3 g fiber, 0 g sugars

Caesar Side Salad: 370 calories, 2 g fiber, 1 g sugars

7-oz Top Sirloin with Mushroom Sauce: 420 calories, 1 g fiber, 2 g sugars

Chicken Fingers Appetizer: 420 calories, 2 g fiber, 2 g sugars

Vegetable Burger: 380 calories, 8 g fiber, 6 g sugars

SONIC

Sugar Bombs

Caramel Malt (mini): 540 calories, 0 g fiber, 59 g sugars

Carolina Pulled-Pork Sandwich: 730 calories, 4 g fiber, 20 g sugars

Chicago Dog (6"): 410 calories, 2 g fiber, 17 g sugars

Onion Rings (medium): 440 calories, 3 g fiber, 14 g sugars

SuperSonic Double Cheeseburger with Ketchup: 1,130 calories, 2 g fiber, 11 g sugars

Smarter Choices

Fries or Tots: 220 calories, 2 g fiber, 0 g sugars

Jr. Breakfast Burrito: 280 calories, 0 g fiber, 0 g sugars

Super Crunch Chicken Strips (3 pieces): 330 calories, 2 g fiber, 0 g sugars

Jr. Burger: 330 calories, 1 g fiber, 3 g sugars

Grilled Chicken Wrap: 430 calories, 2 g fiber, 4 g sugars

Three Solutions to Restaurant Sabotage

Ever notice that many restaurants crank up the music to an unpleasant volume and the air conditioning to goose bump levels? Even the lighting can seem unnervingly bright.

It's no accident. These choices are made with one goal in mind: cranking up your appetite, according to a study from Cornell University's Food and Brand Lab and the Georgia Institute of Technology.

In this study, participants ate a meal in two nearly identical settings. The catch: One setting had dimmer lighting and softer music. People eating in the toned-down environment consumed 200 *fewer* calories—or roughly 18 percent less food—than those seated in the brightly lit room. Why? The more-relaxed environment increased the diners' satiety.

Music and lighting are just two of the tricks restaurants employ to ramp up your appetite. Here are three more—and solutions for each.

Sabotage: Alcohol pushing. Ever wonder why servers are so gung ho to keep the drinks flowing? Turns out that drinking booze just before a meal boosts short-term appetite and food consumption, according to a study from the University of Sussex. Researchers say alcohol may temporarily impair your body's ability to feel full. **Solution:** Don't imbibe until your dinner arrives.

Sabotage: TVs at the bar. A University of Minnesota study found that watching TV distracts diners, which leads to a bump in the amount of food consumed. **Solution:** Avoid bellying up to the bar to watch the tube.

Sabotage: Arctic temperatures. Researchers found that lowering the temperature of a dining room by 10 degrees boosted food consumption nearly 20 percent. Apparently your appetite-controlling hormones are impaired when the temperature drops. **Solution:** Along with your salad dressing, bring a sweater with you.

STARBUCKS

Sugar Bombs

Caramel Ribbon Crunch Frappuccino Blended: 290 calories, 0 g fiber, 58 g sugars

Reduced-Fat Banana Chocolate Chip Coffee Cake: 400 calories, 4 g fiber, 50 g sugars

White Chocolate Mocha: 310 calories, 0 g fiber, 44 g sugars

Greek Yogurt with Honey Parfait: 300 calories, 1 g fiber, 32 g sugars

Turkey Rustico Panini: 480 calories, 4 g fiber, 13 g sugars

Smarter Choices

Bacon and Gouda Artisan Breakfast Sandwich: 350 calories, 0 g fiber, 0 g sugars

Ham and Swiss Panini: 340 calories, 2 g fiber, 1 g sugars

Cappuccino with 2% Milk: 90 calories, 0 g fiber, 8 g sugars

Iced Caffe Latte: 100 calories, 0 g fiber, 9 g sugars

Almond Cookie: 230 calories, 2 g fiber, 14 g sugars

SUBWAY

Sugar Bombs

Sweet Onion Chicken Teriyaki Chopped Salad with Dressing: 240 calories, 4 g fiber, 22 g sugars

Subway Club Salad with Honey Mustard Dressing: 220 calories, 4 g fiber, 20 g sugars

6" Sweet Onion Chicken Teriyaki: 370 calories, 5 g fiber, 16 g sugars

6" Chicken Cordon Bleu Melt: 410 calories, 5 g fiber, 13 g sugars

6" Meatball Marinara: 480 calories, 8 g fiber, 12 g sugars

Smarter Choices

6" Veggie Delite: 230 calories, 5 g fiber, 6 g sugars

6" BLT: 320 calories, 5 g fiber, 6 g sugars

Black Forest Ham Salad with Oil and Vinegar: 370 calories, 4 g fiber, 6 g sugars

6" Tuna: 480 calories, 5 g fiber, 6 g sugars

6" Buffalo Chicken with Ranch Dressing: 420 calories, 6 g fiber, 8 g sugars

TACO BELL

Sugar Bombs

Brownie Sandwich: 400 calories, 3 g fiber, 38 g sugars

Cantina Double Steak Quesadilla: 960 calories, 9 g fiber, 10 g sugars

Cantina Burrito—Veggie: 720 calories, 17 g fiber, 8 g sugars

XXL Grilled Stuft Burrito—Steak: 840 calories, 10 g fiber, 7 g sugars

Fiesta Taco Salad—Chicken: 730 calories, 8 g fiber, 7 g sugars

Smarter Choices

Tostada: 270 calories, 8 g fiber, 1 g sugars

MexiMelt: 260 calories, 4 g fiber, 2 g sugars

Fresco Crunchy Tacos (2 tacos): 300 calories, 6 g fiber, 2 g sugars

Cool Ranch Doritos Locos Tacos (2 tacos): 320 calories, 6 g fiber, 2 g sugars

Cinnamon Twists: 170 calories, 1 g fiber, 10 g sugars

TONY ROMA'S

Sugar Bombs

Boneless Chicken Bites—Thai Chili Sauce:
979 calories, 0 g fiber, 57 g sugars

Original Baby Back Ribs (half slab):
511 calories, 0 g fiber, 57 g sugars

BBQ ½ Chicken: 685 calories, 0 g fiber,
40 g sugars

**Fire-Kissed Peach and Country Style
Chicken Salad (without dressing):**
874 calories, 6 g fiber, 37 g sugars

Turkey Cheddar Melt Sandwich:
1,025 calories, 3 g fiber, 26 g sugars

Smarter Choices

Norwegian Salmon—Blackened or Grilled:
536 calories, 2 g fiber, 0 g sugars

Filet Medallions—Asiago Crust:
348 calories, 0 g fiber, 0 g sugars

Dinner Caesar Side Salad: 215 calories,
2 g fiber, 3 g sugars

**Chicken Spinach Stack with Wild Rice
Blend:** 594 calories, 2 g fiber, 3 g sugars

**Chipotle Sausage and Roasted Vegetable
Soup:** 150 calories, 1 g fiber, 4 g sugars

UNO CHICAGO GRILL

Sugar Bombs

Mega-Sized Deep Dish Sundae:
2,700 calories, 10 g fiber, 244 g sugars

Chopped Power Salad: 540 calories,
9 g fiber, 51 g sugars

Thin Crust BBQ Chicken Pizza:
1,030 calories, 3 g fiber, 28 g sugars

Beef Chili: 410 calories, 10 g fiber,
10 g sugars

**Roasted Eggplant, Spinach, and Feta Pizza
on Traditional Crust Appetizer (half
size):** 440 calories, 6 g fiber, 8 g sugars

Smarter Choices

Herb-Rubbed Breast of Chicken:
490 calories, 1 g fiber, 0 g sugars

Stuffed Mushrooms Appetizer:
140 calories, 1 g fiber, 2 g sugars

Tuscan Pesto Minestrone Soup:
150 calories, 4 g fiber, 3 g sugars

Deep Dish Prima Pepperoni Pizza:
1,750 calories, 5 g fiber, 6 g sugars

Mini Chocolate Peanut Butter Cup:
360 calories, 2 g fiber, 28 g sugars

WENDY'S

Sugar Bombs

Caramel Frosty Shake (small):
650 calories, 0 g fiber, 96 g sugars

Strawberry Frosty Shake (small):
540 calories, 1 g fiber, 86 g sugars

**Apple Pecan Chicken Salad with Blue
Cheese Crumbles, Roasted Pecans, and
Pomegranate Vinaigrette Dressing:**
570 calories, 7 g fiber, 37 g sugars

¼ lb Single with Cheese: 600 calories,
3 g fiber, 10 g sugars

**6-Piece Regular Chicken Nuggets with
Sweet and Sour Sauce:** 320 calories,
1 g fiber, 10 g sugars

Smarter Choices

Crispy Chicken Caesar Wrap: 440 calories,
2 g fiber, 1 g sugars

**6-Piece Regular Chicken Nuggets with
Ketchup:** 280 calories, 1 g fiber,
2 g sugars

Jr. Bacon Cheeseburger: 390 calories,
2 g fiber, 5 g sugars

Vanilla Frosty Waffle Cone: 290 calories,
1 g fiber, 34 g sugars

Chocolate Frosty (small): 290 calories,
2 g fiber, 40 g sugars

LOW-SUGAR ETHNIC CHOICES

While most ethnic cuisine is healthy, the way it's prepared in American restaurants may not be. To limit your sugar intake when you eat Italian, Mexican, or other ethnic food, use the simple cheat sheet below. It offers a sampling of healthy options and terms to look for when making your selections, as well as sugar bombs to sidestep.

CHINESE

- *Zheng* (steamed)
- *Jum* (poached)
- *Kao* (roasted)
- "Stock velveted" (cooked in seasoned water rather than oil)
- Brown rice, not white (or skip the rice entirely)

Sugar bombs: General Tso's chicken; sweet and sour dishes; and high-sugar duck, plum, and hoisin sauces

GREEK/MIDDLE EASTERN

- Greek salad with lemon and oil dressing (request feta cheese and dressing on the side)
- Plaki (fish cooked in tomatoes and onions)
- Souvlaki or kebab (marinated meat on a skewer with vegetables, broiled or grilled); hold the rice
- Tabbouleh (bulgur wheat salad with lemon and mint)

Sugar bombs: baklava and moussaka (ground meat and oily eggplant covered with a rich, creamy topping)

INDIAN

- Tandoori (chicken, meat, or fish cooked in a clay oven with spices)
- *Raita* (flavorful yogurt sauce)
- Vegetable curries prepared without *ghee* (clarified butter)

Sugar bombs: chutney; fried breads, such as *poori;* and dishes made with coconut milk

ITALIAN

- Red sauces
- Piccata (thin slices of meat sautéed in a lemon and butter sauce)
- Mussels *fra diavolo*
- Lightly sautéed
- Grilled

Sugar bombs: pasta (the ultimate Sugar Mimic); try a red sauce over steamed spinach or grilled veggies instead

JAPANESE

- Broiled or grilled fish
- *Oshitoshi* (steamed spinach)
- Yakitori (grilled chicken)
- Sashimi (raw fish)

Sugar bombs: rice (a Sugar Mimic), teriyaki sauce, soy sauce, and yakitori sauce

MEXICAN

- *Seviche* (fresh fish or shrimp marinated with lime juice)
- Rice and black beans
- Salsa or picante sauce
- Soft corn tortillas

Sugar bombs: chimichangas and flan

THAI

- Papaya salad
- Satay (skewer of grilled meat or poultry)
- Water-based curries (*gaeng pah*), which are prepared with water rather than coconut milk

Sugar bombs: sweet coconut rice and dishes prepared with coconut milk or peanut sauces

Grocery Shopping the Sugar Smart Way

When you're out shopping, it can be hard to decipher which items contain healthy amounts of sugar. Keeping this in mind, we've provided the guide below to help you stay on track as you eliminate your sugar belly for good.

As always, stay away from items listed as "Sugar Bombs"; these can send you into sugar overload. Instead, pick "Smarter Choices," which contain lower amounts of sugar.

The Sugar Smart Diet is all about making good choices. So, be sure to reference this handy guide as you navigate the aisles of your supermarket. It will help you achieve the sugar freedom you've been craving so that you can live the Sugar Smart sweet life!

GROCERY ITEMS

BOTTLED TEA

Sugar Bombs

Nestea Iced Tea with Lemon Flavor (20 oz): 225 calories, 0 g fiber, 55 g sugars

SoBe Energize Green Tea (20 oz): 200 calories, 0 g fiber, 51 g sugars

Nantucket Nectars Half and Half (17.5 oz): 190 calories, 0 g fiber, 46 g sugars

Lipton Green Tea with Citrus (20 oz): 180 calories, 0 g fiber, 46 g sugars

Arizona Arnold Palmer Half and Half Iced Tea Lemonade, Lite (20 oz): 120 calories, 0 g fiber, 32 g sugars

Smarter Choices

Gold Peak Iced Tea, Unsweetened (12 oz): 0 calories, 0 g fiber, 0 g sugars

Honest Tea Just Green Tea (16 oz): 0 calories, 0 g fiber, 0 g sugars

Pure Leaf Iced Tea, Unsweetened (8 oz): 0 calories, 0 g fiber, 0 g sugars

Sweet Leaf Unsweet Tea, Lemon and Lime (16 oz): 0 calories, 0 g fiber, 0 g sugars

GT's Organic Raw Kombucha, Multi-Green (16 oz): 70 calories, 0 g fiber, 4 g sugars

CEREAL

Sugar Bombs

Kellogg's Low-Fat Granola with Raisins (¾ cup): 259 calories, 5 g fiber, 19 g sugars

Kellogg's Cracklin' Oat Bran (¾ cup): 200 calories, 6 g fiber, 14 g sugars

General Mills Wheaties Fuel (¾ cup): 190 calories, 8 g fiber, 14 g sugars

General Mills Oatmeal Crisp Hearty Raisin (¾ cup): 173 calories, 4 g fiber, 14 g sugars

Kellogg's Frosted Mini-Wheats (21 biscuits): 190 calories, 6 g fiber, 11 g sugars

Smarter Choices

General Mills Fiber One, Original (¾ cup): 90 calories, 21 g fiber, 0 g sugars

Post Shredded Wheat Spoon-Size Wheat 'n Bran (¾ cup): 120 calories, 5 g fiber, 0 g sugars

General Mills Cheerios (¾ cup): 75 calories, 2 g fiber, <1 g sugars

General Mills Kix (¾ cup): 66 calories, 2 g fiber, 2 g sugars

Nature's Path Organic Heritage Flakes (¾ cup): 120 calories, 5 g fiber, 4 g sugars

CONDIMENTS AND SAUCES

Sugar Bombs

Roland Major Grey's Mango Chutney (2 Tbsp): 80 calories, 0 g fiber, 18 g sugars

A Taste of Thai Pad Thai Sauce (2 Tbsp): 90 calories, 0 g fiber, 16 g sugars

Famous Dave's BBQ Sauce, Sweet and Zesty (2 Tbsp): 70 calories, 0 g fiber, 16 g sugars

Gold's Sweet and Sour Duck Sauce (1 oz): 60 calories, 0 g fiber, 11 g sugars

Peter Luger Steak House Old Fashioned Sauce (1 Tbsp): 30 calories, 0 g fiber, 7 g sugars

Smarter Choices

Grey Poupon Dijon Mustard (1 tsp): 0 calories, 0 g fiber, 0 g sugars

La Choy Stir-Fry Teriyaki Sauce and Marinade (1 Tbsp): 10 calories, 0 g fiber, 1 g sugars

Newman's Own Mild Salsa (2 Tbsp): 10 calories, <1 g fiber, 1 g sugars

Annie's Naturals Organic Honey Mustard (1 tsp): 10 calories, 0 g fiber, 2 g sugars

Sir Kensington's Gourmet Scooping Ketchup, Classic Flavor (1 Tbsp): 15 calories, 0 g fiber, 2 g sugars

COOKIES

Sugar Bombs

Mrs. Fields Triple Chocolate Cookies (1 cookie): 210 calories, 1 g fiber, 19 g sugars

Nabisco Double Stuf Oreos (2 cookies): 140 calories, 1 g fiber, 13 g sugars

Pepperidge Farm Soft-Baked Santa Cruz Oatmeal Raisin Cookies (1 cookie): 130 calories, 2 g fiber, 13 g sugars

Manner Lemon Cream Filled Wafers (5 wafers): 150 calories, <1 g fiber, 12 g sugars

Newman's Own Newman-O's Wheat-Free, Dairy-Free Cookies (2 cookies): 130 calories, 2 g fiber, 11 g sugars

Smarter Choices

Aleia's Ginger Snaps (1 cookie): 60 calories, 0 g fiber, 5 g sugars

Tate's Bake Shop All Natural Cookies, Chocolate Chip Walnut (1 cookie): 80 calories, 0 g fiber, 5 g sugars

Pamela's Lemon Shortbread (1 cookie): 120 calories, 0 g fiber, 5 g sugars

Kashi Chocolate Almond Butter Cookies (1 cookie): 130 calories, 4 g fiber, 7 g sugars

Nabisco Newtons Fruit Thins, Lemon Crisp (2 cookies): 140 calories, 1 g fiber, 7 g sugars

CRACKERS

Sugar Bombs

Keebler Sandwich Crackers, Club and Cheddar (1 package): 190 calories, <1 g fiber, 6 g sugars

Special K Multi-Grain Crackers (24 crackers [30 g]): 120 calories, 3 g fiber, 6 g sugars

Pepperidge Farm Baked Naturals Toasted Wheat Crisps (17 crackers [30 g]): 140 calories, 2 g fiber, 5 g sugars

Wheat Thins Zesty Salsa (15 crackers [32 g]): 140 calories, 3 g fiber, 5 g sugars

Keebler Wheatables Toasted Honey Wheat (17 crackers [30 g]): 140 calories, 1 g fiber, 4 g sugars

Smarter Choices

RyKrisp Natural or Multi-Grain Crackers (4 crackers [28 g]): 100 calories, 6 g fiber, 0 g sugars

Special K Cracker Chips, Sea Salt (30 crackers [30 g]): 110 calories, 3 g fiber, 0 g sugars

Triscuit Original Thin Crisps (15 crackers [30 g]): 130 calories, 3 g fiber, 0 g sugars

Mary's Gone Crackers Organic Chipotle Tomato Pretzels (15 pieces [30 g]): 150 calories, 4 g fiber, 0 g sugars

Annie's Organic Cheddar Classics (12 crackers [30 g]): 150 calories, 1 g fiber, 0 g sugars

FROZEN MEALS

Sugar Bombs

PF Chang's General Chang's Chicken (1): 410 calories, 4 g fiber, 29 g sugars

Kashi Sweet and Sour Chicken (1): 320 calories, 6 g fiber, 25 g sugars

Smarter Choices

Marie Callender's Comfort Bakes Savory Chicken and Rice (1): 330 calories, 2 g fiber, 0 g sugars

FROZEN MEALS (*cont.*)

Sugar Bombs

Lean Cuisine Grilled Chicken and Penne Pasta (1): 330 calories, 6 g fiber, 24 g sugars

Marie Callender's Fresh Flavor Steamers Sesame Chicken (1): 400 calories, 5 g fiber, 22 g sugars

Lean Cuisine Ranchero Braised Beef (1): 240 calories, 2 g fiber, 22 g sugars

Smarter Choices

Smart Ones Slow Roasted Turkey Breast (1): 200 calories, 2 g fiber, <1 g sugars

Evol Fire-Grilled Steak (1): 400 calories, 9 g fiber, 1 g sugars

Amy's Black Bean Vegetable Enchilada (1): 160 calories, 4 g fiber, 2 g sugars

Cedar Lane Garden Vegetable Lasagna (1): 180 calories, 2 g fiber, 2 g sugars

FRUIT DRINKS AND JUICE

Sugar Bombs

Welch's 100% Grape Juice (1 cup): 140 calories, 0 g fiber, 40 g sugars

Langers Pomegranate Blueberry Plus (1 cup): 140 calories, 0 g fiber, 32 g sugars

Ocean Spray Cran-Apple (1 cup): 130 calories, 0 g fiber, 32 g sugars

Simply Lemonade (1 cup): 120 calories, 0 g fiber, 28 g sugars

V8 V-Fusion Peach Mango (1 cup): 120 calories, 0 g fiber, 26 g sugars

Smarter Choices

R.W. Knudsen Family Just Cranberry (1 cup): 70 calories, 0 g fiber, 9 g sugars

Tropicana Trop 50 Some Pulp Orange Juice (1 cup): 50 calories, 0 g fiber, 10 g sugars

V8 V-Fusion Light Pomegranate Blueberry (1 cup): 50 calories, 0 g fiber, 10 g sugars

V8 V-Fusion + Tea, Pineapple Mango Green Tea (1 cup): 50 calories, 0 g fiber, 10 g sugars

Lakewood Organic Lemonade (1 cup): 80 calories, 0 g fiber, 16 g sugars

GRANOLA/ENERGY BARS

Sugar Bombs

PowerBar Performance Energy Bar, Vanilla Crisp (1 bar): 240 calories, 1 g fiber, 26 g sugars

Quaker Oatmeal to Go Apples with Cinnamon (1 bar): 220 calories, 5 g fiber, 22 g sugars

Odwalla Banana Nut Bar (1 bar): 220 calories, 5 g fiber, 17 g sugars

Nature Valley Crunchy Oats 'n Honey Granola Bar (1 package [2 bars]): 190 calories, 2 g fiber, 12 g sugars

Nature's Path Organic Chococonut Chewy Granola Bar (1 bar): 140 calories, 2 g fiber, 11 g sugars

Smarter Choices

Quaker 25% Less Sugar Chewy Chocolate Chip Granola Bars (1 bar): 100 calories, 3 g fiber, 5 g sugars

Kashi Honey Almond Flax Chewy Granola Bar (1 bar): 140 calories, 4 g fiber, 5 g sugars

KIND Nuts and Spices Maple Glazed Pecan and Sea Salt (1 bar): 210 calories, 5 g fiber, 5 g sugars

Kellogg's FiberPlus Antioxidants Caramel Coconut Fudge (1 bar): 130 calories, 9 g fiber, 7 g sugars

Larabar Uber Sticky Bun, Sweet and Salty Fruit and Nut Bar (1 bar): 220 calories, 3 g fiber, 7 g sugars

HOT CEREAL

Sugar Bombs

Quaker Oatmeal Express, Baked Apple (1 packet): 200 calories, 4 g fiber, 19 g sugars

Quaker Oatmeal Express, Cinnamon Roll (1 packet): 200 calories, 4 g fiber, 17 g sugars

Quaker Instant Oatmeal, Apple Crisp (1 packet): 150 calories, 3 g fiber, 14 g sugars

McCann's Instant Irish Oatmeal, Maple and Brown Sugar (1 packet): 160 calories, 3 g fiber, 13 g sugars

Quaker Instant Oatmeal, Maple and Brown Sugar (1 packet): 160 calories, 3 g fiber, 12 g sugars

Smarter Choices

Bob's Red Mill Organic High Fiber Hot Cereal (⅓ cup dry): 150 calories, 10 g fiber, 0 g sugars

Quaker Old Fashioned Oats (½ cup dry): 150 calories, 4 g fiber, 1 g sugars

Quaker Steel Cut Oats (¼ cup dry): 150 calories, 4 g fiber, 1 g sugars

Quaker Lower Sugar Instant Oatmeal, Maple and Brown Sugar (1 packet): 120 calories, 3 g fiber, 4 g sugars

Kashi GoLean Creamy All Natural Instant Hot Cereal, Truly Vanilla (1 packet): 140 calories, 7 g fiber, 6 g sugars

ICE CREAM

Sugar Bombs

Graeter's Chocolate Chocolate Chip (½ cup): 300 calories, 0 g fiber, 30 g sugars

Ben & Jerry's Chocolate Peppermint Crunch (½ cup): 300 calories, 2 g fiber, 30 g sugars

Magnum Double Chocolate Ice Cream Bar (1 bar): 340 calories, 2 g fiber, 29 g sugars

Häagen-Dazs Dulce de Leche (½ cup): 270 calories, 0 g fiber, 27 g sugars

Ben & Jerry's FroYo Cherry Garcia Frozen Yogurt (½ cup): 200 calories, <1 g fiber, 27 g sugars

Smarter Choices

Edy's Slow-Churned Chocolate (½ cup): 100 calories, 1 g fiber, 13 g sugars

Edy's Slow-Churned Mint Chocolate Chip (½ cup): 120 calories, 0 g fiber, 13 g sugars

Diana's Bananas Banana Babies, Dark Chocolate (1 bar): 130 calories, 1 g fiber, 14 g sugars

Breyers Natural Vanilla (½ cup): 130 calories, 0 g fiber, 14 g sugars

Turkey Hill Light Recipe Moose Tracks (½ cup): 140 calories, 1 g fiber, 15 g sugars

MILK ALTERNATIVES

Sugar Bombs

Pacific Organic Oat Vanilla Beverage (1 cup): 130 calories, 2 g fiber, 20 g sugars

Blue Diamond Almonds Almond Breeze Chocolate Almond Milk (1 cup): 120 calories, 1 g fiber, 20 g sugars

Smarter Choices

Blue Diamond Almonds Almond Breeze Unsweetened Vanilla Almond Milk (1 cup): 40 calories, 1 g fiber, 0 g sugars

So Delicious Dairy-Free Unsweetened Vanilla Coconut Milk Beverage (1 cup): 45 calories, 1 g fiber, 0 g sugars

MILK ALTERNATIVES (*cont.*)

Sugar Bombs

Silk Soymilk, Chocolate (1 cup):
120 calories, 2 g fiber, 17 g sugars

Silk Almond Milk, Vanilla (1 cup):
90 calories, 0 g fiber, 16 g sugars

Rice Dream Enriched Vanilla (1 cup):
130 calories, 0 g fiber, 12 g sugars

Smarter Choices

Soy Dream Original, Enriched (1 cup):
100 calories, 2 g fiber, 4 g sugars

Blue Diamond Almonds Almond Breeze Almond Milk Coconut Milk Blend (1 cup):
60 calories, 1 g fiber, 6 g sugars

Silk Soymilk, Vanilla (1 cup): 100 calories, 1 g fiber, 8 g sugars

NUT BUTTER AND JELLY/JAM/FRUIT SPREAD

Sugar Bombs

Nutella Hazelnut Spread (2 Tbsp):
200 calories, 1 g fiber, 21 g sugars

Bonne Maman Four Fruits Preserves (1 Tbsp): 50 calories, 0 g fiber, 13 g sugars

Welch's Concord Grape Jelly (1 Tbsp):
50 calories, 0 g fiber, 13 g sugars

Peter Pan Natural Honey Roast Creamy Peanut Butter (2 Tbsp): 220 calories, 2 g fiber, 8 g sugars

SunButter Natural Omega-3 Sunflower Seed Spread (2 Tbsp): 203 calories, 3 g fiber, 4 g sugars

Smarter Choices

Barney Bare Almond Butter (2 Tbsp):
200 calories, 4 g fiber, 1 g sugars

Smucker's Organic Natural Creamy Peanut Butter (2 Tbsp): 210 calories, 2 g fiber, 1 g sugars

Crazy Richard's Chunky Peanut Butter (2 Tbsp): 190 calories, 3 g fiber, 2 g sugars

Justin's Honey Almond Butter (2 Tbsp):
190 calories, 3 g fiber, 3 g sugars

Smucker's Low-Sugar Strawberry Preserves (1 Tbsp): 25 calories, 0 g fiber, 5 g sugars

PASTA SAUCE

Sugar Bombs

Bertolli Vineyard Premium Collections Marinara with Burgundy Wine (½ cup):
90 calories, <1 g fiber, 12 g sugars

Bertolli Tomato and Basil Sauce (½ cup):
70 calories, 3 g fiber, 12 g sugars

Ragu Mama's Special Garden Sauce (½ cup): 90 calories, 2 g fiber, 11 g sugars

Prego Fresh Mushroom Pasta Sauce (½ cup): 70 calories, 3 g fiber, 11 g sugars

Ragu Chunky Tomato, Onion, and Garlic Pasta Sauce (½ cup): 90 calories, 1 g fiber, 10 g sugars

Smarter Choices

Monte Bene All-Natural Garlic Marinara Pasta Sauce (½ cup): 40 calories, 2 g fiber, 0 g sugars

Cucina Antica Garlic Marinara (½ cup):
40 calories, 1 g fiber, 1 g sugars

Progresso White Clam Sauce with Garlic and Herb (½ cup): 120 calories, 1 g fiber, 1 g sugars

Classico Sundried Tomato Alfredo Pasta Sauce (¼ cup): 60 calories, 0 g fiber, 2 g sugars

Rao's Homemade Vodka Sauce (½ cup):
80 calories, 1 g fiber, 4 g sugars

SALAD DRESSING

Sugar Bombs

Wish-Bone Light Western Dressing (2 Tbsp): 70 calories, 0 g fiber, 12 g sugars

Annie's Lite Poppy Seed Dressing (2 Tbsp): 70 calories, 0 g fiber, 9 g sugars

Kraft Creamy Catalina Sweet Honey Dressing (2 Tbsp): 100 calories, 0 g fiber, 8 g sugars

Kraft Classic Catalina Salad Dressing (2 Tbsp): 90 calories, 0 g fiber, 8 g sugars

Ken's Steak House Lite Asian Sesame Dressing (2 Tbsp): 70 calories, 0 g fiber, 7 g sugars

Smarter Choices

Walden Farms Honey Dijon Dressing (2 Tbsp): 0 calories, 0 g fiber, 0 g sugars

Bolthouse Farms Chunky Blue Cheese Dressing (2 Tbsp): 35 calories, 0 g fiber, 1 g sugars

Ken's Steak House Lite Northern Italian Dressing (2 Tbsp): 45 calories, 0 g fiber, 1 g sugars

Bolthouse Farms Caesar Parmigiano Dressing (2 Tbsp): 45 calories, 0 g fiber, 2 g sugars

Annie's Naturals Lite Herb Balsamic Dressing (2 Tbsp): 50 calories, 0 g fiber, 2 g sugars

SOUP

Sugar Bombs

Campbell's Slow Kettle Style Soups, Tomato and Sweet Basil Bisque (1 cup): 260 calories, 3 g fiber, 22 g sugars

Campbell's Gourmet Bisques, Golden Butternut Squash (1 cup): 110 calories, 3 g fiber, 12 g sugars

Campbell's Go Moroccan Style Chicken with Chickpeas (1 cup): 160 calories, 6 g fiber, 11 g sugars

Wolfgang Puck Organic Signature Tortilla Soup (1 cup): 140 calories, 6 g fiber, 8 g sugars

Campbell's Chunky Healthy Request Savory Vegetable Soup (1 cup): 120 calories, 4 g fiber, 8 g sugars

Smarter Choices

Campbell's Healthy Request Homestyle Chicken Noodle Soup (½ cup): 60 calories, 1 g fiber, 1 g sugars

Progresso Light Zesty Santa Fe Style Chicken Soup (1 cup): 80 calories, 2 g fiber, 1 g sugars

Pacific Organic Creamy Butternut Squash Soup (1 cup): 90 calories, 3 g fiber, 4 g sugars

Amy's Organic Fire-Roasted Southwestern Vegetable Soup (1 cup): 140 calories, 4 g fiber, 4 g sugars

Campbell's V8 Tomato Herb Soup* (1 cup): 90 calories, 3 g fiber, 12 g sugars

This is purposefully in the Smarter Choices category; it has significantly less sugar than the Sugar Bombs tomato soup.

YOGURT

Sugar Bombs

Stonyfield Organic Fat-Free French Vanilla (8 oz): 170 calories, 0 g fiber, 33 g sugars

Fage Total 2% Greek Yogurt with Honey (5.3 oz): 190 calories, 0 g fiber, 29 g sugars

Dannon Fruit on the Bottom, Mixed Berries (6 oz): 150 calories, <1 g fiber, 27 g sugars

Yoplait Original Low-Fat Mountain Blueberry Yogurt (6 oz): 170 calories, 0 g fiber, 26 g sugars

Stonyfield Organic Greek 0% Honey Yogurt (5.3 oz): 120 calories, 0 g fiber, 17 g sugars

Smarter Choices

Fage Total 0%, Plain (6 oz): 100 calories, 0 g fiber, 7 g sugars

Siggi's Icelandic-Style Skyr, Strained Nonfat Yogurt, Vanilla (5.3 oz): 100 calories, 0 g fiber, 9 g sugars

Siggi's Icelandic-Style Skyr, Strained Nonfat Yogurt, Acai and Mixed Berry (5.3 oz): 100 calories, 0 g fiber, 9 g sugars

Dannon All Natural Nonfat, plain (6 oz): 80 calories, 0 g fiber, 12 g sugars

Fage Total 0% with Blueberry (5.3 oz): 120 calories, 0 g fiber, 16 g sugars

APPENDIX C

Cooking the Sugar Smart Way

In the last two sections, we've given you the information you need to stay sugar smart when you're out at restaurants or at your local supermarket. And Chapter 11 provides you with an abundance of recipes sure to keep you on track. But what happens when you get home late and still need to make dinner or realize you have to host a last-minute get-together for friends and family?

Well, don't worry, because we've got you covered. The following pages feature 100 of the easiest, fastest, and best-tasting sugar smart recipes you could ever need. Divided into 10 different categories, you'll find everything from the best snacks to dinner options to desserts. We've even provided a special section on the best recipes for entertaining!

Even better, all of these recipes (with the exception of the desserts) adhere to the Phase 1 guidelines, which means they'll work for you no matter where you are in your sugar smart journey. And here's the best news yet: Nearly all of these recipes can be made in 20 minutes or less! So get ready to dig in and enjoy the sweet life!

10 Best Snacks

Spiced Cheesy Popcorn

PREP TIME: 5 minutes ● **TOTAL TIME:** 5 minutes

Makes 1 serving

2 cups air-popped popcorn
1½ teaspoons olive oil
1 teaspoon grated Parmesan cheese
¼ teaspoon chili powder
⅛ teaspoon salt

In a medium bowl, drizzle the popcorn with the oil. Sprinkle with the cheese, chili powder, and salt and toss to coat.

Nutrition per serving: 132 calories, 3 g protein, 14 g carbs, 2 g fiber, 0.5 g total sugar, 8 g fat, 1.5 g saturated fat, 317 mg sodium

Spiced Pumpkin Seeds

PREP TIME: 5 minutes ● **TOTAL TIME:** 15 minutes

Makes 12 servings

2 cups raw pumpkin seeds (pepitas)
1 tablespoon olive oil
½ teaspoon pumpkin pie spice
¼ teaspoon sea salt

Preheat the oven to 350°F.

In a small bowl, combine the seeds, oil, and pumpkin pie spice and toss to coat well. Spread on a large baking sheet. Sprinkle with the salt. Bake for 10 minutes, or until lightly browned.

Nutrition per serving: 135 calories, 5 g protein, 3 g carbs, 1 g fiber, 0 g total sugar, 12 g fat, 2 g saturated fat, 28 mg sodium

Chipotle Nuts

PREP TIME: 5 minutes ● **TOTAL TIME:** 5 minutes + cooling time

Makes 4 servings

1 teaspoon olive oil
⅓ cup unsalted almonds
¼ cup unsalted cashews
1 teaspoon salt-free chipotle seasoning

In a large skillet over medium heat, heat the oil. Cook the almonds, cashews, and the chipotle seasoning, shaking the skillet occasionally, for 2 minutes, or until the nuts are well coated. Let cool completely.

Nutrition per serving: 128 calories, 3 g protein, 5 g carbs, 2 g fiber, 1 g total sugar, 11 g fat, 1.5 g saturated fat, 2 mg sodium

Veggies with Creamy Caper Dip

PREP TIME: 5 minutes ● **TOTAL TIME:** 5 minutes

Makes 1 serving

¼ cup 0% plain Greek yogurt
1 teaspoon capers, drained and chopped
Pinch of salt-free lemon-pepper seasoning
1 small red bell pepper, sliced
6 asparagus spears, blanched

In a small bowl, stir together the yogurt, capers, and lemon-pepper seasoning. Serve with the bell pepper and asparagus.

Nutrition per serving: 73 calories, 8 g protein, 11 g carbs, 4 g fiber, 7 g total sugar, 0.5 g fat, 0 g saturated fat, 171 mg sodium

Edamame Dip and Pepper Strips

PREP TIME: 10 minutes ● **TOTAL TIME:** 20 minutes

Makes 4 servings

8 ounces frozen shelled edamame, thawed
4 cups water
2 tablespoons olive oil
1 tablespoon lemon juice
Dash of hot-pepper sauce (optional)
2 red, yellow, or green bell peppers, cut into strips

In a medium saucepan over high heat, bring the edamame and water to a boil. Reduce the heat to medium-low, cover, and cook for 5 minutes, or until very tender. Remove and reserve ½ cup of the water. In a sieve, drain the edamame and rinse under cold water for 3 minutes.

In a food processor or blender, combine the edamame, oil, lemon juice, and ¼ cup of the reserved water. Process or blend until smooth, adding more water if needed. Place in a serving bowl and stir in the hot-pepper sauce, if using. Serve with the pepper strips.

Nutrition per serving: 148 calories, 7 g protein, 10 g carbs, 4 g fiber, 2 g total sugar, 9 g fat, 1 g saturated fat, 172 mg sodium

Smoked Salmon Bites

PREP TIME: 5 minutes ● **TOTAL TIME:** 10 minutes
Makes 1 serving

1 tablespoon cream
   cheese, softened
½ teaspoon prepared
   horseradish
8 slices cucumber
   rounds, about ½" thick
1 ounce smoked salmon,
   cut into 8 pieces

In a small bowl, mix together the cheese and horseradish. Arrange the cucumber slices on a plate. Divide the cheese mixture among the slices. Top each with 1 piece of the salmon.

Nutrition per serving: 142 calories, 19 g protein, 2 g carbs, 0.5 g fiber, 1 g total sugar, 7 g fat, 2.5 g saturated fat, 73 mg sodium

Asian Chicken Lettuce Cups

PREP TIME: 5 minutes ● **TOTAL TIME:** 5 minutes
Makes 4 servings

8 leaves Bibb lettuce
½ cup cooked shredded
   chicken
1 tablespoon rice wine
   vinegar
1 tablespoon reduced-
   sodium soy sauce
½ teaspoon toasted
   sesame oil
¼ teaspoon red-pepper
   flakes
1 cup shredded red
   cabbage

Arrange the lettuce leaves in a single layer on a serving plate. Divide the chicken evenly among the leaves.

In a small bowl, whisk together the vinegar, soy sauce, oil, and red-pepper flakes. Add the cabbage and toss to coat. Divide the cabbage mixture among the lettuce leaves. Roll each leaf into a wrap.

Nutrition per serving: 73 calories, 12 g protein, 2 g carbs, 0.5 g fiber, 1 g total sugar, 2 g fat, 0.5 g saturated fat, 175 mg sodium

Coconut-Peanut Butter Celery

PREP TIME: 5 minutes ● **TOTAL TIME:** 5 minutes

Makes 1 serving

2 tablespoons creamy,
   natural, unsalted
   peanut butter
⅛ teaspoon ground
   cinnamon
1 large rib celery
1 tablespoon rolled oats
½ teaspoon shredded
   coconut

In a small bowl, stir together the peanut butter and cinnamon. Spread the peanut butter mixture into the celery and top with the oats and coconut.

Nutrition per serving: 130 calories, 5 g protein, 8 g carbs, 2 g fiber, 2 g total sugar, 9 g fat, 1 g saturated fat, 32 mg sodium

Almond Yogurt with Oats

PREP TIME: 5 minutes ● **TOTAL TIME:** 5 minutes

Makes 1 serving

½ cup 0% plain Greek
   yogurt
1 tablespoon almond
   butter
1 tablespoon rolled oats

In a small bowl, stir together the yogurt and almond butter. Stir in the oats and enjoy.

Nutrition per serving: 153 calories, 15 g protein, 10 g carbs, 1 g fiber, 4 g total sugar, 6 g fat, 1 g saturated fat, 41 mg sodium

Turkey Roll-Ups

PREP TIME: 5 minutes ● **TOTAL TIME:** 5 minutes

Makes 1 serving

3 slices turkey breast
½ ounce goat cheese
1 scallion, cut into strips
   lengthwise

Place the turkey slices on a work surface. Divide the goat cheese among the slices and spread to cover. Divide the scallion strips among the turkey slices. Roll the turkey around the scallion strips. Cut each in half.

Nutrition per serving: 153 calories, 15 g protein, 10 g carbs, 1 g fiber, 4 g total sugar, 6 g fat, 1 g saturated fat, 41 mg sodium

10 Best Fish Dinners

Pan-Seared Halibut

PREP TIME: 5 minutes ● **TOTAL TIME:** 20 minutes

Makes 4 servings

⅓ cup fresh cilantro
    leaves
1 tablespoon lime juice
2 tablespoons olive oil,
    divided
4 skinless halibut fillets
    (5 ounces each)
⅛ teaspoon ground black
    pepper
¼ teaspoon salt

In a blender, combine the cilantro, lime juice, and 1 tablespoon of the oil and blend until smooth. Place the halibut fillets on a baking sheet. Drizzle with the cilantro mixture and, using your hands, rub on all sides of the fillets.

In a large nonstick skillet over medium-high heat, heat the remaining 1 tablespoon oil. Sprinkle the halibut with the pepper and salt. Cook for 10 minutes, turning once, or until the fish flakes easily.

Nutrition per serving: 191 calories, 26 g protein, 0.5 g carbs, 0 g fiber, 0 g total sugar, 9 g fat, 1 g saturated fat, 244 mg sodium

Garlic-Herb Shrimp

PREP TIME: 5 minutes ● **TOTAL TIME:** 10 minutes

Makes 4 servings

2 tablespoons olive oil,
    divided
3 cloves garlic, minced
2 tablespoons finely
    chopped fresh flat-
    leaf parsley
2 tablespoons finely
    chopped fresh basil
    leaves
1 pound frozen and
    thawed cooked shrimp

In a large nonstick skillet over medium heat, heat 1 tablespoon of the oil. Cook the garlic for 1 minute, or until fragrant and golden. Add the parsley, basil, shrimp, and the remaining 1 tablespoon oil and cook, stirring frequently, for 3 minutes, or until the shrimp are heated through.

Nutrition per serving: 199 calories, 26 g protein, 3 g carbs, 0 g fiber, 0 g total sugar, 9 g fat, 2 g saturated fat, 10 mg sodium

Garlic Shrimp over Zucchini Ribbons

PREP TIME: 10 minutes ● **TOTAL TIME:** 20 minutes

Makes 4 servings

2 cloves garlic, minced
½ teaspoon red-pepper flakes
¼ teaspoon ground black pepper
¼ teaspoon salt
20 large shrimp, peeled and deveined
2 tablespoons olive oil, divided
2 large zucchini, cut lengthwise into ⅛"-thick slices using a mandoline or knife
2 tablespoons lemon juice
1 tablespoon grated Parmesan cheese

In a medium bowl, combine the garlic, red-pepper flakes, black pepper, and salt. Add the shrimp and toss to coat. Set aside.

In a large skillet over medium heat, heat 1 tablespoon of the oil. Cook the zucchini slices, stirring frequently, for 5 minutes, or until softened. Increase the heat to medium-high, if necessary. Transfer to a bowl and cover.

In the same skillet over medium-high heat, heat the remaining 1 tablespoon oil. Add the reserved shrimp in a single layer, working in batches, if necessary. Cook for 4 minutes, or until the shrimp are opaque throughout. Remove from the heat.

Divide the reserved zucchini among 4 plates. Top with the shrimp. Drizzle the lemon juice over the shrimp and sprinkle with the cheese.

Nutrition per serving: 122 calories, 7 g protein, 7 g carbs, 2 g fiber, 4 g total sugar, 8 g fat, 1 g saturated fat, 376 mg sodium

Spicy Tilapia Fillets over Cabbage

PREP TIME: 5 minutes ● **TOTAL TIME:** 20 minutes

Makes 4 servings

4 tilapia fillets (5 ounces each)
2 teaspoons olive oil
¼ teaspoon salt
¼ teaspoon ground black pepper
⅛ teaspoon ground red pepper
¼ cup 0% plain Greek yogurt
2 tablespoons lime juice
2 cups shredded red cabbage

Arrange the top oven rack 6" away from the heat. Preheat the broiler to low. Coat a rimmed baking sheet with cooking spray. Gently pat the fillets dry with a paper towel. Arrange in a single layer on the baking sheet. Drizzle with the oil and turn the fillets to coat on all sides.

In a small bowl, combine the salt, black pepper, and red pepper. Sprinkle over the tilapia.

Broil for 6 minutes, or until the fish flakes easily.

In a large bowl, whisk together the yogurt and lime juice. Add the cabbage and toss to combine. Divide among 4 plates. Top each bed of cabbage with a tilapia fillet.

Nutrition per serving: 177 calories, 30 g protein, 4 g carbs, 1 g fiber, 2 g total sugar, 5 g fat, 1 g saturated fat, 234 mg sodium

Pan-Seared Tuna

PREP TIME: 5 minutes ● **TOTAL TIME:** 20 minutes

Makes 4 servings

2 tablespoons reduced-sodium soy sauce
1 tablespoon lime juice
1 clove garlic, minced
1 teaspoon grated fresh ginger
1 tablespoon toasted sesame oil
4 tuna steaks (4 ounces each)
1 teaspoon sesame seeds

In a small bowl, whisk together the soy sauce, lime juice, garlic, and ginger.

In a large nonstick skillet coated with cooking spray over medium-high heat, heat the oil. Brush the tuna steaks with half of the soy sauce mixture on both sides. Cook for 5 to 6 minutes for medium doneness, turning once and brushing the remaining sauce on the steaks throughout cooking.

Transfer the tuna steaks to a serving platter and sprinkle with the sesame seeds.

Nutrition per serving: 164 calories, 27 g protein, 1 g carbs, 0 g fiber, 0 g total sugar, 5 g fat, 1 g saturated fat, 331 mg sodium

Salmon Quinoa Cakes

PREP TIME: 5 minutes ● **TOTAL TIME:** 30 minutes

Makes 4 servings

3 cans (6 ounces each) wild Alaskan sockeye salmon, drained
1 egg, lightly beaten
½ cup cooked quinoa
4 scallions, finely chopped
2 tablespoons lemon juice, divided
3 tablespoons 0% plain Greek yogurt, divided
1 teaspoon Dijon mustard
½ teaspoon ground cumin
3 teaspoons olive oil, divided

In a medium bowl, combine the salmon, egg, quinoa, scallions, 1 tablespoon of the lemon juice, 1 tablespoon of the yogurt, the mustard, and cumin. Toss with 2 forks to mix evenly. Use your hands to flake the salmon into small pieces. Shape into 8 patties.

In a large nonstick skillet coated with cooking spray over medium heat, heat 1½ teaspoons of the oil. Cook 4 patties for 8 minutes, turning once, or until golden brown. Remove to a plate lined with paper towels. Repeat with the remaining 1½ teaspoons oil and the remaining 4 salmon patties. Divide the cakes among 4 plates.

In a small bowl, whisk together the remaining 1 tablespoon lemon juice and 2 tablespoons yogurt. Top the salmon cakes with a small dollop of the dressing.

Nutrition per serving: 252 calories, 31 g protein, 7 g carbs, 1 g fiber, 1 g total sugar, 11 g fat, 2 g saturated fat, 453 mg sodium

Roasted Salmon Fillet

PREP TIME: 10 minutes ● **TOTAL TIME:** 20 minutes

Makes 1 serving

1 skinless wild salmon fillet (4 ounces)
½ teaspoon stone-ground mustard
⅛ teaspoon ground black pepper

Preheat the oven to 400°F. Coat a baking sheet with cooking spray.

Place the salmon on the baking sheet and brush with the mustard. Sprinkle with the pepper. Roast for 10 minutes, or until the salmon is opaque.

Nutrition per serving: 162 calories, 23 g protein, 0 g carbs, 0 g fiber, 0 g total sugar, 7 g fat, 1 g saturated fat, 82 mg sodium

Fresh Tuna Salad

PREP TIME: 5 minutes ● **TOTAL TIME:** 10 minutes

Makes 1 serving

1 pouch (3 ounces)
  albacore tuna, flaked
1 rib celery, finely
  chopped
1 wedge apple, finely
  chopped
1 tablespoon chopped
  walnuts
1 tablespoon 0% plain
  Greek yogurt
⅛ teaspoon ground black
  pepper
⅛ teaspoon salt

In a small bowl, combine the tuna, celery, apple, walnuts, yogurt, pepper, and salt. Gently fold the mixture until well combined.

Nutrition per serving: 231 calories, 23 g protein, 24 g carbs, 5 g fiber, 17 g total sugar, 7 g fat, 0.5 g saturated fat, 383 mg sodium

Lemon-Herbed Cod

PREP TIME: 5 minutes ● **TOTAL TIME:** 15 minutes

Makes 1 serving

1 tablespoon olive oil
1 cod fillet (5 ounces),
  1" thick
2 teaspoons lemon juice
1 teaspoon dried parsley
½ teaspoon dried thyme

In a large nonstick skillet over medium-high heat, heat the oil. Cook the cod fillet for 6 minutes, turning once, or until golden and the fish flakes easily.

Meanwhile, in a small bowl, combine the lemon juice, parsley, and thyme.

Place the fish on a plate. Drizzle with the lemon mixture.

Nutrition per serving: 201 calories, 17 g protein, 1 g carbs, 0 g fiber, 0 g total sugar, 14 g fat, 2 g saturated fat, 345 mg sodium

Pan-Grilled Tilapia

PREP TIME: 5 minutes ● **TOTAL TIME:** 15 minutes

Makes 1 serving

½ teaspoon chili powder
⅛ teaspoon garlic
   powder
1 tilapia fillet (5 ounces)
2 teaspoons olive oil
1 tablespoon fresh
   cilantro leaves,
   chopped
1 tablespoon lime juice

In a small bowl, combine the chili powder and garlic powder. Rub the mixture on the tilapia fillet.

In a large nonstick grill pan or skillet lightly coated with cooking spray over medium-high heat, heat the oil. Cook the fillet for 6 to 7 minutes, turning once, or until the fish flakes easily and is opaque in the center.

Place on a serving dish and top with the cilantro and lime juice.

Nutrition per serving: 229 calories, 29 g protein, 4 g carbs, 0 g fiber, 0 g total sugar, 11 g fat, 2 g saturated fat, 76 mg sodium

10 Best Chicken Dinners

Grilled Chicken Skewers

PREP TIME: 10 minutes ● **TOTAL TIME:** 20 minutes

Makes 4 servings

3 boneless, skinless
  chicken breast halves
  (4 ounces each), cut
  into ¾" cubes
½ small zucchini, halved
  lengthwise and sliced
  into ½" chunks
½ small red onion, cut
  into large chunks
½ small red bell pepper,
  cut into large chunks
1 pound new potatoes
  (1½" diameter each),
  parboiled and halved
Pinch of salt
Pinch of ground black
  pepper
2 tablespoons olive oil
1 tablespoon chopped
  fresh basil
1 teaspoon chopped
  fresh rosemary

Preheat the grill or a grill pan to medium-high.

On eight 6 to 8" skewers (see note), alternately thread the chicken, zucchini, onion, bell pepper, and potatoes until all the pieces are used. Season with the salt and black pepper.

In a small bowl, stir together the oil, basil, and rosemary. Set aside half the dressing in a separate container. Brush the rest onto the skewers.

Cook for 8 minutes, turning once, or until the chicken is no longer pink and the juices run clear. Then use a clean brush to coat with the reserved dressing and transfer to a serving plate.

Nutrition per serving: 239 calories, 21 g protein, 16 g carbs, 2 g fiber, 2 g total sugar, 9 g fat, 1 g saturated fat, 177 mg sodium

Note: If using wooden skewers, soak them in cold water for at least 10 minutes prior to cooking.

Grilled Lemon and Oregano Chicken Cutlets

PREP TIME: 5 minutes ● **TOTAL TIME:** 20 minutes

Makes 4 servings

4 chicken cutlets
  (4 ounces each),
  ½" thick
3 tablespoons +
  1 teaspoon olive oil,
  divided
3 tablespoons lemon
  juice
2 tablespoons fresh
  oregano, finely
  chopped
¼ teaspoon salt, divided
¼ teaspoon ground black
  pepper, divided
2 zucchini, halved
  lengthwise and cut
  into ¼" slices
2 cups cooked brown
  rice, warmed
4 lemon wedges, for
  garnish

Preheat the grill to medium. Coat a 15" x 11" piece of foil or a grill basket with cooking spray.

Place the chicken cutlets in a single layer in an 11" x 8" glass baking dish. In a small bowl, whisk together 3 tablespoons of the oil, the lemon juice, oregano, ⅛ teaspoon of the salt, and ⅛ teaspoon of the pepper. Drizzle half of the lemon juice mixture over the chicken cutlets, reserving the rest for later use. Turn the cutlets over to coat on all sides. Marinate for 5 minutes.

Cook the chicken for 8 minutes, turning once, or until no longer pink and the juices run clear. Transfer to a plate and cover to keep warm.

Arrange the zucchini slices in a single layer on the foil or grill basket, sprinkle with the remaining ⅛ teaspoon salt and ⅛ teaspoon pepper, and drizzle with the remaining 1 teaspoon oil. Cook for 6 minutes, turning once, or until tender. If the zucchini gets charred quickly while still crisp, gently lift the foil or basket to the top shelf of the grill.

Transfer the chicken and zucchini to a serving platter. Drizzle the reserved lemon juice mixture over the chicken. Serve with the prepared brown rice. Garnish with the lemon wedges, if desired.

Nutrition per serving: 342 calories, 27 g protein, 24 g carbs, 2 g fiber, 1 g total sugar, 15 g fat, 2 g saturated fat, 282 mg sodium

Easy Thai Chicken

PREP TIME: 5 minutes ● **TOTAL TIME:** 10 minutes

Makes 1 serving

1 cup shredded roasted chicken

1 serving Asian Peanut Sauce (page 355)

1 serving Stir-Fried Vegetables (page 341)

2 leaves fresh basil, chopped

In a medium saucepan over medium heat, cook the chicken, sauce, and vegetables, stirring often, for 4 minutes, or until heated through. Top with the basil. Transfer to a medium serving bowl and enjoy.

To prepare using a microwave oven, place the chicken, sauce, and vegetables in a microwaveable dish, stirring slightly, and heat on high power for 1 minute, or until heated through. Top with the basil.

Nutrition per serving: 414 calories, 49 g protein, 14 g carbs, 4 g fiber, 7 g total sugar, 18 g fat, 3 g saturated fat, 812 mg sodium

Chicken Cutlets Topped with Turkey Bacon and Avocado

PREP TIME: 10 minutes ● **TOTAL TIME:** 20 minutes

Makes 4 servings

1 Hass avocado

¼ cup cherry tomatoes, chopped

¼ teaspoon salt, divided

¼ teaspoon ground black pepper, divided

1 teaspoon canola oil

2 boneless, skinless chicken breast halves (8 ounces each), halved lengthwise and pounded to ¼" thickness

2 slices natural turkey bacon, chopped

2 tablespoons fat-free, reduced-sodium chicken broth or water

2 cups mixed greens

In a small bowl, mash the avocado with a fork. Add the tomatoes, ⅛ teaspoon of the salt, and ⅛ teaspoon of the pepper. Stir to combine and set aside.

In a large nonstick skillet over medium-high heat, heat the oil. Season the chicken with the remaining ⅛ teaspoon salt and the remaining ⅛ teaspoon pepper and cook for 6 to 8 minutes, turning once, or until no longer pink and the juices run clear. Transfer to a plate and set aside.

Reduce the heat to medium. Cook the bacon, stirring occasionally, for 4 to 5 minutes, or until crisp. Transfer to a plate and set aside.

In the same skillet, add the broth or water and cook, scraping the bottom to incorporate any browned bits, until the mixture boils and reduces slightly.

Top the reserved cutlets with the reserved avocado mixture and bacon bits. Drizzle with the pan juices. Serve with the mixed greens.

Nutrition per serving: 221 calories, 28 g protein, 4 g carbs, 3 g fiber, 0.5 g total sugar, 10 g fat, 2 g saturated fat, 401 mg sodium

Grilled Chicken Caesar Salad

PREP TIME: 5 minutes ● **TOTAL TIME:** 20 minutes

Makes 4 servings

2 boneless, skinless chicken breast halves (8 ounces each), halved lengthwise and pounded to ¼" thickness

2 tablespoons olive oil, divided

½ teaspoon salt

½ teaspoon ground black pepper

4 hearts romaine, halved and core removed

⅓ cup Caesar dressing

2 tablespoons shaved Parmesan cheese

2 baked potatoes, halved

Preheat the grill to medium-high.

In a medium bowl, toss the chicken with 1 tablespoon of the oil, the salt, and pepper.

Cook for 8 minutes, turning once, or until no longer pink and the juices run clear. Transfer to a cutting board. Cut into ½" slices.

Brush the romaine halves with the remaining 1 table-spoon oil on the cut sides. Place on the grill cut side down and cook for 1 minute, or until slightly wilted and grill marks appear. Remove the romaine halves to a cutting board and coarsely chop.

Divide the lettuce and chicken among 4 plates. Drizzle the dressing over the salads and sprinkle evenly with the cheese. Serve each salad with 1 baked potato half.

Nutrition per serving: 390 calories, 28 g protein, 20 g carbs, 2 g fiber, 2 g total sugar, 22 g fat, 4 g saturated fat, 710 mg sodium

Ginger-Coconut Chicken

PREP TIME: 5 minutes ● **TOTAL TIME:** 20 minutes

Makes 4 servings

1 teaspoon ground coriander

1 teaspoon ground turmeric

¼ teaspoon ground black pepper

4 boneless, skinless chicken thighs (about 1 pound)

½ cup lite canned coconut milk

2 teaspoons grated fresh ginger

2 cups cooked brown rice

Preheat the grill to medium-high.

In a medium bowl, combine the coriander, turmeric, and pepper. Add the chicken thighs and toss to coat. Pour the coconut milk over the thighs and add the ginger. Toss to coat. Marinate for 5 minutes.

Grill the chicken thighs for 8 minutes, turning once, or until the internal temperature reaches 165°F and the juices run clear. Serve each thigh over ½ cup cooked brown rice.

Nutrition per serving: 275 calories, 17 g protein, 24 g carbs, 0 g fiber, 1 g total sugar, 11 g fat, 4 g saturated fat, 212 mg sodium

Chili-Lime Chicken Tacos

PREP TIME: 5 minutes ● **TOTAL TIME:** 10 minutes

Makes 1 serving

1 cup shredded cooked
   chicken breast
1 tablespoon olive oil
2 teaspoons lime juice
⅛ teaspoon chili powder
3 leaves Bibb lettuce
½ avocado, peeled,
   pitted, and chopped
¼ cup cherry tomatoes,
   quartered
2 tablespoons fresh
   cilantro leaves,
   chopped
1 thin slice red onion,
   chopped

In a small microwaveable bowl, microwave the chicken on medium power for 45 seconds, or until hot. If additional time is needed, heat in 15-second intervals.

Add the oil, lime juice, and chili powder and stir to coat the chicken.

Arrange the lettuce leaves on a plate. Divide the chicken mixture among the lettuce leaves. Divide the avocado, tomatoes, cilantro, and onion among the "tacos."

Nutrition per serving: 484 calories, 46 g protein, 10 g carbs, 6 g fiber, 2 g total sugar, 29 g fat, 5 g saturated fat, 117 mg sodium

Zesty Lemon-Pepper Chicken Tenders

PREP TIME: 10 minutes ● **TOTAL TIME:** 20 minutes

Makes 4 servings

1 clove garlic, minced
½ teaspoon salt-free
   lemon-pepper
   seasoning
1 tablespoon fresh
   oregano, chopped
1 tablespoon red wine
   vinegar
2 tablespoons olive oil,
   divided
1 pound chicken tenders

In a large bowl, combine the garlic, lemon-pepper seasoning, oregano, vinegar, and 1 tablespoon of the oil. Add the chicken. With your hands or a fork, toss well to coat all the pieces.

In a large skillet over medium-high heat, heat the remaining 1 tablespoon oil. Cook the chicken tenders for 6 minutes, turning once, or until no longer pink and the juices run clear. Adjust the heat if necessary and turn the chicken more than once if needed.

Nutrition per serving: 162 calories, 24 g protein, 0.5 g carbs, 0 g fiber, 0 g total sugar, 6 g fat, 1 g saturated fat, 132 mg sodium

Buffalo Chicken

PREP TIME: 5 minutes ● **TOTAL TIME:** 10 minutes

Makes 1 serving

1 cup shredded cooked chicken breast

1 tablespoon hot-pepper sauce

2 tablespoons shredded reduced-fat Mexican-blend cheese

1 cup shredded romaine lettuce

Preheat the oven to 400°F. Place the chicken in a small baking dish or ramekin. Stir in the hot-pepper sauce to coat the chicken. Top with the cheese. Bake for 5 minutes, or until the cheese has melted and the chicken is heated through.

Arrange the lettuce on a plate. Carefully spoon the chicken on top of the lettuce.

Nutrition per serving: 282 calories, 48 g protein, 3 g carbs, 1 g fiber, 1 g total sugar, 8 g fat, 3 g saturated fat, 721 mg sodium

Parmesan Chicken Fingers

PREP TIME: 5 minutes ● **TOTAL TIME:** 20 minutes

Makes 4 servings

1 cup rolled oats, divided

¼ cup grated Parmesan cheese

2 tablespoons fresh flat-leaf parsley, chopped

½ teaspoon garlic powder

¼ teaspoon mustard powder

¼ teaspoon salt

¼ teaspoon ground black pepper

1 egg

2 tablespoons olive oil

1 pound chicken tenders, pounded to ¼" thick

In a food processor, pulse ¼ cup of the oats in 10-second intervals until the oats are finely ground almost into flour. Place in a shallow bowl.

In another shallow bowl, combine the cheese, parsley, garlic powder, mustard powder, salt, pepper, and the remaining ¾ cup oats.

In a third shallow bowl, whisk the egg.

In a large nonstick skillet over medium-high heat, heat the oil. Set up the work station in an assembly-line fashion, starting with the bowl of ground oats, then the egg, then the whole oats mixture, with the skillet on the stove at the end.

Dredge each chicken tender into the ground oats to coat lightly. Dip into the egg mixture, shaking off any excess. Lay each tender in the whole oats mixture and turn to coat. Cook for 8 minutes, turning once, or until no longer pink and the juices run clear. Transfer to a serving platter.

Nutrition per serving: 315 calories, 31 g protein, 14 g carbs, 2 g fiber, 1 g total sugar, 14 g fat, 3 g saturated fat, 372 mg sodium

10 Best Beef Dinners

Steak Salad

PREP TIME: 5 minutes ● **TOTAL TIME:** 10 minutes

Makes 1 serving

2 cups chopped romaine lettuce

1 slice red onion, chopped

¼ cup cherry tomatoes, halved

1 ounce crumbled blue cheese

4 ounces sliced cooked steak, cut into bite-size pieces

1 tablespoon Blue Cheese Dressing (page 347)

On a plate, combine the lettuce, onion, tomatoes, and blue cheese. Top with the steak. Drizzle with the dressing.

Nutrition per serving: 314 calories, 35 g protein, 10 g carbs, 3 g fiber, 4 g total sugar, 15 g fat, 8 g saturated fat, 572 mg sodium

Cracked Pepper and Mustard Steak

PREP TIME: 5 minutes ● **TOTAL TIME:** 15 minutes

Makes 1 serving

2 teaspoons Dijon mustard

1 teaspoon olive oil

½ teaspoon cracked black pepper

4 ounces cooked boneless rib-eye steak

In a small bowl, whisk together the mustard, oil, and pepper. Coat the steak with the mustard mixture.

In a small nonstick skillet over medium-high heat, cook the steak for 2 to 3 minutes, turning once, or until heated through.

Nutrition per serving: 237 calories, 23 g protein, 3 g carbs, 0 g fiber, 0 g total sugar, 14 g fat, 4 g saturated fat, 312 mg sodium

Asian Beef Lettuce Cups

PREP TIME: 5 minutes ● **TOTAL TIME:** 5 minutes

Makes 1 serving

2 leaves Boston lettuce

4 ounces hot cooked 95% lean ground beef

½ small red bell pepper, finely chopped

1 scallion, chopped

1 tablespoon fresh cilantro leaves

2 teaspoons reduced-sodium soy sauce

2 teaspoons olive oil

¼ teaspoon red-pepper flakes

Arrange the lettuce leaves on a plate. Divide the beef, bell pepper, scallion, and cilantro between the 2 leaves. In a small bowl, whisk together the soy sauce, oil, and red-pepper flakes. Drizzle over the lettuce cups.

Nutrition per serving: 302 calories, 32 g protein, 5 g carbs, 2 g fiber, 2 g total sugar, 17 g fat, 5 g saturated fat, 464 mg sodium

Loaded Baked Potato with Steak

PREP TIME: 5 minutes ● **TOTAL TIME:** 10 minutes

Makes 1 serving

1 hot baked potato, halved

4 ounces cooked strip steak, thinly sliced and heated

¼ cup cherry tomatoes, halved

1 slice red onion, chopped

1 slice cooked bacon, crumbled

¼ cup shredded Monterey Jack cheese

1 tablespoon reduced-fat sour cream

1 teaspoon chopped fresh chives

Arrange the top oven rack 6" away from the heat. Preheat the broiler to high.

Place the potato halves side by side on a baking sheet lined with foil. Top with the steak, tomatoes, onion, bacon, and cheese. Broil for 1 minute, or until the cheese is melted and golden. Transfer to a serving plate and top with the sour cream and chives.

Nutrition per serving: 623 calories, 44 g protein, 40 g carbs, 4 g fiber, 4 g total sugar, 32 g fat, 15 g saturated fat, 343 mg sodium

Broiled Soy-Ginger Flank Steak

PREP TIME: 5 minutes ● **TOTAL TIME:** 20 minutes

Makes 4 servings

1 pound flank steak
2 tablespoons reduced-sodium soy sauce
1 clove garlic, minced
1 teaspoon grated fresh ginger
1 teaspoon olive oil

Preheat the broiler to high.

Place the steak on a plate. In a small bowl, whisk together the soy sauce, garlic, ginger, and oil. Brush the soy sauce mixture onto the steak on all sides. Use your hands to press the mixture into the steak.

On a broiler pan lightly coated with cooking spray, cook the steak 2 to 3" beneath the heat for 5 minutes, or until the steak is tender but charred. Turn and cook for 5 minutes, or until a thermometer inserted in the center registers 145°F for medium-rare.

Let the steak rest for 5 minutes before slicing against the grain.

Nutrition per serving: 204 calories, 25 g protein, 1 g carbs, 0 g fiber, 0 g total sugar, 11 g fat, 4 g saturated fat, 422 mg sodium

Quick Buffalo-Style Steak

PREP TIME: 5 minutes ● **TOTAL TIME:** 10 minutes

Makes 1 serving

4 ounces cooked filet mignon steak, sliced
2 teaspoons hot-pepper sauce
⅛ teaspoon ground black pepper

In a small bowl, toss the steak, hot-pepper sauce, and black pepper together until coated.

In a nonstick skillet over medium-high heat, cook the steak for 2 to 3 minutes, stirring frequently, or until heated through. You can also reheat the steak in a microwave oven on medium power for 30 seconds to 1 minute.

Nutrition per serving: 63 calories, 8 g protein, 0 g carbs, 0 g fiber, 0 g total sugar, 3 g fat, 1 g saturated fat, 100 mg sodium

Italian Steak Burgers

PREP TIME: 5 minutes ● **TOTAL TIME:** 20 minutes

Makes 4 servings

1 pound 95% lean ground beef
1 tablespoon dried Italian seasoning
1 clove garlic, minced
⅛ teaspoon salt
⅛ teaspoon freshly ground black pepper
4 slices mozzarella cheese
1 zucchini, sliced
1 tablespoon olive oil
½ cup tomato sauce

Preheat the grill to high.

In a large bowl, mix together the beef, Italian seasoning, and garlic. Divide and shape into 4 patties, each ¾" thick. Season both sides with the salt and pepper and place on the grill. Cook for 4 minutes, or until slightly charred. Turn and cook for 3 minutes. Add 1 slice of the cheese to each burger and cook for 1 minute.

In a medium bowl, toss the zucchini slices with the oil. Arrange in a single layer on foil and place on the grill. Cook for 4 minutes, turning once, or until charred and slightly softened.

Meanwhile, pour the tomato sauce into a small glass bowl. Cover with a paper towel and microwave on medium power for 1 minute, stirring after each 15-second increment, or until heated through.

Divide the zucchini among 4 plates. Top with a burger. Top each burger with 2 tablespoons of the tomato sauce.

Nutrition per serving: 279 calories, 31 g protein, 3 g carbs, 1 g fiber, 2 g total sugar, 15 g fat, 7 g saturated fat, 413 mg sodium

Speedy Meatball Dinner

PREP TIME: 5 minutes ● **TOTAL TIME:** 10 minutes

Makes 4 servings

½ cup no-sugar-added marinara sauce
16 hot cooked meatballs (1 ounce each)
2 tablespoons grated Parmesan cheese

In a small saucepan over low heat, warm the marinara. Divide the meatballs among 4 plates. Top with the marinara and cheese.

Nutrition per serving: 248 calories, 21 g protein, 10 g carbs, 1 g fiber, 1 g total sugar, 13 g fat, 5 g saturated fat, 319 mg sodium

Grilled Skirt Steak

PREP TIME: 5 minutes ● **TOTAL TIME:** 20 minutes
Makes 4 servings

1 teaspoon olive oil
½ teaspoon garlic
   powder
¼ teaspoon salt
¼ teaspoon ground black
   pepper
1 pound trimmed skirt
   steak, ¾" thick

Preheat the grill to high.

Combine the oil, garlic powder, salt, and pepper and rub on all sides of the steak.

Cook the steak for 4 minutes, or until golden and charred. Turn and grill for 4 minutes, or until cooked to the desired doneness (145°F for medium-rare). Transfer to a cutting board. Let the steak rest for 5 minutes and then slice against the grain and divide the slices among 4 plates.

Nutrition per serving: 198 calories, 24 g protein, 0 g carbs, 0 g fiber, 0 g total sugar, 10 g fat, 4 g saturated fat, 222 mg sodium

Pan-Seared Strip Steak

PREP TIME: 5 minutes ● **TOTAL TIME:** 15 minutes
Makes 1 serving

¼ teaspoon chili powder
¼ teaspoon ground
   cumin
¼ teaspoon garlic
   powder
⅛ teaspoon salt
2 teaspoons olive oil,
   divided
5 ounces top sirloin
   steak, 1" thick,
   brought to room
   temperature

Preheat the oven to 450°F.

In a small bowl, combine the chili powder, cumin, garlic powder, and salt. Rub ½ teaspoon of the oil on the steak. Rub the spice mixture on all sides.

In a cast-iron skillet or ovenproof skillet over medium-high heat, heat the remaining 1½ teaspoons oil. Cook the steak until a crust forms on the bottom, about 2 to 3 minutes. Turn and cook until a crust forms on the other side, 2 to 3 minutes.

Transfer the skillet into the oven and cook for 3 minutes. Turn and cook for 3 minutes, or until the desired doneness.

Nutrition per serving: 279 calories, 31 g protein, 2 g carbs, 0 g fiber, 0 g total sugar, 16 g fat, 4 g saturated fat, 373 mg sodium

10 Best Pork Dinners

Balsamic Pork Chops

PREP TIME: 10 minutes ● **TOTAL TIME:** 20 minutes

Makes 4 servings

1 tablespoon olive oil
4 boneless pork loin
    chops (5–6 ounces
    each), trimmed
¼ teaspoon salt
1 tablespoon balsamic
    vinegar
1 tablespoon Dijon
    mustard
3 tablespoons water
¼ cup reduced-fat sour
    cream
3 scallions, chopped

In a large nonstick skillet over medium-high heat, heat the oil. Sprinkle the pork chops with the salt and cook for 6 minutes, turning once, or until browned.

In a small bowl, whisk together the vinegar, mustard, and water until blended. Stir into the skillet. Reduce the heat to medium, cover, and simmer for 1 minute, or until a thermometer inserted in the center of a chop registers 160°F, the juices run clear, and the sauce has thickened slightly.

Transfer the pork to a platter. Add the sour cream and scallions to the sauce in the skillet and cook for 1 minute, or until heated through. Spoon the sauce over the pork.

Nutrition per serving: 103 calories, 7 g protein, 2 g carbs, 0 g fiber, 1 g total sugar, 7 g fat, 2 g saturated fat, 209 mg sodium

Asian Pork Burgers

PREP TIME: 5 minutes ● **TOTAL TIME:** 15 minutes

Makes 4 servings

1 pound lean ground
    pork
2 tablespoons reduced-
    sodium soy sauce
2 scallions, finely
    chopped
1 teaspoon grated fresh
    ginger
¼ teaspoon toasted
    sesame oil

In a large bowl, mix together the pork, soy sauce, scallions, ginger, and oil. Form the mixture into 4 patties.

Heat a large nonstick grill pan coated with cooking spray over medium heat. Cook the patties for 10 minutes, turning once, or until a thermometer inserted in the center registers 160°F.

Nutrition per serving: 147 calories, 25 g protein, 2 g carbs, 0 g fiber, 0 g total sugar, 5 g fat, 1.5 g saturated fat, 344 mg sodium

Parmesan Pork Chop

PREP TIME: 5 minutes ● **TOTAL TIME:** 15 minutes

Makes 2 servings

3 tablespoons grated
  Parmesan cheese
½ teaspoon cracked
  black pepper
2 boneless pork loin
  chops (5–6 ounces
  each), trimmed
1 tablespoon olive oil

In a shallow bowl, stir together the cheese and pepper. Dredge the pork chops in the cheese mixture.

In a medium nonstick skillet over medium-high heat, heat the oil. Cook the pork chops for 5 minutes, turning once, or until a thermometer inserted in the center registers 160°F and the juices run clear.

Nutrition per serving: 266 calories, 28 g protein, 1 g carbs, 0 g fiber, 0 g total sugar, 16 g fat, 5 g saturated fat, 166 mg sodium

Pork Cutlets with Green Olive Gremolata

PREP TIME: 10 minutes ● **TOTAL TIME:** 20 minutes

Makes 4 servings

4 boneless pork loin
  cutlets (4 ounces
  each), pounded to
  ¼" thickness
½ teaspoon dried
  oregano
¼ teaspoon salt
2 teaspoons olive oil
2 teaspoons unsalted
  butter
½ small red onion,
  chopped
2 cloves garlic, minced
¼ cup pimiento-stuffed
  green olives, coarsely
  chopped
¼ cup coarsely chopped
  fresh flat-leaf parsley
3 tablespoons orange
  juice

Sprinkle both sides of the pork with the oregano and salt.

In a large nonstick skillet over medium heat, heat the oil. Cook the pork for 6 minutes, turning once, or until browned and the juices run clear. Transfer to a platter. Cover loosely with foil.

In the same skillet, melt the butter. Cook the onion and garlic for 4 minutes, stirring occasionally, or until the onion is tender and lightly browned. Remove from the heat. Stir in the olives, parsley, and orange juice. Spoon over the pork.

Nutrition per serving: 243 calories, 25 g protein, 3 g carbs, 0 g fiber, 1 g total sugar, 14 g fat, 4 g saturated fat, 375 mg sodium

Peppered Pork Tenderloin with Horseradish Sauce

PREP TIME: 10 minutes ● **TOTAL TIME:** 20 minutes

Makes 4 servings

1 pound pork tenderloin
1½ teaspoons coarsely ground black pepper
½ teaspoon salt
¼ teaspoon garlic powder
⅓ cup 0% plain Greek yogurt
2 tablespoons chopped English cucumber
1 teaspoon prepared horseradish
¼ teaspoon Worcestershire sauce

Preheat the oven to 425°F.

Place the pork on a wire rack in a broiling pan or roasting pan and sprinkle with the pepper, salt, and garlic powder. Roast for 20 minutes, or until a thermometer inserted in the center registers 160°F and the juices run clear. Let stand for 5 minutes before slicing.

Meanwhile, in a small bowl, combine the yogurt, cucumber, horseradish, and Worcestershire until well mixed. Serve the sauce with the pork.

Nutrition per serving: 150 calories, 25 g protein, 2 g carbs, 0 g fiber, 1 g total sugar, 4 g fat, 1 g saturated fat, 366 mg sodium

Curried Pork Medallions

PREP TIME: 5 minutes ● **TOTAL TIME:** 20 minutes

Makes 4 servings

2 teaspoons curry powder
¼ teaspoon salt
¾ pound pork tenderloin, cut crosswise into 4 medallions
2 teaspoons olive oil, divided
½ cup 0% plain Greek yogurt

In a shallow bowl, stir together the curry powder and salt. Dredge the medallions in the curry mixture.

In a large nonstick skillet over medium-high heat, heat 1 teaspoon of the oil. Cook half the pork for 5 minutes, turning once, or until the juices run clear. Remove to a plate. Repeat with the remaining 1 teaspoon oil and the remaining pork.

Remove the skillet from the heat and stir in the yogurt until well blended with the pan drippings and heated through. Drizzle over the pork.

Nutrition per serving: 116 calories, 20 g protein, 2 g carbs, 1 g fiber, 2 g total sugar, 3 g fat, 1 g saturated fat, 256 mg sodium

Spicy Pork with Zucchini Ribbons

PREP TIME: 5 minutes ● **TOTAL TIME:** 15 minutes

Makes 4 servings

1 teaspoon cumin
  powder
1 teaspoon adobo sauce
¾ pound pork tenderloin,
  thinly sliced
3 teaspoons olive oil,
  divided
1 zucchini, cut
  lengthwise into
  ⅛"-thick slices using a
  mandoline or knife
1 tablespoon lime juice
¼ teaspoon salt

In a medium bowl, combine the cumin and adobo sauce. Add the pork and toss to coat well.

In a large nonstick skillet over medium heat, heat 2 teaspoons of the oil. Cook the pork for 5 minutes, turning occasionally, or until browned and the juices run clear. Transfer to a plate.

In the same skillet, heat the remaining 1 teaspoon oil. Cook the zucchini, stirring occasionally, for 2 minutes, or until tender. Remove from the heat and sprinkle with the lime juice and salt. Serve with the pork.

Nutrition per serving: 174 calories, 19 g protein, 4 g carbs, 0 g fiber, 2 g total sugar, 9 g fat, 2 g saturated fat, 310 mg sodium

Ginger-Pork Stir-Fry

PREP TIME: 10 minutes ● **TOTAL TIME:** 20 minutes

Makes 4 servings

¾ pound pork tenderloin,
  trimmed and cut into
  thin strips
3 tablespoons reduced-
  sodium soy sauce,
  divided
1 tablespoon cornstarch
3 teaspoons peanut oil,
  divided
1 green bell pepper,
  thinly sliced
1 carrot, thinly sliced
1 sweet onion, sliced
1 tablespoon grated
  fresh ginger

In a medium bowl, toss the pork with 1 tablespoon of the soy sauce and the cornstarch.

In a large nonstick skillet or wok over medium-high heat, heat 2 teaspoons of the oil. Cook the pork for 5 minutes, or until no longer pink. Transfer to a plate and set aside.

In the same skillet or wok, heat the remaining 1 teaspoon oil. Cook the pepper, carrot, onion, and ginger, stirring often, for 5 minutes, or until tender-crisp. Add the reserved pork and the remaining 2 tablespoons soy sauce. Cook, stirring, for 1 minute, or until the pork is heated through.

Nutrition per serving: 314 calories, 25 g protein, 19 g carbs, 4 g fiber, 3 g total sugar, 16 g fat, 3 g saturated fat, 466 mg sodium

Thai Pork Kebabs

PREP TIME: 10 minutes ● **TOTAL TIME:** 20 minutes

Makes 4 servings

½ cup lite coconut milk

2 tablespoons Thai red curry paste

1 tablespoon natural peanut butter

1 pound pork loin, cut into ¾" pieces

1 red or yellow bell pepper, cut into 1" chunks

1 large red onion, cut into wedges

Coat a grill rack or broiler-pan rack with cooking spray. Preheat the grill to medium-high or the broiler to high.

In a medium bowl, whisk together the coconut milk, curry paste, and peanut butter.

On eight 10" metal skewers, alternately thread the pork, pepper, and onion. Place the skewers on the grill or broiler pan and brush with some of the curry mixture. Grill or broil for 8 minutes, brushing occasionally with the curry mixture and turning once, or until browned and the pork is no longer pink.

Nutrition per serving: 234 calories, 28 g protein, 9 g carbs, 2 g fiber, 4 g total sugar, 9 g fat, 3 g saturated fat, 465 mg sodium

Pork Tenderloin with Pineapple Salsa

PREP TIME: 10 minutes ● **TOTAL TIME:** 20 minutes

Makes 4 servings

1 tablespoon olive oil

2 teaspoons chili powder

½ teaspoon ground cumin

¼ teaspoon salt

1 pound pork tenderloin

4 slices (½" thick) fresh pineapple, cored

1 small red onion, finely chopped

1 jalapeño pepper, minced (wear plastic gloves when handling)

1½ cups fresh cilantro, chopped

2 tablespoons lime juice

Coat a grill rack or broiler-pan rack with cooking spray. Preheat the grill or broiler to high.

In a small bowl, combine the oil, chili powder, cumin, and salt. Rub over the tenderloin.

Place the pork and pineapple slices on the grill or broiler pan. Cook the pineapple for 5 minutes, turning once. Remove to a cutting board. Cook the pork for 10 more minutes, turning once, or until a thermometer inserted in the center registers 160°F and the juices run clear.

Meanwhile, chop the pineapple and place in a medium bowl. Add the onion, pepper, cilantro, and lime juice and toss to coat. Serve with the pork.

Nutrition per serving: 207 calories, 25 g protein, 14 g carbs, 2 g fiber, 8 g total sugar, 6 g fat, 1 g saturated fat, 210 mg sodium

10 Best Sides

Cilantro-Lime Rice Pilaf

PREP TIME: 5 minutes ● **TOTAL TIME:** 15 minutes
Makes 4 servings

2 tablespoons olive oil
1 small red bell pepper, chopped
3 cups cooked brown rice
¾ cup loosely packed fresh cilantro leaves, chopped
2 tablespoons lime juice
1 teaspoon ground cumin

In a medium saucepan over medium-high heat, heat the oil. Cook the pepper, stirring occasionally, for 5 minutes, or until softened.

Reduce the heat to medium. Add the rice, cilantro, lime juice, and cumin and toss to combine. Cook, stirring often, for 2 minutes, or until heated through.

Nutrition per serving: 232 calories, 4 g protein, 36 g carbs, 3 g fiber, 1 g total sugar, 8 g fat, 1 g saturated fat, 10 mg sodium

Make it a meal: Add 4 ounces cooked chicken breast and 1 grilled corn on the cob to each serving.

Snap Peas and Carrots with Ginger

PREP TIME: 10 minutes ● **TOTAL TIME:** 20 minutes
Makes 4 servings

3 carrots, quartered crosswise, then quartered lengthwise
½ pound sugar snap peas, trimmed
1 tablespoon toasted sesame oil
2 scallions, thinly sliced diagonally
3 cloves garlic, thinly sliced
1" piece of fresh ginger, peeled and cut into thin matchsticks
2 tablespoons reduced-sodium soy sauce

Place a steamer basket in a large saucepan with 2" of water. Bring to a boil over high heat. Steam the carrots and snap peas in the basket, covered, for 5 minutes, or until the carrots are tender. Remove the carrots and peas with a skimmer or tongs, drain well, and place on a serving plate.

In a large skillet over medium heat, heat the oil. Cook the scallions, garlic, and ginger, stirring, for 2 to 3 minutes, or until the garlic is golden brown. Stir in the soy sauce and bring to a boil. Cook, stirring constantly, for 1 to 2 minutes, or until lightly thickened. Spoon the sauce over the peas and carrots.

Nutrition per serving: 83 calories, 3 g protein, 10 g carbs, 3 g fiber, 4 g total sugar, 4 g fat, 0.5 g saturated fat, 321 mg sodium

Make it a meal: Add 4 ounces cooked salmon and ½ cup cooked quinoa to each serving.

Greek Salad

PREP TIME: 10 minutes ● **TOTAL TIME:** 10 minutes

Makes 4 servings

2 large heirloom
　tomatoes, coarsely
　chopped
3 tablespoons chopped
　pitted kalamata olives
1 small cucumber,
　quartered lengthwise
　and cut into ¾" chunks
½ small red onion, thinly
　sliced
2 tablespoons olive oil
1 teaspoon red wine
　vinegar
¼ teaspoon ground black
　pepper
2 tablespoons chopped
　fresh oregano
¼ cup crumbled feta
　cheese

In a medium serving bowl, combine the tomatoes, olives, cucumber, and onion. Toss with the oil, vinegar, pepper, and oregano. Top with the cheese.

Nutrition per serving: 152 calories, 3 g protein, 7 g carbs, 2 g fiber, 4 g total sugar, 13 g fat, 3 g saturated fat, 342 mg sodium

Make it a meal: Add 4 ounces sliced flank steak and ½ cup cooked farro to each serving.

Green Beans with Pesto and Parmesan

PREP TIME: 5 minutes ● **TOTAL TIME:** 10 minutes

Makes 4 servings

¼ cup water
1 pound fresh green
　beans, trimmed
2 tablespoons
　refrigerated pesto
2 tablespoons shredded
　Parmesan cheese

In a large nonstick skillet over high heat, bring the water to a boil. Reduce the heat to a simmer. Cook the green beans, covered, for 2 minutes, or until tender-crisp. Remove the lid and cook until the water has evaporated, about 3 minutes.

Remove from the heat and add the pesto. Toss to coat and transfer to a serving dish. Top with the cheese.

Nutrition per serving: 79 calories, 4 g protein, 8 g carbs, 3 g fiber, 4 g total sugar, 4 g fat, 1 g saturated fat, 116 mg sodium

Make it a meal: Add 4 ounces cooked tilapia fillet and ½ cup cooked wild rice to each serving.

Buffalo-Style Potato Salad

PREP TIME: 5 minutes ● **TOTAL TIME:** 20 minutes
Makes 4 servings

1 pound small new
 potatoes, quartered
⅓ cup 0% plain Greek
 yogurt
2 tablespoons reduced-
 fat sour cream
2 tablespoons hot-
 pepper sauce
½ teaspoon ground black
 pepper
3 ribs celery, chopped
3 scallions, thinly sliced

In a large pot of boiling salted water, cook the potatoes for 10 minutes, or until almost tender.

Meanwhile, in a large bowl, stir together the yogurt, sour cream, hot-pepper sauce, and black pepper.

Drain the potatoes well. Transfer to the bowl with the yogurt mixture. Add the celery and scallions and toss to combine. Serve warm or at room temperature.

Nutrition per serving: 114 calories, 5 g protein, 21 g carbs, 4 g fiber, 3 g total sugar, 1 g fat, 1 g saturated fat, 308 mg sodium

Make it a meal: Add 4 ounces grilled chicken breast and 1 cup leafy greens side salad to each serving.

Summer Corn Salad

PREP TIME: 10 minutes ● **TOTAL TIME:** 20 minutes
Makes 4 servings

4 ears corn, husked
1 summer squash, thinly
 sliced
1 zucchini, thinly sliced
3 tablespoons olive oil,
 divided
1 cup cherry tomatoes,
 halved
3 tablespoons chopped
 fresh basil
1 teaspoon chili powder
¼ teaspoon garlic
 powder
¼ teaspoon ground black
 pepper
⅛ teaspoon salt

Coat a large grill rack or basket with cooking spray. Preheat the grill to medium-high.

In a large bowl, toss the corn, squash, and zucchini with 1 tablespoon of the oil.

Place the corn, squash, and zucchini on the grill rack or in the basket. Reserve the bowl. Grill the squash and zucchini for 2 to 3 minutes, turning once, or until softened and slightly charred. Grill the corn for 5 minutes, turning often, or until lightly browned. Transfer the squash and zucchini to a serving bowl and the corn to a cutting board.

Over the reserved bowl, cut the kernels from the corn, discarding the cobs. Add the kernels, tomatoes, and basil to the serving bowl with the squash and zucchini. Drizzle with the remaining 2 tablespoons oil and toss to coat. Sprinkle with the chili powder, garlic powder, pepper, and salt and toss again to coat.

Nutrition per serving: 208 calories, 5 g protein, 25 g carbs, 4 g fiber, 9 g total sugar, 12 g fat, 2 g saturated fat, 94 mg sodium

Make it a meal: Add 3 cups cooked shredded chicken and 2 cups cooked brown rice. Stir everything together.

Braised Radicchio

PREP TIME: 5 minutes ● **TOTAL TIME:** 20 minutes

Makes 4 servings

2 small heads radicchio, quartered lengthwise
1 teaspoon chopped fresh thyme leaves
⅛ teaspoon salt
⅛ teaspoon ground black pepper
2 teaspoons extra-virgin olive oil
2 tablespoons white wine vinegar

Preheat the oven to 400°F. Coat a large rimmed baking sheet with cooking spray.

Arrange the radicchio quarters in a single layer on the baking sheet. Sprinkle with the thyme, salt, and pepper. Drizzle with the oil and vinegar and toss gently to coat on all sides. Roast for 12 minutes, or until the leaves are slightly wilted and charred. Transfer to a serving platter.

Nutrition per serving: 22 calories, 0 g protein, 0 g carbs, 0 g fiber, 0 g total sugar, 2 g fat, 0.5 g saturated fat, 74 mg sodium

Make it a meal: Add 4 ounces cooked pork chop and 1 cup cooked whole grain penne pasta to each serving. Cut up the radicchio and toss with the pasta for a delicious accompaniment to the pork!

Fennel and Arugula Salad with Pecans and Blue Cheese

PREP TIME: 10 minutes ● **TOTAL TIME:** 10 minutes

Makes 4 servings

2 tablespoons olive oil
1 tablespoon white wine vinegar
2 teaspoons Dijon mustard
¼ teaspoon salt
⅛ teaspoon ground black pepper
1 cup arugula
1 bulb fennel, trimmed and thinly sliced
¼ cup coarsely chopped pecans
2 ounces crumbled blue cheese

In a large bowl, whisk together the oil, vinegar, mustard, salt, and pepper. Add the arugula and fennel and toss to combine. Transfer to a serving bowl and top with the pecans and blue cheese.

Nutrition per serving: 179 calories, 5 g protein, 6 g carbs, 3 g fiber, 0.5 g total sugar, 16 g fat, 4 g saturated fat, 435 mg sodium

Make it a meal: Add 4 ounces cooked sirloin steak and ¾ cup cooked bulgur to each serving.

Cheesy Spaghetti Squash

PREP TIME: 10 minutes ● **TOTAL TIME:** 20 minutes

Makes 4 servings

1 medium spaghetti squash (2 pounds), halved lengthwise and seeded
¼ cup water
2 tablespoons olive oil
1 shallot, finely chopped
2 cloves garlic, chopped
1 tablespoon chopped fresh flat-leaf parsley
1 tablespoon chopped fresh basil
¼ cup part-skim ricotta cheese
2 tablespoons grated Parmesan cheese
½ teaspoon salt
½ teaspoon ground black pepper

Pierce the outside of the squash a few times with a fork. Place the squash cut side down in a large microwaveable baking dish. Pour the water around the squash. Cover and microwave on high power for 10 minutes, or until very tender when pierced with a fork. Let cool for 5 minutes.

Meanwhile, in a large nonstick skillet over medium-high heat, heat the oil. Cook the shallot for 3 minutes, or until softened and lightly golden. Add the garlic and cook for 1 minute, or until fragrant and golden.

With a fork, scrape the spaghetti-like strands of the squash into the skillet. Cook for 2 minutes, stirring gently, or until heated through. Stir in the parsley and basil.

Divide the squash mixture evenly among 4 plates. Top each with 1 tablespoon of the ricotta cheese. Sprinkle with the Parmesan cheese, salt, and pepper.

Nutrition per serving: 148 calories, 3 g protein, 16 g carbs, 3 g fiber, 6 g total sugar, 9 g fat, 2 g saturated fat, 372 mg sodium

Make it a meal: Add 4 ounces cooked turkey meatballs (4 meatballs), ⅓ cup marinara sauce, and 1 cup mixed greens to each serving.

Stir-Fried Vegetables

PREP TIME: 5 minutes ● **TOTAL TIME:** 15 minutes

Makes 4 servings

2 teaspoons canola oil

2 cloves garlic, minced

½ pound bok choy, cut into ¼" slices

2 cups broccoli florets, cut into bite-size pieces

2 red bell peppers, sliced

2 tablespoons water

1 tablespoon rice wine vinegar

2 teaspoons reduced-sodium soy sauce

2 teaspoons toasted sesame oil

1 teaspoon Asian chili-pepper sauce

In a large skillet over medium-high heat, heat the canola oil. Cook the garlic for 1 minute, stirring until fragrant. Add the bok choy, broccoli, bell peppers, water, vinegar, soy sauce, sesame oil, and chili-pepper sauce. Cover and cook for 4 minutes, or until the vegetables begin to soften. Uncover and cook, stirring frequently, for 3 minutes, or until the vegetables are tender-crisp.

Nutrition per serving: 84 calories, 3 g protein, 8 g carbs, 3 g fiber, 4 g total sugar, 5 g fat, 0.5 g saturated fat, 155 mg sodium

Make it a meal: Add 4 ounces cooked shredded chicken and 1 cup cooked brown rice to each serving.

10 Best Desserts

Bananas Canadienne

PREP TIME: 5 minutes ● **TOTAL TIME:** 15 minutes

Makes 4 servings

2 large bananas, halved lengthwise and cut crosswise into 4 pieces
1 tablespoon fresh lemon juice
2 tablespoons maple syrup
2 tablespoons finely chopped hazelnuts

Preheat the oven to 325°F. Coat a 9" x 9" baking dish with cooking spray.

Place the bananas cut side up in a single layer in the baking dish. Drizzle with the lemon juice and maple syrup. Sprinkle with the hazelnuts.

Bake for 10 minutes, or until the bananas are lightly browned and glazed.

Nutrition per serving: 114 calories, 1 g protein, 23 g carbs, 2 g fiber, 15 g total sugar, 3 g fat, 0 g saturated fat, 2 mg sodium

Fruit Kebabs with Raspberry Yogurt Dip

PREP TIME: 15 minutes ● **TOTAL TIME:** 15 minutes

Makes 4 servings

1 cup raspberries
½ cup 2% plain Greek yogurt
1 tablespoon honey
1½ cups strawberries, halved if large
1 cup cubed cantaloupe
1 cup cubed watermelon
½ cup seedless green or red grapes
1 tablespoon finely chopped almonds

In a blender, combine the raspberries, yogurt, and honey. Process until blended and the raspberries are pureed. Pour into a small serving dish. Cover and refrigerate while assembling the kebabs.

On eight 6" wooden skewers, alternately thread the strawberries, cantaloupe, watermelon, and grapes.

When ready to serve, sprinkle the almonds onto the dip.

Nutrition per serving: 117 calories, 4 g protein, 24 g carbs, 4 g fiber, 18 g total sugar, 2 g fat, 0 g saturated fat, 21 mg sodium

Strawberry Yogurt Cup

PREP TIME: 5 minutes ● **TOTAL TIME:** 5 minutes

Makes 1 serving

½ cup 0% plain Greek yogurt
½ teaspoon grated orange peel
½ cup sliced strawberries
1 tablespoon low-fat granola

In a small bowl, combine the yogurt and orange peel. Place all but 3 strawberry slices in the bottom of a parfait glass. Top with the yogurt mixture. Sprinkle with the granola. Garnish with the reserved strawberry slices.

Nutrition per serving: 112 calories, 11 g protein, 16 g carbs, 2 g fiber, 10 g total sugar, 1 g fat, 0 g saturated fat, 58 mg sodium

Vanilla Malt

PREP TIME: 5 minutes ● **TOTAL TIME:** 5 minutes

Makes 2 servings

¼ cup Edy's slow-churned vanilla ice cream
1 cup fat-free milk
2 tablespoons malted milk powder
1 teaspoon maple syrup
1 tablespoon vanilla extract

In a blender, combine the ice cream, milk, malted milk powder, maple syrup, and vanilla. Blend until smooth. Pour into 2 glasses and serve immediately.

Nutrition per serving: 101 calories, 5 g protein, 17 g carbs, 0 g fiber, 15 g total sugar, 1 g fat, 1 g saturated fat, 77 mg sodium

Homemade Fruity Yogurt Pops

PREP TIME: 10 minutes ● **TOTAL TIME:** 10 minutes + 6 hours chilling time

Makes 8 servings

2 large mangoes, cut into chunks
2 cups 0% plain Greek yogurt
½ cup fat-free milk

In a blender, pulse the mangoes, yogurt, and milk until smooth. Pour the mixture into eight 4-ounce popsicle molds. Insert a wooden stick into each and freeze for 6 hours.

Unmold before serving.

Nutrition per serving: 86 calories, 6 g protein, 16 g carbs, 1 g fiber, 14 g total sugar, 0 g fat, 0 g saturated fat, 28 mg sodium

Chocolate-Pistachio-Dipped Apricots

PREP TIME: 10 minutes ● **TOTAL TIME:** 15 minutes

Makes 12 servings

2 ounces bittersweet or semisweet chocolate (¼ cup), chopped
1½ tablespoons finely chopped pistachios
24 dried apricots (4 ounces)

Place the chocolate in a small microwaveable cup. Microwave on high power for 30 seconds, stirring every 10 seconds, or until melted and smooth.

Place the pistachios on a sheet of waxed paper and line a plate with waxed paper.

Dip each apricot into the melted chocolate to coat two-thirds of the apricot. Dip lightly, coated end down, into the pistachios and place on the lined plate.

Nutrition per serving: 51 calories, 1 g protein, 7 g carbs, 1 g fiber, 5 g total sugar, 2 g fat, 1 g saturated fat, 2 mg sodium

Grapes with Sour Cream

PREP TIME: 10 minutes ● **TOTAL TIME:** 10 minutes

Makes 4 servings

2 tablespoons sour cream
2 tablespoons 0% plain Greek yogurt
2 teaspoons maple syrup
1 cup seedless red grapes, halved
1 cup seedless green grapes, halved
½ teaspoon grated orange peel

In a small bowl, mix together the sour cream, yogurt, and maple syrup.

In a medium bowl, combine the red grapes, green grapes, and orange peel and toss to coat. Serve the grape mixture with a dollop of the sour cream mixture.

Nutrition per serving: 76 calories, 1 g protein, 16 g carbs, 1 g fiber, 14 g total sugar, 1.5 g fat, 1.5 g saturated fat, 9 mg sodium

Walnut-Cranberry Oatmeal Drops

PREP TIME: 10 minutes ● **TOTAL TIME:** 20 minutes

Makes 36 cookies

2 cups rolled oats
½ cup whole grain pastry flour
¾ teaspoon baking soda
½ teaspoon ground cinnamon
¼ teaspoon salt
½ cup firmly packed light or dark brown sugar
⅓ cup canola oil
3 egg whites
2 teaspoons vanilla extract
1 cup cranberries, coarsely chopped
2 cups chopped walnuts

Preheat the oven to 350°F. Coat 2 large baking sheets with cooking spray.

In a large bowl, combine the oats, flour, baking soda, cinnamon, and salt.

In a separate bowl, whisk together the sugar, oil, egg whites, and vanilla. Pour into the flour mixture and stir until well blended. Fold in the cranberries and walnuts.

Drop the batter by rounded teaspoons onto the baking sheets. Bake the cookies for 6 to 8 minutes, or until golden brown. Transfer to a rack to cool completely.

Nutrition per cookie: 98 calories, 2 g protein, 8 g carbs, 1 g fiber, 3 g total sugar, 7 g fat, 1 g saturated fat, 48 mg sodium

Raspberry Tiramisu

PREP TIME: 10 minutes ● **TOTAL TIME:** 10 minutes

Makes 1 serving

3 tablespoons part-skim ricotta cheese
¼ teaspoon instant espresso powder
1 teaspoon maple syrup
Dash of vanilla extract
1 soft ladyfinger
1 teaspoon strong brewed coffee
3–4 raspberries for topping

In a small bowl, stir together the cheese, espresso powder, maple syrup, and vanilla. Let stand for 5 minutes to allow the espresso powder to dissolve.

Place the ladyfinger on a small plate and brush with the coffee. Spoon the cheese mixture on top. Top with the raspberries.

Nutrition per serving: 115 calories, 6 g protein, 13 g carbs, 0.5 g fiber, 8 g total sugar, 4 g fat, 2 g saturated fat, 109 mg sodium

Rice Pudding

PREP TIME: 5 minutes ● **TOTAL TIME:** 30 minutes

Makes 4 servings

1¾ cups 2% milk
½ cup instant brown rice
1 tablespoon maple
    syrup
1 tablespoon golden
    raisins
¼ teaspoon ground
    cinnamon
¼ teaspoon ground
    nutmeg
¼ teaspoon salt
1½ teaspoons vanilla
    extract

In a heavy saucepan, combine the milk, rice, maple syrup, raisins, cinnamon, nutmeg, and salt. Heat the rice mixture over medium heat, stirring constantly, for 5 minutes, or until it comes to a slow boil. Reduce the heat to low. Cover and simmer for 20 minutes, stirring occasionally, or until the rice is very tender. Stir in the vanilla. Serve warm or refrigerate to serve cold.

Nutrition per serving: 124 calories, 5 g protein, 19 g carbs, 1 g fiber, 11 g total sugar, 3 g fat, 1 g saturated fat, 199 mg sodium

10 Best Dressings

Blue Cheese Dressing

PREP TIME: 5 minutes ● **TOTAL TIME:** 5 minutes

Makes 4 servings

½ cup 0% plain Greek yogurt
¼ cup blue cheese crumbles
1 teaspoon lemon juice
1 teaspoon white wine vinegar
¼ teaspoon garlic powder
⅛ teaspoon salt
⅛ teaspoon ground black pepper
Fat-free milk, if needed

In a small bowl, whisk together the yogurt, blue cheese, lemon juice, vinegar, garlic powder, and salt and pepper to taste. Refrigerate, covered, for the flavors to blend. Just before serving, whisk in some milk, if necessary, to loosen the dressing. Store any extra dressing in an airtight container in the refrigerator.

Nutrition per serving: 46 calories, 4 g protein, 2 g carbs, 0 g fiber, 1 g total sugar, 2 g fat, 1.5 g saturated fat, 201 mg sodium

Presto Pesto

PREP TIME: 5 minutes ● **TOTAL TIME:** 5 minutes

Makes 8 servings

1 cup fresh basil leaves
1 cup baby arugula
2 cloves garlic, minced
3 tablespoons grated Pecorino Romano cheese
2 tablespoons toasted and coarsely chopped walnuts
¼ cup vegetable broth
¼ cup olive oil
⅛ teaspoon salt
⅛ teaspoon ground black pepper

In a food processor, combine the basil, arugula, garlic, cheese, and walnuts. Process, gradually adding the broth and oil, until smooth. Season with the salt and pepper to taste. Store any extra dressing in an airtight container in the refrigerator.

Nutrition per serving: 84 calories, 2 g protein, 1 g carbs, 0 g fiber, 0.5 g total sugar, 8 g fat, 2 g saturated fat, 135 mg sodium

Basil-Lemon Vinaigrette Dressing

PREP TIME: 5 minutes ● **TOTAL TIME:** 5 minutes

Makes 6 servings

¼ cup fresh basil leaves

2 tablespoons white balsamic vinegar

1 clove garlic, minced

1 tablespoon fresh lemon juice

¼ teaspoon ground black pepper

2 tablespoons olive oil

1 tablespoon vegetable broth

In a blender or food processor, combine the basil, vinegar, garlic, lemon juice, pepper, oil, and broth. Blend or process until smooth. Store any extra dressing in an airtight container in the refrigerator.

Nutrition per serving: 66 calories, 0 g protein, 1 g carbs, 0 g fiber, 0 g total sugar, 7 g fat, 1 g saturated fat, 73 mg sodium

Steakhouse Dressing

PREP TIME: 5 minutes ● **TOTAL TIME:** 5 minutes

Makes 4 servings

2 tablespoons extra-virgin olive oil

2 tablespoons cider vinegar

¼ cup unsweetened ketchup

¼ teaspoon paprika

¼ teaspoon garlic powder

¼ teaspoon onion powder

¼ teaspoon Worcestershire sauce

⅛ teaspoon salt

In a small bowl, combine the oil, vinegar, ketchup, paprika, garlic powder, onion powder, Worcestershire sauce, and salt. Store any extra dressing in an airtight container in the refrigerator.

Nutrition per serving: 72 calories, 0 g protein, 2 g carbs, 0 g fiber, 0 g total sugar, 7 g fat, 1 g saturated fat, 136 mg sodium

Creamy Dill Dressing

PREP TIME: 5 minutes ● **TOTAL TIME:** 5 minutes

Makes 6 servings

¾ cup 0% plain Greek yogurt
2 scallions, white part only, finely chopped
1 clove garlic, minced
1 tablespoon chopped fresh dill
¼ teaspoon salt
2 tablespoons lemon juice

In a blender or food processor, combine the yogurt, scallions, garlic, dill, salt, and lemon juice. Blend or process until completely smooth. Store any extra dressing in an airtight container in the refrigerator.

Nutrition per serving: 19 calories, 3 g protein, 2 g carbs, 0 g fiber, 1 g total sugar, 0 g fat, 0 g saturated fat, 109 mg sodium

Parmesan-Pepper Dressing

PREP TIME: 5 minutes ● **TOTAL TIME:** 5 minutes

Makes 8 servings

¼ cup fat-free plain yogurt
½ cup 1% cottage cheese
¼ cup buttermilk
⅓ cup grated Parmesan cheese
2 tablespoons white wine vinegar
2 cloves garlic, minced
½ teaspoon ground black pepper

In a blender or food processor, combine the yogurt, cottage cheese, buttermilk, Parmesan cheese, vinegar, garlic, and pepper. Blend or process until smooth. Store any extra dressing in an airtight container in the refrigerator.

Nutrition per serving: 32 calories, 4 g protein, 2 g carbs, 0 g fiber, 1 g total sugar, 1 g fat, 1 g saturated fat, 149 mg sodium

Red Wine Vinaigrette

PREP TIME: 5 minutes ● **TOTAL TIME:** 5 minutes

Makes 4 servings

¼ cup red wine vinegar
2 teaspoons Dijon mustard
1 clove garlic, minced
½ teaspoon dried oregano
½ teaspoon dried basil
⅛ teaspoon salt
⅛ teaspoon ground black pepper
2 tablespoons extra-virgin olive oil
2 tablespoons water (optional)

In a medium bowl, whisk together the vinegar, mustard, garlic, oregano, basil, salt, and pepper. Slowly whisk in the oil. Add the water if dressing needs thinning. Store any extra dressing in an airtight container in the refrigerator.

Nutrition per serving: 70 calories, 0 g protein, 1 g carbs, 0 g fiber, 0 g total sugar, 7 g fat, 1 g saturated fat, 134 mg sodium

Two-Mustard Vinaigrette

PREP TIME: 5 minutes ● **TOTAL TIME:** 5 minutes

Makes 4 servings

1 clove garlic, minced
1 teaspoon Dijon mustard
2 teaspoons brown mustard
3 tablespoons cider vinegar
⅛ teaspoon ground black pepper
2 tablespoons extra-virgin olive oil

In a small bowl, combine the garlic, mustards, vinegar, and pepper. Drizzle in the oil while whisking continuously. Store any extra dressing in an airtight container in the refrigerator.

Nutrition per serving: 70 calories, 0 g protein, 1 g carbs, 0 g fiber, 0 g total sugar, 7 g fat, 1 g saturated fat, 56 mg sodium

Creamy Italian Dressing

PREP TIME: 5 minutes ● **TOTAL TIME:** 5 minutes

Makes 8 servings

½ cup fat-free plain yogurt
½ cup buttermilk
3 tablespoons grated Parmesan cheese
1 teaspoon dried basil
½ teaspoon dried oregano
½ teaspoon minced garlic
⅛ teaspoon ground black pepper

In a small bowl, whisk together the yogurt, buttermilk, cheese, basil, oregano, garlic, and pepper. Store any extra dressing in an airtight container in the refrigerator.

Nutrition per serving: 21 calories, 2 g protein, 2 g carbs, 0 g fiber, 2 g total sugar, 1 g fat, 0.5 g saturated fat, 37 mg sodium

Herbed Mustard Dressing

PREP TIME: 10 minutes ● **TOTAL TIME:** 10 minutes

Makes 4 servings

2 tablespoons chopped fresh basil
2 tablespoons lemon juice
1 tablespoon Dijon mustard
1½ teaspoons chopped fresh oregano
⅛ teaspoon salt
⅛ teaspoon ground black pepper
2 tablespoons olive oil
2 tablespoons vegetable broth

In a small bowl, combine the basil, lemon juice, mustard, oregano, salt, and pepper. Whisk until well blended. Whisk in the oil and broth in a slow, steady stream. Transfer to a small jar and refrigerate until ready to serve. Store any extra dressing in an airtight container in the refrigerator.

Nutrition per serving: 66 calories, 0 g protein, 1 g carbs, 0 g fiber, 0 g total sugar, 7 g fat, 1 g saturated fat, 163 mg sodium

10 Best Sauces

Creamy Lemon-Caper Sauce

PREP TIME: 5 minutes ● **TOTAL TIME:** 5 minutes

Makes ½ cup

½ cup 0% plain Greek
    yogurt
1 clove garlic, minced
2 teaspoons lemon juice
1 teaspoon capers,
    drained and chopped
⅛ teaspoon salt
⅛ teaspoon ground black
    pepper

In a medium bowl, whisk together the yogurt, garlic, lemon juice, capers, salt, and pepper until well blended.

Nutrition per serving (2 tablespoons): 19 calories, 3 g protein, 2 g carbs, 0 g fiber, 1 g total sugar, 0 g fat, 0 g saturated fat, 103 mg sodium

Chimichurri Sauce

PREP TIME: 5 minutes ● **TOTAL TIME:** 5 minutes

Makes 2 cups

¾ cup fresh flat-leaf
    parsley
¾ cup fresh cilantro
3 cloves garlic
3 tablespoons fresh lime
    juice
½ teaspoon salt
1 tablespoon olive oil
½ cup water

In a food processor or blender, combine the parsley, cilantro, garlic, lime juice, and salt. Process or blend until finely chopped. Add the oil and water and process or blend until combined.

Nutrition per serving (⅓ cup): 33 calories, 1 g protein, 3 g carbs, 1 g fiber, 0 g total sugar, 2 g fat, 0 g saturated fat, 234 mg sodium

Marinade for Vegetables

PREP TIME: 5 minutes ● **TOTAL TIME:** 5 minutes
Makes 1¼ cups

½ cup olive oil
⅓ cup white wine vinegar
¼ cup finely chopped
    fresh flat-leaf parsley
2 cloves garlic, minced
½ teaspoon dried
    oregano
½ teaspoon dried basil

In a screw-top jar, combine the oil, vinegar, parsley, garlic, oregano, and basil. Cover and shake well.

Nutrition per serving (1 tablespoon): 52 calories, 0.5 g protein, 1 g carbs, 0.5 g fiber, 0.5 g total sugar, 6 g fat, 0.5 g saturated fat, 19 mg sodium

Mustard-Balsamic Glaze

PREP TIME: 5 minutes ● **TOTAL TIME:** 20 minutes
Makes 1¼ cups

1 cup balsamic vinegar
2 tablespoons Dijon
    mustard
1 clove garlic, minced
½ teaspoon ground black
    pepper

In a medium saucepan over high heat, bring the vinegar to a boil. Reduce the heat to medium-low, cover, and simmer for 10 minutes. Stir in the mustard, garlic, and pepper. Cook for 5 minutes, or until thick enough to coat the back of a spoon and reduced to ½ cup. Remove from the heat.

Cool to room temperature and transfer to a jar with a tight-fitting lid.

Nutrition per serving (2 tablespoons): 26 calories, 0 g protein, 5 g carbs, 0 g fiber, 4 g total sugar, 0 g fat, 0 g saturated fat, 78 mg sodium

Creamy Cheese Sauce

PREP TIME: 5 minutes ● **TOTAL TIME:** 15 minutes

Makes 1 cup

¾ cup fat-free milk

8 ounces light cream cheese, cut into small cubes

1 shallot, finely chopped

1 clove garlic, minced

2 tablespoons grated Parmesan cheese

½ teaspoon ground black pepper

In a small saucepan over medium heat, bring the milk to a simmer. Stir in the cream cheese. Cook, stirring, for 3 minutes, or until the cream cheese melts. Add the shallot, garlic, Parmesan cheese, and pepper and cook for 5 minutes, or until the mixture thickens.

Nutrition per serving (¼ cup): 93 calories, 4 g protein, 4 g carbs, 0 g fiber, 2 g total sugar, 7 g fat, 4 g saturated fat, 124 mg sodium

Spinach-Ricotta Sauce

PREP TIME: 5 minutes ● **TOTAL TIME:** 15 minutes

Makes 1 cup

3 teaspoons extra-virgin olive oil, divided

1 small clove garlic, minced

2 tablespoons water

1 cup fresh baby spinach, chopped

1 cup part-skim ricotta cheese

⅓ cup 1% milk

2 tablespoons chopped fresh flat-leaf parsley

½ teaspoon red-pepper flakes

In a medium saucepan over medium heat, heat 2 teaspoons of the oil. Cook the garlic for 1 minute, or until golden and fragrant. Add the water and spinach and cook for 1 minute, or until wilted. Transfer the spinach mixture to a small bowl and set aside.

Reduce the heat to medium-low, and cook the ricotta cheese, milk, and the remaining 1 teaspoon oil for 4 minutes, or until heated through. Stir in the reserved spinach mixture, the parsley, and red-pepper flakes until combined.

Nutrition per serving (¼ cup): 131 calories, 8 g protein, 5 g carbs, 0.5 g fiber, 1 g total sugar, 9 g fat, 3.5 g saturated fat, 97 mg sodium

Asian Peanut Sauce

PREP TIME: 5 minutes ● **TOTAL TIME:** 5 minutes

Makes ¾ cup

¼ cup creamy, natural, unsalted peanut butter

¼ cup fat-free evaporated milk

1 tablespoon reduced-sodium soy sauce

1 teaspoon Asian chili-pepper paste

1 scallion, thinly sliced

In a small saucepan over medium-high heat, combine the peanut butter, milk, soy sauce, chili-pepper paste, and scallion and bring to a boil. Cook, stirring frequently, for 3 minutes, or until slightly thickened and hot.

Nutrition per serving (3 tablespoons): 116 calories, 5 g protein, 6 g carbs, 1 g fiber, 3 g total sugar, 8 g fat, 1 g saturated fat, 180 mg sodium

Mushroom Sauce

PREP TIME: 5 minutes ● **TOTAL TIME:** 20 minutes

Makes 2 cups

1 tablespoon olive oil

8 ounces cremini mushrooms, rinsed, trimmed, and sliced

1 tablespoon butter

1 cup reduced-sodium beef broth

¼ cup 0% plain Greek yogurt

2 tablespoons chopped fresh flat-leaf parsley

⅛ teaspoon salt

⅛ teaspoon ground black pepper

In a large saucepan over medium-high heat, heat the oil. Cook the mushrooms for 5 minutes, or until softened and golden brown. Transfer to a bowl and set aside.

Reduce the heat to medium and melt the butter. Slowly whisk in the broth and then the yogurt. Reduce the heat to low and cook, stirring frequently, for 5 minutes, or until slightly thickened. Stir in the parsley, salt, pepper, and the reserved mushrooms.

Nutrition per serving (½ cup): 80 calories, 3 g protein, 3 g carbs, 0.5 g fiber, 1 g total sugar, 7 g fat, 2.5 g saturated fat, 138 mg sodium

Cheesy Roasted Red Pepper Sauce

PREP TIME: 5 minutes ● **TOTAL TIME:** 15 minutes

Makes 2 cups

3 tablespoons olive oil, divided

1 small onion, finely chopped

1 clove garlic, minced

6 jarred whole roasted red bell peppers

1 tablespoon balsamic vinegar

3 tablespoons reduced-sodium vegetable broth

¼ cup fresh basil leaves, chopped

3 tablespoons grated Parmesan cheese

¼ teaspoon salt

¼ teaspoon freshly ground black pepper

In a large nonstick skillet over medium-high heat, heat 1 tablespoon of the oil. Cook the onion and garlic for 1 minute, or until golden and fragrant. Remove from the heat. Transfer to a blender. Add the bell peppers, vinegar, broth, and the remaining 2 tablespoons oil and pulse until smooth.

Return to the skillet over medium-low heat. Add the basil, cheese, salt, and black pepper and cook for 3 minutes, or until the cheese has melted and the sauce is heated through.

Nutrition per serving (½ cup): 134 calories, 2 g protein, 7 g carbs, 2 g fiber, 4 g total sugar, 12 g fat, 2 g saturated fat, 256 mg sodium

Quick and Tasty Tomato Sauce

PREP TIME: 5 minutes ● **TOTAL TIME:** 10 minutes

Makes 2 cups

1 tablespoon olive oil

1 clove garlic, minced

1 can (14.5 ounces) no-salt-added diced tomatoes

4 fresh basil leaves, chopped

1½ teaspoons dried Italian seasoning

½ teaspoon ground black pepper

¼ teaspoon salt

In a medium saucepan over medium heat, heat the oil. Cook the garlic for 1 minute, or until golden and fragrant. Reduce the heat to medium-low. Add the tomatoes, basil, Italian seasoning, pepper, and salt and cook for 5 minutes to allow the flavors to blend.

Nutrition per serving (½ cup): 56 calories, 1 g protein, 5 g carbs, 1 g fiber, 3 g total sugar, 4 g fat, 0.5 g saturated fat, 157 mg sodium

10 Best Recipes for Entertaining

Cheese and Bacon Stuffed Cherry Tomato Bites

PREP TIME: 10 minutes ● **TOTAL TIME:** 10 minutes
Makes 4 servings

¼ cup cream cheese, softened
1 tablespoon olive-oil mayonnaise
1 slice cooked bacon, crumbled
2 teaspoons finely chopped fresh chives
16 cherry tomatoes
1 teaspoon chopped fresh chives (for garnish)

In a small bowl, stir together the cheese and mayonnaise. Add the bacon crumbles and chives and stir to combine.

Cut a thin slice off the bottom of each tomato, just enough to allow the tomato to stand up straight without cutting into the membrane. Then, cut a thin slice off the top of each tomato and use a small spoon to scoop out the seeds and membrane. Fill each tomato with 1 teaspoon of the cheese mixture. As the tomatoes are filled, arrange them on a serving platter. Sprinkle the platter with chopped chives for garnish, if desired.

Cover loosely with plastic wrap and chill for 1 hour before serving.

Nutrition per serving: 72 calories, 3 g protein, 3 g carbs, 1 g fiber, 2 g total sugar, 5 g fat, 2 g saturated fat, 115 mg sodium

Roasted Red Pepper Hummus

PREP TIME: 5 minutes ● **TOTAL TIME:** 15 minutes
Makes 8 servings

1 can (15 ounces) chickpeas, rinsed and drained
1 clove garlic, minced
¼ cup tahini
3 tablespoons lemon juice
¼ teaspoon salt
¼ teaspoon ground black pepper
1 whole roasted red bell pepper
¼ teaspoon red-pepper flakes

In a food processor, combine the chickpeas, garlic, tahini, lemon juice, salt, and black pepper. Pulse in 5-second intervals until the chickpeas are mashed. Add the bell pepper and red-pepper flakes and pulse until smooth. Let stand for 5 minutes to blend the flavors. Transfer to a serving bowl.

Nutrition per serving: 78 calories, 2 g protein, 6 g carbs, 2 g fiber, 1 g total sugar, 5 g fat, 1 g saturated fat, 156 mg sodium

No-Fuss Chilled Cucumber Salad

PREP TIME: 5 minutes ● **TOTAL TIME:** 10 minutes

Makes 4 servings

2 cucumbers, thinly sliced

2 slices red onion, finely chopped

½ cup 0% plain Greek yogurt

1½ tablespoons white vinegar (or more, if desired)

½ teaspoon smoked paprika

¼ teaspoon salt

¼ teaspoon ground black pepper

In a serving bowl, combine the cucumbers and onion.

In a small bowl, whisk together the yogurt, vinegar, paprika, salt, and pepper. Add to the cucumber mixture and stir together to coat the cucumbers. Cover and chill until being served.

Nutrition per serving: 40 calories, 4 g protein, 6 g carbs, 2 g fiber, 3 g total sugar, 0 g fat, 0 g saturated fat, 156 mg sodium

Anti-Pasta Skewers

PREP TIME: 5 minutes ● **TOTAL TIME:** 10 minutes

Makes 4 servings

2 canned whole artichoke hearts, drained and quartered

4 cherry tomatoes, halved

8 pitted black olives

4 bocconcini, halved

2 pepperoncini peppers, seeded and cut into 8 pieces

2 slices thin-sliced prosciutto, cut crosswise into 8 pieces

2 tablespoons refrigerated pesto

On eight 4" wooden skewers, alternately thread the artichokes, tomatoes, olives, bocconcini, peppers, and prosciutto. Brush the finished skewers with the pesto and serve.

Nutrition per serving: 199 calories, 10 g protein, 4 g carbs, 1 g fiber, 1 g total sugar, 16 g fat, 7 g saturated fat, 730 mg sodium

Roast Beef and Horseradish Bites

PREP TIME: 5 minutes ● **TOTAL TIME:** 5 minutes

Makes 4 servings

4 slices roast beef, halved

4 teaspoons prepared horseradish

4 ounces sharp white Cheddar cheese, cut into 8 cubes

½ cup arugula

Lay out the roast beef slices on a clean cutting board or work area. Spread each with ½ teaspoon of the horseradish.

Place the cheese in the center of each roast beef slice. Divide the arugula among the 8 slices. Tightly wrap up the roast beef around the arugula and cheese and use a wooden pick to hold closed. Repeat with the remaining 7 slices.

Serve on a small platter.

Nutrition per serving: 150 calories, 11 g protein, 1 g carbs, 0 g fiber, 0.5 g total sugar, 11 g fat, 7 g saturated fat, 329 mg sodium

Balsalmic Salad Cups

PREP TIME: 10 minutes ● **TOTAL TIME:** 15 minutes

Makes 4 servings

8 hearts romaine lettuce

½ small cucumber, chopped

½ small red onion, chopped

4 ounces fresh mozzarella, cubed

2 plum tomatoes, chopped

3 tablespoons balsamic vinaigrette

Arrange the romaine hearts on a serving platter. In a medium bowl, mix together the cucumber, onion, mozzarella, and tomatoes. Add the vinaigrette and stir to coat. Allow this mixture to sit for 5 minutes. Spoon the mixture on top of the hearts of romaine and serve.

Nutrition per serving: 109 calories, 7 g protein, 5 g carbs, 1 g fiber, 3 g total sugar, 8 g fat, 3 g saturated fat, 141 mg sodium

Chicken Caesar Wraps

PREP TIME: 5 minutes ● **TOTAL TIME:** 5 minutes

Makes 4 servings

4 leaves romaine lettuce
½ cup shredded romaine lettuce
1 cup hot cooked shredded chicken
2 tablespoons grated Parmesan cheese
2 tablespoons Caesar dressing

Arrange romaine leaves on a serving platter.

In a medium bowl, toss together the shredded romaine, chicken, cheese, and dressing. Divide among the leaves. Wrap up the lettuce leaves and serve.

Nutrition per serving: 110 calories, 12 g protein, 1 g carbs, 0 g fiber, 0 g total sugar, 6 g fat, 1 g saturated fat, 154 mg sodium

Grilled Mesquite Shrimp Skewers

PREP TIME: 5 minutes ● **TOTAL TIME:** 15 minutes

Makes 4 servings

16 large shrimp, peeled and deveined
1 tablespoon olive oil
1 tablespoon mesquite seasoning
1 lime, halved
2 tablespoons chopped fresh cilantro (for garnish)

Preheat the grill to medium-high.

Pat the shrimp dry with a paper towel. In a medium bowl, toss the shrimp with the oil. Sprinkle with the mesquite seasoning and toss to coat.

On four 8" skewers, thread 4 shrimp each. (See note on page 320 if using wooden skewers.) Grill for 4 minutes, turning once, or until the shrimp are opaque.

Transfer to a serving platter and squeeze the lime juice over the shrimp. Garnish with the cilantro.

Nutrition per serving: 54 calories, 4 g protein, 1 g carbs, 0 g fiber, 0 g total sugar, 4 g fat, 0.5 g saturated fat, 159 mg sodium

Spinach and Parmesan Peppers

PREP TIME: 5 minutes ● **TOTAL TIME:** 20 minutes

Makes 4 servings

¼ cup frozen chopped spinach, thawed

4 ounces light cream cheese, softened

1 tablespoon grated Parmesan cheese

1 teaspoon lemon juice

1 clove garlic, minced

8 mini bell peppers, seeded and halved

Preheat the oven to 400°F. Coat a baking sheet with cooking spray.

Use paper towels to press the spinach to remove excess water. In a medium bowl, mix together the spinach, cream cheese, Parmesan cheese, lemon juice, and garlic.

Divide the cheese mixture among the peppers, using a spoon or butter knife to stuff them. Place on the baking sheet and roast for 15 minutes, or until softened. Transfer to a serving plate and enjoy.

Nutrition per serving: 99 calories, 4 g protein, 5 g carbs, 1 g fiber, 3 g total sugar, 7 g fat, 4 g saturated fat, 139 mg sodium

Steak and Potato Bites

PREP TIME: 5 minutes ● **TOTAL TIME:** 15 minutes

Makes 4 servings

2 tablespoons olive oil

1 large baked potato, cooled and cut into 16 (¼") slices

⅛ teaspoon salt

¼ teaspoon ground black pepper

8 ounces grilled strip steak, cut into 16 cubes

1 tablespoon Worcestershire sauce

5 tablespoons 0% plain Greek yogurt

1 teaspoon prepared horseradish

In a large skillet over medium-high heat, heat the oil. Add the potato slices and sprinkle with the salt and pepper. Cook for 5 minutes, turning once, or until both sides are golden brown. Transfer to a serving platter and arrange in a single layer.

In the same skillet, cook the steak and Worcestershire sauce, stirring frequently, for 2 minutes, or until heated through. Remove from the heat.

In a small bowl, combine the yogurt and horseradish. Spread a small teaspoonful over each potato slice. Top each with a piece of steak. Serve immediately.

Nutrition per serving: 296 calories, 19 g protein, 18 g carbs, 2 g fiber, 2 g total sugar, 16 g fat, 5 g saturated fat, 167 mg sodium

INDEX

Underscored page references indicate boxed text and tables. **Boldface** references indicate photographs.

C

Chocolate (*cont.*)
  Chocolate-Pistachio-Dipped Apricots, 344
  controlling cravings for, <u>85</u>, <u>96</u>, <u>134</u>
  Creamy Dark Chocolate-Banana-Coconut Pudding, 243
  dark
    health benefits of, <u>114</u>, 180, <u>186</u>
    sugar in, <u>61</u>, <u>83</u>, <u>167</u>
  Hershey's Kisses, 202
  Homemade Chocolate Milk, 202
  Lindt Excellence Cocoa, 202
  Microwave S'more, 202
  Nutty Choco-Banana Oatmeal, 200
  Pinto Bean Brownies, 247
Cholesterol levels
  fructose and, 37
  high
    from added sugars, 39
    exercise preventing, 253, <u>261</u>
  in metabolic syndrome, 36
  Sugar Smart Diet lowering, <u>26</u>, <u>54</u>, <u>68</u>, <u>96</u>, <u>134</u>, <u>154</u>
Chronic diseases
  contributors to, xix, <u>4</u>, 20
  preventing, xv, xvi, xviii, <u>261</u>
Chronic inflammation, 30, <u>198</u>
Cinnamon, 60, 62, 124–25
Circle breathing, for stress relief, 113
Cirrhosis, 34
Cleveland Clinic, vi
Cobbler
  Easy Cinnamon-Apple Cobbler, 241
Coffee
  fat-free latte, 131
  PB&J Toast and Café au Lait, 168
  Vanilla Latte, <u>121</u>
Coffee drinks, 188, 191
Collagen, sugar damaging, <u>40</u>
Comfort, sugar associated with, 66–67
Comfort eaters, xvi
Condiments, 185, 301
Cookies
  Barnum's Animals Crackers, 202
  Carr's Ginger Lemon Cremes, 202
  No-Bake Oatmeal Cookies, 244
  Oreos, 202
  Pepperidge Farm Milano Cookies, 202
  Pepperidge Farm Nantucket Cookies, 202
  Sugar Smart choices of, 302
Coping strategy, for sticky situations, 194
Core training, 257. *See also* Sugar Smart Workout, Sugar Belly Blaster
Corn
  Summer Corn Salad, 338

Corn syrup, vs. high-fructose corn syrup, <u>4</u>. *See also* High-fructose corn syrup (HFCS)
Coronary artery disease, vi, 36
Cortisol, as stress hormone, 63, 258, 259
Crackers
  Honey Maid Graham Crackers, 202
  Microwave S'more, 202
  Sugar Smart choices of, 302
Cravings
  analyzing, 82
  carbohydrate, experiment on, 47–49
  chocolate, <u>85</u>, <u>96</u>, <u>134</u>
  controlling, xvi–xvii, 166
  emotions and, 76
  exercise reducing, 65–66, 253
  flours causing, 22
  nonfood treats soothing (*see* Cravings Crushers; Rewards Card, for soothing cravings; Sweet Freedom strategies)
  in Phase 1, 101, 105–6, 112
  in Phase 3, 163, 166
  sugar
    after splurges, 195
    from blood sugar swings, 103, <u>114</u>
    brain's role in, 45–47
    disappearance of, 163
    foods satisfying, <u>198</u>
    from meal skipping, 60
    preventing or reducing, 59, 60, <u>83</u>, <u>140</u>, <u>198</u>
    from sleep deprivation, 64–65
  sugar causing, xiv, 5, <u>15</u>
  Sugar Smart Diet reducing, <u>26</u>, <u>54</u>, <u>96</u>, <u>134</u>, <u>154</u>, <u>176</u>
Cravings Crushers, 101, 141, 163
  calcium and vitamin D supplements, 106–7
  cinnamon, 124–25
  peanut butter for breakfast, 112–13
  reading, 115
  tea, 115
  vinegar, 118–19
  water, 121–22
Cucumbers
  Cool Cucumber, Tomato, Black Bean, and Barley Salad, 128
  Crudités and Hummus, 130
  Cucumber-Jalapeño Quencher, <u>121</u>
  Greek Salad, 337
  No-Fuss Chilled Cucumber Salad, 358
  Tuna Salad Cucumber Stackers, 171

D

Dehydration, 121
Denny's, Sugar Smart choices at, 290–91
Depression, 51

R

Radical acceptance exercise, 119–20
Radicchio
    Braised Radicchio, 339
RAIN technique, for controlling cravings, 166
Raspberries
    Fruit Kebabs with Raspberry Yogurt Dip, 342
    Raspberry Tiramisu, 345
Reading, for stress reduction, 115
Red Robin, nutrition calculator of, 290
Red wine vinegar
    Red Wine Vinaigrette, 350
Restaurant dining. See Dining out guidelines
Reward regions, of brain, 46, 83, 90, 137, 253
Rewards Card, for soothing cravings, 90–92, 93,
    101, 105, 199
Rhodiola, for stress relief, 164
Rice, brown
    Cilantro-Lime Rice Pilaf, 336
    Loaded Shrimp Fajita Bowl with Brown Rice, 169
    Rice Pudding, 346
Rosemary, for energy, 110
Running, 261

S

Salad dressings
    oil and vinegar, 11, 118
    restaurant, 190, 287
    Sugar Smart choices of, 185, 305
    10 best
        Basil-Lemon Vinaigrette Dressing, 348
        Blue Cheese Dressing, 347
        Creamy Dill Dressing, 349
        Creamy Italian Dressing, 351
        Herbed Mustard Dressing, 351
        Parmesan-Pepper Dressing, 349
        Presto Pesto, 347
        Red Wine Vinaigrette, 350
        Steakhouse Dressing, 348
        Two-Mustard Vinaigrette, 350
Salads
    Asian Quinoa Salad, 233
    Balsamic Salad Cups, 359
    Beer BBQ Chicken Thighs with Corn and
        Tomato Salad, 228
    Blue Cheese, Walnut, Chicken, and Quinoa
        Salad, 129
    Buffalo-Style Potato Salad, 338
    Cool Cucumber, Tomato, Black Bean, and
        Barley Salad, 128
    Crunchy Turkey-Pear Salad Sandwich, 168
    Fennel and Arugula Salad with Pecans and
        Blue Cheese, 339

Fiesta Egg Salad, 128
Fresh Tuna Salad, 318
Greek Salad, 337
Grilled Chicken Caesar Salad, 323
Grilled Shrimp Salad with Potato, Sunflower
    Seeds, and Goat Cheese, 130
No-Fuss Chilled Cucumber Salad, 358
Poached Eggs with Fruity Wheat Berry Salad,
    232
Roasted Veggie, Bulgur, and Chickpea Salad
    with Feta Dressing, 222
Spinach and Grapefruit Salad with Wheat
    Berries and Grilled Chicken, 146
Steak Salad, 326
Summer Corn Salad, 338
Tangy Mediterranean Tuna Salad, 128
Tuna Salad Cucumber Stackers, 171
Whole Wheat Tuna Pasta Salad over Mixed
    Greens, 146
Salsa
    Fish Tacos with Mango-Lime Salsa in Crispy
        Corn Tortillas, 223
    Pork Tenderloin with Pineapple Salsa, 335
Sandwiches
    Crunchy Turkey-Pear Salad Sandwich, 168
    Roast Beef, Swiss, and Arugula Sandwich, 169
    Turkey Burger with Broccoli-Wheat Berry
        Toss, 169
Sauces
    low-sugar swaps for, 185
    pasta, Sugar Smart choices of, 306
    Phase 1, 309
        Sugar Smart Marinara Sauce, 234
    Phase 3
        Panko-Crusted Chicken Tenders with
            Honey-Mustard Dipping Sauce, 229
        Sugar Smart Asian Peanut Dressing, 235
        Sugar Smart BBQ Sauce, 234
        Sugar Smart Teriyaki Sauce, 235
    Sugar Smart choices of, 301
    10 best
        Asian Peanut Sauce, 355
        Cheesy Roasted Red Pepper Sauce, 356
        Chimichurri Sauce, 352
        Creamy Cheese Sauce, 354
        Creamy Lemon-Caper Sauce, 352
        Marinade for Vegetables, 353
        Mushroom Sauce, 355
        Mustard-Balsamic Glaze, 353
        Quick and Tasty Tomato Sauce, 356
        Spinach-Ricotta Sauce, 354
Sausage
    Chicken Sausage and Veggie Pita Pizza, 147
    Potato, Pepper, and Chicken Sausage Sauté,
        129

W

Waffles
  Peaches 'n' Cream Waffles, 200
Walking
  benefits of, <u>110</u>, 253, 260–62, <u>261</u>
  for controlling chocolate cravings, <u>85</u>
  for hunger suppression, 259–60
  proper form for, <u>255</u>
Water drinking, 121–22
Watermelon
  Watermelon and Feta Salad, 238
Waters, flavored, <u>121</u>, 164, 188
Weight, effect of sugar on, 5
Weight gain, vii, <u>21</u>
Weight loss
  fiber and, 138
  from Sugar Smart Diet, xvi, xix, 102 (*see* also
    Success stories)
Weight-loss maintenance, exercise for, 253
Weil, Andrew, xv, xviii, <u>61</u>, **61**
Wendy's, Sugar Smart choices at, 297
Wheat berries
  Poached Eggs with Fruity Wheat Berry Salad,
    232
  Spinach and Grapefruit Salad with Wheat
    Berries and Grilled Chicken, 146
  Turkey Burger with Broccoli-Wheat Berry
    Toss, 169
Whole grain products. *See* also Grain products
  problems with, 20, 22
  quick digestion of, 31
  reintroducing, 25, 139, <u>163</u>
  sugar in, xiv, xvii, 2, 89
Whole grains, FDA definition of, 22
Wild rice
  Cranberry-Walnut Wild Rice Pilaf, 240
Wine, <u>125</u>
Wraps
  Apricot-Almond Breakfast Wrap, 145
  Chicken Caesar Wrap, 360
  Tuna-Potato Wrap, 237
  Turkey, Roasted Pepper, and Avocado Roll-Up
    with Edamame, 170

Turkey and Cheese Wrap, 130
Turkey Sausage, Spinach, and Cheddar Wrap,
  145

X

Xylitol, <u>21</u>

Y

Yoga, <u>111</u>, 125–26, 165, 259. *See* also Sugar Smart
    Workout, Energizing Yoga; Sugar Smart
    Workout, Relaxing Yoga
Yogurt
  allowed in Sugar Smart Diet, <u>100</u>
  Almond Yogurt with Oats, 313
  Blueberry and Honey Yogurt Parfait, 168
  Blue Cheese Dressing, 347
  Cashew-Coconut Muesli Yogurt, 127
  Creamy Dill Dressing, 349
  Creamy Italian Dressing, 351
  Creamy Lemon-Caper Sauce, 352
  Crunchy Almond Yogurt, 127
  Fruit Kebabs with Raspberry Yogurt Dip,
    342
  Homemade Fruity Yogurt Pops, 343
  identifying added sugar in, <u>18–19</u>
  low-sugar swaps for, 187
  Parmesan-Pepper Dressing, 349
  PB&J Yogurt, 147
  Peaches 'n' Cream Waffles, 200
  Roasted Lemon-Ginger Pears with Pecan
    Yogurt, 242
  Strawberry-Kiwi Crunch Yogurt, 145
  Strawberry Yogurt Cup, 343
  Sugar Smart choices of, 307
  Yogurt-Covered Blueberries, 243

Z

Zucchini
  Garlic Shrimp over Zucchini Ribbons,
    315
  Spicy Pork with Zucchini Ribbons, 334